Confronting Past Human Rights Violations

This book examines what makes accountability for previous abuses more or less possible for transitional regimes to achieve. It closely examines the other vital goals of such regimes against which accountability is often balanced. The options available are not simply prosecution or pardon, as the most heated polemics of the debate over transitional justice suggest, but a range of options, from complete amnesty through truth commissions and lustration or purification to prosecutions. The question, then, is not whether accountability can be achieved, but what degree of accountability can be achieved by a given country.

This book examines five countries' experiences in detail – El Salvador, Honduras, Argentina, South Africa, and Sri Lanka – and offers a comparative survey of nearly 30 countries' experiences. It discusses three factors that affect the accountability achieved: international or external influences, the balance of forces between civilians and the military and or government and opposition forces, and the extent and nature of previous rights abuses. The book also examines strategies of transition, trade-offs and compromises that regimes (and international actors assisting them) may make in an attempt to achieve greater accountability or greater stability. The focus is on the politics of transition: what makes accountability more or less feasible and what strategies are deployed by regimes to achieve greater accountability (or alternatively, greater reform). The result is a more nuanced understanding of the different conditions and possibilities that countries face, and the lesson that there is no one-size-fits-all prescription that can be handed to transitional regimes.

Chandra Lekha Sriram is Lecturer in the School of International Relations at the University of St. Andrews, where she teaches international relations and international law, and human rights. She obtained her doctorate from Princeton University in 2000.

THE CASS SERIES ON PEACEKEEPING

ISSN 1367–9880

General Editor: Michael Pugh

This series examines all aspects of peacekeeping, from the political, operational and legal dimensions to the developmental and humanitarian issues that must be dealt with by all those involved with peacekeeping in the world today.

1. **Beyond the Emergency: Development within UN Missions**
edited by Jeremy Ginifer

2. **The UN, Peace and Force**
edited by Michael Pugh

3. **Mediating in Cyprus: The Cypriot Communities and the United Nations**
by Oliver P. Richmond

4. **Peacekeeping and the UN Agencies**
edited by Jim Whitman

5. **Peacekeeping and Public Information: Caught in the Crossfire**
by Ingrid A. Lehman

6. **US Peacekeeping Policy under Clinton: A Fairweather Friend?**
by Michael MacKinnon

7. **Peacebuilding and Police Reform**
edited by Tor Tanke Holm and Espen Barth Eide

8. **Peacekeeping and Conflict Resolution**
edited by Oliver Ramsbotham and Tom Woodhouse

9. **Managing Armed Conflicts in the 21st Century**
edited by Adekeye Adebajo and Chandra Lekha Sriram

10. **Women and International Peacekeeping**
edited by Louise Olsson and Torunn L. Tryggestad

11. **Recovering from Civil Conflict: Reconciliation, Peace and Development**
edited by Edward Newman and Albrecht Schnabel

12. **Mitigating Conflict: The Role of NGOs**
edited by Henry F. Carey and Oliver P. Richmond

13. **Ireland and International Peacekeeping 1960–2000: A Study of Irish Motivation**
Katsumi Ishizuka

14. **Peace Operations after September 11, 2001**
edited by Thierry Tardy

15. **Confronting Past Human Rights Violations: Justice vs. Peace in Times of Transition**
Chandra Lekha Sriram

Confronting Past Human Rights Violations

Justice vs Peace in Times of Transition

Chandra Lekha Sriram

FRANK CASS
LONDON and NEW YORK

First published in 2004 in Great Britain by Frank Cass
2 Park Square, Milton Park, Abingdon, Oxon OX14 4RN

Simultaneously published in the USA and Canada
by Frank Cass
270 Madison Avenue, New York, NY 10016

Transferred to Digital Printing 2006

Typeset in Erhardt by
Keystroke, Jacaranda Lodge, Wolverhampton

British Library Cataloguing in Publication Data
A catalogue record for this book is available from the British Library

Library of Congress Cataloging in Publication Data
Sriram, Chandra Lekha, 1971–
Confronting past human rights violations : justice vs. peace in times of transition / Chandra Lekha Sriram. – 1st ed.
p. cm. – (The Cass series on peacekeeping, ISSN 1367–9880 ; 14)
Includes bibliographical references and index.
1. Truth commissions–Case studies. 2. Human rights–Case studies. 3. Crimes against humanity–Case studies. 4. War crimes–Case studies. 5. Government liability–Case studies. 6. Restorative justice–Case studies. 7. Amnesty–Case studies. I. Title. II. Series.

JC580 . S65 2004
323 .4'9–dc22 2004002936

ISBN10: 0–7146–5599–6 (hbk)
ISBN10: 0–415–40758–3 (pbk)

ISBN13: 978–0–7146–5599–4 (hbk)
ISBN13: 978–0–415–40758–8 (pbk)

Contents

Preface

The basic questions that this book asks are 'What makes accountability for past abuses more or less possible in transitional regimes that still face serious resistance from elements of the old regime?' and 'Against what other goals is accountability likely to be balanced?' I begin with the continuum of possible outcomes: the options are not simply prosecution or pardon, as the most heated polemics of the debate over transitional justice might have us believe, but a range of options – from complete amnesty through truth commissions and lustration or purification to prosecutions. The question, then, is not whether or not accountability can be achieved, but what point on the accountability continuum can be achieved by a given country. I hypothesize that there are three factors that make accountability more or less feasible in a particular country: international/external influences, the balance of forces between civilians and the military and or government and opposition forces, and the extent and nature of previous rights abuses. Then, as the relatively small literature that does address factors affecting accountability runs the risk of being too deterministic, I argue that there are also strategies of transition, trade-offs and compromises that regimes (and international actors assisting them) may make in an attempt to achieve greater accountability or greater stability. It is these last two practical aspects that the book emphasizes, articulating and investigating hypotheses about what makes accountability more or less feasible and what strategies can be deployed to achieve greater accountability (or, alternatively, greater reform). The result is a more nuanced understanding of the different conditions and possibilities that countries face, and the lesson that there is no one-size-fits-all prescription that can be handed to transitional regimes considering the legacy of the past.

Acknowledgements

A project of this size cannot be undertaken, much less completed, without the support of many people. I am grateful to my friends and colleagues, for support both intellectual and emotional, during the protracted development, research and editing of this book, and particularly to the support and advice provided by my advisers and dissertation committee.

Any list is bound to be incomplete given the vast number of people who have contributed. Any errors of fact or judgement are, of course, my own. I would like to thank, first and foremost, my primary advisers, Professors Michael Doyle and Richard Falk of Princeton University. Their advice, criticism and encouragement continuously enabled me to refine my argument and consider novel theoretical approaches. I am also very indebted to two committee members who provided insights and helpful discussions nearer the completion of the project, Professor Gary Bass and Alexandra Barahona de Brito. The book has since benefited immeasurably from the comments of anonymous reviewers, and from my editors at Frank Cass, Sian Mills, Sally Green and Andrew Humphrys.

Innumerable colleagues, in my department as well as around the world, have pushed me further, enabling me to think about my argument in new contexts, and with new frameworks. A special and heartfelt thanks is due to an extraordinary man and politician, Dr Neelan Tiruchelvam, whose graciousness and support were matched only by his dedication to human rights and reform in Sri Lanka. He was assassinated by an LTTE suicide bomber in 1999, and the world is much the poorer for the loss.

I am also particularly grateful for extended conversations and advice from Amy Ross, Ram Manikkalingam, Amanda Dickins, Angela Tsay, Jonathan Allen and Pete Furia, as well as more recent conversations that have provoked me to think further while revising, with Brad Roth, Donald Rothchild, Marie-Joelle Zahar, Stephen Brown, Jamie Mayerfeld, Ramani Muttetuwegama, Laila Manji, Jamal Benomar, John Clarke, Ben Reilly, Elizabeth Cousens, Bronwyn Leebaw and Rama Mani. I gained much insight from colleagues at the Instituto de Derechos Humanos at the Universidad Centroamericana, in particular Boris Solorzano, and the Centre for Human Rights at the University of Colombo, in particular Ravindra Fernando and of course from all of my interviewees. I am especially grateful for the hospitality and insights of Manouri Muttetuwegama.

I have benefited particularly from my time at the International Peace Academy (IPA), both in the quality of my colleagues and the support shown by the institution as I sought to revise this book while carrying on work on conflict prevention. For this I owe a debt of gratitude to the management of IPA, particularly David Malone, John Hirsch and Necla Tschirgi. I have gained much from working with and learning from all of my colleagues at IPA, but I particularly want to thank Karin Wermester, Karen Ballentine, Zoe Nielsen, Sorrel Osborne, Lotta Hagman, Angela Muvumba, Marlye Gelin-Adams, Adekeye Adebajo, Jake Sherman, Jilla Moazami and Simon Chesterman for friendship, ideas and support.

I am happy to count so many of those above as good friends as well as colleagues, but am perhaps most indebted to many friends who had no stake at all in this project or set of issues except as my friends. Their support, and often their insights and questions, as persons expert in completely different areas, have enriched my life and this project. I especially want to thank Stephanic Harves, Michael Siu, Janet Klein, Andy Bye, Robin Huffstutter, Sean Corner, Wayne Snow, Mira Seo, LaTanya Rucker, Nick Tolwinski, Florian Becker, David Kasunic, Michael D'Alba, Patrick Shorb, Olivier Pauluis, John Normand, Antonio Garcia, Jenny Tsien, Sal Mustafa, Elizabeth Letcher, Jill Cetina, Credence Fogo, Karen DeLeon-Jones, Dani Eurynome, Margaret Lo, Ping Foong, Rebel McKinley, Susan Nicastro, Kim Germain, Bridget Guarasci, Andrew Croce, Yvan Fitch, Alan Adkins, Anna Lau and the late Moshe Levy. And of course I wish to thank my mother, Carolyn Nikkal, for continuously believing in me even when I didn't.

Last but certainly not least, this project would not have been possible without financial support from a number of sources. These include my graduate support at Princeton University, specific grants from the Princeton Department of Politics and the Stafford Fund, from the Princeton University Center for International Studies and the Mellon Foundation, from the Social Science Research Council and MacArthur Foundation and from the Institute for the Study of World Politics.

List of abbreviations

ANC	African National Congress (South Africa)
ANSP	Academia Nacional de Seguridad Pública (national police academy, El Salvador)
CES	Cuerpo Especial de Seguridad (special security body, Honduras)
CIA	Central Intelligence Agency
CNDH	Comisionado Nacional para la Protección de los Derechos Humanos(national commission for the protection of human rights, Honduras)
CNJ	Consejo Nacional de la Judicatura (national judicial council, El Salvador)
CODESA	Convention for a Democratic South Africa
CONADEP	Comisión Nacional sobre Desaparición de Personas (national commission for the disappeared, Argentina)
COPAZ	Comisión Nacional para la Consolidación de la Paz (national commission for the consolidation of peace, El Salvador)
CSCE	Conference on Security and Cooperation in Europe
DIC	Dirección de Investigacion Criminal (criminal investigation agency, Honduras)
DNI	Dirección Nacional de Investigaciones (national investigation agency, Honduras)
DNS	doctrine of national security
EU	European Union
FAES	Fuerzas Armadas de El Salvador
FMLN	Farabundo Martí National Liberation Front (El Salvador)
FSP	Fuerza de Seguridad Pública (public security force, Honduras)
ICCPR	International Convention on Civil and Political Rights
ICITAP	International Criminal Investigative Training Program
IFP	Inkatha Freedom Party (South Africa)
IPA	International Peace Academy
IPKF	Indian peacekeeping force (Sri Lanka)
JVP	Janata Vimukthi Peramuna (Sri Lanka)
KGB	Committee of State Security (USSR)
KR	Khmer Rouge (Cambodia)

LTTE	Liberation Tigers of Tamil Eelam (Sri Lanka)
MPNP	Multi-Party Negotiating Process (South Africa)
NATO	North Atlantic Treaty Organization
NGO	non-government organization
NP	National Party (South Africa)
NSF	National Salvation Front (Romania)
OAS	Organization of American States
OAU	Organization of African Unity
ONUSAL	UN Observer Mission in El Salvador
PA	People's Alliance (Sri Lanka)
PAC	Pan-Africanist Conference
PNC	Policía Nacional Civil (national civilian police)
PSO	Public Security Ordinance (Sri Lanka)
PTA	Prevention of Terrorism Act (Sri Lanka)
SADF	South African Defence Force
SANDF	South African National Defence Force
SAP	South African Police
SLFP	Sri Lankan Freedom Party
TEC	Transitional Executive Council
TRC	Truth and Reconciliation Commission (South Africa)
TSE	Tribuna Supremo Electoral (supreme electoral tribunal, El Salvador)
TULF	Tamil United Liberation Front (Sri Lanka)
UCA	Universidad Centroamericano (El Salvador)
UDF	United Democratic Front (South Africa)
UN	United Nations
UNP	United National Party (Sri Lanka)
UNTAC	United Nations Transitional Authority for Cambodia
URNG	Unidad Revolucionaria Nacional Guatemalteca (Guatemalan National Revolutionary Unity Guatemala)

Introduction

Truth, justice, and accountability

> Our common sense seems to support both positions: that a voluntarily committed criminal act is deserving of punishment, and that the social consequences of applying this punishment must be considered. It would be irrational to impose a punishment when the consequences of doing so, far from preventing future crimes, might cause greater social harm than that caused by the crime itself or by the absence of punishment. It would be unjust, however, to seek merely to avoid future crimes without taking into account, when applying the penalty, whether the person who committed the misdeed deserves to be punished.
>
> Former president of Argentina, Raúl Alfonsín[1]

The dilemma: justice vs. peace

'No justice, no peace.' From the riots in Los Angeles following the first verdict in the Rodney King beating case in 1992 to the outcry in England over the botched inquiry into the murder of Stephen Lawrence in 1993, there is a widespread intuition that justice and peace are inextricably linked. Furthermore, a vast literature expanding upon this intuition has developed.[2] Where there is justice, there can be peace, and peace justice; but the absence of one may necessarily result in the absence of another. Can one imagine a generally functioning court system such as that of the USA in the context of civil or external war where stability is gone and national security supersedes individual security? And, after the riots in Los Angeles, can one imagine peace following what appears to be a gross miscarriage of justice? In stable, established democracies such as the USA or the UK, the linkage of peace and justice appears quite logical.

However, citizens of countries emerging from civil war, authoritarian, totalitarian or military governments (or some combination of these) may rightly view the relationship between peace and justice quite differently. Having suffered vast human losses through conflict, repression, torture and disappearances, they desire peace, or at least an end to the conditions that led to these losses. They will also, however, desire some type of justice or accountability for the losses they sustained. They then desire justice *and* peace but, in the dozens of nations that have undergone such transitions since the early 1970s, the people and their new democratic leaders often learn that peace and justice cannot be achieved simultaneously in such situations. The difficulty is that in the near term, these two goods may be at odds, even though in the long term a just and stable society requires that they be united.[3]

Consider, for example, the situation faced by President Raúl Alfonsín in Argentina in 1983. Following the 'dirty war', a period of repression under a military dictatorship which sought to eliminate all opposition under the guise of fighting communist subversives, he was faced with two contradictory impulses: to ensure stability and consolidate democracy, and to punish members of the junta and others for the appalling human rights violations that they committed. He quickly found that pursuing justice could come at the cost of peace: in response to prosecutions and arrests, the military staged several coups and threatened more, and Alfonsín retrenched, vastly limiting the scale of prosecutions.

Argentina's experience is at once unique and typical. It is unique in that, alone among the cases examined in depth here, there was no significant external involvement in the transition. This absence of external actors may well have increased the challenges faced by Alfonsín. It is typical, nonetheless, in that the tensions faced and trade-offs made in Argentina look not dissimilar from those in Honduras, or El Salvador, for example.

However, while Alfonsín's experience illustrates the difficulty of achieving justice and peace in transitional times, it does *not* mean that transitional regimes can pursue *either* peace and stability, *or* justice, but not both. To the contrary, consolidating democracies have a wide range of options with regard to justice and accountability: they can pursue selective prosecutions, purges and even commissions of inquiry that lay bare the legacy of the past. These measures may not provide complete justice, but they may be the best option available. Wise leaders will recognize that there is a balance to be struck between justice and peace, and tread carefully.

Justice and peace: lessons

The purpose of this book is to provide lessons and guidance for policymakers, internal and external, facing the *justice vs. peace* dilemma so that they might be able to achieve as much of each as possible. However, not every new regime is born in the identical domestic military and political, or international context. Further, regimes experience differing constraints as they move through frequently protracted periods of transition. Thus it is important to understand what sort of constraints different regimes face as they move to democracy.

This book first seeks to identify the military, political, historical and international factors that make it more or less possible for a regime to pursue accountability without running the risk of instability or even reversion to non-democratic rule. For example, El Salvador at the time of its transition was formally democratic but in the end-stages of a brutal civil war, and the military dominated political life. It not only began the screening of its security forces, but did so under the auspices of a UN-brokered and monitored peace accord. Thus, while it faced constraints with regard to the pursuit of justice, we can expect those to be different from those faced by Honduras, a formally democratic state where the military still carries much political weight and which is still struggling to assert civilian control over the military, and where external actors have played a much smaller role in aid of democratization.

Once we identify the constraints that a new democracy faces, we can then ask exactly how it might choose to strike a balance between peace and justice. While any sacrifice of justice to peace may seem repugnant, the reality is that countries from southern Europe to South America have felt compelled to make it, so it is worthwhile to determine what they might gain in the bargain. I therefore seek to identify the goods beyond the simple absence of active conflict (negative peace) that a state might achieve by pursuing lesser accountability. Most importantly, the state might seek to entrench democracy and prevent a recurrence of the violence in the long term, particularly by subordinating the military to civilian control, engendering the preconditions for eventual positive peace.

Transitional justice and peacebuilding: moving beyond common debates

There is a vast literature on both transitional justice and peacebuilding and, while this book seeks to build upon that literature, it also moves beyond it. Arguments about appropriate approaches to past abuses have taken several forms. These have been normative (examples include work by Martha Minow and Mark Osiel, cited in this introduction), empirical but case-specific (examples include the work of Malamud-Goti and of Barahona de Brito, cited in this introduction) and empirical and overarching but non-comparative (such as the excellent work of Hayner, which offers extended comparisons, but not structured qualitative comparative analysis such as I have tried to engage in here). All of these have made important contributions to thought and policy with regard to transitional justice, but there remains a gap. That is an exploration of the issue that is undergirded by normative considerations, and that examines empirical cases, but which does so in a comparative context. This approach lends methodological credibility to claims about which outcomes are likely to obtain, and also provides deeper insights for those confronting choices about transition, both local actors and the international peacekeepers and peacebuilders that seek to assist them. While many of the difficult choices about transition must be taken by local actors, and all must be taken with reference to local needs, the reality is that many are taken, *de facto*, by international peacekeeping and peacebuilding actors, ranging from the United Nations to bilateral donors. Only such cross-case comparisons that provide generalizable propositions with a deep understanding of specific needs in context can provide guidance for these actors.

Much of the work in transitional justice pursues explicitly normative claims about what is good for societies and victims, or simply what is 'right'. This is the case in the work of, for example, Neier, Minow and Osiel, of Crocker and of Cohen. This is an important foundation for developing policy, but may well be too narrow. In particular, such approaches only occasionally offer insights into the prerequisites for peacebuilding.[4] This may be in part because considerations of stability are perceived to be at odds with justice, rather than necessary for and complementary to it. As I suggest throughout this book, while there are trade-offs, the choice is not simply either peace or justice.

There is also a vast number of article- and book-length examinations of the single experience of one or another country that experienced this choice, and/or of the role of international peacekeepers and peacebuilders that sought to assist them; the work of Johnstone on El Salvador[5] or Malamud-Goti on Argentina are good examples. Such studies have yielded important insights regarding the specific challenges in those cases, and are often asserted to be generalizable. However, little work has sought to systematically compare cases across time and space to develop propositions that may be reliably extended to future cases.

Drawing upon a host of cases, other literature has developed general propositions about what is feasible or appropriate with regard to accountability. For example, the crucial role of the truth commission in mediating at least in part the peace/justice divide has been elaborated upon or examined by Hayner, Rotberg and Thompson. The function of public discourse in aiding reconciliation through commissions and beyond has been articulated by Osiel. Much of that work, however, refers to the rich experiences of myriad countries by way of illustration only, and thus, while important, may be more wide than deep. As a result, while it enables us to develop important generalizations about the subject, it may fail to take sufficient account of the differences among cases.

This study engages in structured, focused, comparative examination of five very different country experiences, in which national actors, and in most instances external actors engaged in peacekeeping or peacebuilding, faced similar dilemmas. A close examination of each enables me to develop general claims about the preconditions that make accountability more or less feasible, *and* about the trade-offs among various goals that are entailed. A further examination of nearly 30 national experiences allows me to substantiate my claims with reference to a broader set of cases, including the very distinct transitions in southern Europe and eastern Europe. This approach allows me, then, to develop an argument based upon evidence that is both wide and deep.

While the book argues for policies about accountability that are responsive to local needs and capacities, the reality is that in most instances local actors do not act alone, but rather are supported or hindered in their transitions by a host of external actors engaged in peacekeeping or peacebuilding. In only one of the five cases I examine in depth were international actors not deeply involved in the transitional period. This is the case of Argentina, yet, as I discuss in Chapter

4, it engaged in roughly the same set of choices as those where international actors were more involved. This consistency would seem to substantiate the argument I develop about the general sets of trade-offs in which states engage, with or without external assistance. Examination of this case in depth, as well as a number of the nutshell cases in southern Europe and elsewhere, in which external actors were not heavily involved, may also help to control for the possibility of bias by external actors, that they systematically promote a particular resolution of the tensions between peace and justice.

Peace vs. justice: learning from experience

This book addresses the peace/justice divide at the level of theory *and* practice, offering lessons for transitional regimes and those who would seek to help them. I have discussed elsewhere the moral objections to sacrificing justice to stability, and do not delve deeply into that complex issue here.[6] I address here the practical continuum of outcomes: the options are not simply prosecution or pardon, as the most heated polemics of the debate might have us believe, but a wide range of options from complete amnesty through truth commissions and lustration (purification or purges) to prosecutions. The question, then, is not whether or not accountability can be achieved, but what point on the accountability continuum can be achieved by a given state at a given point in time. I articulate factors that make accountability more or less likely in a given country, which are further illustrated by the case studies. Finally, I argue that, despite the importance of these factors for accountability, there are also strategies of transition, trade-offs and compromises that regimes (and international actors assisting them) may make in an attempt to achieve greater accountability or stability. The emphasis here is on these two practical aspects: what makes accountability more or less feasible, and what trade-offs are engaged in by transitional regimes and the external actors that seek to help them? The result is a more nuanced understanding of the different conditions and possibilities that new democracies face, and the lesson that there is no one-size-fits-all prescription that can be handed to transitional regimes considering the legacy of the past.

It is worth pointing out that what is feasible varies not simply with the particular context of each country, but with the 'period' of transition the country is in. That is to say, measures that might not be feasible during peace negotiations or initial transitional stages may become feasible as democracy becomes increasingly consolidated over time. For example, Argentina scaled back attempts at accountability in response to coup attempts and threats by the military in the mid-1980s, but the prospect of further prosecutions was raised again in 1995, more than a decade after the formal transition to democracy began. Democratization is a *process* rather than a moment, and this study examines countries in the period leading up to transition – the exit of militaries from formal or informal control of governance, the end of a civil war, or the end of an authoritarian regime. It examines their experiences through relevant negotiations, explicit and implicit, and articulates the compromises that are struck throughout. There is no set terminus to the examination of any case, other than (a) the apparent waning of strong demands for, or opposition to, accountability, or (b) the completion of activities of the research project in December 1999.

It is worth noting in passing that an important phenomenon on the rise, particularly since the detention of General Augusto Pinochet Ugarte in Great Britain on an arrest warrant issued by a Spanish magistrate, that of internationalization of justice, is too recent to be examined in great detail here, although I have examined the proliferation of cases based upon universal jurisdiction elsewhere.[7] Over the next few years it is likely to be the case that increasing pressure from external legal proceedings will affect domestic choices about transitional justice in ways good and ill; to date it is only in Chile that we have seen a significant effect.[8] The theory I articulate here may be adapted to include this phenomenon as it develops – the types of international/external effects that have included traditional power politics and positive and negative incentives may also include in future the internationalization of justice and the effects it has on domestic processes.

Peace vs. justice: beyond simple dichotomies

I have already laid out the basic potential conflict between peace and justice, and have sought to illustrate that it is more complex than an either/or choice. However, many transitional leaders seem to believe, or are told by other internal and external actors alike, either that they must pursue justice because a good polity cannot be built upon a foundation of injustice, or that they must sacrifice justice for the sake of stability or reconciliation. Such arguments are heard from international and domestic human rights organizations or, at the other end of the spectrum, from members of military organizations fearing prosecution. I address these arguments in more detail below.[9] In Chapter 1 I turn to the question of what makes accountability more or less feasible for a particular nation, and strategies that new democracies might deploy to strike a balance between peace and justice.[10] The remainder of the book fleshes out these claims through case studies drawn from countries around the world. I must turn first, however, to the peace vs. justice debate in slightly more detail, in order to begin to lay bare what is really at stake in this stark dilemma.

Seeking peace, seeking justice: arguments for punishment and amnesty

Those who argue that past human rights abuses must be punished are often concerned with the value of retribution, deterrence, how the victims themselves feel, and the impact on society (social pedagogy).[11] Conversely, those who argue for amnesty argue for the need for national reconciliation or stability. I begin by spelling out the ethical and practical arguments underpinning the defence of punishment and accountability before turning to the defence of amnesty. It is worth noting that there are myriad ways in which the case for and against different modes of punishment can be categorized; this synopsis is meant to categorize the most common rationales and approaches.[12]

Practical and ethical bases for punishment

International human rights groups such as Amnesty International and Human Rights Watch, as well as domestic groups such as the Madres de la Plaza de Mayo (the mothers of the disappeared in Argentina) place great pressure on new regimes to address the abuses of the past through prosecution or other forms of accountability. The arguments they make for punishment fall into several categories: retributivism, deterrence, victims' rights and the pedagogic effect of trials for society.

Retributivism, in plain language, requires that past abusers, such as members of the junta in Argentina, be punished for one simple reason: their actions were reprehensible. There is no concern here with deterrence or bolstering the rule of law: the goal is simply to make clear that wrongdoing must be punished. On this account, then, selective prosecutions like those carried out in Argentina are unacceptable,[13] because any wrongdoing requires punishment,[14] and thus even low-level criminals must be prosecuted,[15] even if they are less accountable than those who actually ordered them to commit murder or other heinous acts.[16] Thus, the sort of legislation passed in Argentina allowing certain offenders the defence of superior orders is also unacceptable.

Alternatively, retributive approaches may demand punishment not just because of the atrocious nature of the crime (that goes without saying), but also because failure to punish invites repetition, though this point is more important for deterrence, addressed next[17] and is not a purely retributive argument.[18] It has been heard quite commonly in arguments for the war crimes tribunal in the former Yugoslavia: to fail to punish ethnic cleansing is to invite Milosevic and leaders elsewhere in the world to look upon it as a legitimate policy tool. For our purposes, however, the central concern of retributivism is that it is the wrongness of the act that calls forth punishment, not effects on societies, victims or even criminals.

However, pursuing prosecution for such reasons may prove problematic in practice. Such punishment by its very nature may continue the abuse of the legal system by the previous regime. Not all perpetrators can possibly be punished, so instead somewhat specious distinctions among state actors are made: some of the guilty may be punished, but others are untouched and, by implication, innocent. A pure punishment/prosecution approach to the problem simply continues socially embedded habits of blaming and divisive 'us vs. them thinking' that were adopted under the previous regime: all the blame is put on a select few who are punished; the rest go free, and the justice system remains suspect. It may be argued that such a situation occurred with the selective prosecutions in Argentina.[19]

Punishment might also prove counterproductive if it provokes a response from elements of the old regime that may undermine the nascent democracy, weakening its legitimacy and undermining its authority over the security forces.[20]

Alternatively, a transitional regime may wish to punish past abuses if it has positive behavioural and societal effects – that is, if it helps to deter future abuses. Given a clear proscription of certain behaviour, and the punishment of that behaviour when it occurs, future violators will be deterred; complementarily, a larger societal deterrent is expected to result from the reinforcement of the rule of law, human rights and democratic processes. The idea is that, for example, another dirty war is prevented not only because members of the former junta (or potential copycats) fear punishment but also because the rule of law is so entrenched as to make the return to lawlessness or abuse of law virtually impossible.

Thus, punishment may serve to restore (or install) democracy, the rule of law and respect for human rights, by making it clear that certain actions are not only proscribed by law, but subject to punishment.[21] On the other hand, an amnesty might encourage future abuses by appearing to condone them. The point is to demonstrate that the rules of a civilized society 'cannot be flouted'.[22] Both Amnesty International and Human Rights Watch officially state that it is the responsibility of new regimes to prosecute, lest abuses recur, or a self-perpetuating cycle of violence be set in motion by those seeking vengeance for prior wrongs, but using similar means.[23] However, both note that, where this is not feasible, at the very least a public airing of the truth must take place, as a sort of second-best deterrent measure.

Prosecution, then, has the effect of deterring potential individual violators, and strengthening societal respect for the rule of law and new democratic institutions. Failure to punish perpetrators will weaken the new state by raising serious doubts about the legitimacy and efficacy of the judicial system.[24] Successful punishment will not only enhance the credibility of the new regime, but also aid its consolidation and reform efforts.[25] While not every crime must be punished, at least some exemplary punishments are necessary for deterrent purposes.[26]

However, as we have already noted, rather than reinforce the foundations of a nascent democracy, attempts at prosecution could undermine them.[27] The possibility that seeking accountability will lead to instability and even a return to abusive authoritarianism is at the very heart of the dilemma that transitional regimes face.

Prosecuting perpetrators as a deterrent may also seem morally unsatisfactory, lacking a moral justification of the *right* to punish.[28] This could have undesirable effects – what seem to be clearly morally bad actions are not punished because they do not serve the cause of deterrence.

Finally, however, there is a practical problem with the hope that prosecution will deter future abuses: it is based on the assumption that the perpetrator knew or believed her/himself to be wrong, and many leaders and active participants in authoritarian and abusive regimes have by all accounts not believed themselves to be doing something wrong. For example, many former military officials in Argentina continue to insist that the 'dirty war' was a justifiable war against subversion. If this is indeed the case, then such abuses are undeterrable, since potential abusers will see such punishments as unjustifiable, or simply as punishment of behaviour not analogous to their own.[29]

There is another powerful reason to pursue prosecutions: the costs that the victims have already incurred, and the future costs that may be incurred by failing to acknowledge their claims.[30] Victims may lose their sense of control and autonomy, and often feel isolated. After state-sponsored human rights abuses, victims may feel especially isolated, as others in the community will often have distanced themselves from victims of such abuses, contending that 'they must have done something to deserve this', or fearing a sort of guilt by association.[31]

The paramount concern, then, should perhaps be to lessen victims' suffering in ways responsive to the harm they have suffered: the state should help them regain a sense of control and help them reintegrate into society. It is also important that the process of helping them involve their active participation, helping them to find meaning and a catharsis following what was frequently seemingly random victimization,[32] and restore their dignity by giving them 'their day in court'.[33]

To aid victims, any measures taken should promote the perception of procedural fairness and participation of the victims by allowing them to tell their own stories to the greatest extent possible. However, though a formalized adversarial setting is important, the process does not necessarily have to lead to incarceration for perpetrators or compensation for the victims. This is because a significant portion of the benefit for victims comes in publicly telling the truth and having it formally acknowledged and pronounced: the 'truth' about abuses is often known, but what is important is the official acknowledgement of the truth;[34] further, public disclosure of the identities of perpetrators is a form of punishment in itself.[35] Truth commissions may be one tool to address the pain of the victims: in South Africa many have argued that simply having a commission with the trappings of officialdom provided some catharsis for victims; in El Salvador the truth commission made a point of naming the names of certain perpetrators in full recognition of the improbability of prosecutions.

While punishment is useful, then, it is not the only, or even frequently the best solution, if one's concern is the aid of victims. Trials may be of use, but so may truth-telling procedures such as truth commissions. Victims may benefit by having a public platform, by having the truth officially endorsed, and by being compensated.[36]

Of course, while this approach may have significant benefits for those directly victimized by previous abusive regimes, it may ignore larger societal needs, such as the re-establishment of the rule of law and faith in the legitimacy of the regime through public accountability (through prosecutions or lustration, for example). In so failing to establish the new regime's commitment to human rights and the rule of law, it might inadvertently undermine deterrence and send the wrong message to potential coup-makers.[37] Lingering resentments over the past may also resurface later, posing problems for the new regime.[38]

Trials may do more than deter abuses, set past harms right or satisfy the victims: they may strengthen a new democracy through their educational impact.[39] They are a public spectacle that fosters discussion and forces society to face its recent past; such discussion, it might be hoped, could help prevent a reversion to the patterns of abuse that occurred in the past. The goal of a trial need not be solely to construct a single narrative of victims and victimizers, but rather an open dialogue that embodies and enables the liberal virtues of toleration and respect.[40]

However, prosecutions on this basis are still risky: it may just as easily destabilize a new regime to have a trial conducted for pedagogic purposes as it would to have a trial conducted for deterrence or pure punishment. Instead of fostering dialogue, this approach may widen and reify rifts in society. Actors that one might seek to re-educate are likely to be resistant to assertions that what they did might have been morally wrong.

Practical and moral grounds for amnesty

At the same time, there may be multiple reasons to promote amnesties, including: concerns for social peace, reconciliation and stability.

Pragmatic considerations loom large in any consideration of this dilemma. While human rights advocates and many new democrats, as well as those who seek to help them in the UN and elsewhere might ideally desire to punish perpetrators of abuses, the fear of retribution by those perpetrators may convince even the staunchest human rights advocate that amnesties are preferable to coups. For example, while President Carlos Menem of Argentina had been persecuted during the dirty war and vowed not to pardon military figures convicted of human rights abuses, he did just that when faced with a restive military.

There may also be more normative reasons for amnesty: should accountability be made a top priority by a nascent, fragile democracy, a rebellious military could easily end the democratic experiment, and democratic stability and the goods it protects may be viewed as moral goods themselves.[41] The future stability of a state in which the rule of law reigns and human rights abuses do not take place might be reasonably placed above the satisfaction and legitimation generated by prosecutions and punishments, although that trade-off is not cost-free.[42] This trade-off will be apparent to reforming democrats even before a transition, and likely affect the sacrifices they seek from the authoritarian regime, particularly in negotiated transitions: reformers will recognize that the chances of a handover are slim where members of the current regime fear future retribution.[43] There is a very real danger that prosecutions intended to strengthen the rule of law and nascent democracy could have the reverse effect; thus reformers may have to accept amnesties and other compromises.[44]

Finally, in many countries punishing all of those responsible for human rights abuses may not be feasible because violators abound: this was a serious concern, for example, in the Uruguayan transition. Defenders of the amnesty there cited the number of potential defendants, as well as the likely destabilizing effect on the nation of pursuing all of them.[45] As the newly elected president of Guatemala said in 1985, 'We're not going to be able to investigate the past. We would have to put the entire army in jail.'[46]

Argentina, facing a large number of potential defendants, took a tiered approach to prosecutions: only those who gave orders or directly carried them out were targeted. Even the president's human rights adviser at the time now argues that the tactic of selective prosecution, chosen because of the vast number of perpetrators, was a mistake: it split the military, and generated further resentment against the civilian regime. Many saw the strategy as mere scapegoating, and the authority of the judicial system was undermined. Instead, in a country with a history of structural violence and social scapegoating, the courts were seen as an instrument of revenge rather than justice.[47] In such situations, amnesty might well be preferable; perhaps the past must simply be pardoned, and society must focus on the future.

Amnesty for the purpose of 'national reconciliation' is often suspect, based as it may be on cynical self-serving arguments made by officials of abusive regimes.[48] Locating the normative core of the 'national reconciliation' defence of amnesty is difficult: at the base of most arguments are the practical concerns discussed previously. Meanwhile, many so-called 'laws of national reconciliation' are frequently nothing more than final-hour self-amnesties by outgoing regimes, padded with rhetoric about a societal need to forgive if not forget.

However, one might argue forgiveness is a part of social healing: in its absence, trials might perpetuate an unhealthy cycle of blame and scapegoating. In countries where massive abuses have occurred, mistrust of fellow citizens and the justice system is widespread, so prosecutions might be counterproductive. It might be preferable to pass an amnesty law, and attempt to begin social healing by focusing on the future rather than the past. In some instances it might be healthier for all concerned to forgive if not forget, and move forward.[49] It might be the case that reconciliation is not a moral 'second-best' because there is no practical preferable option. There may still be some moral virtue in the process of reconciling narratives and attempting to reconcile groups and persons.[50]

Social reconciliation, while it may necessitate amnesty, does not preclude other forms of 'punishment'. The revelation of the truth, it is sometimes claimed, may both enable the victims to heal, and also serve to 'shame', and thus punish, the perpetrators. It may also serve to enable national debate over past events that can eventually enable reconciliation. For this to be the case, of course, amnesties need to be crafted carefully, so that they allow for a measure of accountability and revelation of the truth, rather than simply shielding perpetrators.[51]

However, amnesty on any grounds will still be highly suspect. Perhaps amnesty does not enable stability, and a stable democracy cannot be built on such a weak foundation: a government that begins its term by rejecting the rule of law and accountability undermines its own claims to legitimacy. And it might be the case that social reconciliation cannot be achieved by simply turning a blind eye to the past: victims and victimizers alike need a *process* to achieve reconciliation – at least a public outing of the truth, perhaps prosecutions as well. Further, it may be that, even if forgiveness and reconciliation is the 'right' approach, it is for the victims, not the government, to approve this path.

Frequently, new democracies choose a compromise approach: the truth commission. National reconciliation, or at the very least stability, is sought through offering elements of the old regime amnesty, but at the same time the various benefits to victims and society as a whole through outing the truth are sought through a formalized mechanism of truth-telling. There were at least 15 truth commissions, some government sponsored, some not, between 1974 and 1994, and more have been developed since, most notably in Guatemala and South Africa.[52] This particular compromise has been especially common following transitions in Latin America, where old authoritarian and/or military rulers retained significant control over the process of transition, limiting the political feasibility of accountability efforts beyond truth-telling.[53]

These efforts sought to reap the putative benefits of truth-telling that have been discussed to this point: in particular vindication of the victims,[54] and official acknowledgement of the truth and in some cases the identity of the perpetrators. While acknowledged to be compromise results in the face of political obstacles, truth commissions, say their advocates, aid reconciliation and stability.[55] They may further do so where the mandate of the commission empowers its members to recommend specific measures of judicial, military, police or other institutional reform. It is worth recognizing the limits of truth commissions, both as substitutes for justice and where they are simply badly implemented.[56] They are, notwithstanding their flaws, popular solutions, and are seldom the only tool deployed, as the cases in this book illustrate.

Choosing between peace and justice while seeking long-term peace and justice

It is not my intention at this stage to contend that one or another of these approaches to the peace/justice dilemma is correct, or even to suggest that none of them is correct and propose my own comprehensive solution to the dilemma.

I do suggest, however, that one needs to look at competing interests before formulating a policy: some states may need public articulation of the truth, some states amnesty, some states prosecution, and most a complex admixture of several. Thus, rather than arguing that one or another approach is universally the best, a case-by-case analysis is called for, both to assess what is needed and, as I address shortly, what is feasible. There are numerous competing goods or goals to be sought, and it may be reasonable to make principled trade-offs among them.[57]

In the remainder of the book I deal with historical cases and practical considerations. In Chapter 1, I discuss the practical aspects of the dilemma: given that there will be a wide spectrum of cases in which accountability is more or less feasible, it is worth attempting to establish what features of the state itself or of international politics affect the range of possible outcomes. I then discuss those factors that appear most salient, drawing on lessons from the comparative study of civil–military relations and transitional regimes.

As I discussed above, I seek to build on the existing literature on transitional justice as well as relevant literature on peacekeeping and peacebuilding, but to add to it by emphasizing a question it fails to address in a truly systematic fashion: what makes accountability more or less possible?[58]

The range of options available to a transitional regime will depend, not surprisingly, on the type of transition it has undergone:[59] for example, whether a country has experienced the complete overthrow of a military regime, or has seen a negotiated exit from power, or the old regime has orchestrated its own exit affects the strength of status quo elements and thus affects the accountability that is feasible. This is undoubtedly the case; however, to tell a fuller story, I seek to articulate conditions and pressures prior to, during and shortly after the period of transition that affect the choices made.

I suggest that the level of accountability that is feasible is dependent upon the nature of civil–military relations and/or the balance of power between the government and opposition, the nature of international involvement in the transition, and the nature of past abuses.[60] While the last varies significantly across cases, it is less clear what effect it ultimately has on outcomes.

Does the importance of such pre-existing factors mean that transitional regimes have no meaningful options with regard to justice? I argue that we should not be overly deterministic in our assessment of the avenues open to regimes, and point to possible trade-offs that they may engage in – with or without the aid of international organizations or non-government organizations (NGOs) – to pursue reform and accountability. If civil–military relations are a central element of a new regime's stability,[61] then their 'corporate interests' will be of great concern.[62] I suggest that regimes that attempt to take on the question of accountability will face recalcitrant members of the old regime, and particularly of the military, not just on this issue but on other issues that are generally high on the reform agenda of new regimes: the size and budgets of militaries and their force structure, doctrine and education. For example, in El Salvador, while prosecution was essentially impossible, the new regime made bold moves in curtailing the military's autonomy, subordinating it to civilian control and a new doctrine, reducing its size and budget, and separating it from the police, which even came to include former rebels.

While addressing these issues that affect military autonomy may be a central part of consolidating civilian rule and preventing a renaissance of the culture of abuse, new regimes must recognize that moves on these issues will be viewed with suspicion by the military and that some trade-offs may need to occur. I return to this question in the case studies, illustrating the delicate compromises that new regimes tend to make on the issues of accountability, budgets and institutional reform of the security forces.

In Chapter 2, I provide thumbnail sketches of a variety of nations not discussed in further detail here, to help flesh out the universe of approaches to the dilemma that recent decades have seen. For each case, I suggest which of the factors I have articulated were salient and how, as well as identify the outcomes reached on the question of accountability.

Finally, I turn to my five cases, and allow the stories to speak for themselves, before attempting to analyse the choices each transitional regime made. In the conclusion I attempt to provide a rough set of prescriptions that vary by case-type.

The bulk of the book addresses five cases in detail, drawing on literature dealing with civil–military relations, transitions and democratization in particular. I go about examining the choices tackled by each regime through a combination of legal documents, historical and journalistic narrative, and interviews with relevant political players. I rely not just on what the actors said their intentions were in constructing particular mechanisms of accountability or other transitional processes, but on the structural or institutional products and practical effects of these efforts as well.

Drawing lessons from such a small number of cases is, of course, a risky proposition. I have sought to make this somewhat more defensible by examining cases that differ in terms of (a) international involvement, (b) balance of forces and (c) nature of violations.[63] Finally, I examine experiences beyond Latin America, where the bulk of the cases arose until eastern Europe began to face the issue, by including South Africa and Sri Lanka as case studies.

The findings and lessons

As I have explained, there are two strands of argument developed in this study, which are further examined through five in-depth case studies. First, location on the spectrum of accountability that a country can choose will depend on its context and history. I argue that international factors, the balance of forces, and the nature and extent of past abuses and strife affect the degree to which accountability can be attained. Second, accountability might be traded against other goods a transitional regime seeks to attain, such as military reform and reduction, which may contribute to democracy and stability. These strategies do not simply entail the abandonment of justice for some other political end, but the considered weighing and trading of important goals. One must ask not only what is feasible in a given country, a question I seek to shed light on here, but also how desired goals are to be attained.

Notes

1 Raúl Alfonsín, 'Never Again in Argentina', *Journal of Democracy*, 4, 1 (January 1993).

2 The literature is vast and expanding, and any listing will necessarily be incomplete. In addition to works cited throughout this chapter, further key volumes include Robert I. Rotberg and Dennis Thompson (eds), *Truth v. Justice: The Morality of truth commissions* (Princeton, NJ: Princeton University Press, 2000); Edward Newman and Albrecht Schnabel (eds), 'Recovering from Civil Conflict: Reconciliation, Peace, and Development' *International Peacekeeping*, 9, 2 (Summer 2002) (special issue); Carla Hesse and Robert Post (eds), *Human Rights in Political Transitions: Gettysburg to Bosnia* (New York: Zone Books, 1999); M. Cherif Bassiouni and Madeline H. Morris (eds), 'Accountability for International Crimes and Serious Violations of Fundamental Human Rights', *Law and Contemporary Problems*, 59 (1996) (special issue); Richard Louis Siegel, 'Transitional Justice: A Decade of Debate and Experience', *Human Rights Quarterly*, 20 (1998), pp. 431–54; Michelle Parlevliet, 'Considering Truth: Dealing with a Legacy of Gross Human Rights Violations', *Netherlands Quarterly of Human Rights*, 16 (1998), pp. 141–74.

3 See, on the necessity of marrying peace and justice, Rama Mani, *Beyond Retribution: Seeking Justice in the Shadows of War* (Cambridge: Polity, 2002).

4 For the challenges of peacebuilding, see Elizabeth M. Cousens and Chetan Kumar, with Karin Wermester (eds), *Peacebuilding as Politics: Cultivating Peace in Fragile Societies* (Boulder, CO: Lynne Rienner, 2001); John Paul Lederach, *Building Peace: Sustainable Reconciliation in Divided Societies* (Washington, DC: US Institute of Peace, 1997); compare a critique of the traditional assumptions of peacebuilding in Roland Paris, 'Peacebuilding and the Limits of Liberal Internationalism', *International Security*, 22 (1997), pp. 54–89.

5 Ian Johnstone, *Rights and Reconciliation: UN Strategies in El Salvador* (Boulder, CO: Lynne Rienner, 1995).

6 Chandra Sriram, 'Truth Commissions and Political Theory: Tough Moral Choices in Transitional Situations', *Netherlands Quarterly of Human Rights*, 18, 4 (December 2000).

7 Chandra Lekha Sriram, 'Contemporary Practice of Universal Jurisdiction: Disjointed and Disparate, yet Developing', *International Journal of Human Rights*, 6, 4 (2002); Sriram, 'Externalizing Justice Through Universal Jurisdiction – Problems and Prospects', *Finnish Yearbook of International Law* XII (2001).

8 For considered views on both sides of this issue, see Juan E. Mendez, 'National Reconciliation, Transnational Justice, and the International Criminal Court', and Brad R. Roth, 'Peaceful Transition and Retrospective Justice: Some Reservations', in *Ethics and International Affairs*, 15, 1 (2001), pp. 25–50.

9 See, for example, Nigel S. Rodley, 'The International Legal Consequences of Torture, Extra-legal Execution, and Disappearance' and Ellen Lutz, 'After the Elections: Compensating Victims of Human Rights Abuses', in Ellen L. Lutz, Hurst Hannum and Kathryn J. Burke (eds), *New Directions in Human Rights* (Philadelphia, PA: University of Pennsylvania Press, 1989). I do not, however, deal with the obligation to prosecute under international law; see Diane Orentlicher, 'Settling Accounts: The Duty to Prosecute Human Rights Violations of a Prior Regime', *Yale Law Journal*, 100 (1991), pp. 2537–615. See also Margaret Popkin and Nehal Bhuta, 'Latin American Amnesties in Comparative Perspective: Can the Past be Buried?', *Ethics and International Affairs*, 13 (1999), pp. 100–3; Carlos S. Nino, 'The Duty to Punish Past Abuses of Human Rights Put into Context: The Case of Argentina', *Yale Law Journal*, 100 (1991). On the degree to which these international obligations are applied by states, see Naomi Roht-Arriaza, 'The Developing Jurisprudence on Amnesty', *Human Rights Quarterly*, 20 (1998),

pp. 843–5. See also Steven R. Ratner and Jason S. Abrams (eds), *Accountability for Human Rights Atrocities in International Law: Beyond the Nuremberg Legacy* (Oxford: Oxford University Press, 2001).

10 Jose Zalaquett, 'Balancing Ethical Imperatives and Political Constraints: The Dilemma of New Democracies Confronting Past Human Rights Violations', *Hastings Law Journal*, 43 (1992), p. 1430 articulates this balance well, as one between the Weberian ethics of responsibility and ethics of conviction.

11 Less common are arguments that refer to the inherent normative value of upholding the rule of law; it is more common to argue for the importance of the rule of law only in the context of reinforcing democracy and stability. But see Stanley Cohen, 'State Crimes of Previous Regimes: Knowledge, Accountability, and the Policing of the Past', *Law and Social Inquiry*, 20, 1 (Winter 1995), p. 22. I elaborate on the value of the rule of law and 'doing justice' in itself elsewhere, in Sriram, 'Truth Commissions and Political Theory'.

12 In this I distinguish my categories from, for example, those offered by Mani in *Beyond Retribution*, which emphasizes rule of law, rectificatory justice and distributive justice. While I concur with her thesis that long-term justice and peace entail distributive justice, and that their absence is a contributor to conflict, I here emphasize the structural needs not merely of rule of law, but of the larger security situation, without which long-term positive peace will also be impossible to attain. Such an emphasis should not enable a minimalist approach to international assistance that focuses on thin institution-building, but a thick understanding of a host of societal and individual needs, which include broad security.

13 Nino, 'The Duty to Punish Past Abuses', pp. 2619–21, though this is not the normative position that he takes.

14 Ronald J. Rychlak, 'Society's Moral Right to Punish: A Further Exploration of the Denunciation Theory of Punishment', *Tulane Law Review*, 65, 2 (December 1990), pp. 325–31.

15 Rychlak, 'Society's Moral Right', pp. 326–27. This approach leads to Kant's infamously perverse notion of a criminal's 'right' to be punished. Nino, while not agreeing with retributivism, in essence takes this logic one step further in an attempt to reconcile liberalism with punishment, by conceiving of punishment as resulting from consent or contract: Carlos S. Nino, 'A Consensual Theory of Punishment', *Philosophy and Public Affairs*, 12, 4 (Fall 1983), pp. 289–306.

16 Aryeh Neier, *War Crimes: Brutality, Genocide, Terror, and the Struggle for Justice* (New York: Random House/Times Books, 1998), pp. 83–4, makes the retributivist case.

17 Jamal Benomar, 'Justice After Transitions', *Journal of Democracy*, 4, 1 (January 1993), p. 4. See also Neier, *War Crimes*, p. 222 on the utility of trials, even a small number of exemplary ones, towards these ends. I would argue that these arguments that point to the external effects rather than the nature of the crime or offender ought to be separate from pure retributivist arguments. See Alfonsín, 'Never Again in Argentina', treating retribution and deterrence motivations as opposed; J. L. Mackie, 'Morality and the Retributive Emotions', *Criminal Justice Ethics*, 1, 1 (Winter/Spring 1982), p. 4.

18 But see Mackie, 'Morality and Retributive Emotions', who begins with the intuitive emotional appeal of retribution and seeks to derive a moral account to justify punishment. For a similar claim, that adds that there may be times when it is morally inappropriate to forgive, see Jeffrie Murphy, 'The Retributive Emotions', and 'Forgiveness and Resentment', in Jeffrie G. Murphy and Jean Hampton, *Forgiveness and Mercy* (Cambridge: Cambridge University Press, 1988), but see Hampton, 'Forgiveness, Resentment, and Hatred,' in the same volume. For a defence of punishment based on deserts that is not strictly retributive, but depends rather upon the balancing of benefits and burdens dealt the criminal and victim, see

Wojciech Sadurski, 'Distributive Justice and the Theory of Punishment', *Oxford Journal of Legal Studies*, 5, 1 (1985), pp. 47–59. See also Martha Minow, *Between Vengeance and Forgiveness: Facing History after Genocide and Mass Violence* (Boston, MA: Beacon Press, 1998), which acknowledges the value of both extremes, but seeks to identify other purposes and paths between them.

19 This argument is made particularly forcefully in the Argentine context by Jaime Malamud-Goti, *Game Without End: State Terror and the Politics of Justice* (Norman, OK: University of Oklahoma Press, 1996), pp. 187–98.

20 Mani, *Beyond Retribution*, pp. 33–6, 54–86, elaborates upon this with an emphasis on restoring rule of law, but not larger structural/institutional reordering. Lynn Berat and Yossi Shain, 'Retribution or Truth Telling? Legacies of the Transitional Phase', *Law and Social Inquiry*, 20, 1 (Winter 1995), p. 166; Nino,'The Duty to Punish Past Abuses', p. 2639.

21 I elaborate upon this in Sriram, 'Truth Commissions and Political Theory'. See also Mani, *Beyond Retribution*, pp. 32–3; Jon M. Van Dyke and Gerald W. Berkley, 'Redressing Human Rights Abuses', *Denver Journal of International Law and Policy*, 20, 2 (1992), pp. 244–5. Alfonsin, 'Never Again', p. 19; compare Rychlak, 'Society's Moral Right to Punish', pp. 299–338. While Rychlak's denunciation theory is presented as preferable to deterrence theory, the concern with the effects on society do overlap somewhat: see pp. 331–5.

22 Neier, *War Crimes*, p. 222, 'Symposium: Transitions to Democracy', p. 1056 (remarks of Diane Orentlicher). It should be noted that deterrent concerns may also underpin calls for truth-telling, for similar reasons: fear of discovery may help deter future abusers. See Cohen, 'State Crimes of Previous Regimes', p. 19.

23 Human Rights Watch, 'Policy Statement on Accountability for Past Abuses', and Amnesty International, 'Policy Statement on Impunity', in Neil J. Kritz (ed), *Transitional Justice: How Emerging Democracies Reckon with Former Regimes* (Washington, DC: United States Institute of Peace Press, 1995), vol. I, pp. 217–19. It should be noted, however, that the position of Amnesty International is conflicted on the question of amnesty, flatly opposing pre-conviction, but not post-conviction, amnesties. 'Symposium: Transitions to Democracy and the Rule of Law', *American University Journal of International Law and Policy*, 5, 4 (Summer 1990), pp. 1044–5 (remarks of Nigel Rodley).

24 Diane F. Orentlicher, 'Settling Accounts: The Duty to Prosecute Human Rights Violations of a Former Regime', in Kritz (ed), *Transitional Justice* vol. I, p. 377. See also 'Symposium: Transitions to Democracy', p. 1040 (comments of Jaime Malamud-Goti), and Jaime Malamud-Goti, 'Punishment and a Rights-based Democracy', *Criminal Justice Ethics*, 10 (Summer/Fall 1991), pp. 1–13.

25 See Malamud-Goti, remarks in 'Symposium: Transitions to Democracy', pp. 1040–1.

26 Orentlicher, 'Settling Accounts', pp. 407–9. See also Jaime Malamud-Goti, 'Transitional Governments in the Breach: Why Punish State Criminals?' in Kritz (ed.), *Transitional Justice*, pp. 189–93, although it is worth noting that his more recent work points to serious flaws in the strategy of selective prosecution.

27 Van Dyke and Berkley, 'Redressing Human Rights Abuses', p. 246.

28 Rychlak, 'Society's Moral Right to Punish', pp. 322–5. See also, in connection with this dilemma, the commentary on the Kantian critique of the utilitarian defence of punishment in David Little, 'A Different Kind of Justice: Dealing With Human Rights Violations in Transitional Societies', *Ethics and International Affairs*, 13 (1999), p. 67. The philosophical issue of the underpinnings of a right to punish is beyond the scope of this inquiry for the moment.

29 Naomi Roht-Arriaza, 'The Legal Setting', in Naomi Roht-Arriaza, *Impunity and Human Rights in International Law and Practice* (New York: Oxford University Press, 1995), p. 14; Rychlak, 'Society's Moral Right to Punish', pp. 309–10.

30 See, in particular, Naomi Roht-Arriaza, 'Punishment, Redress, and Pardon: Theoretical and Psychological Approaches', and Jaime Malamud-Goti, 'Punishing Human Rights Abuses in Fledgling Democracies: The Case of Argentina', in Roht-Arriaza, *Impunity and Human Rights*.

31 Roht-Arriaza, 'Punishment, Redress, and Pardon', p. 19; Malamud-Goti, 'Punishing Human Rights Abuses in Fledgling Democracies', pp. 166–8, and generally Malamud-Goti, *Game Without End*; Cohen, 'State Crimes of Previous Regimes', p. 19; Minow, *Between Vengeance and Forgiveness*, p. 21.

32 Roht-Arriaza, 'Punishment, Redress, and Pardon', p. 19; a related claim can be found in Kenneth Bloomfield, 'How Should we Remember? The Work of the Northern Ireland Victims Commission', in Brandon Hamber (ed.), *Past Imperfect: Dealing with the Past in Northern Ireland and Societies in Transition* (Derry/Londonderry, Northern Ireland: INCORE, 1998), pp. 50–6, a volume that deals generally with the issues of remembering and forgetting the past and the needs of victims.

33 Van Dyke and Berkley, 'Redressing Human Rights Abuses', p. 244; Berat and Shain, 'Retribution or Truth Telling in South Africa?', p. 166. See also Juan E. Mendez, 'In Defense of Transitional Justice', in A. James McAdams (ed.), *Transitional Justice and the Rule of Law in New Democracies* (Notre Dame: University of Notre Dame Press, 1997).

34 The difference between 'knowledge' and official 'acknowledgement' is well articulated by Aryeh Neier, 'What Should be Done About the Guilty?', *New York Review of Books*, 1 February 1990, p. 34; it is also attributed to Thomas Nagel's remarks in Aspen Institute, Justice and Society Program, *State Crimes: Punishment or Pardon?* (Wye Center, CO: Aspen Institute, 1989); see also Priscilla Hayner, 'Fifteen truth commissions – 1974 to 1994: A Comparative Study', *Human Rights Quarterly*, 16 (1994), pp. 607–9; and Hayner, *Unspeakable Truths: Confronting State Terror and Atrocity* (London: Routledge, 2000). But see Benomar, 'Justice After Transitions', p. 10; Minow, *Between Vengeance and Forgiveness*, pp. 52–79 generally.

35 Roht-Arriaza, 'Punishment, Redress, and Pardon', pp. 19–21; Van Dyke and Berkley, 'Redressing Human Rights Abuses', p. 246. In some instances the findings of a commission may be used to facilitate regular judicial proceedings: see Popkin and Roht-Arriaza, 'Truth as Justice', p. 105–7.

36 These are just three of the eight goals or goods that one analyst suggests are to be pursued in such transitional situations. See David A. Crocker, 'Reckoning with Past Wrongs: A Normative Framework', *Ethics and International Affairs*, 13 (1999), pp. 47–62.

37 Naomi Roht-Arriaza, 'Conclusion: Combating Impunity', in Roht-Arriaza (ed.), *Impunity and Human Rights*, p. 292.

38 Berat and Shain, 'Retribution or Truth Telling in South Africa?', pp. 166–7.

39 Mark Osiel, *Mass Atrocity, Collective Memory, and the Law* (New Brunswick: Transaction Publishers, 1997).

40 Osiel, *Mass Atrocity*, p. 2.

41 This is articulated as the 'reconciliation view' in Jamal Benomar, 'Justice After Transitions', in Kritz (ed.), *Transitional Justice*, vol. I, pp. 32–3. See also Orentlicher, 'Settling Accounts', p. 379; Roht-Arriaza, 'Conclusion: Combating Impunity', p. 296.

42 But see Mani, *Beyond Retribution*, pp. 53–86, on the limits of relying upon rule of law alone.

43 Van Dyke and Berkley, 'Redressing Human Rights Abuses', p. 246.

44 Cohen, 'State Crimes of Previous Regimes', p. 34–5.

45 Van Dyke and Berkley, 'Redressing Human Rights Abuses', p. 252.

46 Quoted in Cohen, 'State Crimes of Previous Regimes', p. 7.

47 Malamud-Goti, *Game Without End*, esp. pp. 167–98.
48 Cohen, 'State Crimes of Previous Regimes', p. 36.
49 Van Dyke and Berkley, 'Redressing Human Rights Abuses', p. 246; Cohen, 'State Crimes of Previous Regimes', pp. 41–2; Donald W. Shriver Jr, *An Ethic for Enemies: Forgiveness in Politics* (New York: Oxford University Press, 1995).
50 Susan Dwyer, 'Reconciliation for Realists', *Ethics and International Affairs*, 13 (1999).
51 Mani, *Beyond Retribution*, pp. 111–13; Cohen, 'State Crimes of Previous Regimes', pp. 36–7.
52 Hayner, 'Fifteen truth commissions'.
53 Margaret Popkin and Naomi Roht-Arriaza, 'Truth as Justice: Investigatory Commissions in Latin America', *Law and Social Inquiry*, 20, 1 (Winter 1995), pp. 79–116.
54 Popkin and Roht-Arriaza, 'Truth as Justice', pp. 100–1.
55 Popkin and Roht-Arriaza, 'Truth as Justice', p. 83.
56 Mani, *Beyond Retribution*, pp. 101–9, states these limits well.
57 Crocker, 'Reckoning with Past Wrongs', pp. 47–62.
58 For some exceptions see Alexandra Barahona de Brito, *Human Rights and Democratization in Latin America* (Oxford: Oxford University Press, 1997), and Luc Huyse, 'Justice After Transition: On the Choices Successor Elites Make in Dealing with the Past', in 'Symposium: Law and Lustration: Righting the Wrongs of the Past', in *Law and Social Inquiry*, 20, 1 (Winter 1995). For more general overviews, see Guillermo O'Donnell and Philippe C. Schmitter, *Transitions from Authoritarian Rule: Tentative Conclusions about Uncertain Democracies* (Baltimore, MD: Johns Hopkins University Press, 1991) and Kritz (ed.), *Transitional Justice*.
59 See, for example, Samuel P. Huntington, *The Third Wave: Democratization in the Late Twentieth Century* (Norman, OK: University of Oklahoma Press, 1991), esp. pp. 112–61; Huntington, 'How Countries Democratize', *Political Science Quarterly*, 106, 4 (1991–92), pp. 579–616; Terry Lynn Karl, 'Dilemmas of Democratization in Latin America', *Comparative Politics*, 23 (October 1990), pp. 1–21.
60 This is a category that will vary widely, and may be too complex to ultimately have a clear causal role to play. It may include everything from the duration of a conflict and casualties sustained by all, to the way in which killings were done (were people killed or were they disappeared?), whether torture was involved, and the proportion of the population affected by or implicated in the abuses.
61 See, for example, Morris Janowitz, *The Professional Soldier: A Social and Political Portrait* (Glencoe, IL: Free Press, 1960); Samuel Huntington, *The Soldier and the State: the Theory and Politics of Civil: Military Relations* (Cambridge, MA: Belknap/Harvard University Press, 1964); Huntington, 'Reforming Civil–Military Relations', *Journal of Democracy*, 6, 4 (October 1995), pp. 9–17; Samuel E. Finer, *The Man on Horseback: The Role of the Military in Politics* (Boulder, CO: Westview, 1962, 1988); Eric A. Nordlinger, *Soldiers in Politics: Military Coups and Governments* (Englewood Cliffs, NJ: Prentice-Hall, 1977).
62 Alfred Stepan, *Rethinking Military Politics: Brazil and the Southern Cone* (Princeton, NJ: Princeton University Press, 1988) and several essays in Constantine P. Danopoulos (ed.), *From Military to Civilian Rule* (London: Routledge, 1992).
63 Gary King, Robert O. Keohane and Sidney Verba, *Designing Social Inquiry: Scientific Inference in Qualitative Research* (Princeton, NJ: Princeton University Press, 1994), pp. 137–8. Such selection on the independent explanatory variable is designed to compensate for the small number of cases.

1 What makes accountability possible?

Introduction

The debate over 'law and lustration' or the treatment of wrongdoers by successor (often democratic) state regimes has focused on the relative merits of prosecution, amnesty and truth commissions. However, this literature largely focuses on desirable outcomes and what is sacrificed given significant state and/or military opposition to any or all of these measures.[1] Few studies have considered the preconditions under which these measures become more feasible. In this chapter, I set forth factors that I hypothesize affect the outcome that can be attained. I also address strategies of transition that may be adopted both by transitional states and by the international community, and which are informed by my discussion of the previously discussed factors.

Accountability outcomes can be seen, in one sense, as a function of will and capacity. A sheer desire by many to see justice done following a regime change may not make it occur, given practical obstacles like, say, a strong military. On the other hand, there may be cases where, even though the military is no longer an obstacle, there are powerful reasons not to pursue full-scale accountability, for example, because vast sections of society are implicated in the abuses. My goal, here, is to spell out what limits or enables new regimes in the pursuit of accountability: what are political obstacles, and for what other reasons might they choose to forgo justice? Alternatively, what steps can be taken to enhance the degree of accountability achievable?

In this chapter, I develop the hypotheses that the following factors affect the degree to which accountability can be attained:

- the level/nature of international involvement,
- the balance of forces between the rulers and civilian/guerrilla opposition, and
- the nature of past human rights abuses, repression and/or civil strife.

This mode of analysis is temporally prior to the more common emphasis on 'transition type' and, I argue, more sensitive to differences among cases. However, this is not simply a deterministic analysis: while the factors I set forth may set the parameters of state action, there are strategies that states can employ to achieve more accountability or, if they prefer, to achieve greater reform to prevent future abuses. I argue that states will end up in a delicate balancing act, trading off the goods of accountability, and the reform and the reduction of security forces against each other in most cases.

The dilemma

A specific dilemma drives case selection: the concern here is the actions of successor regimes dealing with previous human rights abuses in the face of recalcitrant elements of the government or the military. In these instances, there has been a precarious transition, and the military often still commands great power. Governments are faced with the demands of victims and their families, as well as domestic and/or international human rights organizations and other external groups, to prosecute such perpetrators. However, they know that while such actions would satisfy many, and lend legitimacy to the nascent regime, powerful officials and generals could feel so threatened that they would be provoked to seize power. Therefore, governments face this putative dilemma: they must choose between 'peace' and 'justice'. There is a range of measures from which they can choose: from the strongest, prosecution, through truth commissions, to the least strong, amnesty for perpetrators.

The existing literature

Much of the existing literature on justice in transitional states consists of case studies documenting the choices that governments have made, and following closely their implementation or non-implementation, and their outcomes. These studies often treat rather well the agonizing choices faced by successor regimes, and the compromises democratic regimes may make with holdover militaries in particular. One can find any number of typologies of measures that may be taken, and analysis of the merits of each. What seems to be missing, however, is an analysis of the forces that drive these outcomes.

A key foundation for examining the ways that transitional regimes behave with regard to human rights violations is an understanding of the larger context of democratization itself. Therefore, it is useful to turn to the democratization literature, in particular that of Samuel Huntington with regard to the 'third wave' of democratization in the late 1980s and 1990s.

The literature on democratization, and on transitional justice more generally, has emphasized the impact of the nature of the transition from authoritarianism on the range of options that the new government has.[2] While this observation is useful, I suggest that the nature of the transition is a mediating factor, a product of the variables I discuss below, as well as a factor in the outcomes of interest to this study. Here, I briefly discuss the literature on transition types, and discuss its relation to my hypotheses.

Huntington articulates four transition types: transformation, transplacement, replacement and intervention. He suggests that the level of accountability will range from minimal in transformations, which are initiated by the old regimes, to substantial in replacements and interventions. In Chapter 2 I categorize a larger number of countries' experiences using some of his typology, so it bears brief examination here.

According to Huntington, the least amount of accountability will be achieved in situations of transformation from above, where 'those in power in an authoritarian regime take the lead and play the decisive role in ending that regime and changing it into a democratic system'.[3] Slightly more accountability will be achieved in a transplacement, where 'democratization is produced by the combined actions of government and opposition'; while the status quo elements aren't willing to initiate change, they will ultimately recognize the need to negotiate it.[4] Replacement occurs when the old regime is ultimately replaced by the opposition through a struggle, frequently coup or civil war; here accountability, according to Huntington, is particularly feasible.[5] Finally, interventions by external forces may bring about a change in regime and in regime type; as I explain below, for our purposes here they can be placed into an aggregate category, 'effective overthrow', with replacements.

It should now be apparent that, while transition type is important, we must begin our inquiry at the stage before the transition, and understand the balances of power between civilian and military, government and opposition, as well as international factors. It is these factors that truly affect accountability, although the nature of the transition is an important, and visible, mediating factor.

Given the presence of strong demands for accountability, what are the factors that affect which measures are actually selected? Little extant work seeks to specify the conditions, and most of it does not systematically operationalize them.[6]

Factors affecting accountability

I argue that the relevant factors to be considered are:

(1) the protractedness and intensity of the prior conflict or abuses, in other words the nature and extent of repression, rights abuses and the impact of war;
(2) the prior state of civil–military relations, as well as subsequent reform; and
(3) the effect of international factors and politics on the peace/justice process.

First, the nature of human rights violations. Ex ante, it would appear that a long and bloody conflict could contribute to the prosecution of crimes, or hinder them. Certainly the desire for justice on the part of the victims could increase with the aggregation of abuses;[7] on the other hand, exhaustion from the conflict could lead many to compromise with former abusers and grant amnesty. Thus the number of years the conflict endured and the casualties incurred matters, but the nature of violations also matters: disappearances and torture have different psychological, social and political effects from killings where the location of the dead is acknowledged or detentions that do not result in deaths.

A related issue is the strength of domestic opposition/guerrilla groups. This would, clearly, have an effect on the protractedness of a conflict, but the presence of an alternative centre of power can be expected to influence outcomes in its own right. The relative strengths of governments and opposition movements are better dealt with in the next category, civil–military relations, which may be cast as a larger category dealing with the 'balance of forces'.

Next, civil–military relations and the 'balance of forces'. It seems obvious that where a military establishment has kept a civilian government subordinate, or where the government was a military one, the transition and prosecutions will be more difficult, since the perpetrators will be in possession of the power to halt change. Similarly, the degree to which a military has reformed may affect the degree of justice possible, though this factor is at least partially contingent upon the former nature of civil–military relations. Justice may be limited generally where the military has penetrated civil society and civilian political life. Furthermore, military reform and the pursuit of justice may be traded off against one another. The corporate interests of the military are likely to be protected in at least one of three aspects: the protection of members from prosecution, the maintenance of large military budgets, and the defence of institutional prerogatives.[8] Progress may be achieved on one or two, but probably not all three, of these areas. I discuss these 'strategies of transition' below.

The relative strengths of government and opposition/guerrilla groups will be important, as they will affect the amount of leverage each has in a transition, negotiated or otherwise. While much attention has been paid to the role of military opposition, civilian opposition should not be discounted. In many countries opposition was led by political parties, or human rights NGOs, or church groups, placing pressure at pivotal moments on repressive regimes.

Finally, international/external factors. Not only international involvement in a conflict and its resolution, but also shifts in the structure of international politics, may affect the nature of transitions. It may be the case that international factors are permissive of or more directly manipulative of regime change.[9] Regimes may change because the external environment has changed (for example, a patron ceases to support a repressive regime), in part as a result of shifting norms, or examples set by neighbours, in response to pressure such as aid conditionality, or because of the forces of transnational non-state actors. While permissive conditions are certainly important in that they create unique historical opportunities for change, they cannot frequently be created; thus my discussion of strategies of transition focuses only on those international factors that seem more manipulable. I touch only briefly on the permissive conditions that were perhaps especially important in the so-called 'third wave' of democratization.

Broad shifts in international politics, in particular the end of the Cold War, affected a number of transitional states: many repressive regimes lost guarantees of external support, and in the former Soviet bloc the threat that the Soviet Union would intervene to quash liberalization was removed. Conversely, the vanishing of the Soviet threat, real or perceived, altered US policies towards states under its influence.

Another external factor that undoubtedly played an enabling role is what is sometimes referred to as the 'human rights revolution'. The proliferation of NGOs, both domestic and international, as well as the increase in numbers of conventions on rights and signatories to them, as well as United Nations, (UN), European Union (EU) and Organization of American States (OAS) bodies monitoring and occasionally enforcing these rights can be said to have changed the environment in which state actors worked. While the Cold War may have protected dictators in either sphere of influence from accountability for a time, with its end the new norms were able to play a greater, even unexpected, role.[10]

Arguably, to the degree that external arbiters are involved in the negotiation of peace, greater justice might be possible, since militaries might be cowed by the fear of further intervention. Conversely, however, external players may be more willing to make compromises about justice. In discussing 'strategies of transition', I address possible strategies that international actors and transitional regimes might employ to facilitate transitions and transitional justice.

The players in transitions

Two distinct sets of actors may be involved in framing strategies for transitions: international actors such as the UN (or strong actors like the USA), and the transitional states themselves. After examining the various factors that enhance or impede the possibility of imposing accountability, I address the ways that some of these factors may be manipulated by transitional strategies.

International or external actors such as the UN or the USA can have significant effects on transitions in several ways. First, they may pressure regimes to liberalize, or warring factions to negotiate, through 'good offices', or more active negotiations such as those undertaken by the 'friends of the secretary-general' in Cambodia and El Salvador. They may condition aid on altered policies. Such actions may help tip the 'balance of force' if not in favour of the opposition, at least in favour of negotiation. Finally, they may provide funds for mechanisms of accountability, such as the significant contributions made to the Salvadoran truth commission by the UN, and in particular member states such as the United States.

Democratizing regimes themselves may wish to develop strategies that reassure militaries that their corporate status is protected. This will, of course, be more important where there has been significant military involvement in or domination of politics; militaries may be eased out of power only with certain guarantees regarding protection of their budgetary allocations, or amnesties of at least a few high-ranking officers, or promises that the military itself will not be radically restructured.

The factors in depth: theoretical discussion

The nature of past abuses and conflict

The duration of a conflict or its intensity[11] may affect the choices available at a transition in a number of ways. An intense conflict may reach a stalemate in which, out of exhaustion, the parties are more amenable to political compromises. Simultaneously, however, a prolonged conflict may mean that there are many victims and perpetrators, such that while the demand for accountability may be intense, the obstacles to judicial or other action may also be greater.

Compromises may also be more attainable when the parties reach what is referred to as a 'hurting stalemate'.[12] The conditions may be most ripe for a peace accord when both parties to a civil conflict have become exhausted, and it appears that no resolution is available in which either side 'wins'.[13] It may take some time for this stalemate to be reached, however, because rebels and governments have different aims: governments win by defeating the rebels, while rebels win simply by enduring. For negotiations to begin, both sides need to have lost faith in the possibility of a military victory and be seeking a way to cut their losses through a negotiated compromise.[14] At this point third-party mediators may become particularly useful, especially in holding a negotiating party to its changed perception of incentives.[15] El Salvador in late 1989 appears to have reached such a stalemate, so that international mediation was more likely to yield results. Alternatively, exhaustion may even incite an authoritarian regime not faced with a strong military opponent to initiate transition. This may be particularly true, as we shall see, with military regimes that begin to feel that their own institutional efficacy is being undermined by the burdens of governance.

However, prolonged conflicts also frequently generate more victims, making a reckoning significantly more risky. Victims and their families may clamour for punishment, but not only are there powerful perpetrators objecting, there are a vast number of them. This may mean that, at best, some sort of selective approach must be pursued, as with the selective prosecutions in Argentina. Additionally, where repression was not only institutionalized but pervaded the society, it may be particularly difficult and dangerous to pursue all perpetrators and collaborators.[16] Thus accountability may be particularly hard to seek in instances where repression was prolonged and/or intense. It matters too, as I have already discussed, what form the repression took. Disappearances may be more difficult to overlook because of the trauma felt by not knowing the locations of loved ones; outright killings may be brutal, but at least this issue is resolved. Similarly, in some countries killings may have been relatively few, but the number of detentions large, as in Uruguay: this may or may not make forward-looking policies easier.

The role of external and international factors

Pressures on a transitional regime may derive from a regional or other superpower or from international organizations or both. I discuss the possibilities of these two types of influence in turn.

Transitional regimes may be subject to the influences of either a regional power or a great power. In most of the cases examined, the power was the USA, though in the case of Sri Lanka the influence of India on its tiny neighbour should not be underestimated. Not surprisingly, the influence of a great power may cut both ways. The USA was heavily involved in the domestic and military politics of its Latin American neighbours, frequently to the detriment of human rights. However, there was always a countercurrent, deriving in particular from congressional opinion, that occasionally led US policy to pressure recipients of military aid to respect human rights. While this latter policy was not always successful, or of a high priority, the political landscape changed significantly with the end of the Cold War.[17] The US conceptualization of its interests in the region changed significantly: it no longer saw communism as a threat and thus concerns that its allies and military aid recipients (at least in the region) were non-democratic or abusive of human rights came to the fore. This change in interests or the conception of interests meant that US influence was at times now shifted to encouraging peace accords and promoting human rights: I next discuss some of the functional ways that external influence might shape domestic accords.

Institutions (or regional or global superpowers playing an analogous role) may help promote peace agreements and/or human rights accountability in two related ways: they may help lower transactions costs and thus facilitate negotiations, and they may apply pressure to induce compromises. Institutions may enable compromise and agreements; they reduce transactions costs and enable cooperation.[18] In particular, they provide neutral fora for interactions, and more importantly may lessen the risks of cheating by increasing transparency. In many of the current transition cases, the impact is increased because of the monitoring roles institutions may play.[19] Institutions may also facilitate agreement because they are perceived as relatively neutral actors in politically charged contexts, and because they in turn create transitional institutions within the country: for example, the peace negotiations in El Salvador created the transitional body, the national commission for the consolidation of peace (COPAZ).[20]

Not only may institutions (or large powers) facilitate and monitor agreements, they may help induce them by altering the incentives of the parties. Through the use of carrot and stick, such as aid or the denial of it, external actors may manipulate parties. Institutions such as the UN may have fewer direct aid dollars to use as carrot or stick, but may still be important for the role that their agencies play in creating programmes and funnelling aid dollars into post-conflict development.[21]

In addition, it might be argued that the spread of norms of democracy and human rights aid transitions to democracy and encourage governments to respect human rights and reform civil–military relations.[22] While the influence of norms on political actors should not be discounted, it is of course notoriously hard to measure, and I focus on the more tangible or observable influences exerted by great powers and international bodies.

Civil–military relations and the balance of forces

The 'balance of forces' element turns out, when unpacked, to be rather more complex than it appears at first glance. It is no more than tautology that regimes where militaries are subordinate to civilians are regimes where militaries do not intervene in politics. What is more interesting is why, when a military has intervened in politics, directly or indirectly, it might choose to withdraw. There are really two steps to this question: what sort of resistance from below might push a military to withdraw from politics, and, once the decision is taken, how much reform will the military allow? I call these steps, respectively, the question of balance of forces and the question of corporate interests.

The 'balance of forces' level of analysis itself has two elements: civil–military relations and the relative strengths of state security forces and resistance (for example, guerrilla) groups.

Civil–military relations themselves are a key factor. It is generally acknowledged that there is something unique about militaries in comparison to other institutions, even highly disciplined and hierarchical state structures. The military is separated from the rest of society by virtue of its education, socialization and training, by the values assumed by its members, and by its extremely rigid and vertical hierarchy.[23] However, as is discussed in greater detail below, while this separation and specialization can make for 'good' professionalism in some countries, it can make for 'bad' or praetorian professional militaries in some developing societies.[24]

In many developing countries the traditional isolation of the military from society was compounded by the effects of the so-called doctrine of national security (DNS), particularly in Latin American states. The DNS can be understood as a direct result of the east–west ideological and geopolitical struggle between the USA and the USSR in the postwar era. With the advent of the bilateral nuclear threat, the USA's strategic conceptions shifted, particularly with respect to the countries in its sphere of influence, from an emphasis on total war to that of flexible response. The security threat was seen to be not simply from external attack, but from internal, inevitably viewed as communist, subversion. American security policy with respect to the region was, therefore, concerned with aiding local governments and militaries in combating such internal subversion.[25]

The specific result of this regional strategy was the creation, beginning in the early 1950s, of mutual defence pacts and an extensive programme of training local military members by the USA either in the USA or at extraterritorial bases.[26] The revolution in Cuba fanned the flames of anticommunist paranoia and of the DNS. Secretary of Defense McNamara articulated the policy in June of 1963 in the following way: it would serve American interests to provide aid to local armies to face local conflicts and subversion.[27] Despite some shifts in application, the doctrine remained intact into the Reagan administration.[28]

The content of the DNS itself can, in retrospect, be seen to be a precursor to the repression that many of these regimes would adopt in the name of 'security'. The communist threat was thought to be everywhere, and, most insidiously, to come from within, in the form of subversives and guerrillas who would destroy the state and the security of the region.[29] Thus, there was a heavy emphasis on rooting out not only active subversives, but elements of the civilian population that might support them. This concern necessitated the creation of elaborate and secret communications and intelligence.[30] Further, and somewhat counterintuitively, some variants of the DNS drew on French counterinsurgency doctrine in Indochina, which viewed various nationalisms as also potentially subversive.[31]

Also relevant is the strength of civil society and the level of civilian opposition. Obviously, guerrilla groups are not the only form of opposition to military or otherwise repressive regimes. Civilian opposition may come in the form of human rights and other NGOs, opposition political parties, or other social networks of resistance. Many expect that civic traditions and various civilian interactions and organizations would serve as a shield against authoritarian rule or, should it come, perhaps help to eventually bring it down. That is, where people are linked through trust, norms and networks, they can overcome collective action problems to defend rights and democracy. Alternatively, where they are relatively atomized, such coordination will be much harder.[32]

While it is not the purpose of this study to examine or test for the effects of 'civil society' per se, I observe where this phenomenon appears to be more or less important. Thus, where there has been a longer tradition of democracy one might expect it to be more difficult for an authoritarian regime to entrench itself; one might also expect that strong NGO or other political opposition play a significant role in the generation and nature of the transition.

Even before authoritarian and/or military regimes step down, the question of the relative strengths of government and opposition is a salient one. Elites do not operate in a vacuum, but rather their hold on power will depend on the degree to which they have consolidated and institutionalized it and the degree of opposition offered by other societal forces. Regimes may not simply choose to leave power, but rather the transition may be initiated by the shifting nature of domestic politics and power alliances.[33]

Obviously where a military/authoritarian regime has actually been ousted it will be in a particularly weak position vis-à-vis the forces of reform. However, the situations examined in this book are more nuanced. Further, it is worth noting that even where the military remains relatively strong within an authoritarian regime it may not necessarily oppose a democratic transition: it might even lead it if it views such a transition as in its interests.[34] Nonetheless, the military will be concerned to protect its own interests: as we shall see, this self-protection will affect the level of accountability for past abuses that can be achieved, and also may limit the extent of other reforms that civilians can effectuate.

Strategies and trade-offs of transition: lessons from military corporatism

Having discussed the basic factors that affect the degree to which accountability is possible, I now turn to a key area where careful strategy is required, but where levels of accountability (or other goods) may be manipulated to some degree by new regimes or their international mentors. At issue here is what provokes military intervention in politics, the way that militaries are moved 'back to the barracks', and the role of military corporate culture. From these I derive lessons about the ways that these players can and do make trade-offs among goods/ends of which militaries will be fiercely suspicious: accountability, institutional/doctrinal reform and budgetary reduction.

Naturally, to some degree the possibilities for change in any of these arenas will be affected by the larger context, that is, the nature of the transition.[35] For example, transitional regimes will have much greater leeway where previous regimes (and, where the regime itself is not military, their military supporters) have been replaced. However, many cases will be those of negotiated transition, where military forces allow a civilian government to come to power, or refrain from intervention as a civilian authoritarian government democratizes.[36] Thus it becomes important why the move back to the barracks takes place.

It has been argued that to move soldiers back to the barracks, nothing more is needed than to reverse the processes that provoked the military to intervene in the first place. However, the reasons adduced for the original intervention are wide-ranging – from sectional, class or ethnic interests to a belief that the government is inefficient or pursuing dangerous policies.[37] By contrast, in many cases the return to the barracks depends upon the militaries themselves, and results from the breakdown of military regimes and the recognition of this breakdown.[38] More recently, some have recognized the need to reassure officers about the maintenance of their institutional positions. However, even this instructive analysis may not tell the entire story: militaries and security agencies may be worried about their 'corporate status', but may be worried about some elements of it more than others.

Following Stepan, in the book I analyse three issue areas of concern to militaries in transitional situations: how the new regime handles the legacy of human rights violations, how it deals with the organizational mission, structure and control of the military, and how it handles the military budget.[39] A closer examination of cases will reveal the compromises that transitional regimes must make in arenas of deep concern to militaries. Encroachment on one traditional area of military power (say, the budget) will likely be simultaneous with significant compromise in another area (say, accountability). While it is possible to further disaggregate areas of military concern into sub-issue areas, that is not necessary for our purposes.[40]

Militaries, society and intervention

Clearly, the level of professionalization of the military matters, as does instability in society and politics, although the reasons for intervention in and withdrawal from politics are more complex. Some emphasize the level of professionalization of the military and, in particular, the officer corps,[41] arguing that attaining objective civilian control would result from maximizing military professionalism, making it a tool of the state and keeping it out of politics,[42] in opposition to earlier claims that intervention is more likely to occur where there was a tradition of military involvement in politics or where there were low levels of social mobilization.[43] It may also be the case that democracies are able to reform civil–military relations with the diffusion of norms of civilian control that has taken place around the globe, and where civilianizing is in the interests of both militaries and civilians (because military control of the state is difficult and distracts militaries from their core functions), and because, other than the costs imposed on militaries themselves, military reform is virtually cost-free to societies.[44]

The impact of professionalism may be disputed: it can just as easily provide an impetus to intervention by the military, not least because the corporate loyalty that is integral to professionalism also generates an autonomous corporate interest that may be served by intervention.[45] Given the many advantages which militaries have over civilians, including superiority in organization, emotionalized symbolic status and a monopoly of arms, perhaps the interesting question is why we ever see civilian governments. The answer may be found in the political weaknesses of militaries: they lack legitimacy and the technical capacity to administer any but the most primitive community.[46] Several factors inhibit intervention, including the (Janus-faced) professionalism, fear of loss (of fighting capacity, of a civil war) and a belief in the principle of civilian supremacy.[47]

On the other hand, intervention results from a confluence of factors, including motive, mood of the military, and opportunities presented for intervention. Motives include various sectional interests, and claims about the 'national interest', as well as claims about the role of soldiers as saviours of countries.[48] 'Mood' factors are related to 'self-importance', or the degree to which militaries consider themselves superior to civilians.[49] Finally, opportunities to intervene arise where civilians are more dependent on militaries, or where there are domestic crises or power vacuums.[50] Intervention will happen most frequently where soldiers do not believe in civilian supremacy, and civilians are dependent upon the military.[51]

Conditions include the disintegration of the original conspiratorial group, the growing divergence of interest between the junta of rulers and the military who head active fighting services, and the political difficulties of the regime.[52] Conditions of military withdrawal may include, *inter alia*, a lack of self-confidence, a belief in civilian supremacy, adequate protection of corporate interests, and a civilian organization that can assume power. The case studies illustrate this logic: African scholars argue that the lack of political order is endemic, and is a key enabling factor for military intervention.[53] Alternatively, some argue that handbacks occur where the military's unity is threatened, or where there is a civilian renewal.[54] Thus many argue intervention is more likely where it is seen to be in the corporate interests of the military, and where civilians are weak and there is disorder. Militaries are generally not pushed back to the barracks by civilian pressure, but by internal rifts that make governing difficult.

Militaries, transitions and democratization: more recent arguments

The more recent literature on intervention and withdrawal makes somewhat different arguments. Militaries' corporate interests still matter, but so does the strength of civilian players and the role of outside players.[55] First, there are factors attributable to civilian actors and societal dynamics. There is widespread consensus that intervention is facilitated by weak civilian rulers, and that return to civilian rule may occur when civilians resolve their differences, and the military begins to lack performance legitimacy.[56] Such indigenous forces aid democratization generally, by pushing for it and highlighting the declining legitimacy of authoritarian regimes in a world where democracy is increasingly valued.[57] Military corporate interests also play a role. Military rulers may initiate change in response to internal divisions; they will also prioritize military corporate concerns;[58] concerns about corporate interests that may have incited intervention in the first place are not likely to have waned.[59] Finally, international factors play an important role. These include outside pressure on regimes regarding human rights records, pressure to democratize in order to join the North Atlantic Treaty Organization (NATO), and loss or embarrassment in an international conflict.[60]

Militaries and transitions: hypotheses about strategies and trade-offs

What, then, are the issues of greatest concern to militaries in transitions? I am less interested here in external factors that might prompt militaries to try to reform, than in the processes by which such reform is implemented, and the interests that are defended or not defended.[61] According to many analysts, militaries will take care to protect their corporate interests in any transitional period. Thus, one would expect them to take measures to ensure their continued institutional prerogatives, sufficient budgets and the protection of members from retribution for past deeds.[62] Each term merits some additional degree of explication here.

The treatment of members with regard to past human rights violations, or accountability, encompasses measures beyond attempts at prosecution. It includes lustration or purges, in which groups of those accountable for abuses are removed from posts or barred from holding further public office, criminal accountability and even the naming of some perpetrators by truth commissions. While the last is only debatably a true punishment, those responsible will resist it because of the damage it does to their status and the potential that one type of accountability could lead to another.

Members of the security forces will be wary about any cut in their budget because, in the context of shrinking missions, they fear that they could be eliminated or pared down beyond recognition. Bodies that once acted with impunity internally, when limited to defence of territorial sovereignty and facing no plausible external threats, will fear that the guns/butter trade-off will turn increasingly to their disadvantage. They will thus seek not only to maintain high budgets but control over the budgetary process.

Institutional reform will restrict long-standing institutional prerogatives that security forces may be concerned with protecting. Reforms are liable to include civilian control over the armed forces, ranging from who heads the ministry of defence to who selects the heads of the various branches of the armed forces. Another concern is the reform of the institutions themselves, for example the separation of the police from the military and the appointment of a civilian to head the police, and changes in doctrine and education in both bodies. They will be concerned that institutional essence will be harmed, and that civilians will interfere heavily in traditions that, in the minds of officers, have always worked.

A few caveats are in order here. The argument I am making is certainly *not* that accountability ought to be completely jettisoned in order to move militaries out of power. It is also not a claim that instituting institutional reform alone will safeguard against further abuses or facilitate social peace.[63] It is, rather, a claim that such structural reforms are a vital component underpinning stability, without which social justice and positive peace cannot be achieved.

As the cases I examine further suggest, militaries may be more concerned about some of these interests than others. For example, in Argentina and El Salvador, members of the military were at various points subject to some degree of retribution for past behaviour.[64] At least part of the explanation may be that concern for corporate interests does not extend to all members, but generally pertains to the interests of the elite. Thus, one might argue, the military itself is left intact, and many officers are left unpunished, while individuals may be called to account for crimes of a prior regime.[65]

In fact, trade-offs may be made among the three sorts of interests held by the military, in corporate autonomy, treatment of its members, and in budgetary allocations. As Stepan argues, '[i]n a democratizing regime the degree of articulated contestation by the military is strongly affected by the extent to which there is intense dispute or substantial agreement' concerning the three issue areas.[66]

In this inquiry, I examine and apply the thesis that, as the recent 'back to the barracks' literature suggests, there is a range of concerns held by militaries that must be satisfied if civilian rule is to be stable. These concerns fall into roughly three categories: budgetary levels, institutional prerogatives and the treatment of members accused of human rights violations. New regimes may be able to force compromise of some or all of these issues, but will have to compromise as well. In order to force long-term institutional reform, punishment might be sacrificed. Alternatively, budgets might be maintained at an unnecessarily high level so that some form of reckoning with past abuses can take place.[67]

Conclusions

In this chapter I have set forth two sets of hypotheses regarding the possibilities for transitional regimes, with or without the assistance of external players, to achieve accountability. I first laid out hypotheses about what factors make accountability more or less possible in a given country. These are the role of international actors, the balance of forces and the nature of past abuses and conflicts. In the case studies, I articulate the role of each of these factors, and identify which appear to be the most salient.

The second set of hypotheses asks how regimes and/or aid-givers might seek to achieve more accountability, or partial accountability along with reform. Drawing on the literature dealing with military corporatism, I suggest that regimes will have to make trade-offs among accountability, institutional/doctrinal reform and military budget levels. More accountability may be achieved by sacrificing some elements of reform; alternatively, lesser measures of accountability may enable reform measures that might help entrench stability and democratic civil–military relations. In my five case studies, I examine the trade-offs that each country made on these issues.

The next chapter contains nutshell case studies of about 30 countries that have confronted the dilemma I examine, describing them in terms of the history of abuses, the nature of the transition, the factors I have articulated, and the outcomes. The attempt is to capture the general contours of the larger set of cases; the in-depth studies go into greater detail and analysis.

Notes

1 See Huyse, 'Symposium: Law and Lustration'; Roht-Arriaza, *Impunity and Human Rights*.
2 Huntington, *The Third Wave*, pp. 112–61; Huntington, 'How Countries Democratize'; Zalaquett in Kritz (ed.), *Transitional Justice*, vol. I, pp. 18–19; Karl, 'Dilemmas of Democratization'.
3 Huntington, *The Third Wave*, p. 124; see pp. 124–41 on transformations generally.
4 Huntington, *The Third Wave*, p. 151.
5 Huntington, *The Third Wave*, pp. 142–51. Compare Zalaquett's more nuanced set of transition types. For our purposes, however, Huntington's simpler categories will suffice.
6 While I build on the few pieces that do, I seek to make my factors as specific as possible without articulating an unwieldy number of them. Compare Barahona de Brito, *Human Rights and Democratization*, pp. 33–4, 191, which identifies factors such as the legacy of military rule, the political nature of the transition, and political conditions in the successor regime; see also Huyse, 'Justice After Transition',

emphasizing past legacies, the international legal context and the mode of transition. Both are rich sets of criteria, but somewhat difficult to operationalize.

7 Berat and Shain, 'Retribution or Truth Telling in South Africa?', p. 176. Stepan argues that the lesser brutality in Brazil (as compared to Argentina) made it easier for the victims and members of the opposition to accept amnesties: *Rethinking Military Politics*, p. 64.

8 This I call generally institutional reform.

9 The various modes of international influence over regime change are characterized by Philippe C. Schmitter in 'The International Context of Contemporary Democratization', *Stanford Journal of International Affairs* (Fall/Winter 1993), pp. 1–34, as control, contagion, conditionality and consent.

10 I am again grateful to Alexandra Barahona de Brito for her discussions with me of this point.

11 This is partially indicated by the number of deaths in armed conflict or the number of victims of government or opposition group-sponsored human rights abuses, as well as the length of time that the conflict endured.

12 I. William Zartman (ed.), *Elusive Peace: Negotiating an End to Civil Wars*, (Washington, DC: Brookings, 1995), especially Zartman, 'Dynamics and Constraints in Negotiations in Internal Conflicts'.

13 Fen Osler Hampson, *Nurturing Peace: Why Peace Settlements Succeed or Fail* (Washington, DC: United States Institute of Peace, 1996), pp. 11–21, 23 and *passim*.

14 Zartman, 'Dynamics and Constraints', p. 18.

15 Zartman, 'Dynamics and Constraints', p. 19.

16 This problem, compounded with serious concerns about the rule of law and retroactive justice, pervaded the eastern European transitions.

17 On the possibilities and limits of US influence over recipients of military aid, see Richard L. Millett, 'The Limits of Influence: The United States and the Military in Central America and the Caribbean', in Louis W. Goodman, Johanna S. R. Mendelson and Juan Rial (eds), *The Military and Democracy: The Future of Civil–Military Relations in Latin America* (US: Lexington Books, 1990), pp. 123–40. Noting the impact of the shift in regional or international power balances with the onset of détente or the end of the Cold War, see generally Hampson, *Nurturing Peace*.

18 Robert O. Keohane, *After Hegemony: Cooperation and Discord in the World Political Economy* (Princeton, NJ: Princeton University Press, 1984) focuses on the inter-state negotiation.

19 See Hampson, *Nurturing Peace*, p. 23, and on the Salvadoran case, pp. 129–37.

20 Hampson, *Nurturing Peace*, pp. 221–2.

21 Institutions may also set the stage for a transition through other sorts of conditionality, according to Schmitter, 'The International Context', pp. 22–3.

22 On the last issue, see Samuel P. Huntington, 'Reforming Civil–Military Relations', in Larry Diamond and Marc F. Plattner, *Civil–Military Relations and Democracy* (Baltimore, MD: Johns Hopkins University Press, 1996), pp. 3–11.

23 Janowitz, *The Professional Soldier*, pp. 175–95; Finer, *The Man on Horseback*. See also Juan Rial, 'The Armed Forces and the Question of Democracy in Latin America', in Goodman *et al.*, *The Military and Democracy*, p. 15. On contemporary third world strongmen more generally, see Barry Rubin, *Modern Dictators: Third World Coup-makers, Strongmen, and Populist Tyrants* (New York: McGraw-Hill, 1987).

24 For example, Michael Desch argues that countries generate the 'good' professionalism when they face real outside threats, but the bad kind when those are lacking: 'Threat Environments and Military Missions', in Diamond and Plattner (eds), *Civil–Military Relations and Democracy*, pp. 12–29.

25 Ernesto Lopez, *Seguridad Naciónal y Sedición Militar* (Buenos Aires: Editorial Legasa, 1987), pp. 41–50; Frederick M. Nunn, *The Time of the Generals: Latin American Professional Militarism in World Perspective* (Lincoln, NE: University of Nebraska Press, 1992). See also Consejo Episcopal Latinamericano, *La Seguridad Naciónal: Doctrina o Ideología?* (Bogotá: CELAM, no date given), pp. 16–18.

26 Lopez, *Seguridad Nacional*, pp. 55–63. See also Simón Lázara, *Poder Militar: Origen, Apogeo y Transición* (Buenos Aires: Editorial Legasa, 1988), p. 29; Carina Perelli, 'The Military's Perception of Threat in the Southern Cone of Latin America', in Goodman *et al.*, *The Military and Democracy*, pp. 94–101.

27 Moisés Cherñavsky, *La Seguridad Nacional y el Fundamentalismo Democrático* (Buenos Aires: Centro Editor de America Latina, 1993), p. 13.

28 Cherñavsky, *La Seguridad Nacional*, pp. 13–20, discusses the DNS over time.

29 Lázara, *Poder Militar*, pp. 35–7; Juan Rial, 'Armies and Civil Society in Latin America', in Diamond and Plattner, *Civil–Military Relations*, pp. 47–65; Perelli, 'The Military's Perception', pp. 96–101; Virginia Gamba-Stonehouse, 'Missions and Strategy: The Argentine Example', in Goodman *et al.*, *The Military and Democracy*, p. 165.

30 Lopez, *Seguridad Nacional*, pp. 148–56.

31 Lopez suggests that it was this French twist that enabled the demonization of Peronism as subversive in the Argentine case: *Seguridad Nacional*, p. 156.

32 On the role of civic traditions, see Robert D. Putnam, *Making Democracy Work: Civic Traditions in Modern Italy* (Princeton, NJ: Princeton University Press, 1993); see also Gabriel Almond and Sidney Verba, *The Civic Culture: Political Attitudes and Democracy in Five Nations* (Princeton, NJ: Princeton University Press, 1963).

33 Gerardo L. Munck, *Authoritarianism and Democratization: Soldiers and Workers in Argentina, 1976–83* (University Park, PA: Pennsylvania State University Press, 1998).

34 Gabriel Aguilera, 'The Armed Forces, Democracy, and Transition in Central America', in Goodman *et al.*, *The Military and Democracy*, pp. 24–31 notes that militaries may take this opportunity to set boundaries and rules for the transition.

35 The larger context includes a variety of processes that are integral to democratization, ranging from police and security apparatus reform to the strengthening of labour organizations. For a fuller discussion of these factors, as well as a discussion of them in the case of El Salvador, see Robert C. Orr, *Paradigm Lost? US Approaches to Democracy Promotion in Developing Countries* (PhD dissertation, Princeton University, Woodrow Wilson School of Public and International Affairs, Princeton, NJ, November 1996). However, since my focus more generally is on human rights violations and accountability, it makes sense to narrow the focus to actors with more direct influence over the treatment of those issues, such as the police and the military.

36 For a useful typology, see José Zalaquett's six-level hierarchy in Kritz (ed.), *Transitional Justice*.

37 For a brief overview of theories, see Donald Horowitz, *Coup Theories and Officers' Motives: Sri Lanka in Comparative Perspective* (Princeton, NJ: Princeton University Press, 1980), pp. 4–6; he points not to corporate or other sectional interests but a belief by officers that the government was pursuing dangerous policies and contributing to a national crisis, pp. 146, 208. Even if Horowitz is right about what provokes (at least some) officers to attempt to seize power, the concerns that militaries want addressed before stepping down differ thanks to events that have occurred during their tenure (abuses, centralization of power and undermining of civilian oversight over military activities) that they do not want addressed or reversed.

38 Robert H. Dix, 'The Breakdown of Authoritarian Regimes', *Western Political Quarterly*, 35, 2 (1982), pp. 568–9 identifies a chain of events leading to breakdown,

from delegitimation through the strengthening of opposition and divisions opening within elites through the actual regime exit.

39 Stepan, *Rethinking Military Politics*, pp. 68–69. An alternate, but not contradictory conception is articulated by Aguilera, 'The Armed Forces', p. 32, who suggests that they are concerned with institutional autonomy and immunity for past abuses, but also with the prevention of what they consider inappropriate reform of the political system.

40 David Pion-Berlin, 'Military Autonomy and Emerging Democracies in South America', *Comparative Politics*, 25, 1 (October 1992), pp. 83–102, lists 12 areas of interest to militaries, arguing that some are political and some professional concerns, and that 'core professional functions' will be more aggressively defended than others. However, it is not possible to draw a bright line between political and professional concerns and, as this argument is based on five South American countries, it may apply less well in other regional, historical and political contexts. This is recognized by Philip J. Williams and Knut Walter, *Militarization and Demilitarization in El Salvador's Transition to Democracy* (Pittsburgh, PA: University of Pittsburgh Press, 1997), pp. 158–9.

41 Huntington, *The Soldier and the State*; but see Tom Skauge, 'Contraction and Detraction: Non-equilibrium Studies of Civil–Military Relations', *Journal of Peace Research*, 31, 2 (1994), pp. 189–203, arguing that Huntington's analysis is too static, and there are constantly recalibrations in the level of military autonomy, and that there is never a bright line between the military profession and the state.

42 Huntington, *The Soldier and the State*, p. 83.

43 With statistical support from the 1969–78 period for this claim, see J. Mark Ruhl, 'Social Mobilization, Military Tradition, and Current Patterns of Civil–Military Relations in Latin America: Testing Putnam's Major Conclusions', *Western Political Quarterly*, 35, 2 (1982), pp. 574–86.

44 Huntington, 'Reforming Civil–Military Relations', pp. 9–17.

45 Finer, *The Man on Horseback*, pp. 20, 41, 188.

46 Finer, *The Man on Horseback*, pp. 5, 12.

47 Finer, *The Man on Horseback*, pp. 20–6.

48 Finer, *The Man on Horseback*, pp. 28–49. See also Nordlinger, *Soldiers in Politics*, pp. 66–71, arguing that these corporate interests include budgetary support, military autonomy, absence of functional rivals and the survival of the military.

49 Finer, *The Man on Horseback*, pp. 55–63.

50 Finer, *The Man on Horseback*, pp. 64–6.

51 Finer, *The Man on Horseback*, pp. 79–80.

52 Finer, *The Man on Horseback*, p. 174.

53 See, for example, the essays in Henry Bienen (ed.), *The Military Intervenes: Case Studies in Political Development* (New York: Russell Sage Foundation, 1968), particularly Bienen, 'Public Order and the Military in Africa: Mutinies in Kenya, Uganda, and Tanganyika' and Aristide R. Zolberg, 'Military Intervention in the New States of Tropical Africa: Elements of Comparative Analysis'. See also Bienen, *Armies and Parties in Africa* (New York: Africana Publishing, 1978), arguing that the real impetus for a return to civilian rule is the internal fragmentation of the military.

54 Christopher Clapham and George Philip (eds), *The Political Dilemmas of Military Regimes* (Totowa, NJ: Barnes & Noble, 1985), pp. 11–12.

55 See Danopoulos, 'Intervention, Withdrawal, and Civilian rule: Notes and Perspectives', in Danopoulos (ed.), *From Military to Civilian Rule*, p. 4, arguing that societal, professional military and international factors are responsible for bringing about and maintaining long-term military disengagement.

56 Danopoulos, 'Intervention, Withdrawal, and Civilian Rule', pp. 4–5; Danopoulos, 'Farewell to Man on Horseback: Intervention and Civilian Supremacy in Modern

Greece', in Danopoulos (ed.), *From Military to Civilian Rule*, pp. 38, 51; Dix, 'The Breakdown of Authoritarian Regimes'.

57 Huntington, *The Third Wave*.

58 O'Donnell and Schmitter, *Transitions from Authoritarian Rule*, p. 19. See also Myron Weiner, 'Empirical Democratic Theory and the Transition from Authoritarianism', *PS*, 20 (Fall 1987), p. 864, arguing that for the military to step down it needs to establish that the conditions prompting it to step in will not return.

59 Danopoulos, 'Intervention, Withdrawal, and Civilian Rule', p. 13; Danopoulos, 'Farewell to Man on Horseback', p. 38; Fernando Rodrigo, 'A Democratic Strategy Towards the Military in Post-Franco Spain,' in Danopoulos (ed.), *From Military to Civilian Rule*, pp. 69–70.

60 See, for example, O'Donnell and Schmitter, *Transitions from Authoritarian Rule*, pp. 17–18 (military defeat); Rodrigo, 'A Democratic Strategy', p. 73 (NATO); Danopoulos, 'Intervention, Withdrawal, and Civilian Rule', p. 14; Huntington, *The Third Wave*, p. 219.

61 Elsewhere in this study, I deal more explicitly with the factors of international pressure and the strength of civil society, but here I wish to deal only with the corporate concerns of the military.

62 Stepan, *Rethinking Military Politics*, pp. 68–9.

63 The sceptical view of minimalist rule of law reform is well expressed in Mani, *Beyond Retribution*, chapters 2–3. I, however, broaden my emphasis to encompass not rule of law, police and judicial reform alone, but also focus on military reform as a central component.

64 This point should not be overstated, of course; in El Salvador there were no prosecutions for human rights violations, and in Argentina perpetrators were eventually pardoned.

65 See, for example, Huntington, *The Third Wave*, pp. 211–12, noting that the Greek regime was an exception, in that members of the military regime were prosecuted for high treason.

66 Stepan, *Rethinking Military Politics*, p. 68.

67 This helps to explain the counterintuitive result that, even with the cessation of internal armed conflict or direct military rule, military budgets do not always decline. Or, as another scholar notes, in the Latin American region in particular, budgets may not vary across regime type because militaries exercise a great deal of influence even where they are not in direct control: Merilee S. Grindle, 'Civil–Military Relations and Budgetary Politics in Latin America', *Armed Forces and Society*, 13, 2 (Winter 1987), pp. 255–75.

2 Global experiences in transitional justice

Introduction

In this chapter, I give a brief overview of each of the 26 transitional cases that potentially fall within the scope of my inquiry. Because of space limitations, this book discusses only five countries in detail – El Salvador, Argentina, Honduras, South Africa and Sri Lanka – but it is worthwhile to understand the wide range of actual state experience. In a section detailing the experiences of each country, I describe the history of repression, the balance of forces (civil/military or government/opposition), external influences that may have affected the course of the transition, and the transition type itself (replacement/effective overthrow,[1] transplacement or transformation). Finally, I describe the variety of actions taken in that state to address the 'legacy of the past'. As already discussed in the introduction, which introduces the dilemma, the way I have drawn the parameters of this inquiry excludes certain sorts of cases. I do not investigate cases where a victory of rebels over the government, or external intervention, has so completely quashed likely sources of opposition that my dilemma does not arise. These would include so-called victors' justice cases like the Nuremberg prosecutions as well as instances in Ethiopia where the previous regime was overthrown and then prosecuted. Similarly, if a serious demand for accountability has not been articulated, the dilemma does not arise. A more complex situation is that found in many of the post-communist regimes, where what took place was not an overthrow, but generally transformation or transplacement, but justice was frequently not pursued for legalistic, rather than political reasons. I have nonetheless included the last category of cases here.

Table 2.1 illustrates the challenges faced and choices made by each of the countries outlined here.

Latin America and the Caribbean

El Salvador

Between 1980 and 1992, El Salvador experienced a civil war between the civilian government, in which the military and security forces had significant power, and

Table 2.1 Transitional regimes: factors, outcomes and strategies

Country	Factors	Outcomes	Strategies
El Salvador	**I, B,** H	**C,** L, **A**	R, B
Argentina	I, H	**P, C,** L, A,	R, A, B
Honduras	I, H	**P, C,** A	R, **A**
Uruguay	B	**A**	
Guatemala	**I, B**	**C, A**	R
Chile	B	P, **C, A**	
Brazil	B	**A,** C (non-govt)	
Bolivia	B	P	**A**
Haiti	**I**	P	**R,** A
Greece	**I,** B	**P, L,**	**A,** B
Portugal	I, **B**	L	
Spain	I, **B**	A	R (state not mil.)
Czechoslovakia	I, B	P, C, **L**	R
East Germany	**I,** B	**P, C, L,**	A
Hungary	**I,** B	P, C, L	A
Bulgaria	**I,** B	**P, L,**	R, **A**
Albania	**I,** B	**P, L**	R, A
Poland	**I,** B	P, C, L	R, A
Romania	**I, B**	P, C, A	R, A
Russia	B	none	
Lithuania	I	L	
South Africa	**I, B**	P, **C, A**	**R,** A, B
South Korea	unclear	P, A	A
The Philippines	**I, B**	P, C, A	
Cambodia	**I, B**	P	
Sri Lanka	B, H	**P, C**	**R, A**

Note
This table is naturally schematic at best. I list the factors that seem to have been most salient (whether to support or undermine accountability) in each of the regimes listed in Chapter 2, the outcomes chosen, and the strategies deployed (choices of more or less accountability or more or less reform, etc). The most salient factors are in bold.

Key
factors: I = international or external
B = balance of forces
H = nature and extent of human rights violations
outcomes: P= prosecution
C = commission of inquiry/opening of files
L = lustration/purges
A = amnesty
strategies: R= reform of security forces (structure, doctrine, education)
A = accountability
B = budget reduction/control

the Farabundo Martí National Liberation Front (FMLN), a left-wing guerrilla organization. Some 75,000 people died, and countless numbers were tortured or suffered serious human rights violations. The war came to an end with a UN-brokered peace agreement.

While a civilian government formally came to power in 1983, the military kept a strong grip on political power, an entrenched tradition in El Salvador, where coups were relatively common and high-level military officers held cabinet posts unrelated to defence; the war also strengthened the hand of the military over civilians. The balance between the military and the rebels was more even: although the government forces had access to more resources in the form of US aid, military observers agree that neither side could have won the war.

The influence of the USA was important during the war as well as in its resolution. The doctrine of national security generated an internally oriented conception of security, strengthening the role of the military and police in society. Similarly, with the end of the Cold War the US fear of the global spread of communism faded and the USA began to encourage the government to negotiate. The end of the Cold War also meant declining external support for the FMLN, increasing its incentives to negotiate. Finally, the United Nations was actively involved in brokering accords and monitoring their compliance, including the ground-breaking human rights accord, which allowed the establishment of a UN human rights observer mission even before the final ceasefire was reached.

The Salvadoran transition fits most closely the category of transplacement, which is to say that the old regime was neither overthrown, nor did it initiate reform solely from above: rather the new democratic regime was the direct result of negotiation between the government and the rebels, moderated by the USA and the UN.

In El Salvador, there were two salient outcomes with regard to the treatment of previous human rights abuses. First, the peace accords established a truth commission, which heard testimony and compiled a report pertaining to past abuses which named many of those culpable. Second, while a few prosecutions of human rights abuses did go forward, the new civilian government announced a blanket amnesty, under heavy pressure from the military. Military budgets also remained artificially high, but some reform of the security forces was achieved, with the assistance of the international community.[2]

Argentina

Between 1976 and 1983, Argentina experienced what is now known as the 'dirty war'. Under the military dictatorship, thousands disappeared and nearly 10,000 people were held as political prisoners; many were tortured. After the military's defeat by Great Britain in the Falklands/Malvinas conflict, democratization began.

The military clearly dominated civilian forces in Argentina. There was a long history of military rule, and the military turned to the so-called doctrine of national security to legitimate its role in squashing 'internal subversion'. However, the prestige of the military was severely harmed by the Falklands/ Malvinas debacle, which many argue prompted the government to initiate reform. While there were two opposition guerilla groups, it is unclear what level of threat they posed militarily. Opposition also came from civil society, as human rights advocates gained a public voice and affected the agenda of President Alfonsin. Unlike many other cases examined here, there are no obvious international influences in the transition, save the fallout from the military's loss in an external armed conflict. In the Huntington schema, Argentina's transition was a transplacement. While the regime initiated change, it did not remain entirely in its control.

The tension between societal pressures for accountability and military rejection of such calls led to heavy politicization of the issue of transitional justice. A commission was established to investigate the disposition of the disappeared (CONADEP). While a number of prosecutions against high-level military figures ended in conviction, the restive military staged several coup attempts, and eventually the civilian government chose to institute a number of amnesty laws. However, the issue of past abuses arose again late in 1998, when the ex-ruler Emilio Massera was arrested in connection with the kidnapping of two infants. This is thought to be part of a larger pattern of kidnapping of infants of detained mothers; the infants were then given to couples in the security forces. Another former ruler, Jorge Rafael Videla, is also being held in relation to these kidnappings; Massera is also under investigation in Spain for past abuses.[3] Some military reform and a significant reduction in force size as well as a reduction in budgets was also achieved.

Honduras

Like many Latin American nations, Honduras has a long tradition of military rule. And, like many Central American nations, Honduras was powerfully affected by the intensification of Cold War tensions in that region in the 1980s. Honduras was a strategic country, because the US-trained *contras* fighting the left-wing regime in Nicaragua used Honduras as a base. The Honduran military was in turn the beneficiary of US military aid and training assistance.

From 1980 on, there was a significant increase in human rights abuses, often perpetrated by the infamous Battalion 3–16, which was trained by the Central Intelligence Agency (CIA). Members of opposition groups and others 'disappeared', while others were detained and tortured. Change would be initiated after the inauguration of a civilian president in January 1994, who sought reform of the security forces and accountability for past abuses.

As mentioned above, the military has traditionally been heavily involved in politics in Honduras, frequently to the extent of governing directly, as it did before the 1994 Reina regime. There exists no significant opposition force such as a guerilla group and civil society has formed no significant counterweight.

The Cold War rivalry directly affected Honduran politics, and the waning of tensions had the reverse effect. While there was a decline in direct US influence in support of the military, there has not been a significant US effort to encourage democratization or accountability, although more recently it has provided aid to police reform efforts. The Honduran transition can be characterized as transplacement: while the military permitted the elections that ushered it out of direct political power, further changes have been initiated, if not always successfully completed, by civilians.

Honduras has had prosecutions as well as a variant on the truth commission. In December 1993, a government human rights commission issued a report outlining the history of military and government human rights abuses. President Reina has pledged to separate the police force from the military and place it under civilian authority. Further, attempts at holding human rights abusers accountable for their actions have begun despite the presence of one amnesty law. One officer was convicted in July 1993. In July 1995, ten more officers were indicted on charges of kidnapping and torturing students. In response to the push for accountability, in August the military sent tanks into the streets of the capital in what was widely viewed as a warning against further pursuit of accountability, prompting the president to reconsider his stance against amnesty. While recent steps towards reform of the security forces have been taken, the budget for the military continues to rise.

Uruguay

Prior to the military takeover that lasted from 1973 to 1985, Uruguay had a significant history as a relatively stable liberal democracy.[4] In the face of increased violence by the leftist guerrilla group, the Tupamaros, the armed forces had taken over the police role in fighting the rebels in 1971. In 1973, the armed forces forced the president to dissolve parliament, and military rule was formalized in 1976. While, unlike many other countries in Latin America, disappearances and state-sponsored killings were not common, significant numbers of political prisoners were held, and torture was common; in addition, many civil servants lost their jobs for purely political reasons.[5] After a 1980 plebiscite in which the citizenry rejected a draft constitution that would have institutionalized the role of the armed forces in the national government, the military initiated talks with various political parties regarding a transition to civilian rule.

While the Tupamaro movement was armed, it did not seriously harm the armed forces; when they voluntarily withdrew from power it was intact, and the army strongman General Medina became the new government's defence minister.[6] Thus, as one observer has noted, Uruguay lacked certain features present in countries like Argentina, and change was inhibited because the military left power of its own accord and unbowed.[7] There does not appear to have been a great deal of involvement by international actors in the initiation or execution of the Uruguayan return to civilian rule, though UN and

Inter-American human rights bodies were active in monitoring and protesting abuses and impunity.[8]

The Uruguayan return to civilian rule has reasonably been characterized as transplacement: the transition was initiated at the top by the military government, but negotiated with other Uruguayan political actors. This meant that the military had significant, but not total control over the shape of the future political landscape.

The negotiation process culminated in the August 1984 Naval Club Pact, which provided for free elections. The pact also, according to reports, contained an unofficial agreement that the new government would not seek to prosecute past abuses, but would not stand in the way of action by individual citizens in court.[9] The new civilian president, Sanguinetti, had said throughout the campaign, as had the other candidates, that he would seek accountability for past violations. Upon his election, Sanguinetti rapidly amnestied political prisoners, excepting members of the armed forces charged with human rights violations, and provided for restitution for them as well. An investigative commission into the fate of the disappeared was created, but had a weak mandate and even less political impact.

Private lawsuits against members of the armed forces responsible for human rights abuses also rapidly began in civilian courts, whose jurisdiction the military challenged. The military made it clear that it would not appear before these courts, and pushed for an end to the trials. The government sought to avert a direct confrontation with the armed forces by introducing amnesty bills, which were rejected. Finally, in December 1986, the legislature passed the law nullifying the state's claim to punish certain crimes, which, while not termed an amnesty, effectively protected most military members from the judicial process for human rights abuses. While the law stated that the executive was to investigate all disappearance cases and report back to the plaintiffs, in a further concession to the military, the president later delegated the investigations to the military.[10] In 1989, a group of families of victims sought repeal of the law, and acquired the required number of signatures on petitions to hold a referendum. The military vocally opposed the referendum as did the president; the measure was ultimately defeated in a 58–42 vote.[11] The military budget continued to rise throughout the transition and after.[12]

Guatemala

After a coup by the military in 1954, the government of Guatemala became increasingly repressive and abusive of human rights. The government later became engaged in armed struggle with the guerrilla group, the Unidad Revolucionaria Nacional Guatemalteca (URNG), one which lasted 20 years. The repression reached its height in the early 1980s, when 200 Mayan villages were wiped out and tens of thousands were killed, and thousands more forcibly 'disappeared'.[13]

While the country made the formal transition to civilian rule in 1986, the military remained dominant and human rights violations continued; further, a few days prior to the inauguration of the new civilian president, the military pushed through an amnesty decree.[14] It was not until 1990 that the peace process began, with a preliminary accord by the government of Guatemala and the URNG to seek peace through political means. As with many other nations in transition, the key issues of contention were the treatment of past abuses and the nature of the security forces. While a few low-level military officers have in fact been convicted for abuses, high-level officers have not been affected.

However, as in El Salvador, these issues were not the first ones confronted: instead the first substantive agreement was one in 1994 calling on the UN to establish a human rights verification mission. The government also promised to strengthen the office of the human rights ombudsman, fight impunity by criminalizing acts like forced disappearances and extrajudicial execution, and continue cleansing the armed forces,[15] but particular measures to achieve these goals were not specified. The UN mission is empowered only to monitor the human rights situation subsequent to its arrival, not to address the issue of past abuses.

Also in 1994, the parties agreed to the creation of a variant on the truth commission.[16] According to the terms of the agreement, the commission is to 'clarify' human rights violations and violent acts related to the armed conflict. The commission is not to name names; in fact its findings are not to be used in subsequent prosecutions. Some observers see this agreement as creating a commission that is considerably weaker than others such as that of El Salvador.[17]

Subsequent agreements in December 1996 sought to separate the military and the police: they establish the distinctions between the Policía Nacional Civil (PNC) and the army. In particular, the police are to be professional, respectful of human rights, and trained by a police academy that inculcates these traits. Further, with a significant exception, they are to have exclusive control over matters of internal security. By comparison, the military's sole role is to pertain to the defence of sovereignty and territorial integrity, except in exceptional instances when it might act in aid of internal security, but under civilian command. The accords further establish that the military is to be under the control of the president, though the president is to consult with the congress.[18] These accords also dictate the terms of demobilization and the reduction of the military budget. While these reforms would be significant if fully executed, some observers claim that there has been a complete failure to demilitarize the police.[19] Further, the legacy of political killings made a shocking comeback when a bishop active in human rights who had just completed a report on past abuses was killed under mysterious circumstances in early 1998.[20] Finally, the parties agreed to terms for the legal incorporation of the URNG, and on 29 December, the parties signed the final peace accord.

While the URNG was able to carry on an armed struggle against the government of Guatemala for two decades, some observers have suggested that the weak terms of the peace accord indicate that it was outgunned and thus had to accept some serious compromises.[21] There was heavy international pressure to reach an accord, given that Guatemala had the last internal armed conflict in Central America. Furthermore, the UN took an active part in the peace negotiations, establishing a human rights mission while the negotiations went forward, and continues to monitor the peace accords. Like El Salvador's, Guatemala's transition was a negotiated one between the rebels and the government, something of a transplacement.

Guatemala's transition was a negotiated compromise, and the result was a relatively toothless truth commission, but also a promise to purify the armed forces and reform the police and the military. The move towards accountability showed new vigour, however, in late 1998, when a court found guilty and sentenced to death three pro-government fighters for their part in a 1982 massacre.[22] Civilian control over the military budget was established in the peace accords, and the budget held steady for several years and was set to decline in 1999.[23]

Chile

In 1973, General Augusto Pinochet led a coup, instituting a regime in which there was widespread repression carried out by the intelligence service.[24] While the judiciary remained in place, it did not seriously examine claims of human rights abuses, and in 1978 an amnesty law was enacted which barred prosecutions for abuses between 1973 and 1978. Growing protests through the early 1980s prompted Pinochet to declare a state of siege in 1983. Following a 1986 demonstration that involved an assassination attempt, a new state of siege was imposed and about 15,000 people were arrested. This state was lifted in 1987, prompted in part by the upcoming visit from the pope. In 1988, Pinochet consented to a plebiscite on his continued rule; the 'no' vote was followed by the 1989 elections that made Patricio Aylwin president.[25]

There can be no question that before, during and after the transition the Chilean military wielded overwhelming power over Chilean politics. It did not face a challenge in the form of armed opposition and, even after relinquishing control over the state, it maintained its power base and the capacity to oust the new regime if it so chose. By all accounts it was the fear of confrontation with the armed forces that led the Aylwin administration to take a softer line on the legacy of the past than it had initially promised.[26] A recent observer has argued that civil–military relations remain stalemated.[27] Unlike many other countries that experienced this type of transition, external factors were not particularly salient in the Chilean case, though the issues have recently been internationalized with the detention of Pinochet in the UK.

The Chilean transition is categorized as a transformation, as the change of regime type was initiated at the top and remained in Pinochet's power. Parties were allowed to participate in the transition only if they promised to respect the extant constitutional structure. Even after the transition, key facets of the power of the military and of Pinochet remained intact: the constitution preserved military influence and autonomy,[28] Pinochet was to retain the role of commander in chief of the armed forces through 1997, most of the judiciary had been named by Pinochet, and the upper house of the legislature, the Senate, was packed with military supporters.[29]

The military and Pinochet thus retained a great deal of power, which effectively limited the Aylwin regime in its pursuit of accountability. Though the coalition that had supported the Aylwin campaign had advocated the nullification or derogation of the amnesty law, the new government acknowledged that it did not have the political power to pursue punishment.[30] Aylwin initially proposed that there be trials followed by pardon, but major obstacles were resistant judges and the fear of a restive military.[31] Instead, Aylwin created the national commission on truth and reconciliation, which released a report of its investigation into some 3,000 cases in 1991, naming victims but, unlike some commissions, not naming perpetrators. The government also created an extensive reparations programme.[32]

Accountability would be much harder to achieve: Pinochet warned the new government not to 'touch a single hair of a single soldier' lest the 1973 coup be repeated. In December 1990, he put the army on alert to lend credibility to this threat. In order to appease the military, in 1993 Aylwin proposed legislation that would provide anonymity for military defendants and witnesses in the human rights cases that did come before the courts as well as make permanent the 1978 amnesty. Under heavy fire from human rights groups and families of victims, as well as opposition from the leftists in the governing coalition, he withdrew the proposal.[33] By early 1994, there had been 20 convictions for post-1978 abuses.[34] More recently, the international community and Chile have been forced to reconsider Chile's past with the arrest in London of Pinochet pursuant to a Spanish warrant.[35] In the face of the prospect that Pinochet will at long last face justice, but outside Chile's borders, the foreign minister pledged that his own country would pursue accountability, though that promise has been met with scepticism.[36] Pinochet was returned to Chile to face charges there, but in July 2002 the Chilean Supreme Court terminated the prosecution, finding that he was too ill to stand trial. Other measures of military corporatism, such as Pinochet's continued role in politics and the military until his arrest in London and the relative decline of military spending indicate a mixed result.[37]

Brazil

In 1964, the armed forces of Brazil overthrew the president and held power for the next 21 years.[38] For most of this period legislatures were tolerated, but had no autonomy. The use of torture was widespread, and though the number of 'disappeared' was relatively small at approximately 300, tens of thousands were forced into exile, arrested for political reasons, or forced out of their jobs or schools.

Some limited political activity was permitted during this period, and a political alliance between political and military elites paved the way for a gradual opening beginning in 1974. Throughout this period, the military sought to ensure that it would maintain its influence and avoid accountability for past human rights violations. In January 1985, a new civilian president finally came to power. The military was clearly the dominant actor in the Brazilian transition. While it worked in tandem with civilian elites, it was not forced from power by opposition groups. Rather, it dictated the terms and timetable of the transition. While the USA at one point held great sway, in particular over the Brazilian military, providing training and indoctrination in step with the DNS, by the time the transition began that influence had waned. Nor was there significant international involvement in the transition.

Because of the tight management of the transition by the military, it is described as a transformation. In 1979, the military president put forth and achieved the passage of an amnesty bill both for those who had been imprisoned during the military regime and for those who had committed human rights abuses. Further, there are allegations that the civilian president elected in 1985 had negotiated a deal with the military in which he promised that there would be no official investigation into allegations of human rights abuses during the regime. Indeed, the government did not seek to uncover the past; a private inquiry was undertaken by some in the Catholic church, who produced a report called *Brasil: Nunca Maís*.

As already indicated, there was no official attempt to seek accountability for human rights violations or even to officially acknowledge the abuses of the past through a government-sanctioned investigation. Instead, there was an amnesty and a private report. Furthermore, the high degree of control maintained by the military over the 12-year transition meant that there was a great deal of institutional carryover from the military to the civilian regime. The military budget also rose over the protracted transition.[39] Nonetheless, the issue of past abuses has surfaced recently with a re-examination of a 1981 bombing and a controversy surrounding the nomination for the chief of the federal police of an individual accused of torture.[40]

Bolivia

In Bolivia, the period of authoritarian rule for which accountability is demanded was relatively brief, lasting from 1980 to 1981 when it was ruled by General Luis Garcia Meza.[41] During this period political opponents were 'disappeared' and assassinated, and after civilian rule was restored there were calls for punishment. In 1986, the congress brought criminal charges against the general and members of his junta as well as members of the security forces and military. The general and a number of other defendants then went into hiding, but were tried in absentia. After years of delay, the supreme court convicted the defendants on a variety of charges; the human rights violations for which they were convicted included murder, torture and arbitrary detention. The court referred to one set of killings as a 'genocidal' act, referring to international law. Eleven of those convicted are now imprisoned, but the general is still a fugitive. The military claims to have accepted the trials, though there are accusations that it is sheltering Garcia Meza.

Bolivia presents a somewhat unusual case in that it was the military itself that overthrew Garcia Meza, though it was faced with mass mobilization and protest as well. Thus, one commentator argues that it was rupture or collapse in the old regime that made punishment possible.[42] International influence appears to have been less salient at the time of transition for Bolivia than for some of its neighbours with which it collaborated in Operation Condor, a region-wide effort to quash leftist resistance groups. In many ways, Bolivia appears to present a case of transformation from above, given that it was the military itself that ousted its own dictator, while seeking to protect itself. It is also a relatively rare case in that trials were carried out, convictions were achieved and some individuals are now imprisoned for the human rights violations of the past. Military budgets were also slashed.[43]

Haiti

Haiti has a lengthy history of authoritarian rule punctuated by coups.[44] The country's human rights record was dismal, with high levels of corruption, as well as official brutality in which some 40,000 Haitians died between 1957 and 1971. In 1986, after 31 years of Duvalier rule, first under 'Papa Doc' and later under his son 'Baby Doc', that family's reign finally ended. However, the fall of Baby Doc did not lead immediately to democratization: instead for four years there were regimes backed by the military and the economic elite.

During this period there was a minimal response to calls for accountability for abuses of the past. Some low-ranking military officers and members of the Tonton Macoutes, a brutal private security body, were prosecuted; high-ranking military members and the head of the Tonton Macoutes were allowed to leave the country. In 1990, with significant UN and OAS aid, Haiti finally experienced a free election. With a 75 per cent voter turnout, Jean-Bertrand Aristide was elected by two-thirds of the vote. Aristide immediately initiated measures to reform the security forces and address the legacy of the past: he announced a commission to investigate the human rights abuses of the past, dissolved the 'section chiefs' who reported back to military and ran roughshod over human rights in rural areas, planned retirement of senior military officials responsible for human rights abuses, and planned a new system of rural police untainted by the abuses of the past.

However, the Aristide regime was threatened from the outset: there was an attempted coup before Aristide took office, and there was a series of coup attempts that failed before the final successful one in September 1991. This coup forced Aristide's removal, reversed his reform initiatives, and began a reign of terror in which thousands have been tortured or killed and many more have fled in flimsy boats to the USA. The old system of section chiefs and Tonton Macoutes, now called attachés, was restored. The military coup leaders installed a civilian puppet government.

The international community then became involved in efforts to negotiate the return of Aristide to power and the removal of Raoul Cedras from the military high command. The negotiations repeatedly foundered on the issue of accountability for human rights violations. In 1993, an extensive accord was finally reached which would have provided for an amnesty; and retired Cedras; it would have allowed other coup initiators to remain in the military but posted them abroad. The agreement would also have separated the military and the police, and reformed both. However, Cedras violated the agreement, and the international community was further outraged when the attachés assassinated the minister of justice and Aristide's key financial supporter. The international community responded with sanctions and an oil and weapons embargo, and the USA and others sent warships to the region. Finally, in July 1994, the UN Security Council authorized a US invasion and occupation, which prompted Haiti's de facto leaders to negotiate. As a result, Aristide took power, the military was disbanded and the UN began a police mission in Haiti; in addition a UN–OAS civilian monitoring mission was installed.

While domestic opposition was vocal, the military held the advantage, easily forcing Aristide into exile and terrorizing the civilian population. Obviously external actors were central to the Haitian transition, from international political pressure to active invasion, intervention and monitoring under UN auspices. While the military regime took part in negotiations, it ultimately had little influence in the process once the international community stepped in; thus the Haitian transition looks like a virtual effective overthrow. Haiti has not fully addressed the legacy of the past. Important reforms like the abolition of the military and the training of a more disciplined police force have gone forward, with aid from the international community.[45] However, the few attempts at prosecution have not been vigorously pursued.

Southern Europe

Greece

In April 1967, a junta of mid-level officers seized power, suspending the constitution and parliament.[46] Its rule was marked by torture and arbitrary arrests. In 1974, the military sponsored a coup in Cyprus. Faced with embarrassment and likely defeat there, the military leaders began negotiations for the return to civilian rule, which came in July. The outgoing regime retained a significant degree of power over the transition, passing power to active anti-communist Constantine Karamanlis. The new regime instituted a programme of dejuntafication followed by trials, but the overall policies of democratization were marked by gradualism.

Because the military as an institution remained intact, there were limitations on the degree of change that the new government could impose. The government did free political prisoners and announce an amnesty for political crimes other than those related to the junta, as well as transfer, discipline or dismiss some 100,000 civil servants who had served under the junta, and limit the power of the military police. At the same time, junta leaders and 30 security officials were indicted for deaths in a university uprising in 1973.

Nonetheless, Karamanlis was concerned about confronting the military head on without a popular electoral mandate, and announced elections. Following parliamentary elections that gave the Karamanlis government that mandate, he voided the laws of the junta. In 1975, prosecutions began against 150 persons for actions by the junta, ranging from ministers to military and police officers. At the same time, a similar number of senior officers of the armed forces and security forces were forcibly retired. While many were brought to trial, and three of the coup leaders were sentenced to death, their sentence was commuted to life and only eight other individuals received a similarly severe sentence. Other trials for torture would follow; by December 1976 there had been some 400, but the rate of convictions was low and did not result in particularly serious sentences.

At the same time, the government took measures to avoid a military backlash, setting a deadline for private lawsuits and offering a deal to those who testified for the prosecution: that they would not be prosecuted. Some of those convicted were let off with fines or even suspended sentences. Karamanlis further sought to appease the military by increasing its budget and promising that career evaluations would be based on future, not past, behaviour.

While the junta was clearly dominant in the political realm, its political clout at the time of the handover had been severely damaged by the crisis in Cyprus. Further, the existence of a real threat from Turkey over Cyprus forced the military to become more externally oriented. The crisis in Cyprus was a key factor, both because of its impact on the military's prestige and because of the demands it placed on the military. The transition in Greece was essentially a transformation, initiated from above by the military, with its looming presence placing significant limitations on the actions that a new civilian government could take. Nonetheless, the military's weakened state probably enabled the new government to make the significant strides that it did in instituting trials.

While there were trials of numerous figures, it is worth noting how few actually were convicted or served extensive sentences. There were some purges, but the military's budget actually increased and there were no attempts at institutional reform.

Portugal

Portugal experienced a half-century of authoritarian rule punctuated by a coup by a small number of junior and mid-level officers in 1974, overthrowing that regime.[47] There was a purge of citizens for ideological reasons in 1974–75; the former president and prime minister were exiled. In 1976, however, a new legislature was democratically elected, and reversed these policies, nullifying the purges and seeking to reintegrate purged officials.

The new constitution and regime had to mediate between two contending forces: the right wing, which had held dictatorial power for nearly 50 years, and the left wing, which had briefly run an authoritarian regime. While there was also significant domestic opposition to the regime that occasionally took the form of armed resistance, it was ultimately the coup by the low-level officers that brought the downfall of the regime. There does not seem to have been significant international involvement in the transition, but one salient factor may have been the military's overextension in colonial warfare in Angola, Guinea and Mozambique. The transition seems best classifiable as a replacement through a coup, after which the military would step down.

Purges took place, but the mechanisms like trials and truth commissions that are so familiar today were not utilized. The military budget spiked before the democratic legislature took over, but was then drastically reduced, and the military services were reduced as well.[48]

Spain

The dictatorship of General Franco began in 1939 with his faction's victory in the Spanish Civil War and lasted for the next 46 years.[49] Political repression was widespread, including the elimination of competing political parties, the elimination of those who had supported the republicans, and the banning of nearly all associations save the Catholic church. From 1969 to 1973, the government was administered by the Opus Dei sect of the Catholic church under Admiral Blanco. Under this regime, there was an increase in repressive policies, and in 1971 the Catholic church broke ties with the regime. The assassination of Blanco by Basque separatists in 1973 struck a severe blow to the regime. In 1975, Franco died; the new king he had selected initiated reforms. However, many elements of the previous system would endure. In 1976, the king issued an amnesty for many who had been convicted of political crimes and, in 1977, a new bicameral legislature was elected. However, a substantial part of the old regime was absorbed into the new; police files were not used to purge abusers, but were sealed instead. And in 1977 the new legislature passed an amnesty covering all political crimes committed by both government and opposition. The Francoist political class maintained a strong hand in the project of constitutional reform, obtaining guarantees of personal continuity and striking out some features of reform. The only reform that directly affected the Francoist political machinery was the dissolution of the party created by Franco and of state corporatist interest associations created for workers and capitalists under his regime.

No measures could be taken to address the abuses of the past. The tribunal of public order, a body that was ostensibly created to combat terrorism but was rather used to repress the opposition, was eliminated in 1977. However, the opposition had to abandon its demands for prosecution and punishment of those responsible for abuses under Franco both because of internal divisions that made the opposition weak and continuing threats to democratic reform. There was a continued threat of a coup, given that the military high command was still dominated by men appointed in the Franco years. Further, the upper ranks of civil servants also had a shaky commitment at best to democracy. The transition in Spain was thus very gradual: the military was never truly purged, and maintained a great deal of control over politics, and attempted two coups in the early 1980s; plots for other coups were revealed subsequently. Further, the strife in the Basque region strengthened the military's hand.

There can be no question that the military and Franco had a stranglehold on the nation for nearly half a century, although there was some civilian political opposition as well as a serious threat from the Basque separatists. Nonetheless, the military and upper echelon of civilian Francoists were able to control the initiation and pace of transition. It has been argued by some that liberalization was reinforced by Spain's quest to join the European Economic Community. It applied in February 1962, but that application was rejected because of the nature of the political system. Therefore, the thesis goes, Spain became obsessed with attaining some democratic credibility in order to gain legitimacy in European eyes.[50]

Spain underwent a very protracted transformation from above; as already discussed, the transition was initiated by the king, but both military and civilian elites remained largely untouched; purges of the military were prevented by coup attempts and threats, and large elements of the Francoist bureaucracy remained entrenched into the 1980s. While there was a formal handover of power to democratically elected civilians in Spain, the legacy of Francoism was far from addressed in this long transition. With regard to repression and human rights abuses, there was no process imposing accountability; there were no purges; and there wasn't even a government-sponsored attempt at truth-telling. The military upper echelons and Francoist civil servants also remained in control of the state machinery. The military budget continued to rise steadily throughout the protracted transition, with a three–four year exception.[51]

Eastern Europe

The experience of countries in eastern Europe is different from that of other countries studied in the book for a number of reasons. Most notably, rather than the military running the state or heavily dominating a nominally civilian government, the military was itself heavily dominated by the communist party apparatus. Thus, at the time of the transition, the concern with regard both to accountability and the threat of instability posed by the old guard pertained to the party rather than the army. Second, that party's control withered, at least temporarily, with the decline of its sponsor in the Soviet Union. As a result, while many in the party and state apparatus remained in power at some level, they did not pose the same sort of threat as, say, the military did in post-transition Argentina. Finally, while imposing accountability has been difficult, one of the most common objections has been that retroactive justice violates the rule of law, a very different concern from that frequently voiced in Latin

American transitions.[52] Like their Latin American counterparts, many former Soviet bloc states signed additional human rights instruments. Most importantly, many had signed and ratified the European Convention on Human Rights and accepted the jurisdiction of the European Court of Human Rights.[53]

Czechoslovakia (later the Czech Republic and the Slovak Republic)

In February 1948, the communists seized power in Czechoslovakia.[54] Political prisoners were sent to prisons or labour camps, and thousands were killed by government forces. In early 1968, the country experienced a brief opening when Communist Party leader Alexander Dubcek lifted censorship and promised democratic and economic reforms. That reform was brought to an abrupt halt when troops from Soviet and other eastern bloc countries invaded Czechoslovakia.

The political liberalization from above in the late 1980s in the Soviet Union and parts of eastern Europe enabled the growth of new opposition groups. During November 1989, peaceful demonstrations as well as a workers' strike created heavy pressure on the communist leader to resign. The opposition group, the Civic Forum, entered into negotiations with a seriously weakened communist regime. Some argue that the results achieved were largely dictated by the opposition because of the disarray in the ruling party.[55] By the end of December, the so-called velvet revolution had achieved that resignation and the installation of Vaclav Havel as president. Havel immediately moved to grant amnesty to some 20,000 prisoners.

One of the key political issues in Czechoslovakia was how the abuses of the past should be addressed. In May 1990, a Communist Party official and a number of police officers were convicted and sentenced for their part in putting down a student demonstration the previous November. A lustration law passed in October 1991 barred a large number of persons active under the communist regime or identified as conscious collaborators from a range of elected and appointed state posts until January 1996. The legislation came under heavy domestic and international fire for its expansive nature. In November 1992, the nation's constitutional court struck down the clause relating to 'conscious collaborators'.

Another key item on the new government's agenda was the reform of the police, judiciary and other instruments of power. The state security body, known as the StB, which had been a huge, unwieldy tool of repression, was finally eliminated, though not without numerous scandals. With regard to the judiciary, a screening process was put into place, though it only targeted the most serious collaborators. However, in the economic realm, old communists remained as the heads of a significant number of state-owned industries.

In January 1993, the nation split into the Czech Republic and Slovakia; the lustration legislation was applied with greater vigour in the former than the latter. In July of that year, the parliament of the Czech Republic passed a law lifting the statute of limitations on crimes committed during the communist era which had not been prosecuted for political reasons. In January 1994, the Slovakian constitutional court rejected calls by the prime minister to overturn the lustration law. The Czech Republic went further, establishing an office to investigate the crimes of communism; in early 1998, the government brought charges against three former top communists for their aid in the 1968 invasion.[56] Both nations also took steps to make restitution to victims of the old regime. The Czech Republic, in 1997, passed legislation allowing those who were Czechoslovakian citizens during communism to read their files. Both new republics also took steps to scale back the size of their militaries.[57]

While superficially the state possessed a preponderance of power, the lessening of the Soviet hold on the region combined with swelling public opposition to weaken and delegitimate the regime. Naturally, the single greatest influence from the outside was in the form of the declining influence of the Soviet Union. While in 1968 reform had been crushed by Soviet and allied troops, no such threat was credible this time, leaving the government perhaps no choice but to negotiate. More recently, improved respect for human rights has been driven at least in part by a desire to join the EU.

The Czechoslovak case (and then the cases of the Czech and Slovak republics) may be characterized as a transplacement, because the government initiated negotiations and held some power, but did so under heavy opposition power and made great concessions. The attempts at lustration caused a great public debate, and it can safely be said that the law was not entirely effective. However, in the Czech Republic at least it probably served to keep former top communists out of power. An early prosecution attempt for recent repression was successful; in the Czech Republic a limited prosecution effort for older crimes has begun only recently. In Slovakia, by contrast, the admittedly flawed lustration legislation has generally not taken effect. The law's use or threat of its use may have served to keep those implicated in the abuses of the past out of important state roles. The infamous StB was eliminated, and the judiciary was cleansed in part in both republics; the dominance of ex-communists was less thoroughly eliminated in control over state-owned industries.

The Czech Republic has created the office of a commissioner for human rights, as well as set up an office to document the crimes of the Soviet era: this office has recommended punishment that has been carried out in some cases, and lustration laws continue to bar some from holding public office. In Slovakia, abuses by the successor regime meant that human rights were frequently pushed aside as a priority but, in late 1997, a new government created a new post, the deputy prime minister for human rights and minorities.[58]

East Germany

In 1949, in the Soviet-occupied zone of Germany, the German Democratic Republic was declared.[59] Thus followed some 50 years of a centralized, repressive communist regime. East Germany's Stasi was the most pervasive secret police body in the region, with a vast number of collaborators. It carried out torture and arbitrary arrests and otherwise repressed the opposition.

With the Soviet relaxation of its grip on the region, in May 1989 East Germans began fleeing to the west in huge numbers. By fall 1989, there were demonstrations calling for reunification with West Germany, and political and economic reform. In October, Erich Honecker was replaced as leader by Egon Krenz, who was in turn replaced by Hans Modrow when he failed to push through reforms quickly enough. Modrow initiated discussions with the opposition and, in March 1990, democratic elections were held. The new coalition government was led by pro-unification parties; in October, the two Germanies were reunified.

After the unification, a number of border guards were brought to trial for shooting at fleeing East Germans in the period between the construction of the Berlin wall in 1961 and its fall in 1989. Some 200 East Germans were killed during that time. The trials, which began in October 1990, resulted in the convictions of several guards, though they were given relatively lenient sentences because of their low level of power and the history of propaganda to which they had been subjected.

In January 1992, the Stasi records were opened for public access; as a result thousands of civil servants, including judges and police officers, who had been informers, were dismissed. Civil servants have been screened for past conduct by the Gauck authority, a special body set up by the government to administer the vast Stasi files. Public sector employers can solicit information; they then make their own decisions on a case-by-case basis; the majority of those identified as informers have in fact retained their jobs. In tandem with the opening of the files came the creation of a study commission to examine the legacy of the past.[60]

In November 1992, a trial was opened against Honecker and other former high officials, but charges against all six defendants were dropped due to their ill health. More recently, in 1997, Egon Krenz was sentenced to six years' imprisonment for the 'shoot to kill' policy at the border, along with a number of other former officials.

Like other nations in the region, East Germany was faced with the loss of its patron's support and a rising tide of opposition. These circumstances weakened the strength and legitimacy of the state; that combined with the large number of fleeing East Germans forced the government to negotiate with the opposition. Further leverage was given to advocates of human rights and accountability when the two Germanies merged. East Germany was unique because not only was it in many ways a defeated regime upon reunification, but it was merging with a state with more experience of the rule of law and democracy. As with other cases in the region, the most important influence was probably the lack of Soviet influence. The desire of people in the Germanies to reunify also played a role. The German transition is sometimes described as a replacement; it could reasonably be a transplacement as well. While what makes the East German case unique is its ultimate essential absorption into West

Germany, decisions to initiate the transition were taken at the top of the Communist Party hierarchy, albeit under heavy pressure from domestic opposition. The unified Germany has undertaken a number of high-profile cases against border guards and former high-level officials, though some of the latter cases have been dropped because of the defendants' ill health. The Gauck authority has enabled the screening of public servants for past collaboration; many have been dismissed as a result.

Hungary

In 1945, Soviet troops occupied Hungary, and the Communist Party began taking control of ministries.[61] By 1947, power was consolidated in the head of the party, Matyas Rakosi. In 1953, after the death of Stalin and with the urging of Khrushchev to loosen this centralized control, Rakosi was replaced by Imre Nagy, who implemented a programme of liberal reforms that released political prisoners. A contest for power ensued, and Nagy was replaced by Rakosi; Rakosi, unable to consolidate his power, was then replaced by Erno Gero in 1956. After police fired on a peaceful student march, there was a popular revolt aided by the military, which returned Nagy to power in October. Nagy instituted new reforms and repudiated the Warsaw Pact; in response Soviet troops invaded and Nagy was executed.

The new leader, Janos Kadar, purged some officials and repression was reimposed. In the face of the opening in the Soviet Union and concerned by their own weak economy, reformers within the Communist Party challenged its hierarchy and formulated plans for economic reform and to some degree political reform. These events led to Kadar's downfall, and there were public calls for economic and political reform. As one observer put it, the regime legitimated the opposition by inviting them to a series of round-table talks about radical economic reform from mid- to late-1989.[62] The opposition pushed the discussions beyond the economic realm, winning agreement to free elections. A new constitution in 1989 expanded freedoms of speech, assembly and the press, and free elections were held in 1990. The renamed Communist Party won 10 per cent of the seats in parliament.

The question of addressing the repression of the past, particularly acts surrounding the 1956 invasion, was a hot political and legal issue. In 1991, the legislature passed a law that sought to restart the statute of limitations on crimes of the past such as treason, murder and torture resulting in death that had not been prosecuted for political reasons. A key concern regarding this legislation was that it broke promises that the opposition had made during negotiations with the communists. The point was mooted, however, when it was held unconstitutional. A subsequent resolution declaring that the statute of limitations had been tolled by the flaws of the judicial system was also struck down. However, a new law treating the acts of 1956 as war crimes and crimes against humanity was upheld by the constitutional court in 1993. Following this decision, around a dozen people were arrested for the shootings of civilians in 1956. By February 1998, only three people had been convicted pursuant to this law.[63]

Hungary also set up a restitution programme to return land that had been illegally seized by the government. In 1992, the legislature passed laws voiding convictions for crimes against the state and public order between 1963 and 1989; it also passed legislation to compensate persons or families who for political reasons had been deprived of life or liberty unlawfully between 1939 and 1989. Finally, an executive decree increased the pensions of former political prisoners.

In March 1994, a law was passed that would require screening between 10,000 and 12,000 officials to ascertain whether they had ever been informers for the secret police. In May, following high unemployment and inflation, popular discontent returned the communists to power through elections. In 1997, a narrow lustration law was passed. Under its terms, the records of senior public figures are reviewed by a commission. It requests that they resign; otherwise it exposes their pasts. However, the only power that the commission holds is that of exposure; the prime minister has admitted that he received a negative report, but refuses to resign. Finally, following the German example, Hungary has set up an office to allow people access to their own files.

As with other eastern European countries, in Hungary the ruling party clearly held the upper hand in terms of political and military dominance. However, its political standing was weakened both by harsh economic conditions and actions by reformers within the party. The key factor enabling the opening in Hungary was the new openness in the Soviet Union which made a repeat of the 1956 invasion highly unlikely. Hungary saw a transition initiated from above. While economic problems weakened the standing of the government, it was still in the power of the communists to initiate and direct discussions of political and economic transition. Hungary developed a significant programme of restitution and rehabilitation for the victims of the past. Attempts to prosecute for crimes of the past have been far more limited, though it is worth noting that the constraints have been largely legal. A narrow lustration law was passed, but has had a limited impact.

Bulgaria

In 1947, the Communist Party consolidated power in Bulgaria, leading to over four decades of repression.[64] In the early years of power struggles, there were vast purges of party members, many of whom were sent to labour camps. Repression eased slightly after 1962, but there were still tight restrictions on freedom of the press, speech, religion and assembly, as well as repression of ethnic minorities, in particular ethnic Turks.

A weak economy combined with the new Soviet openness to shake up the Bulgarian Communist Party. The government came under increasing domestic criticism and, in October, there was a large demonstration in the capital coinciding with a meeting about ecology of the Conference on Security and

Cooperation in Europe (CSCE). In November 1989, party members ousted longtime ruler Todor Zhivkov, replacing him with a new ruler who announced a plan of economic, political and legal reform. In 1990, the BCP, now the Bulgarian Socialist Party, won the election, but an opposition party, the Union of Democratic Forces (UDF), won the subsequent 1991 parliamentary and 1992 presidential elections.

Bulgaria faced the same range of issues other eastern bloc nations confronted: how to compensate the victims, whether to prosecute perpetrators, whether to pass lustration legislation, and whether to open the secret files of the security apparatus. In 1990, an amnesty was declared for political prisoners; in 1991, laws were passed providing for their compensation and rehabilitation, and to return property wrongfully confiscated by the state.

In 1992, Zhivkov was sentenced to seven years in prison, but for embezzlement, not human rights abuses. In 1993, however, he and two others were indicted for the campaign to forcibly assimilate ethnic minorities during the 1980s. He was also indicted for setting up labour camps where 147 prisoners died between 1959 and 1962; camp officials were indicted for murder. By 1998, no progress had been made on these cases, and Zhivkov died in August.

The legislature passed two purge laws, which were struck down by the constitutional court in 1992. Finally, in early 1993, the court upheld a law instituting screening requirements for members of scientific organizations. The UDF had campaigned for access to the secret police files, but it closed them in 1993 on national security grounds. The government was clearly weakened by a poor economy and popular discontent, but still maintained the upper hand. As with other cases in the region, the most decisive external factor in Bulgarian reform was the Soviet openness. Bulgaria experienced a transformation from above; it was reformers within the party that ousted Zhivkov and initiated the reforms that led to free elections. Victims of repression were rehabilitated and compensated, but were not allowed access to their secret police files. The lustration legislation was a relatively narrow screening law for a subset of workers. Similarly, while Zhivkov and a number of labour camp officials are charged with abuses, most of the members of the old establishment remain untouched. The ministry of the interior has incomplete but improving control over the police and there have been some reforms aimed at increasing this control.[65]

Albania

Communist forces came to power in 1944 in Albania when the German forces withdrew.[66] The subsequent regime under Enver Hoxha was the most repressive in the region, with political opponents sent to prisons where forced labour was imposed; all sectors of society were subject to periodic purges. After Hohxa's death in 1985, his successor maintained the same type of regime until 1990 when, in response to domestic unrest and the fall of communist regimes elsewhere, the regime initiated some limited reforms. In July, there was a mass demonstration in the capital, and some 4,700 people sought asylum at European embassies. They were allowed to leave, and independent political parties were allowed to seek office.

In 1991, despite a flawed election, the opposition gained one-third of the seats in the legislature. Political prisoners were also released, though despite these reforms human rights abuses continued. In December, as a protest to the socialists' blocking of reform, the opposition parties withdrew from the coalition. An interim government was formed, and in the March 1992 elections the Democratic Party gained two-thirds of the seats in the legislature, and Dr Sali Berisha became president. In 1993, the country began to face the legacy of the past. The legislature passed a law on the restitution of expropriated property. It also passed a law to screen lawyers and deprive them of their licenses for past collaboration, but this law was struck down by the constitutional court.

Numerous charges have been filed against former officials and elites. Hoxha's widow was sentenced to 11 years in prison for misuse of state funds, and a border guard was sentenced to ten years for killing persons attempting to flee the country. In December 1993, ten senior former communist officials were sentenced to prison terms of five to ten years and ordered to repay $60,000. In recent years, NGOs have sought to retrain Albania's police with respect to both technical matters and human rights.

Albania's ruling class still firmly held power at the time of transition, though it faced an increasingly restive population. Albania, having been extremely isolated, was slower to react to the new openness in the region than other countries, but new Soviet policies and the fall of communist regimes in the region were important events enabling change in the regime. Albania experienced a transformation from above. The government was under heavy domestic pressure, but initiated and controlled the pace of the transition. Victims of land expropriation were given restitution, and political prisoners were freed, but no provisions were made for access to secret police files. The one attempt at lustration legislation was struck down by the high court. However, there have been a number of successful prosecutions of former elites, though these cases have focused on corruption as well as repression.

Poland

Following the Second World War, under the Yalta agreement, Poland was to have fair elections, but those held in 1947 were controlled by the Communist Party, leading to the establishment of a communist state.[67] Periodic uprisings by workers and students were harshly put down; the most significant of these would be a workers' movement known as Solidarity. Solidarity was well positioned to take advantage of the new Soviet openness and the weakness of the Polish regime. The regime entered into round-table talks with Solidarity in 1989 after a dismal level of public support. The negotiations resulted in free elections for a new upper house of the legislature, but guaranteed the communists 65 per cent of the lower house. June 1989 elections thus gave the communists dominance of the lower house, but handed them a crushing defeat in the upper house. The agreements had also given the communists the power to designate the ministers of defence and the interior. Otherwise, however, the elections delegitimated the communists further and enabled Solidarity to implement reforms.

Poland moved slowly to confront the abuses of the past, drawing a 'thick line' between the present and the past. There are reports that this slow pace enabled the security forces to destroy hundreds of thousands of documents pertaining to past repression. A parliamentary commission investigating deaths under the old regime received little support from the ministry of the interior, which was still dominated by communists. Plans are now set to open the security files to the populace through a body on the model of Germany's Gauck authority.

In June 1992, the parliament passed an ill-conceived lustration law which was so poorly structured as to cause a great deal of confusion and make future attempts at lustration difficult.[68] It was over five years later, in early 1998, that a new, very narrow lustration law was passed. Individuals seeking high elected or appointed office must declare at the time whether or not they were collaborators. Having been a collaborator does not disqualify a candidate for a job; only lying about one's status can disqualify one from public office for ten years.[69] There have also been sporadic attempts to prosecute individuals for the abuses of the past. General Jaruzelski has been indicted for his actions ordering the shooting of protesting workers in 1970–71, and some other senior figures have been charged with the deaths of workers who were striking in 1981–82.

A number of observations may be drawn out about the Polish experience. While the government was still in control in 1989, it faced a particularly strong and well entrenched opposition group in the form of Solidarity; the opening of the Soviet Union was, of course, a decisive factor in Poland's reform. Poland experienced a transformation from above, and the regime, while ceding power, was also able to maintain some of its influence.

The holdover of ex-communists in power in legislative positions and in the bureaucracy is perhaps one of several reasons why Poland has sought to draw a 'thick line' between the present and the past. The result is that there has been minimal lustration, a few prosecution attempts, and there are now plans to open an archive. However, this lack of lustration also implies a threat to stability. Until recently this was compounded by a general failure to reform the security apparatus, but the government has begun to take steps to restructure the military, increase civilian control and depoliticize it.

Romania

Following the Second World War, the Soviet Union pushed for the inclusion of the Communist Party in the postwar government; it consolidated power and steadily pushed non-communists out of power, until the Romanian People's Republic was declared following the king's abdication in late 1947.[70] Though the state under Ceaucescu in the 1960s became increasingly independent of Moscow, it remained very repressive.

The regime change in Romania was unlike that in other eastern European countries in that it was rapid and bloody. It began with a popular uprising in December 1989, sparked by a protest in a small town that soon served to reveal the lack of support for the country's ruler, Nicolae Ceaucescu. A larger demonstration on 22 December followed in the capital, initially put down by the army and security forces; however they soon joined the crowds instead. The group that took over, the National Salvation Front (NSF), included many former high-ranking Communist Party members and generals, including the future president, Ion Iliescu.

The following day, the arrest of the Ceaucescus was announced by Iliescu. They were not given the benefit of a public, civilian trial; instead they were tried in secret by a military tribunal. Three days after their arrest, national television broadcast images of the couple shot dead. The videotape of the two-hour trial indicated that the couple had been charged with genocide, among other things; they were convicted of undermining state power and the national economy, conspiracy and destroying public assets. The trial displayed anything but due process; the defence lawyers failed to serve their clients, and there was no appeal. The trial also failed to clarify the events that led from the clashes between demonstrators and security forces to their joining together.

Further trials followed that of the Ceaucesus, including the trials of his brother, a general, and of their son. In early 1990, in rehearsed and presumably coerced testimony that the defendants later renounced, four of Ceaucescu's top aides were convicted of genocide for their part in ordering the opening of fire on demonstrations the previous December. However, in 1993, their sentences were reduced and, by 1994, all four had been paroled or released for medical reasons.

In March 1990, 25 police officers and officials from the state security agency were charged with complicity in genocide; nearly two years later, 18 were convicted; of these, ten were pardoned. In July 1990, the entire political executive committee of the Communist Party were brought to trial. After a complex procedural history, all were convicted, but have since been paroled or released for medical reasons. Relatives of the Ceaucescus were also brought to trial; their son was initially convicted of genocide, but on appeal was convicted only of illegal firearms possession, and was released in late 1992.

In early January 1990, the new government issued two amnesty decrees. The first, more broadly phrased, left open the possibility of amnesty not just for those who opposed the regime but for members of the old regime as well; the second specifically excluded those who directed or participated in the past repression. The first amnesty has turned out to be a way to quietly avoid pursuing some past human rights abuses.[71]

A further limitation to the confrontation of the past abuses is that the trials dealt only with the repression of December 1989, not the longer history of abuses under communism. The new government was pressurized by NGOs to initiate some sort of trial of communism, but negotiations on this issue failed. An attempt was made to prosecute key officials under Ceaucescu's predecessor who were responsible for torture, internment and forced labour camps, but after numerous delays the statute of limitations had run and so the indictments were abandoned in early 1994. In April 1993, nine defendants including seven Securitate officers and a former minister of the interior were convicted for carrying out the orders for a summary execution in 1981. Advocacy for further trials, as well as a judgement of the more diffuse repression under communism, has yet to bear fruit.

There have been efforts to address the legacy of the past in other ways. In 1990, a law was passed to compensate former political prisoners. Other efforts have been less than successful: a law to allow access to security files has yet to go through, and a commission set up in 1991 to establish the truth has yet to release a report.

Romania is an unusual case of transition: a popular uprising appears to have been in essence co-opted by elements of the old regime with a dubious interest in change. The new regime should have had a relatively free hand in addressing the abuses of the past, but may also have had powerful incentives not to do so. In fact, in mid-1990, the new regime violently put down peaceful demonstrators who argued that the population sought to eliminate the old regime, not give Communist Party anti-Ceaucescu forces power, and argued that the transitional NSF government members should not be allowed to run for office.

Romania was of course affected by the changes in the former Soviet Union and the region more generally. Further, it may have been more susceptible to external pressure on human rights, in particular from the USA, which examined the record closely in conjunction with Romania's application for most favoured nation trading status. Romania's application for membership in the Council of Europe also subjected it to scrutiny on this matter.

Romania's experience is unusual, and does not fit in comfortably with the other transitions discussed here. Certainly what change has occurred has been entirely controlled by the new regime, which not coincidentally contains leaders who were in the upper echelons of the old communist regime. The ambiguous nature of the transition has led to ambiguous treatment of the past. The most decisive step to confront the abuses of the past was in itself a human rights violation: the sham trial and execution of the Ceaucescus. It seems reasonable to interpret this trial as aimed less at addressing the legacy of abuse and more at appeasing a population calling for real change. Further trials took place, but the effect of the trials was curtailed by the amnesty law, the statute of limitations and health problems of the defendants. Furthermore, for the most part the larger history of abuse was not addressed, only the events during the so-called revolution. This was an approach that seemed to be tailored to appease the population without endangering members of the new regime, ex-communists themselves. Wider attempts at opening the records and truth-telling have also failed to bear fruit thus far. Reforms have shown some success; the new constitution limits the role of the military to defence of territorial integrity and, since

1993, the USA has held limited training of military and civilian officials, emphasizing civilian democratic control over the military. In May 1998, the ombudsman's office for complaints provided for in the 1991 constitution finally began its work.

Russia

The case of Russia differs from those of other eastern bloc nations discussed here in that the repression was imposed purely from within.[72] While repression was widespread throughout the Soviet era, the most significant abuses occurred following the rise to power of Joseph Stalin in 1924. The most severe repression took place in 1937 and 1938, when 8 to 12 million people were deported or interned in prisons or labour camps. Between 1935 and 1945, some 7 million people were executed. A first wave of destalinization took place under his successor, Khrushchev; of more interest for our purposes is the liberalization that occurred after Mikhail Gorbachev rose to power in 1985.

This liberalization was accompanied by a rise in nationalism; between 1988 and 1990, all republics of the then Soviet Union declared independence. In June 1990, Russia declared independence, and a year later Boris Yeltsin was democratically elected. In August 1991, the day before the signing of a treaty passing expanded political and economic powers to the republics a group of military, Communist Party, and Committee of State Security (KGB) officials staged a coup which failed. The Communist Party was abolished during 1991 and 1992, but the constitutional court declared that local branches could re-establish themselves. A second coup attempt took place in October 1993 following a dispute between Yeltsin and the parliament. Members of parliament were arrested, but in February 1994 members of the new parliament passed amnesty legislation covering both coup attempts.

With regard to past abuses, rehabilitation attempts had begun under Khrushchev, but had dwindled before Gorbachev came to power. He pushed through reforms of the rehabilitation process in 1988–89 under public pressure. The inadequacy of the compensation granted to those who were rehabilitated soon became a hot political issue. In 1991, the legislature of the Russian republic passed a law rehabilitating former political prisoners and providing substantial compensation for both moral and material harm done to them.

With regard to past abusers, however, the political situation is more complex. There have been failed attempts to pass a screening law, but nearly all key political groups opposed them. Furthermore, in 1993, the parliament passed a bill making it illegal to identify KGB collaborators. The statute of limitations on the crimes of the past has run, making prosecutions under domestic law virtually impossible. In one instance, a number of prosecutions that were being processed were halted by the statute of limitations; publicity surrounding this event led to the stripping of their positions and degrees. An attempt by an NGO, Memorial, to bring a case rooted in international law, failed when a court denied the case a hearing.

Reform in the former Soviet Union and later Russia was initiated from above. Although there was a growing public call for reform, the two coup attempts indicate the continued strength and recalcitrance of old party members, elements of the military and of the KGB. Further, despite reform efforts, the legacy of the powerful security apparatus endures, according to some analysts.[73] Historians and political scientists will undoubtedly continue to argue for decades about what led to reforms and the breakup of the Soviet Union. Certainly, one key cause was a severe economic slump, brought on in part by structural economic problems and exacerbated by the high costs of competition with the USA. It is less clear the degree to which international and in particular American criticism on issues of human rights and political freedom had an impact on the course of reforms.

The transformation from above enabled various political and economic reforms, including its breakup into independent republics. The ruling class was divided, however: while leaders like Gorbachev and later Yeltsin could initiate reform, they did so at the risk of a backlash from conservative elements, such as was manifested in the coup attempts of 1991 and 1993. The continued influence of these conservative elements is certainly a key reason why Russia has not addressed the issue of past offences more aggressively. Victims have been rehabilitated and compensated, but lustration and prosecution attempts have been frustrated. And, while the historical record is being clarified by a new generation of historians, there is no project like that in Germany and elsewhere to open secret police files to the public.

Lithuania

In 1940, the Soviet Union captured Lithuania and declared it a constituent republic.[74] Some 5,000 Lithuanians were executed, and another 35,000 were deported to Siberia. Lithuania was briefly lost to the Nazis, but the Soviets recaptured it in 1944, and sent another 60,000 to Siberia. In 1949, in order to carry out a programme of forced collectivization, another 60,000 were deported. Until the thaw under Gorbachev, political persecution remained common.

In May 1989, the Lithuanian supreme council declared Lithuanian sovereignty. A rising tide of nationalism in the Baltic states prompted a human chain between the capitals of those states calling for independence. In December, a multi-party system was adopted, and the president who was elected in February 1990 called for autonomy. When Lithuania declared independence in March, the Soviets cracked down. However, following the failed coup in Moscow in August 1991, the Soviet grip on the republics faltered. The international community gave official recognition to the Baltics and, in September, the Soviet Union recognized their independence.

The Lithuanian government moved quickly to cleanse state structures; in November 1991, a government decree barred former KGB employees and informers from holding official posts for five years. The property of the Communist Party was also confiscated, and owners of property nationalized under communism were allowed to petition for its return. However, a broader law that would have banned more collaborators from a wide array of state posts, from economy-related jobs to the armed forces, was rejected in May 1992. And former communists were not banned from office: in 1993 the successor party to the communists captured the presidency.

Lithuania's independence and reforms would have been impossible had not the Soviet Union been weakened and loosened its grip on its constituent republics. A rising tide of nationalism hastened the state's independence. The most obvious external influence on Lithuania's transition was the waning of the Soviet Union. Also important was the role of diplomatic recognition in legitimating the new republic as a sovereign nation. Lithuania could be said to have experienced transformation from above or transplacement, as its release by the Soviet Union was followed by a referendum. Lithuania moved swiftly to implement some purges of the state apparatus, and stripped the Communist Party of its property. It also sought to restore confiscated property to its former owners. However, no strides were taken to prosecute those responsible for past repression or otherwise officially acknowledge the past. A promise to create an international commission for crimes of the past has not been fulfilled; the only trial that has been pursued was against a Nazi war criminal.

Africa

Fewer nations in Africa have faced this dilemma than have done in Latin America or Europe. This is the case in part because fewer nations in the region are experiencing true civilianization and democratization; further, some of those that have replaced dictatorships have done so by overthrowing them. In Ethiopia, for example, the old regime was soundly defeated in a civil war, facilitating the campaign of prosecutions for abuses of the past that has followed.[75] In Uganda, the resistance movement that overthrew the old repressive regime promised to step down after a transition period, but failed to do so; the commission of inquiry it set up to address the abuses of the past had not issued a report after some ten years. In Rwanda, prosecutions have gone forward at the domestic and international level following the civil war and genocide of 1994; the genocide was curtailed only by the overthrow of the regime, but the fighting continues.[76] The recent peace accord in Sierra Leone is fragile, and two earlier ceasefire accords have been broken; nonetheless the amnesty provision has been questioned by human rights organizations and UN officials. A new special court has been created, and will supplement the work of a commission of inquiry.[77]

South Africa

After nearly 50 years of racist, repressive white rule under apartheid, then-President F. W. de Klerk initiated reform in early 1990 by lifting the ban on various anti-apartheid and opposition groups, including the African National Congress (ANC). Negotiations began between the government and these parties shortly thereafter. The government also created a commission of inquiry (the Goldstone Commission) to look into a number of particularly notorious instances of violence; the ANC subsequently created a commission to look into its own abuses.

During the negotiations, the issue of how to deal with the abuses of the past loomed large. The ANC had advocated a purge of the military and opposed an amnesty, while the position of the government and military was directly opposed. The parties finally reached agreement on an interim constitution in late 1993, which provides for majority rule, protects the positions of civil servants and military members, and stipulates that the parliament is to provide for the provisions of an amnesty.

The new ANC government came to power in early 1994, and shortly thereafter created a truth commission, which was unique in that amnesty was given only to those who applied to the commission and came clean about their involvement in the abuses of the past. In addition, old military officers are being retired and ex-ANC guerrillas are joining the military.

Guerrilla threats and international disapproval placed pressure on the government to reform, but it was the government that initiated the reform, which was tolerated by the security establishment. The government was continually mindful of the threat of military or right-wing rebellion. International opposition to apartheid was longstanding and vocal. There are strong disagreements as to the degree to which international sanctions and disapproval affected decisions to reform, but these were not irrelevant, as the South African regime liked to view itself as part of the western world that condemned apartheid. Undoubtedly, the demise of communism helped assuage fears of the leftist tendencies of domestic anti-apartheid groups.

South Africa experienced a transformation from above, initiated and controlled by the de Klerk government, which sought to limit liability for past violations and protect the positions of those who had served the apartheid regime in military and civilian capacities. Agreed procedures largely foreclosed the possibility of prosecutions for the abuses of the past; but, should a person not apply for amnesty they are still vulnerable to prosecution. In addition, the parties agreed to protect the positions of military members and civilians alike from the old regime. However, ex-guerrillas are being integrated into the state security forces now, and officers from the old regime are retiring. Finally, the budget for the military dropped somewhat once the costs of transition have been discounted.

Asia

South Korea

Between 1948 and 1987, South Korea was under authoritarian rule with the exception of a brief period of democratization in 1960–61.[78] During that opening, legislation was passed to enable prosecution of those who had engaged in election-related crimes as well as large numbers of police. The government also planned a purge of high-level officers and a reduction of the military, but the military and the USA vehemently opposed these moves; the regime was overthrown by Major General Park Chung Hee in 1961. In 1987, then-ruler General Chun Doo Hwan agreed to opposition demands, including elections. In late 1988, there were hearings in the legislature regarding abuses under Chung, in particular a notorious massacre at Kwanjgu. As a result, a deal was struck in which Chung apologized on television and went into exile.

In 1994, a prosecutor's office in Seoul determined that Chun and Roh Tae Woo had engaged in a military rebellion in 1979, but prosecution did not follow immediately. The case was reopened in 1995 following the discovery of corruption by Roh; Chun was sentenced to life in prison (reduced from a death sentence) and Roh to imprisonment. However, the new president, Kim Dae Jung, previously persecuted by the former leaders, freed both in December 1997.[79] Subsequent pardons were granted to 12 former army generals who had been close to Roh and Chun.[80]

While there has been domestic political opposition, nothing like an armed opposition exists now to threaten the government. The most salient feature of South Korean political life has been the ongoing rift with North Korea, though it is unclear what role that or the continued US presence played in the return to democratic rule. The transition was a transformation from above, with the military rulers choosing to allow elections to go forward.

South Korea's treatment of Chun and Roh is unusual in that the former leaders no longer seem to have posed a serious threat to stability, yet were treated with some care, with the prosecutor at first declining to pursue the case in 1994, and the case that was pursued arising originally not out of Kwangju or the coup, but corruption, though the other issues were eventually drawn in. Finally, Kim does not seem to have been acting out of fear, but mercy or forgiveness, when he pardoned the two. While the military budget appears to have increased in real terms but decreased as a percentage of GDP, it is unclear what import this has given the heavy role played by the USA in the peninsula.[81]

The Philippines

Between 1972 and 1986, Ferdinand Marcos held dictatorial power over the Philippines.[82] In 1986, he was defeated at the ballot box by Corazon Aquino, the widow of a slain opposition leader who headed the 'people power' movement. However, despite the very real popular nature of her support, many believe that she would not have triumphed without the support of the military. While the military had been a key supporter of Marcos, and with the police had been a major human rights abuser, in 1986 the defence minister and vice-chief of staff of the armed forces switched camps and threw their support to Aquino. This shift proved an immense aid to the popular opposition movement, and thus Aquino's new presidency was beholden to and dependent upon the armed forces.

Given this dependency, serious constraints were placed on the treatment of the abuses of the past: Aquino generally did not pursue prosecutions of human rights abusers, particularly those in the military. Nonetheless, before long the defence minister was planning to oust her. While Aquino survived this and other coup attempts, she became dependent on one faction of the armed forces to protect her. As a result, there has been very little commitment to pursuing cases against the military. Prosecutions before military tribunals have been shams, and prosecutions in civilian courts have been undermined by military and police intransigence. Thus, between 1987 and 1990, 994 complaints were filed resulting in only six convictions.

Despite subsequent accusations that she had forgotten about human rights, Aquino came to power with a strong commitment to address the abuses of the past. She released 500 political prisoners and created a committee on human rights immediately after taking office. The committee's mandate was to investigate abuses of the past and make recommendations, which could include prosecution. However, following comments by Aquino's spokesperson that seeking to prosecute members of the military for rights abuses might be destabilizing, the members of the committee resigned in 1987. An independent commission on human rights was created by the February 1987 constitution, but it had little more power or success. These flaws were exacerbated by the actions of the head of the commission, who treated the abuses of the government and of the rebel army as equivalent, although those of the government and military were of a far greater magnitude.

While the strength of Aquino's popular support cannot be denied, and the rebel army undoubtedly formed some threat to the establishment, it was the defection of a few key military figures that gave Aquino a large boost. This also meant that she was dependent upon the military and vulnerable to coup threats and attempts. The military remained strong through the transition, continued to wage war against rebels, and some elements even gained popularity for their role in ousting Marcos.

The military itself was split between those who wanted a strong, but reprofessionalized military, and those who wanted to retain a larger role in politics. It was this latter group that was responsible for the coup threats and attempts that posed a serious challenge to Aquino's rule.[83] The USA has played a central role in the politics and military of the Philippines for a century. It encouraged the adoption by the military of the doctrine of national security beginning in the 1950s, and sought to push Marcos towards power sharing in 1984–85. The USA eventually courted Aquino openly, putting pressure on the regime during the 1986 election with a congressional delegation. The Filipino transition is a difficult one to categorize, catalysed as it was by a combination of popular opposition and military support. The result, however, was much like that of a transformation from above; the military retained a great deal of control over politics.

As a result, movement to address the human rights abuses of the past was limited. The committee and later the commission on human rights generated reports and suggestions, a few of which developed into prosecutions, but there were even fewer convictions. In 1995, the government offered an amnesty to former rebels and members of the security forces. Abuses by the security forces continue and are also not generally punished.[84] While there has been a significant absolute increase in the military budget, it has not increased as a percentage of GDP.[85]

Cambodia

After receiving its independence from France in 1954, Cambodia experienced a period of political unrest and flux.[86] In 1975, the Khmer Rouge (KR) guerrillas seized power and instituted a 'reorganization' of society, more frequently referred to as genocidal policies, resulting in the deaths of 1 million Cambodians. The severe repression continued through 1978, when Vietnam invaded, replacing Pol Pot's Khmer Rouge regime with one headed by Hun Sen. Three rebel groups formed a government in exile three years later; one of the factions was the KR. While there were efforts at truth-telling about the abuses of the past during this time, prosecutions were rendered impossible by the difficulty of identifying perpetrators, the fact that many had fled the country, and fundamental flaws in the judicial system. Khmer Rouge leaders Pol Pot and Ieng Sary were prosecuted and sentenced to death in absentia, but there was little chance of their capture at that time.

It was only when Vietnam withdrew its troops in 1989 that peace efforts began in earnest. In 1990, the five permanent members of the Security Council presented a peace plan to the parties; the result was the creation of the interim supreme national council. In October 1991, the parties to the Cambodian conflict and 18 other nations signed a peace treaty; a UN advance team was sent in a month later. The agreement itself, to the degree that it touched on human rights, focused largely on future protection. Although the past genocide loomed large, a key concern was convincing the KR to disarm, and the USA and China, in particular, insisted that the KR could not be excluded from participation in a future government. Thus, political concerns led the parties, domestic and international, to effectively foreclose the possibility of accountability for the genocide. The role of a large UN peacekeeping force was to supervise the cantonment and demobilization of combatants, effectively control the government and police until a new government was elected and installed, and ensure greater protection for human rights.

In March 1992, the UN peacekeeping force, to number over 20,000, began deployment. However, the KR demonstrated increasing intransigence: it violated provisions regarding cantonment and demobilization and took UN troops hostage. In early 1993, the KR announced that it would boycott upcoming elections and intensified its attacks. Elections went forward nonetheless, and a new government was installed. Through early 1994, the government sought to negotiate with the KR, but launched an offensive against it when that failed.

Pol Pot himself was eventually captured by members of his own group, but died before prosecutions could go forward. However, several former top Khmer Rouge leaders have been charged, and one has already been sentenced to life in prison, with plans for further proceedings to be televised.[87] The government rejected a UN proposal to turn over other former leaders to an international tribunal, but more recently a UN plan has proposed the creation of a joint national– international tribunal.[88]

The Cambodian situation is rather complex, due in part to external forces. But for the Vietnamese invasion, it is impossible to say how long the KR might have remained in power; even after it was ousted, it remained a force to be reckoned with, forcing even international partners in the peace negotiations to accept the prospect of future KR participation in politics. Its defection from the peace process posed a serious threat to the newly elected government.

International involvement has been extensive, with the UN force in the country supervising elections, and continuing to place public pressure on the government to address the legacy of the past, particularly with the offer to create a tribunal to prosecute past abusers. The Khmer Rouge was effectively overthrown, but by an outside force, so that the new nation has continually faced the threat of a resurgence of the party. This has necessarily resulted in concessions to the group on numerous issues.

The question of how to address past abuses was revived in late 1998 and early 1999 with the surrender of two former leaders of the Khmer Rouge and outrage at the fact that they were not only not being punished but vacationing at a remote town. These events sparked renewed demands for trials for crimes against humanity.[89] Reports suggested that Prime Minister Hun Sen favoured a tribunal, which he later rejected; King Sihanouk expressed willingness to face a tribunal for his past acts.[90] The UN and the Cambodian government have developed a plan for a tribunal, though it remains to be seen whether it will come into being. The military budget rose significantly in 1997 but was scheduled to drop in 1999.[91] While the United Nations Transitional Authority for Cambodia (UNTAC) included a civilian police monitoring element, problems with the security forces were not resolved.[92]

Sri Lanka

Sri Lanka, unlike most of the cases examined here, has been a democracy since independence, but has experienced a civil war since the early 1980s.[93] Progressive restrictions on civil rights have been imposed with the continuation of the war, a brutal one that has taken over 55,000 lives. Following an electoral administration shift in 1994, commissions of inquiry into past abuses were created and some prosecutions began; the government also created a human rights commission and a cabinet-level commission to combat harassment. Several convictions have been obtained against members of the security forces in high-profile disappearance cases.

Sri Lanka is an unusual case in that it has not experienced a traditional transition, and in that the primary constraint on accountability is not the fear of military reaction. While it faces a strong separatist rebel movement that can neither win nor be totally defeated, and has a strong military that is loath to face accountability or reform, this may not be the most salient limitation on accountability. Indeed, there seems to be no risk that the security forces of Sri Lanka would stage a coup; civilians are limited because they are dependent upon the military to wage the war and do not wish to limit their actions or undermine morale. Sri Lanka is different too in that the international influence it is subject to is not that of the USA or the UN, but India, which in 1987 sent an ill-fated peacekeeping force to the island. Ethnic links between the rebels and a populous state in the south of India brought on India's involvement in the 1980s; however, in recent rounds of reform, accountability and negotiation with the rebels, India has been far less involved.

It may be something of a misnomer to refer to transition in Sri Lanka, as there has been no transition from authoritarianism to democracy; nonetheless we see an important policy shift following an electoral regime change. Sri Lanka took the common routes of prosecution and truth commission; attempts at constitutional and security force reform have been less successful. Little can be extrapolated from the continuing rise in military budgets as the civil conflict continues.

Notes

1 Because of the nature of the cases examined here, the importance of this category is negligible, as we shall see.

2 William Stanley and Robert Loosle, 'El Salvador: The Civilian Police Component of Peace Operations', in Robert B. Oakley, Michael J. Dzidzic and Eliot M. Goldberg, *Policing the New World Disorder: Peace Operations and Public Security* (Washington, DC: National Defense University Press, 1998).

3 'Argentina: Ex-ruler Held in Kidnappings', *New York Times* (26 November, 1998), p. A10; Clifford Krauss, 'Spanish Judge Investigating Rights Abuses in Argentina', *New York Times* (29 November, 1998), p. 4.

4 Lawrence Weschler, *A Miracle, A Universe: Settling Accounts with Torturers* (New York: Pantheon, 1990); Van Dyke and Berkley, 'Redressing Human Rights Abuses', pp. 251–4; Hayner, 'Fifteen truth commissions', p. 616.

5 Estimates place the number of Uruguayans who disappeared after being arrested at 164; however, it is also estimated that, by the late 1970s, one in 500 citizens were sent to jail for political reasons, giving Uruguay the highest per-capita rate of political prisoners in the world. Further, some 30,000 civil servants were apparently dismissed for ideological reasons. See Van Dyke and Berkley, 'Redressing Human Rights Abuses', p. 251; Roht-Arriaza, 'Case Studies: Latin America', in *Impunity and Human Rights*, p. 148; and the editor's introduction 'Uruguay', in Kritz (ed.), *Transitional Justice*, vol. II, p. 383. Further, estimates are that some three to four hundred thousand Uruguayans, of a population that stood at 3 million in 1970, went into exile. Weschler, *A Miracle, A Universe*, pp. 87–8.

6 Americas Watch, 'Challenging Impunity: The Ley de Caducidad and the Referendum Campaign in Uruguay', reprinted in Kritz (ed.), *Transitional Justice*, vol. II, p. 386.

7 Weschler, *A Miracle, A Universe*, p. 166.

8 For example, the Inter-American Commission on Human Rights found that the amnesty law violated basic provisions of the American Convention of Human Rights and the American Declaration of the Rights and Duties of Man: Robert K. Goldman, 'Amnesty Laws and International Law', reprinted in Kritz (ed.), *Transitional Justice*, vol. II, p. 412.

9 Privately, some officials of the subsequent Sanguinetti government claim that the Naval Club Pact secretly promised the military an effective amnesty: Weschler, *A Miracle, A Universe*, pp. 166–7.

10 The military prosecutor who took up the investigation was, as feared, not impartial, concluding in the only six cases he looked into that the security forces were not implicated in abuses: Americas Watch, 'Challenging Impunity', pp. 391–2.

11 Carlos Varela, 'The Referendum Campaign in Uruguay: An Unprecedented Challenge to Impunity', *Human Rights International Reporter*, 13, 1 (Spring 1989), pp. 16–18 discusses the ultimately failed referendum movement.

12 International Institute of Strategic Studies (IISS), *The Military Balance* (London: International Institute of Strategic Studies, 1982–90).

13 Roht-Arriaza, 'Case Studies: Latin America', in Roht-Arriaza (ed.), *Impunity and Human Rights*, pp. 155–9; *Acuerdos de Paz* (Guatemala City, Guatemala: Universidad Rafael Landivar–Instituto de Investigaciones Económicas y Sociales, 1997). See also US Department of State, 'Guatemala Country Report on Human Rights Practices for 1998' (26 February 1999), available at http://www.state.gov/www/global/human_rights/1998_hrp_report/guatemal.htm.

14 Van Dyke and Berkley, 'Redressing Human Rights Abuses', p. 255.

15 'Acuerdo Global Sobre Derechos Humanos', in *Acuerdos de Paz*, points 3 and 4.

16 'Acuerdo sobre el establecimiento de la comisión para el esclarecimiento histórico de las violaciónes a los derechos humanos y los hechos de violencia que han causado sufrimiento a la población guatemalteca', in *Acuerdos de Paz*.

17 Roht-Arriaza, 'Case Studies: Latin America', pp. 157–9.

18 'Acuerdo sobre fortalecimiento del poder civil y función del ejército en una sociedad democrática', 'Acuerdo sobre reformas constitucionales y régimen electoral', in *Acuerdos de Paz*.

19 Roht-Arriaza, 'Case Studies: Latin America', p. 158.

20 Larry Rohter, 'Guatemala Cover-up Charged in Killing of Bishop', *New York Times* (23 October 1998), p. A3.

21 Roht-Arriaza, 'Case Studies: Latin America', pp. 158–9.

22 'Guatemala: 3 Sentenced to Death', *New York Times* (2 December 1998), p. A8.

23 International Institute of Strategic Studies, *The Military Balance* (London: International Institute of Strategic Studies, 1995–99).

24 Zalaquett, 'Balancing Ethical Imperatives and Political Constraints', pp. 1432–8; Jorge Correa Sutil and Francisco Jimenez, '"No Victorious Army Has Ever Been Prosecuted": The Unsettled Story of Transitional Justice in Chile', in McAdams (ed.), *Transitional Justice*, pp. 123–44; Hayner, 'Fifteen truth commissions', pp. 621–3, and Van Dyck and Berkley, 'Redressing Human Rights Abuses', pp. 249–51.

25 'Editor's Introduction: 'Chile', in Kritz (ed.), *Transitional Justice*, vol. II, pp. 453–4.

26 Jorge Mera, 'Chile: Truth and Justice under the Democratic Government', in Roht-Arriaza (ed.), *Impunity and Human Rights*, p. 171. See also Sutil and Jimenez, 'No Victorious Army', p. 124, arguing that the problem was that the Chilean military was defeated only in the ballot box, not on a battlefield.

27 Mark Ensalaco, 'Military Prerogatives and the Stalemate of Chilean Civil–Military Relations', *Armed Forces and Society*, 21, 2 (Winter 1995), pp. 255–70.

28 Pinochet ensured that this would be the case by stipulating that in order to participate in the plebiscite, political parties had to pledge to accept the constitution of 1980 and not to change it except according to its own terms. Jorge Correa,

'Dealing with Past Human Rights Violations: The Chilean Case after Dictatorship', in Kritz (ed.), *Transitional Justice*, vol. II, p. 456.

29 Kritz, 'Chile', p. 454.

30 Correa, 'Dealing with Past Human Rights Violations', pp. 458–9.

31 Correa, 'Dealing with Past Human Rights Violations', pp. 459–60.

32 In 1992, the legislature created a reparations programme for families of victims named in the report of the truth commission. David Weissbrout and Paul W. Fraser, 'Book Review: Report of the Chilean National Commission on Truth and Reconciliation', reprinted in Kritz (ed.), *Transitional Justice*, vol. II, p. 470. The reparations fund is to provide pensions: it is expected to spend about $22 million annually. Mera, 'Chile: Truth and Justice', p. 173.

33 Mera, 'Chile: Truth and Justice', p. 181.

34 Kritz, 'Chile', p. 454.

35 Clifford Krauss, 'Chile Renders a Verdict on Pinochet: Let's Move On', *New York Times* (22 November 1998), p. 6.

36 Warren Hoge, 'Chilean Official Says His Country Will Pursue Justice Against Pinochet', *New York Times* (30 November 1998), p. A10; Hoge, 'British Court Rules Against Pinochet: Now Cabinet Must Weigh Extradition', *New York Times* (26 November 1998), pp. A1, A8; Barbara Crossette, 'Dictators (and Some Lawyers) Tremble', *New York Times* (29 November 1998), sec. 4, pp. 1, 3; Tim Weiner, 'U.S. Will Release Files on Crimes Under Pinochet', *New York Times* (2 December 1998), pp. A1, A8; Warren Hoge, 'Law Lords in London Open Rehearing of Pinochet Case', *New York Times* (19 January 1999), p. A3.

37 See United Nations Development Programme (UNDP), *Human Development Report 1996* (New York: Oxford University Press, 1996); shows a significant real rise in expenditures between 1985 and 1994, but a decline by more than half as a percentage of GDP. See also James W. Wilkie and Jose Guadalupe Ortega (eds), *Statistical Abstract of Latin America*, vol. 33 (Los Angeles, CA: UCLA Latin American Center Publications, University of California, 1997), p. 286.

38 Stepan, *Rethinking Military Politics*; Robert G. Wesson, *The United States and Brazil: Limits of Influence* (New York: Praeger, 1981); 'Editor's Introduction: Brazil,' in Kritz (ed.), *Transitional Justice*, vol. II, pp. 431–2.

39 Guillermo O'Donnell, 'Challenge to Democratization in Brazil', in Kritz (ed.), *Transitional Justice*, vol. II, pp. 433–42. The budget doubled in real terms and as a percentage of GDP; see UNDP, *Human Development Report 1996*, p. 174. But see the figures in Wilkie and Guadalupe Ortega (eds), *Statistical Abstract of Latin America*, p. 286.

40 Larry Rohter, 'Past Military Rule's Abuse is Haunting Brazil Today', *New York Times* (11 July 1999), p. 12.

41 Rene Antonio Mayorga, 'Democracy Dignified and an End to Impunity: Bolivia's Military Dictatorship on Trial', in McAdams (ed.), *Transitional Justice*, pp. 61–82; Roht-Arriaza, 'Case Studies: Latin America', in Roht-Arriaza (ed.), *Impunity and Human Rights*, pp. 151–3. The president who was democratically elected in 1997 began facing calls for accountability more recently for a small number of deaths that occurred under his earlier military dictatorship: Clifford Krauss, 'Bolivian's Dark Past Starts to Catch Up With Him', *New York Times* (14 March 1999), p. 3.

42 Mayorga, 'Democracy Dignified', p. 66.

43 UNDP, *Human Development Report 1996*, p. 174. But compare Wilkie and Guadalupe Ortega (eds), *Statistical Abstract of Latin America*, p. 286.

44 Irwin P. Stotzky, 'Haiti: Searching for Alternatives', in Roht-Arriaza (ed.), *Impunity and Human Rights*, pp. 185–97; US Department of State, 'Haiti Country Report on Human Rights Practices for 1998' (26 February 1999), available at http://www.state.gov/global/human_rights/1998_hrp_report/haiti.htm.

45 Michael Bailey, Robert Maguire and J. O'Neil G Pouliot, 'Haiti: Military–Police Partnership for Public Security', in Oakley *et al.*, *Policing the New World Disorder.*

46 Nicos C. Alivizates and P. Nikiforos Diamandouros, 'Politics and the Judiciary in the Greek Transition to Democracy', in McAdams (ed.), *Transitional Justice*, pp. 27–51; P. Nikiforos Diamandouros, 'Regime Change and the Prospects for Democracy in Greece: 1974–83'; Harry J. Psomiades, 'Greece: From the Colonels' Rule to Democracy'; Amnesty International, 'Torture in Greece: The First Torturers' Trial, 1975'; 'Editor's Introduction: Greece', in Kritz (ed.), *Transitional Justice*, vol. II; Roht-Arriaza, 'Case Studies: Europe', in Roht-Arriaza (ed.), *Impunity and Human Rights*, pp. 78–80.

47 D. L. Raby, *Fascism and Resistance in Portugal: Communists, Liberals and Military Dissidents in the Opposition to Salazar, 1941–1974* (Manchester: Manchester University Press, 1988); Kenneth Maxwell, 'Regime Overthrow and the Prospects for Democratic Transition in Portugal'; Antonio Costa Pinto, 'The Radical Right in Contemporary Portugal', and 'Editor's Introduction: Portugal', in Kritz (ed.), *Transitional Justice*, vol. II, pp. 283–96.

48 IISS, *The Military Balance* (1972–79).

49 Raymond Carr and Juan Pablo Fusi Aizipurua, *Spain: Dictatorship to Democracy* (London: George Allen & Unwin, 1981); Jose Maria Maravall and Julia Santamaria, 'Political Change in Spain and the Prospects for Democracy', Edward Malefakis, 'Spain and its Francoist Heritage', and 'Editor's Introduction: Spain', in Kritz (ed.), *Transitional Justice*, vol. II, pp. 297–322.

50 Carr and Aizipurua, *Spain: Dictatorship to Democracy*, p. 175.

51 IISS, *The Military Balance* (1977–87). There was a reduction at the time Spain joined NATO, and the budget remained flat for several years thereafter.

52 See generally Helga A. Welsh, 'Dealing with the Communist Past: Central and East European Experiences after 1990', *Europe–Asia Studies*, 48, 3 (1996), pp. 413–28; Claus Offe, 'Disqualification, Retribution, Restitution: Dilemmas of Justice in Post-communist Transitions', *Journal of Political Philosophy*, 1, 1 (1993), pp. 17–44; Judy Batt, *East Central Europe from Reform to Transformation* (London: Pinter, 1991).

53 In 1995, 14 members from the Soviet bloc had joined; and, by 1996, ten had ratified the convention and incorporated it into domestic law. See Andrew Drzemczewski, 'Ensuring Compatibility of Domestic Law with the European Convention on Human Rights Prior to Ratification: The Hungarian Model', *Human Rights Law Journal*, 16, 7 (November 1995), p. 241 and appendix A; Jorg Polakiewicz, 'The Application of the European Convention on Human Rights in Domestic Law', *Human Rights Law Journal*, 17, 12 (December 1996), pp. 405–11.

54 Kathleen E. Smith, 'Decommunizations after the "Velvet Revolutions" in East Central Europe', in Roht-Arriaza (ed.), *Impunity and Human Rights*, pp. 82–98; Timothy Garton Ash, 'The Truth about Dictatorship', *New York Review of Books* (19 February 1998), pp. 35–40; Adam Michnik and Vaclav Havel, 'Confronting the Past: Justice or Revenge', Michael Kraus, 'Settling Accounts: Post-communist Czechoslovakia', Jan Obrman, 'Czech Parliament Declares Former Communist Regime Illegal', and 'Editor's Introduction: Czechoslovakia', in Kritz (ed.), *Transitional Justice*, vol. II, pp. 533–88.

55 Kraus, 'Settling Accounts', pp. 543–4.

56 This followed an attempt to bring similar charges which was barred because the statute of limitations had run; the legislation lifting the statute of limitations in certain cases cleared the way for this round of prosecutions.

57 The plan was to reduce forces that had once totalled 200,000 to 65,000. Compulsory military training was also cut from two years to one. In the Slovak Republic, plans were made to cut the budget and reduce forces from 42,000 to 36,000. See US Department of State, 'Background Note: Czech Republic, July 1994' and 'Background Note: Slovak Republic, April 1998', available at http://www.dosfan.

lib.uic.edu/ERC/bgnotes/eur/czechrepublic9407.html and /slovakrepublic9804.html.

58 US Department of State, 'Czech Republic Country Report on Human Rights Practices for 1998' and 'Slovak Republic Country Report on Human Rights Practices for 1998', available at http://www.state.gov/www/global/human_rights/1998_hrp_report/czechrepublic.html and /slovakre.html.

59 McAdams, 'Communism on Trial: the East German Past and the German Future', in McAdams (ed.), *Transitional Justice*, pp. 239–52; Garton Ash, 'The Truth about Dictatorship'; Smith, 'Decommunization'; 'Accountability for State-sponsored Human Rights Abuses in Eastern Europe and the Soviet Union' (panel discussion), *Boston College Third World Law Journal*, 12, 2 (Summer 1992), pp. 246–52; Suzanne Walther, 'Problems in Blaming and Punishing Individuals for Human Rights Violations: The Example of the Berlin Wall Shootings', in Roht-Arriaza (ed.), *Impunity and Human Rights*, pp. 99–112; Commission on Security and Cooperation in Europe, 'Human Rights and Democratization in Unified Germany' and 'Editor's Introduction: East Germany', in Kritz (ed.), *Transitional Justice*, vol. II, pp. 593–691.

60 Hayner, 'Fifteen truth commissions', p. 627.

61 Gabor Halmai and Kim Lane Scheppele, 'Living Well is the Best Revenge: The Hungarian Approach to Judging the Past', in McAdams (ed.), *Transitional Justice*, pp. 155–84; Garton Ash, 'The Truth about Dictatorship'; Smith, 'Decommunization'; Judith Pataki, 'Dealing with Hungarian Communists' Crimes', Alexander H. Platt, Imtiaz T. Ladak, Alan J. Goodman and Matthew R. Nicely, 'Compensating Former Political Prisoners: An Overview of Developments in Central and Eastern Europe', and 'Editor's Introduction: Hungary', in Kritz (ed.), *Transitional Justice*, vol. II, pp. 645–92.

62 Smith, 'Decommunization', p. 85.

63 Garton Ash, 'The Truth about Dictatorship', p. 37.

64 Commission on Security and Cooperation in Europe, 'Human Rights and Democratization in Bulgaria'; Helsinki Watch, 'Democratization in Bulgaria'; Kjell Engelbrekt and Duncan M. Perry, 'The Conviction of Bulgaria's Former Leader' and 'Editor's Introduction: Bulgaria', in Kritz (ed.), *Transitional Justice*, pp. 693–711. US Department of State, 'Bulgaria Country Report on Human Rights Practices for 1998' (26 February 1999), available at http://www.state.gov/global/human_rights/1998_hrp_report/bulgaria.htm.

65 US Department of State, 'Bulgaria Country Report on Human Rights Practices for 1998'.

66 US Department of State, 'Albania Country Report on Human Rights Practices for 1998' (26 February 1999), available at http://www.state.gov/www/global/human_rights/1998_hrp_report/albania.htm; Commission on Security and Cooperation in Europe, 'Human Rights and Democratization in Albania' and 'Editor's Introduction: Albania', in Kritz (ed.), *Transitional Justice*, vol. II, pp. 723–9.

67 US Department of State, 'Background Note: Poland, August 1994', available at http://dosfan.lib.uic.edu/ERC/bgnotes/eur/poland9408.html. Andrzej S. Walicki, 'Transitional Justice and the Political Struggles of Post-communist Poland', in McAdams (ed.), *Transitional Justice*, pp. 185–226; Smith, 'Decommunization'; and Garton Ash, 'The Truth about Dictatorship'.

68 The attempt to cleanse the parliament failed because the files obtained from the security forces listed all members, whether they had been collaborators or targets. After a great deal of confusion and anger, the parliament voted the government out of power for favouring lustration: Smith, 'Decommunization', p. 96.

69 Garton Ash, 'The Truth about Dictatorship', p. 38.

70 Edwin Rekosh, 'Romania: A Persistent Culture of Impunity', in Roht-Arriaza (ed.), *Impunity and Human Rights*, pp. 129–44; 'Accountability for State-sponsored

Human Rights Abuses in Eastern Europe and the Former Soviet Union', pp. 252–6. See also US Department of State, 'Background Note: Romania, June 1997', available at http://www.dosfan.lib.uic.edu/ERC/bgnotes/eur/romania9701.html; and US Department of State, 'Romania Country Report on Human Rights Practices for 1998', available at: http://www.state.gove/www/global/human_rights/1998_hrp_report/romania.html.

71 Rekosh, 'Romania', pp. 135–6.

72 Kathleen E. Smith, 'Destalinization in the Former Soviet Union', in Roht-Arriaza (ed.), *Impunity and Human Rights*, pp. 113–28; Robert Sharlet, 'The Russian Constitutional Court: The First Term', Platt *et al.*, 'Compensating Former Political Prisoners', Victor Yasmatin, 'Legislation on Screening and State Security in Russia' and 'Editor's Introduction: Russia', in Kritz (ed.), *Transitional Justice*, vol. II, pp. 735–61.

73 'Accountability for State-sponsored Human Rights Abuses in Eastern Europe and the Soviet Union', pp. 257–65.

74 'Editor's Introduction: Lithuania', in Kritz (ed.), *Transitional Justice*, vol. II, pp. 763–69. US Department of State, 'Lithuania Country Report on Human Rights Practices for 1998' (26 February 1999), available at http://www.state.gov/global/human_rights/1998_hrp_report/lithuani.htm.

75 See US Department of State, 'Ethiopia Country Report on Human Rights Practices for 1998' (26 February 1999), available at http://www.state.gov/www/global/human_rights/1998_hrp_report/ethiopia.htm; 'Ethiopia', in Human Rights Watch, *World Report 1999*, available at http://www.hrw.org/worldreport99/africa/ethiopia.html.

76 US Department of State, 'Rwanda Country Report on Human Rights Practices for 1998' (26 February 1999), available at http://www.state.gov/www/global/human_rights/1998_hrp_report/rwanda.htm; 'Rwanda', in Human Rights Watch, *World Report 1999*, available at http://www.hrw.org/worldreport99/africa/rwanda.html; and International Criminal Tribunal for Rwanda, Press and Public Affairs Unit, 'Introduction to the International Criminal Tribunal for Rwanda (ICTR), available at http://www.ictr.org/english/factsheets/introduction.htm; the statute of the tribunal is available at http://www.ictr.org/statute.html. For a thorough account of the history of the events leading up to, including and subsequent to the genocide, see Human Rights Watch, *Leave None to Tell the Story: Genocide in Rwanda* (March 1999), available at wysiwyg://93/http://www.hrw.org/reports/1999/rwanda/.

77 Paul Lewis, 'Amnesty in Sierra Leone Opposed by Rights Group', *New York Times* (26 July 1999), p. A7. See also www.specialcourt.org.

78 Sung-Joo Han, 'The Failure of Democracy in South Korea', 'The Experiment in Democracy' and 'Editor's Introduction: South Korea', in Kritz (ed.), *Transitional Justice*, vol. II, pp. 208–39.

79 Neier, *War Crimes*, p. 87.

80 US Department of State, 'Republic of Korea Country Report on Human Rights Practices for 1998', available at http://www.state.gov/www/global/human_rights/1998_hrp_report/southkor.htm.

81 UNDP, *Human Development Report 1996*, p. 174.

82 Gretchen Casper, *Fragile Democracies: The Legacies of Authoritarian Rule* (Pittsburgh, PA: University of Pittsburgh Press, 1995); Belinda A. Aquino, 'The Human Rights Debacle in the Philippines', in Roht-Arriaza (ed.), *Impunity and Human Rights*, pp. 231–51; Hayner, 'Fifteen truth commissions', pp. 620–1.

83 Casper, *Fragile Democracies*, pp. 161–7.

84 US Department of State, 'Philippines Country Report on Human Rights Practices for 1998' (26 February 1999), available at http://www.state.gov/www/global/human_rights/1998_hrp_report/philippi.htm.

85 UNDP, *Human Development Report 1996*, p. 174 and UNDP, *Human Development Report 1997/98*, p. 188.

86 Michael W. Doyle, *UN Peacekeeping in Cambodia: UNTAC's Civil Mandate* (Boulder, CO: Lynne Rienner, 1995); Dennis McNamara, 'UN Human Rights Activities in Cambodia: An Evaluation', in Alice H. Henkin (ed.), *Honoring Human Rights and Keeping the Peace: Lessons from El Salvador, Cambodia, and Haiti* (Washington, DC: Aspen Institute, 1995), pp. 57–82; Michael Vickery and Naomi Roht-Arriaza, 'Human Rights in Cambodia', in Roht-Arriaza (ed.), *Impunity and Human Rights*, pp. 243–51; US Department of State, 'Cambodia Country Report on Human Rights Practices for 1998' (26 February 1999), available at http://www.state.gov/www/global/human_rights/1998_hrp_report/cambodia.htm.

87 'Cambodia: Khmer Rouge Officer Gets Life', *New York Times* (8 June 1999), p. A8; 'Cambodia: TV Trial for Khmer Rouge', *New York Times* (26 June 1999), p. A5.

88 Seth Mydans, 'Of Top Khmer Rouge, Only One Awaits Judgment', *New York Times* (14 March 1999), p. 6; Philip Shenon, 'UN Plans Joint War Crimes Tribunal for Khmer Rouge', *New York Times* (12 August 1999), p. A8.

89 Seth Mydans, '20 Years On, Anger Ignites Against Khmer Rouge', *New York Times* (10 January 1999), pp. 1, 6.

90 'Resolution: Cambodia and the Khmer Rouge', *Far Eastern Economic Review*, 162, 2 (14 January 1999), p. 86; P. S. Suryanaraya, 'Cambodia Planning a truth commission', *The Hindu* (17 January 1999), p. 17; 'Tutu Will Help Cambodia', *Daily Mail and Guardian*, (18 January 1999).

91 IISS, *The Military Balance* (1996–99).

92 James A. Schear and Karl Farris, 'Policing Cambodia: The Public Security Dimensions of UN Peace Operations', in Oakley *et al.*, *Policing the New World Disorder*.

93 See Chapter 7 on Sri Lanka generally; for a current overview of the human rights situation, see US Department of State, 'Sri Lanka Country Report on Human Rights Practices for 1998', (26 February 1999), available at http://www.state.gov/www/global/human_rights/1998_hrp_report/srilanka.htm.

3 El Salvador

'Negotiated revolution' and the truth commission

Introduction

El Salvador is a fertile case for us to examine because it provides myriad outcomes: it experienced amnesty, a truth commission, reform of the security forces and nominal purification. In addition, the factors leading to the transition seem to be multiple, including a virtual military stalemate leading both sides of the civil conflict to see the virtues of negotiation, and the active pressure and facilitation of the USA and the UN. This does not mean, however, that full accountability and reform could be achieved: an amnesty was pushed through, limiting accountability, but the reform of the armed forces was rather more successful, as we shall see.

A brief history

From 1980 to 1991, El Salvador was engaged in a brutal civil war between government forces and the Farabundo Martí National Liberation Front (FMLN). Thousands were killed, and massive human rights violations were perpetrated during this period.[1] Those responsible were largely members of the military and security forces. Although the regime during this period was not technically a military one, the military exerted extraordinary power and influence over the political process, and the transition would face many of the same obstacles that transition from military rule faces.

While underlying social and economic complaints went largely unaddressed, and prosecution of those responsible for crimes was not pursued, the final peace accord included an agreement to purge responsible officers, abolished two repressive security forces, and established a new civilian police, the Policía Nacional Civil (PNC).[2] Perhaps most importantly, however, the agreement established a commission on the truth to investigate past abuses and make recommendations. Because this commission, and the Salvadoran model in general, are often offered up as models for resolution of other disputes, their successes and failures are worth examining here.[3]

Negotiating peace: events and accords

In El Salvador, the road to peace was long, and often foundered in the face of military intransigence and opposition to the imposition of responsibility for human rights violations. Before 1992, there was a long line of attempted peace accords, but the process leading to the final peace began in 1990 with an agreement reached in Costa Rica, which established minimum human rights standards and envisioned the establishment, achieved six months later, of ONUSAL (UN Observer Mission in El Salvador), a UN human rights verification mission. A 1991 accord reached in New York established the national commission for the consolidation of peace (COPAZ), provided for the demobilization of the FMLN, and for the future access of FMLN members to the PNC.[4] Finally, agreements reached in the last hours of 1991 in New York made the 1992 Chapultepec peace accords possible.

In this section, I give a detailed account of the context and history of the peace negotiations, and the shifting positions of both Salvadoran parties, as well as the role played by international actors. I do this to illustrate more fully the compromises that were made by both the FMLN and the government of El Salvador, as well as the influence of actors like the USA and the UN, and the shifting international climate.

Late 1989 is thought by many to mark the turning point in the long process leading to peace in El Salvador, as important domestic, regional and international events took place.

First, the FMLN launched a massive new initiative in November 1989, demonstrating that, though it might be unable to defeat the armed forces, the military conflict had reached an impasse.[5] In time, this would convince not just the Fuerzas Armadas of El Salvador (FAES), but also their key patron, the USA, that their confidence in eventual defeat of the FMLN was misplaced, and that negotiation was the only solution. Thus, by February of 1990, the US Senate had passed a resolution calling for UN and OAS mediation for an immediate ceasefire, and the US Department of State also called on President Cristiani to consider a ceasefire.[6]

Shortly after the FMLN offensive began, on 16 November, there was an attack at the Universidad Centroamericana (UCA), killing six Jesuit priests, a domestic worker and her daughter, that was subsequently linked to the armed forces. What might have been simply another instance of serious human rights abuses turned out to have international consequences. The US Congress, in particular, expressed outrage at this crime, not least because it was perpetrated by the Batallion Atlacatl, of whose members about 1,000 had been trained in the USA.[7]

Another key event enabling political change was the winding down of the Cold War. The end of the Cold War signalled ideological and material changes that profoundly altered the political climate in Central America, among other places. Waning of Soviet international support for communist regimes and revolutionary rhetoric meant not only that any communist threat in the region was disappearing, but also that the USA could perceive that it was waning.[8] This would mean, in time, not only that Soviet aid to Nicaragua would end, but that Nicaragua would have free elections replacing the Sandinistas, and that Sandinista aid to the FMLN would end. Not only would the Soviets begin championing negotiations, but the USA was increasingly able to see the FMLN as a party that could be negotiated with, rather than part of an all-encompassing communist threat. The electoral triumph of Violeta Barrios de Chamorro in Nicaragua was also part of historic changes in the international and regional environment. In particular, the loss of Sandinista backing was expected to weaken the FMLN significantly.[9]

1989 also brought a shift in the political and ideological landscape. The FMLN moved from calling for socialist revolution to calling for pluralist democracy after a great deal of internal debate. As a result, its negotiating demands de-emphasized socio-economic issues and called for institutional reform. There was a simultaneous moderation in the government camp. While the new president, Alfredo Cristiani, was part of the conservative ARENA party, the party itself was split between hard-liners and those who advocated a negotiated settlement to the war; Cristiani's campaign had promised to seek negotiations.[10] Some place particular importance on the perspective of Cristiani, which was perhaps in part motivated by the belief that peace would bring foreign investment and economic development.[11]

Thus, a number of domestic, regional and international factors were important: military stalemate in the country; regional changes arising from the US invasion of Panama, the elections in Nicaragua and elections of conservative governments in other countries in the region; interests of local entrepreneurs in stability for the sake of growth; a shift in US policy due to the apparent waning of the communist threat, as well as a recognition that its Salvadoran strategy had neither defeated the rebels nor democratized the society; and a shift in Soviet foreign policy. These are thought to be the key factors that enabled negotiations to begin in earnest; once started, they were strengthened by the participation of a wide array of international actors.[12] All of these events, then, were important preconditions for the negotiations: I turn now to a discussion of each of the key peace accords and the negotiating tactics employed by both sides in reaching them, as well as the intervention of members of the international community.

The Geneva accords, reached on 4 April 1990, dealt with little substance, but laid the groundwork for further negotiations, and active involvement of the United Nations and member governments. Setting a precedent that would be followed throughout the negotiations, military activity escalated during the negotiations, as each side sought to improve its negotiating position with a strengthened military position.[13]

Meanwhile, congressional opinion in the USA became increasingly critical of the Salvadoran government, and of American support of the government and armed forces of El Salvador. For the first time, Congress named a delegation to examine human rights abuses in El Salvador, the Moakley commission, headed by Representative Joseph Moakley, which investigated the killings at UCA.[14]

Congressional outrage at the UCA massacre was also articulated in a way more likely to directly influence the policy of the Salvadoran government: on 26 April, the US House of Representatives voted for a 50 per cent reduction in military aid to El Salvador for fiscal years 1991 and 1992. The conditions for reinstatement of aid were that the government must engage in talks in good faith with the FMLN, and prosecute those responsible for the UCA massacre. Cristiani's immediate response to this cut was to assert that it would send the wrong message to the FMLN, and to say that money would simply be diverted from other government projects to continue the war.[15]

The Bush administration began to send similar signals to the Salvadoran government: Secretary of State James Baker said that the UCA case had become the decisive issue in the history of El Salvador, and White House Chief of Staff John Sununu told Cristiani that the handling of the UCA case would have a significant impact on US aid. At this point, some argue, a new US policy was developing, in conjunction with the recognition that ten years of war and billions of dollars in US aid had not altered the correlation of forces enough to ensure a FAES victory.[16]

This growing US pressure may have accelerated the shifting perspectives of the FAES, whose rhetoric moved from assertions of the certainty of imminent victory to recognition of the need to end the war by political means. This did not mean it greeted FMLN proposals warmly: the FMLN insisted that for peace and democratization to succeed, the armed forces would have to be reformed, a claim rejected both by President Cristiani and Colonel Rene Emilio Ponce, who stated flatly that the military would not be a subject of negotiations.[17]

While in July 1990, an important agreement was reached in Costa Rica regarding human rights, the armed forces continued to be a key point of contention in subsequent rounds. In the San Jose accords, protection of key human rights such as liberty and bodily integrity, protection against reprisals for exercise of legitimate political rights, and protection of the right to habeas corpus, *inter alia*, were agreed to. The parties also agreed to the creation of a UN mission to monitor the human rights agreement. However, the future status of the armed forces was not resolved. The government advocated an amnesty for past abuses, and that no one lose their positions of power or privilege for past acts.[18]

However, in this as in the August San Jose round, the FMLN rejected this position. In the August round, the FMLN demanded that the Fuerzas Armadas as well as the FMLN symmetrically disappear, giving way to a new, civilian public security force. And, on the question of impunity, the FMLN argued that there must be a process of *depuración* that would also establish the truth. These demands, as well as the elimination of the Batallion Atlacatl, the national guard and the treasury police, all notorious human rights violators, were part of an 18-point FMLN proposal in this round.[19]

The government adamantly rejected these demands, pointing out that the existence of the FAES was recognized in the constitution, and arguing that the best method of change was its professionalization, without traumatic ruptures. It responded with its own 33-point proposal, which included, *inter alia*, a *punto final* (full stop) law to halt human rights prosecutions, and transfer, rather than elimination, of the treasury police, national guard and the national police to the supervision of extant ministries, as well as the transfer, rather than elimination, of the Dirección Nacional de Inteligencia (the National Intelligence Agency known for abuses) to the authority of the Casa Presidencial (presidential house). Similarly, rapid reaction battalions were to be transferred rather than eliminated. Some important concessions, however, were the proposals to disarm the patrols of the Defensa Civil (civil defense) and paramilitary forces, to end forcible recruitment, and to open a military university.[20] And shortly thereafter, coinciding with the naming of Colonel Ponce as minister of defence, there were signs that the armed forces might be retreating slightly, as several high-level officials thought to be responsible for corruption or human rights abuses, or heads of notorious institutions like the head of the treasury police, were transferred to posts abroad.[21]

US pressure on the Salvadoran government increased when, on 19 October, the US Senate adopted a military aid package that included the Dodd–Leahy amendment to regulate it, with the same provisions regarding the El Salvador war and peace process as the bill passed by the House of Representatives in June.[22] The military expressed fears that the cut in aid would undermine its advantage over the FMLN. Military actions by both camps subsequently increased dramatically, but the balance of forces did not alter despite a significant FMLN offensive in late November. While the USA worried that the offensive would give the FMLN increased power, the FMLN maintained that its actions were merely meant to strengthen its hand at the negotiating table. Nonetheless, on 7 December, Department of State spokeswoman Margaret Tutwiler announced that the Bush administration planned to speed the delivery of the fiscal year 1991 aid, as well as disburse the remaining 1990 aid, to help the FAES replace lost equipment, in particular that lost to the FMLN's anti-aircraft missiles.[23]

The US policy on aid would change further following the FMLN shoot-down of an American helicopter on 2 January 1991. The FMLN subsequently captured the two American advisers that had been in the craft, and executed them, prompting President Bush, on 7 January, to call for the Congress to unfreeze aid to the Salvadoran government. On 16 January, President Bush announced that the FMLN had violated the conditions of the appropriations act and that he would unfreeze aid, but that he would wait 60 days for the completion of local elections.[24]

Despite the serious setback to negotiations dealt by the FMLN actions, the negotiations continued in Mexico in early February. Key differences now existed between the parties with regard to, *inter alia*, impunity, constitutional reform and the negotiation of a ceasefire. With regard to the proposed ad hoc commission to carry out *depuración* of military officers, the FMLN argued that the UN should generate a list of candidates for membership, with either party able to veto, while the government wanted Cristiani to choose the members with FAES participation. With regard to accountability for rights abuses, the FMLN argued that the emphasis should be placed first on FAES actions, and later on FMLN violations, while the government demanded parallel action. The issue of constitutional reform was more complex, having to do with the timing and structure of reforms to the constitution, which were somewhat hamstrung by the constitution's article 248. This article stipulated rather forbidding regulations for constitutional reform, which also necessitated swift action.[25]

The FMLN perceived the government's stance as increasingly intransigent, as a result of several advantages: increased US hegemony after the Gulf War, logistical problems faced by the FMLN with the political changes in Nicaragua, the expectation that ARENA would be the big winner in upcoming local elections, and the anticipation of a new military campaign by the government. This last factor would be aided significantly by the recent receipt of half of the US aid, the expected unfreezing of the other half, and a recent delivery by the USA to the Fuerza Aerea of new combat planes and helicopters. And indeed, on 14 March, President Bush announced that, as the 60-day grace period had passed and the FMLN had failed to negotiate in good faith, the other half of the aid would be unfrozen.[26]

Serious disagreements continued with regard to the nature of any ceasefire as well. While the FMLN envisioned it as an armed peace, with both sides ceasing hostilities, but keeping their arms and territorial positions while awaiting definitive accords, the government wanted the FMLN to concentrate its forces in special zones and disarm before purification or restructuring of the armed forces or constitutional reform.[27] Despite these disputes, an accord was eventually reached.

The Mexico accords, signed on 27 April 1991, contained significant advances on several critical issues. First, with regard to the armed forces, the parties agreed that there would be constitutional reforms aimed at: clarifying the subordination of the FAES to civilian power, creating the Policía Nacional Civil (PNC), which would expressly be independent of the FAES, creating an intelligence unit independent of the FAES, and redefining military justice to narrow its jurisdiction to strictly military matters. Agreement was also reached on constitutional reforms to reorganize the supreme court, with new rules for appointing judges, restructuring the Consejo Nacional de la Judicatura (CNJ) to ensure its independence from state organs or political parties, and the creation of the Procurador Nacional para la Defensa de los Derechos Humanos (the human rights ombudsman). In the arena of electoral reform, the parties agreed to the creation of the Tribunal Supremo Electoral (TSE), to replace the old electoral council; the TSE was to have greater administrative authority. Finally, the parties agreed to the creation of the Comisión de la Verdad (truth commission), to be made up of three persons chosen by the UN secretary-general, with input from the parties, to hear evidence of grave acts since 1980.[28]

In the Mexico round, the parties also reached agreements regarding the development of constitutional reform and the functioning of the truth commission. The day after the Mexico accords were signed, President Cristiani submitted a constitutional reform package to implement the agreements. Thus, the Mexico accords would eventually be expressed in, *inter alia*, the reform of article 212 of the Salvadoran constitution articulating the sole role of the FAES as defence of territory and sovereignty.[29]

On 20 May 1991, in Resolution 693 the UN Security Council finally established the mandate for the UN observer mission (ONUSAL) that had been agreed in the San Jose accords. While the San Jose accords specified that the mission not be established before a ceasefire, many national sectors, including the government and the FMLN, requested that it be put in place before a ceasefire. The mission would arrive on 26 July.[30]

As negotiations continued, the issue of US military aid continued to be salient. On 26 May, via Radio Venceremos, the FMLN announced a new condition for a ceasefire: the complete suspension of US aid to the FAES. A group of American congresspersons, attempting to prevent Bush's plans to unfreeze aid, sent a letter to the US president arguing that such an act would take the pressure off the government to make concessions in negotiations. In June, Cristiani visited the USA, in part to lobby for the unfreezing of aid; Bush subsequently announced the release of $21 million, or about half of the frozen aid.[31]

The issue of ceasefire timing was bound up not only with the question of US military aid, but also with the issue of future incorporation of FMLN members into Salvadoran society and politics. The government argued that, so long as the FMLN maintained an army it could not become a political party; the FMLN's political committee, meanwhile, entered into private talks in August with heads of political parties and heads of business, hoping to clear the way for the emergence of the FMLN as a political party. The key problem was that, while the government simply hoped to turn the FMLN into an unarmed political party, the FMLN wanted concessions like purification and, as the UN's Alvaro de Soto noted, guarantees would be needed before it would be reasonable to expect the rebels to put down their arms. Furthermore, the FMLN continued to demand incorporation into the military structure, a demand adamantly rejected by the government.[32]

Thus, as the September date for negotiations in New York approached, a number of thorny issues remained: purification, the conditions for a ceasefire, as well as the UCA case and the question of amnesty. Cristiani, on a tour of the Southern Cone, had allegedly said that he would provide amnesty to military members implicated in the UCA case; under heavy political fire he denied this charge, but said that he could offer amnesty as part of the peace process.[33]

When the New York negotiations opened, the parties remained deadlocked over the incorporation of the FMLN into the military; however, on 19 September, the FMLN dropped this demand and instead asked that its members have the chance to join the new PNC, with a set quota to ensure its position.[34] It also asked that FMLN members of the PNC be the nucleus of forces in areas traditionally under the FMLN's control, and that the new director and officials of the PNC be chosen by negotiation between the two parties. The government rejected this proposal the next day, arguing that in order to maintain 'verticality' Cristiani alone must have the power to appoint such officials.

According to one account, it was the intervention of the 'group of friends' of the secretary-general the following evening that forced the FMLN to recognize that no government worried about institutionality could accept such stipulations about the appointment of high officials. On 22 September, the secretary-general proposed, *inter alia*, that ex-FMLN members could join the PNC in their individual capacity, a proposal that the FMLN accepted but the government rejected, the latter continuing to insist on the surrender of the FMLN in exchange for a vague promise of future participation in the political process and an amnesty for the FMLN.

On 24 September, the government finally agreed to give the FAES a limited role in its own purification, and to grant the Comisión Nacional para la Consolidación de la Paz (COPAZ) a fundamental role in selecting the new heads of the police. Finally, on 25 September, the New York accords were signed, with the government having agreed to most of the secretary-general's proposals of 22 September, pertaining to purification, reduction, doctrine and education of the FAES, as well as to the creation of COPAZ and the ad hoc commission to supervise the purification of the military.

Several key features of the New York accords need to be elaborated. First, they created COPAZ, which was to supervise compliance with the political accords. Membership of COPAZ was to include equal numbers (two) of representatives from the GOES and the FMLN, as well as one from the FAES and one from each of the parties of coalitions in the Assembly. According to a separate set of confidential understandings, COPAZ was to have a key role in restructuring the doctrine and educational system of the FAES and in the configuration of the new PNC.[35]

The accords also stipulated that the parties agreed to the purification of the FAES on the basis of recommendations by the ad hoc commission, and that military participation would be limited to two members, who would have limited access to testimony. The parties also agreed to reach criteria for the reduction of the armed forces, and to reach an accord on redefining the doctrine of the FAES. The doctrine was to include the recognition that the FAES was subordinate to constitutional authorities, that it was to respect human rights, that its duty was to the nation, and that its role was to protect sovereignty. The parties agreed to give full force to the April Mexico agreement to reform the educational system of the FAES to emphasize democratic values, human dignity and the subordination of military bodies to constitutional authority.[36] Finally, and of key importance to the FMLN, there was agreement on land transfer to campesinos, a government promise to extend agrarian reform, and other measures to alleviate social and economic problems.[37]

In subsequent negotiations in Mexico, the participation of the FMLN in the PNC, and the reduction of the FA, remained in dispute. Vice-minister of public security, Colonel Inocente O. Montano, maintained that given the academic levels required for entrance into the PNC, former FMLN members would be barred from entry, adding that other aspects of the New York accords were 'anti-constitutional'. And, while the FMLN wanted to propose guidelines for the reduction of the armed forces, Colonel Vargas of the government delegation declared that demand unacceptable.[38] The round concluded without the resolution of either of these key issues, which carried over to the next Mexico round.

In this round, the two issues remained unresolved. While Joaquim Villalobos of the FMLN argued that participation by ex-rebels was a necessary condition for peace, the government insisted that there would be no chairs reserved in the PNC for ex-FMLN members. Similarly, while the government insisted that reduction of the FAES should come as a natural result of the signing of a definitive ceasefire, the FMLN proposed the establishment of a calendar of reduction as part of the accords, to be linked to the reinsertion of the rebels into civilian life.[39]

With the close of the year and the imminent departure of Secretary-General Perez de Cuellar, pressure mounted for the completion of accords in El Salvador. Shortly before midnight on New Year's Eve in New York, the parties agreed to resume negotiations in the new year and, if positive results weren't seen by 10 January, they would accept the resolution of pending issues by the secretary-general. This provision provided important leverage to force the parties into agreement on the two main pending issues. In January, the parties agreed to resolve the remaining issues in order to sign the peace accord in Mexico by 16 January.[40] The New York Acts, I and II, thus did not resolve any substantive issues, but cleared the way for the final accord to be signed at the Castle of Chapultepec in Mexico.

Even at the Chapultepec meeting, the parties remained divided over the reduction of the FAES and rapid reaction battalions. The FAES wanted a reduction of 50.2 per cent over two years (to 31,000 from 63,175), but the FMLN saw this proposal as a trick. However, because of the provision for the UN secretary-general to resolve pending matters left unresolved after 10 January, the issues were finally resolved.[41] Under a plan proposed by the GOES and accepted by the secretary-general, FAES personnel were to be reduced by 50 per cent, and installations converted or eliminated. The Chapultepec accord further called for the dissolution of the rapid reaction battalions, the paramilitary entity the Defensa Civil, the treasury police and the national guard, and also called for the regulation of the reserve forces of the FAES and private security forces. The accord provided for the replacement of the notorious Dirección Nacional de Inteligencia with the Organismo de Inteligencia de Estado (state intelligence organ), which would be directly under the control of the executive, supervised by the legislature and not linked to military power. The accord also provided for the recommendation of purification of members of the armed forces involved in grave human rights abuses by the ad hoc commission, to be made up of three civilians chosen by the secretary-general in consultation with the parties. Finally, the accord reiterated the new doctrine of the FAES, subordinate to civilian power, and outlined a new educational system for the FAES based on doctrinal changes.[42]

Agreement was also finally reached with regard to the PNC. Chapter II of the Chapultepec accords provides for the creation of the new civilian police, stipulating that it is to operate under democratic principles, be a professional body, and be independent of the FAES or any political party. The accords further provide that, in the exercise of their duties, PNC members are to respect human dignity and human rights, and not to employ or tolerate the use of torture. The accords also provide for the creation of the Academia Nacional de Seguridad Pública (ANSP), whose director would be named by the president, and with a civilian academic council. Perhaps most important, the parties agreed that ex-combatants of the FMLN could be incorporated into the PNC provided they complied with the criteria and procedures for entry; similarly ex-members of the national police could join the PNC following evaluation and provided they met criteria for joining the PNC. While no quotas were set in the public agreements, it is widely known that membership of FMLN ex-combatants and ex-national police members (properly screened) was set at 20 per cent each.[43]

The accords also reaffirmed and amplified previous commitments regarding the creation of a Procurador Nacional para la Defensa de Derechos Humanos (a human rights ombuds office), judicial and electoral reform, as well as land transfer. The accords provided for the reinsertion of ex-combatants of the FMLN into civilian and political life, including the right of the FMLN to participate as a political party, with mediums of communication assured.[44] Last but not least, the accords provided for the cessation of conflict, the separation of forces and the calendarization of the disarming of the FMLN and reduction of the FAES under ONUSAL observation.[45] The calendarization was structured so as to provide reassurance to both sides regarding cheating: key actions were staggered and thus linked. Cheating would be rapidly detectable in this way. For example, the national guard and treasury police were to be eliminated before the demobilization of the first 20 per cent of the FMLN, assuaging FMLN fears.[46]

Developments after the peace accords

The Salvadoran peace accords created two bodies to confront the legacy of human rights violations and abuse of power by the government, armed forces and FMLN: the UN-sponsored truth commission, and the *internal* ad hoc commission to review the human rights records of military officers and recommend removal of officers where necessary. I discuss the actions of these commissions and the response of the government and military towards the consequent demands for accountability.

The ad hoc commission

While the ad hoc commission was expected to issue a relatively mild report, its (non-public) report called for the removal of nearly all of the military high command, and the removal or transfer of many more. Those whose removal was recommended included Minister of Defence Rene Emilio Ponce and Vice-Minister of Defence Juan Orlando Zepeda, prompting accusations by the military that the report was part of a leftist plot and a refusal to comply with the recommendations.[47] President Alfredo Cristiani, attempting to avoid instability, delayed implementation of the recommendations, retaining eight officers whose removal had been recommended, and transferring seven more to posts abroad.[48] And, in March 1992, when the treasury police and the national guard were to have been abolished, the government secured passage of legislation that prevented this. Further, counter to the provisions of the accord, some 1,000 members of these forces were transferred to the PNC. The implementation of the recommendations of the ad hoc commission were repeatedly delayed but, by the end of 1993, spurred by pressure from the USA, action was taken on the recommendations for purge or removal.[49]

Just a week after the accords were signed, the law of national reconciliation provided for an amnesty covering most political crimes, with the notable exception of cases decided by jury trial and those in which the truth commission might recommend prosecution. However, the law also provided that, six months after the commission issued its report, the assembly could issue another amnesty.[50]

The truth commission

The truth commission itself was just that: its mandate was to uncover and publicize the truth about atrocities committed during the civil war. Although the commission had no power to force prosecutions or purges, it was hoped that the uncovering of the truth would encourage the acceptance of responsibility and reconciliation, and the commission was empowered to make recommendations.[51]

The truth commission began work in July 1992, soliciting testimony from citizens all over the country. Its work was undermined, however, by a right-wing campaign depicting it as 'designed to destroy the armed forces', and by partial compliance by the government with requests for information. Ponce and Minister of the Presidency Oscar Alfredo Santamaria began pressuring the commission to leave the names of perpetrators out of the report, to propose a 'full stop' law that would prevent or limit prosecutions of state agents, and to delay release of the report.[52]

The members of the commission resisted these pressures, and the report was released as scheduled on 15 March 1993. In justifying its decision to name names in the report, the commission emphasized that in the peace agreements, the parties expressed their desires that the whole truth be known, and that this could not be achieved without the naming of perpetrators of crimes.[53] Even before the report's release, it had an impact: it became known that Defence Minister Ponce would be named in the report, and he made a pro forma offer of resignation, which was declined by the president. One day before the release of the report, President Cristiani requested a blanket amnesty, asking for an 'immediate, general and total amnesty that will end the temptation to seek revenge'.[54]

The wide-ranging report itself was built on the evidence of some 2,000 witnesses, with cases ascribed to both government and FMLN forces. The vast majority were ascribed to government forces. The report discussed the work of death squads run by the government, as well as some renowned cases of murder and kidnapping by the FMLN. The report contained a number of important and wide-ranging recommendations, of which I discuss only six here. First, it recommended that those named in the report be removed from positions of authority, and not allowed to hold public office for ten years. Second, it proposed that all members of the supreme court should resign immediately. Third, it stated that an investigation of private armed groups should be made to prevent the rise of new death squads. Fourth, it argued that the peace accord provisions dealing with reform of the armed forces and judiciary ought to be implemented. Fifth, it recommended that judges be named by an independent council on the judiciary. Sixth, it stated that a special fund should be created to compensate victims.[55]

It is noteworthy that the commission did not recommend prosecutions of those responsible for atrocities. However, it did not consider prosecutions a viable option, given the 'glaring deficiencies of the judicial system'.[56] The commission did not decide that pardons were the best thing prudentially or ethically: it simply lamented the impossibility of fair trials. It did advocate what it termed a more universal pardon, not a formal sort, but what it referred to as a collective determination that abuses would not recur. This ought, in an ideal situation, to include punishment of the guilty. The truth commission, therefore, saw the road to reconciliation not as built on forgiving and forgetting, but on the revelation of the truth, (impracticable) punishment and reparations. While forgiveness was thought to be indispensable, so was accountability.[57]

The executive, judicial and military responses to the report were swift and negative. President Cristiani called for a full amnesty; General Ponce derided the report as unjust; and members of the supreme court asserted that the report lacked objectivity and refused to resign. Opponents of the report described it as an attack by outsiders on Salvadoran sovereignty. The military released a statement on the report that was reprinted in newspapers arguing that the commission had exceeded the mandate granted to it under the peace accords, asserting that the report was unjust, unethical, illegal and biased.[58]

Just five days after the release of the report, led by the ruling ARENA party, the assembly passed the law of general amnesty for the consolidation of peace, containing 'broad, absolute and unconditional amnesty' for crimes of a political nature committed before 1 January 1992. Following the passage of the amnesty, a number of individuals in jail for human rights violations were released.[59]

The amnesty law was challenged with the aid of the Instituto de Derechos Humanos (institute of human rights) of the UCA, but the Sala de lo Constitucional (constitutional chamber) of the Corte Suprema de Justicia (supreme court of justice), which hears challenges to the constitutionality of laws, essentially refused to reach the merits of the case on the grounds that it raised a non-justiciable political question. According to the logic of the decision, the Sala is not empowered to hear purely political questions, which the case raises because it deals with the question of amnesty or 'grace'. The court argued that this was a power attributable to sovereignty, and thus resided in the people, and formed part of a social and political struggle that the court could not enter. It finally observed that the legislature assembly, under article 131 of the constitution, possesses the exclusive exercise of this political power, hence the refusal of the court to reach the merits of the case.[60]

El Salvador today: 'UN success story'

Despite the grim outlook after the release of the truth commission report, El Salvador has become something of an unexpected UN success story. Despite what many have seen as the sacrifice of justice to peace, and the failure of the government to acknowledge culpability, many of the worst perpetrators have been purged, former FMLN members are now members of the legislature, and new supreme court justices have taken office. In March 1995, citing the reduction in complaints of human rights violations, the UN Human Rights Commission removed El Salvador from its list of countries subject to permanent monitoring. In January 1996, COPAZ officially closed, affirming that the task of overseeing the transition had diminished. El Salvador has ratified four of the six international human rights treaties recommended by the truth commission.[61]

The success story is far from complete: accusations of fraud were raised in the spring 1994 elections.[62] Perhaps more ominously, a spate of assassinations in late 1993 widened the gulf between ARENA and the FMLN, and the pattern suggested the resurgence of death squads. While political killings appeared to wane, extrajudicial killings without political motives occurred. Nonetheless, members of the PNC have been implicated in these killings. The PNC has been a frequent subject of human rights complaints, approximately 1,800 in 1995, largely dealing with excessive use of force against demonstrations.[63] Furthermore, a former MINUSAL (UN Mission in El Salvador, the smaller successor to the ONUSAL observer mission) director claimed that the PNC has incorporated large numbers of former members of the security forces, and that many of these former members have been given administrative posts, contrary to the peace accords.[64] In May 1993, an illegal arms dump linked to the FMLN was found.[65] An issue that the truth commission report and the peace accords generally left untouched was that of children abducted by government forces during the war, some of whom were killed, some of whom were adopted.[66]

It is yet too early to assess the long-term effects of the peace accords, the truth commission investigations and the failure to prosecute perpetrators. Even if peace has been achieved, anecdotal evidence attests to the degree to which ordinary citizens are still haunted by the war. And, even if stability persists, such citizens may have lost faith in the accords and in democratic reforms in light of Cristiani's flouting of the truth commission's recommendations.[67] At the very least, however, the commission's report probably served as an important first step for, as UN Secretary-General Boutros-Ghali stated, 'in order to put behind them the trauma of the war, the Salvadorans have to go through the catharsis of facing the truth . . . There can be no reconciliation without the public knowledge of the truth.'[68]

Further signs of the greater entrenchment of democracy and peace and the civilianization of the armed forces are the 1997 election results and the reactions to them. On 16 March, in mayoral and legislative elections, the FMLN outpolled the ruling party, ARENA. Notable were not only the great strides made by the FMLN, but the 30 per cent drop in votes for ARENA since 1994.[69] Equally notable is the acceptance of the results by the FAES and ARENA.

Trade-offs of transition

As discussed earlier, an examination of the literature on civil–military relations and intervention of militaries in politics may enable one to hypothesize about the types of concerns that must be assuaged in order to coax militaries 'back to the barracks'. These are, of course, the treatment of members charged with serious human rights violations, institutional integrity and autonomy, and budgetary levels. The first has already been discussed in some detail; the other two require further discussion.

First, however, a caveat. El Salvador does not, technically, provide us with a case in which a new civilian regime coaxed the military back to the barracks; rule in El Salvador has been formally civilian since 1982, and change was instituted by an extant civilian regime. However, many of the issues are analogous because of El Salvador's history of military-led coups, and the high degree of influence held by the military and security forces in the civilian government, which I discuss further below.[70]

Accountability for rights abuses

El Salvador had something of a mixed record with regard to accountability for past human rights violations. Prosecutions were not directly provided for in the accords, and blanket amnesties ultimately protected those responsible for past violations. However, the creation of the Truth Commission was not a bar to potential prosecutions, though the commission itself suggested they would not be ideal under the circumstances. Many were removed or transferred based upon the recommendations of the ad hoc commission, and the truth commission recommended a temporary bar on government service by those named in its report.

Budgetary concerns

Of course, the treatment of prior human rights violations was just one issue of relevance to the Salvadoran military's corporate interests. Also of concern was its measure of the budget. In light of its traditional autonomy and influence over politics, there was no tradition of subjecting the defence budget to public scrutiny, making the task of bringing spending under control particularly difficult.[71] In 1993, the military's budget was 1.7 per cent of the country's GDP, well below the 3.7 per cent level of 1989, but still well above prewar levels. By 1995, the budget sank still further, to just 1.2 per cent of GDP.[72] And, what some saw as artificially high military spending after the end of the war may have been justifiable as part of the cost of demobilization. Nonetheless, the budget remained surprisingly high given the drastic reduction of forces, the absence of an external or internal enemy, and the plummeting of US military aid.[73]

Institutional reform

Finally, the concerns for institutional integrity, or fear of institutional reform, are in part reflected in concerns for the fate of members accused of human rights violations. Here, the record is clearly mixed, as amnesties were passed, but the truth commission was able to name particular perpetrators. More generally, the military's role in public security was curtailed by the peace accords. Under the terms of the accord, the PNC contained some members of the old military, but contained an equal percentage of former FMLN members. Through various ruses, the old security forces were able to place more of their members in the new forces than permitted by the accords.[74] Further, the failure to fully dissolve repressive security forces enabled the military to retain autonomy despite institutional change. And, despite a significant increase in civilian oversight, some commentators have argued that not enough oversight was provided for in the accords.[75] On the other hand, in addition to the elimination of certain repressive security forces, the accords provided for a drastic cut in the membership of the armed forces, a reduction by half, which has been achieved.[76]

The institutional changes in the public security forces are worth discussing in more detail, as they were some of the most highly contested aspects of the peace accords, and appear to constitute the biggest sacrifices by the government. In spite of problems of cheating discussed above, these changes, it is to be hoped, will help form the foundation for lasting change.[77]

Police reform

A key sacrifice was the civilianization of the police force. While previously the line between the police and the military had been somewhat blurred, the constitutional and doctrinal reforms have attempted to de-link the two forces. First, the reform of the constitution's article 212 emphasizes the new role of the armed forces: to defend the sovereignty of the nation. This is a significant shift from prior perspectives on security, fostered by the so-called doctrine of national security as well as the fact of civil war, that enemies were as likely to come from within as without, and the military's role was to stop internal subversion as well as repel external invasion.

Further, the new doctrine of the PNC emphasized the importance of democratic principles and respect for human rights: the institutional doctrine states that the PNC is subordinated to democratic principles, setting aside political, ideological or social considerations;[78] the *Ley Orgánica* expressly prohibits the infliction or toleration of human rights abuses, and bars the use of superior orders as an excuse.

The changes to the police were not only in norms and doctrines; important institutional changes were also made. The *Ley Orgánica* establishes an inspector-general of the police, under the vice-minister of public security, whose job it is to watch and control police officers' behaviour with respect to human rights, and to make reports every six months to the Procurador para la Defensa de Derechos Humanos on the matter. It also dictates the organization within the PNC of a consulting office made up of professionals specializing in, *inter alia*, security, constitutional rights, human rights and politics. Furthermore, the director-general of the PNC is to be named by the president every three years, and the legislature can recommend that he or she be removed for grave violations of human rights.[79]

Naturally, such formal safeguards are necessary, but not sufficient, to effect a change in police behaviour, hence the new Academia Nacional de Seguridad Pública (ANSP), replacing the academy of the old national police. It was through this academy that the ex-FMLN combatants and ex-national police members would pass in order to become members of the new PNC; in this politicized situation training would be particularly important.[80] The curriculum of the ANSP emphasizes respect for human rights and citizens in general, and has been aided significantly by international support and participation: many of the instructors are from other countries, and programmes like the US Department of Justice International Criminal Investigative Training Program (ICITAP) as well as aid from the EU have provided important resources.[81] Finally, reforms articulated in the peace accords have already been discussed: the inclusion of ex-FMLN members in the PNC and the elimination of bodies like the treasury policy, national guard and the DNI constitute important sacrifices that should not be underestimated.

Reform of the armed forces

In order to appreciate the magnitude of reforms made to the Salvadoran armed forces, we must first recall the extent and depth of the military's influence over Salvadoran society, as well as the nature of military institutions and beliefs. The

FAES's adherence to the doctrine of national security' effectively eliminated the common distinction between internal public security problems and external military threats. As many scholars of Latin American militaries have noted, many nations in both Central and South America faced relatively few external military threats in the twentieth century, but had to cope with significant problems with internal order. Thus, the role of the military in such nations was frequently political, and oriented towards internal rather than external security. Scholars disagree about the exact source and effect of the doctrine, but concur that militaries in the region played central roles in state politics, whether as direct or indirect rulers.[82]

Nations embraced this doctrine in response to internal instability: in the face of economic crises, internal rebellions and civil wars, militaries were seen as the only source of stability, and the mystique of the military as primary protector of the national project became embedded in state politics. As a result, military leaders undermined democracy and perpetrated severe human rights abuses because they often failed to distinguish between legitimate threats to security, such as terrorism and guerrillas, and legitimate opposition movements made up of students, unions or opposition political parties.[83] The traditional concept of a professional military; one disengaged from politics and respectful of civilian rule, did not apply; the 'new professionalism', in which militaries see their professional role as that of protecting against internal enemies, allowed these armies to intervene in politics. The doctrine was arguably reinforced by Cold War pressures, with US concerns about the spread of communism affecting military aid priorities.[84] The doctrine and the role of US pressure and aid were discussed in more detail in Chapter 2.

In El Salvador, the doctrine was particularly salient, especially as the volume of US aid increased. By the 1970s, the Salvadoran armed forces held a strong belief in the need to protect western values, a vision of the world as divided into two irreconcilable blocs, a definition of democracy in terms of internal security and anticommunism, a valorization of security defined as the status quo, and a view of the military as the only guarantee of security. The doctrine had a significant impact on the Salvadoran concept of security, as did the East/West confrontation. Thus, in El Salvador, the threat to internal security, the FMLN, was part of a larger geopolitical crisis.[85]

These beliefs were given form through direct and indirect intervention in politics by the Salvadoran military. Even before the coup in October 1979, military officers occupied important cabinet and bureaucratic posts, including many unrelated to defence or security matters: for example, in 1977–79, the head of the ministry of labour and the head of ANTEL, the telephone company, to name just two, were military men.[86]

Even after the 1982 elections and the return to at least nominally civilian rule, the Salvadoran military's tendency towards intervention and non-democratic behaviour was buttressed by a belief in the doctrine of national security and increased US military aid and presence in the form of military advisers. These tendencies were reinforced by the hierarchical structure of the military and the *tanda* system, under which military officers of the same generation are promoted as a bloc, taught blind loyalty to one another and the belief that the dominant *tanda* represents the military and the nation. The dominance of the so-called *tandona*, the largest group of graduating officers from the Escuela Militar (Military School), the class of 1966, increased the tendency to hierarchy and non-democratic structure within the military.[87] The 47-officer tandona came to dominate the military, including not just Defence Minister Ponce but 12 of the 15 most important military posts. It should perhaps come as no surprise that nearly all members of the *tandona* could also be found on the ad hoc commission's list of officers to be removed or given early retirement.[88]

Given the traditional role of dominance of the military in Salvadoran society, it becomes more apparent why reduction and reform of the military were both difficult and significant. Reforms encompassed not just the military proper, but the array of public security forces functionally, if not always formally, within its ambit. Further, doctrinal and constitutional reform explicitly excluded the participation by members of the armed forces, with specified objections, in internal security matters. This marks a drastic departure from previous doctrine, which gave the FAES a broad mandate in the rather vague domain of public security.[89] Thus, if one wishes to tally the victories and defeats meted out to the FAES during the peace negotiations and subsequent political wrangling, they might be arrayed as follows.

Losses for the armed forces included the radical cut in size and budget, and the elimination of rapid reaction battalions, the treasury police, the Defensa Civil, the DNI and various paramilitary forces. They also included doctrinal shifts limiting the role of the armed forces to the defence of territorial integrity and the creation of an academic council comprised of civilians as well as military members for the Escuela Militar, and the civilianization of the police force and the inclusion of ex-FMLN members within it. Finally, they included the naming of names in the truth commission report and the possibility of lustration by the ad hoc commission.

However, many of these formal losses were mitigated by real-world politics, both embodied in the accords as well as represented by concessions by the Cristiani government after the accords. These included, within the accords, the lack of adjudicatory power possessed by the truth commission, and the resistance to the FMLN's demands for participation in the armed forces and for a wide purge of those responsible for human rights violations. After the accords, the armed forces and security forces regained yet more ground with the amnesty law, the failure of *depuración*, and the effective smuggling of members of banned security forces into the new PNC and other new civilianized institutions.

Nonetheless, the structural and doctrinal changes should not be ignored, and have been reinforced through educational reform. A portion of all courses given in the Comando de Doctrina y Educación Militar (military doctrine and education command) is devoted to the theme of human rights and their place in wartime; at all levels, from basic training through the course required for advancement from the rank of sergeant to sergeant-major, courses have a significant number of hours devoted to the laws of war, international humanitarian law and the role of the FAES under the constitution.[90]

The military and the transition

Following the theories discussed in Chapter 2, to ensure that militaries return to and stay in the barracks, several sets of factors are relevant: international factors, social/civilian factors, and corporate interest factors. For the purposes of this analysis, the factor of interest is the military's corporate interests, and the way that transitional regimes do and do not cater for these interests. The corporate interest is manifested in concern about three issues in particular: institutional reform, budgetary allocations and the treatment of members in human rights proceedings. In the case of El Salvador, the record seems to be mixed.

Institutional reform was pursued extensively: the peace accords promised to purge officers responsible for grave human rights violations and two security forces were to be abolished. The truth commission recommended that those named in its report be barred from service for ten years. Furthermore, the new security force, the PNC, incorporates former enemies of the military, ex-FMLN members. Nonetheless, last-minute actions and blatant violations of the accords have meant that the repressive old security forces remained intact, and that the new PNC retained members from these forces. When the defence minister offered to resign, the offer was declined. In essence, though the peace accords themselves had the potential to significantly impinge on military autonomy, in practice their effects were ameliorated.

A similarly mixed record can be seen in the treatment of human rights violations, which posed the potentially most direct challenge to the military's corporate interest. The peace accords do not provide for prosecutions: both the ad hoc and truth commissions were empowered to report information and make recommendations, but little more. The creation of these bodies did not, however, preclude the possibility of prosecutions. In some ways, however, the reports of each commission can be seen as stronger than those envisioned by the accords (or by the military). The amnesties passed subsequent to each report negated some of the possible effects of these wide-ranging reports, meaning that the threat to the military's interest in preventing retribution against its members was more or less removed. Finally, the relatively high level of spending on the military may indicate a concession to the military, though the level has clearly declined, and some of those allocations may be justified as part of the costs of transitional demobilization.

Overall, the set of concerns I have articulated seem to match the concerns in play in the Salvadoran case. While the peace accords impinged to a fair degree on the corporate interests of the military, implementation by the transitional regime has softened the effects on the military.

Discussion: key elements of political change

All three of my hypothesized factors played some role in the transition in El Salvador, frequently in interaction with each other. Similarly, the trade-offs one expects from the literature on civil–military relations occurred, leading to partial measures of accountability and reform. I discuss each in turn, and draw out a few preliminary lessons from the Salvadoran experience.

Duration of conflict

The conflict in El Salvador, having gone on a decade and costing 75,000 lives, had reached a hurting stalemate. It had finally become clear that neither side could win. It was this realization by key actors in the Salvadoran military, in particular, which meant that a changed international context and pressure could play catalytic roles.

International factors

The USA played a direct role in the transition through its withholding of aid and application of pressure on the Salvadoran government to address human rights abuses and negotiate in good faith. The USA and the so-called group of friends of the secretary-general provided important pressure on both parties to continue with the negotiations. International actors also act as guarantors of agreements: the ONUSAL mission itself is an example of such a guarantee; also the USA served as a guarantor of the agreements, in particular reassuring the FMLN that it would keep its former client in line.

A key way that international actors may move negotiations forward is not through pressure, but rather mediation. One negotiator in El Salvador has emphasized this is a key contribution of the UN: the proposals of each side were generally unacceptable to the other, but the UN was able to give form to middle or third proposals.

Balance of forces/civil–military issues

In El Salvador, the balance of forces issue was a particularly salient one, as the FMLN, by most accounts, while unable to defeat the FAES, could also not be defeated by it. Thus, the FMLN had important leverage in the negotiations, as well as significant sacrifices to make. As one government negotiator put it, the thrust of the negotiations was certainly to deconcentrate power held by the military and remove it from the political sphere, but also, and equally importantly, to convince the guerrillas to give up their arms and move them *into* the political sphere.[91]

Trade-offs

As we have seen, political pressures and rapid passage of an amnesty law meant that accountability could not be pursued in the form of prosecution, but only in the lesser forms of the naming of names through the truth commission and the partial purges resulting from the recommendations of the ad hoc commission. Significant reforms to the security forces also took place, though budgets remained artificially high.

Lessons

El Salvador provides an illuminating case on several fronts. First, it indicates the importance of two factors (and the supporting role played by a third): without the hurting stalemate that came from the forces being relatively well matched (and the exhaustion produced by a long war), the parties would not have been so prepared to negotiate; without the pressure applied by the USA at a key juncture and the facilitative role played by the USA, the peace might never have been achieved or maintained. Second, it shows us that countries will frequently find themselves not at one extreme or the other of the accountability spectrum, but rather achieve some airing of the truth and purges without judicial punishment. Finally, it indicates the other goods that might be attained in the process of transition: while full accountability may well be impossible, reforms might be achieved that will make future abuses much more unlikely.

Notes

1 See generally Johnstone, *Rights and Reconciliation: UN Strategies in El Salvador*; Thomas Buergenthal, 'The United Nations truth commission for El Salvador', *Vanderbilt Journal of Transnational Law*, 27, 3 (October 1994), pp. 497–544; Popkin and Roht-Arriaza, 'Truth as Justice', pp. 86–9 and Popkin, 'El Salvador: A Negotiated End to Impunity?', pp. 198–217 in Roht-Arriaza (ed.), *Impunity and Human Rights*; Americas Watch/Human Rights Watch, 'El Salvador. Accountability and Human Rights: The Report of the United Nations Commission on the Truth for El Salvador', *News from Americas Watch*, 5, 7 (10 August 1993); Reed Brody, 'The United Nations and Human Rights in El Salvador's "Negotiated Revolution"', *Harvard Human Rights Journal*, 8 (Spring 1995), pp. 153–78.

2 According to many there was a conscious decision to focus on the political and military issues and set aside economic concerns to avoid further divisiveness: Author's interview with Freddy Justiniano of the United Nations Development Programme, (San Salvador, 18 November 1997). See Peace Agreement of 16 January 1992, between the Government of El Salvador and the FMLN, UN Document A/46/864, annex.

3 See, for example, Herman Schwartz, 'What Can We Do about Balkan Atrocities?', *New York Times* (9 April 1993), p. A27, suggesting that a truth commission would be preferable to an international tribunal for the former Yugoslavia. On the negotiations and the role of the UN generally, see T.S. Montgomery, 'Getting to Peace in El Salvador: The Roles of the United Nations Secretariat and ONUSAL', *Journal of Interamerican Studies and World Affairs*, 37, 4 (1995), at p. 139.

4 An early effort was the Arias plan and amnesty of 1987, which covered El Salvador

as well as Nicaragua: John J. Moore Jr, 'Problems with Forgiveness: Granting Amnesty under the Arias Plan in Nicaragua and El Salvador', *Stanford Law Review*, 43 (February 1991), pp. 733–77; David Holiday and William Stanley, 'Building the Peace: Preliminary Lessons from El Salvador', *Journal of International Affairs*, 46 (Winter 1993), pp. 419–20.

5 See, for example, Antonio Martinez Uribe, 'Un Proyecto de Nación Para El Salvador', *Cuaderno de Trabajo No. 02–96* (San Salvador, El Salvador: Colegio de Altos Estudios Estratégicos, May 1996), pp. 1–4; Instituto de Derechos Humanos de la Universidad Centroamericana (IDHUCA), 'José Simeón Cañas', 'Radiografia de Un Proceso de Paz: Borrón y Cuenta Nueva?' (San Salvador, El Salvador: IDHUCA, 1995), pp. 1–10; 'Las Tensiones de la Guerra', *El Salvador Proceso*,' 10, 417 (14 February 1990), p. 5; 'Balance Militar', *El Salvador Proceso*, 11, 457, extraordinario (December 1990), p. 16. On the conduct of the conflict more generally, see Max G. Mainwaring and Court Prisk, 'A Strategic View of Insurgencies: Insights from El Salvador', *Small Wars and Insurgencies*, 4, 1 (Spring/Summer 1993), pp. 53–72.

6 However, the USA recognized the stalemate before the Salvadoran government: while the latter continued that the FMLN was weakening, US Southcom General Maxwell Thurman argued that the FMLN was learning to expand operations beyond the zones of its traditional strengths: 'Las Tensiónes de la Guerra', p. 6. Also, as one analyst notes, until this point negotiations were seen as part of manoeuvres to legitimate their own military strategies, rather than an end in themselves, but this was to change: Ricardo Ribera, 'El Salvador: La Negociacion del Acuerdo de Paz: Un modelo para el Mundo?', *Realidad: Revista de Ciencias Sociales y Humanidades*, 37, (January–February 1993), p. 90. However, others in retrospect date the government's shift in viewpoint to 1989 and the offensive. It has also been claimed that the election of the right-wing ARENA party reassured rightist elements, enabling negotiations to go forward: author's interview with David Escobar Galindo, member of the government negotiating team (San Salvador, 1 July 1998). On the influence of Congress on US policy towards El Salvador even in the early 1980s, see Mark Peceny, 'Culture, Congress, and the Promotion of Democracy in Reagan Policy toward El Salvador: 1981–1984', *Low Intensity Conflict and Law Enforcement*, 3, 1 (Summer 1994), pp. 80–103; 'Vicisitudes Recientes del Proceso de Diálogo', *El Salvador Proceso*, 10, 419 (February 28 1990), p. 6.

7 'Trayectoria del Batallón Atlacatl', *El Salvador Proceso*, 10, 415 (31 January 1990), pp. 11–16. Many have argued that it was the UCA massacre that forced the USA to recognize that its goal of professionalizing the FAES was not succeeding: 'La Guerra Permanente', *El Salvador Proceso*, 11, 432 (13 June 1990), p. 5. See generally Johnstone, *Rights and Reconciliation: UN Strategies in El Salvador*; Buergenthal, 'The United Nations truth commission for El Salvador'; Americas Watch/Human Rights Watch, 'El Salvador: Accountability and Human Rights'.

8 In the admittedly biased opinion of one ex-commandant of the FMLN, it was not strictly the case that the fall of the Soviet Union directly brought about peace, but that it aided the advance of negotiations because, with the end of communism as a threat in the region, the USA no longer had a basis to continue opposing negotiations: 'Entrevista Ex Commandante Jorge Melendez "Jonas",' *Cuadernos del Instituto de Estudios Jurídicos de El Salvador*, 7 (March 1993), p. 174. As David Escobar Galindo put it, the shift in international politics meant that the situation in El Salvador and Central America was in some sense removed from the international agenda and was returned to the sphere of regional and domestic politics: author's interview with David Escobar Galindo (San Salvador, 1 July 1998).

9 'Balance Politico', *El Salvador Proceso*, 11, 457, extraordinario (December 1990), p. 11; 'Más Guerra', *El Salvador Proceso*, 10, 420 (7 March 1990), p. 5.

10 Elisabeth J. Wood, 'The Peace Accords and Postwar Reconstruction', in James K. Boyce (ed.), *Economic Policy for Building Peace: The Lessons of El Salvador* (Boulder, CO: Lynne Rienner, 1996), p. 76.

11 Juan Jose Dalton, 'Los Cambios de la Política: Grietas en ARENA', *Revista Tendencias*, 65 (October/November 1997), p. 32. In particular there was a desire to halt the economic harm caused by FMLN sabotage actions: David Holiday and William Stanley, 'En la Mejor de las Circunstancias: ONUSAL y los Desafíos de la Verificación y el Fortalecimiento Institucional en El Salvador', *Estudios Centroamericanos*, 584 (June 1997), p. 554.

12 Uribe, 'Un Proyecto Para La Nación', pp. 1–4. And the FMLN seems to concur with this analysis. In May 1990 FMLN commandant Jorge Melindez cited the FMLN offensive as a key factor in reopening dialogue, and also noted the importance in the change in US behaviour with the end of the Cold War: 'Convergencia de Diálogos', *El Salvador Proceso*, 10, 430 (30 May 1990), pp. 6–7. Another thesis is that the negotiations themselves had a dynamic of their own that helped push the parties to alter their perceptions and accept new compromises. See, for example, Enrique Baloyra, 'Salvaging El Salvador', *Journal of Democracy*, 3, 2 (April 1992), pp. 60–71; author's interview with David Escobar Galindo (San Salvador, El Salvador, 1 July 1998).

13 Naciones Unidas, *Acuerdos de El Salvador: En El Camino de La Paz* (New York and San Salvador: United Nations, 1992), pp. 1–3; 'Escalada Bélica', *El Salvador Proceso*, 10, 422 (28 March 1990), p. 7; 'Balance Militar', *El Salvador Proceso*, 11, 457, extraordinario (December 1990), pp. 18–19.

14 'Editorial: El Informe de la Comisión Moakley', *El Salvador Proceso*, 10, 426 (2 May 1990), p. 2.

15 Aid was to be cut off entirely if these terms were not complied with, or reinstated if the FMLN did not cooperate in talks: 'Otro Mes de Guerra', *El Salvador Proceso*, 10, 426 (2 May), pp. 5–6. In 1991, this 50 per cent cut amounted to $42.5 million. One editorial noted that while it would not alter the military balance decisively, it could act as a serious spur to negotiations: 'Editorial: La Ayuda en Suspenso', *El Salvador Proceso*, 10, 429 (23 May 1990), p. 2. Many have argued that it was the UCA massacre that forced the USA to recognize that its goal of professionalizing the FAES was not succeeding: 'La Guerra Permanente', *El Salvador Proceso*, 11, 432 (13 June 1990), p. 5. The GOES initially denied military acknowledged the participation of nine military members in the attack on 13 January 1990. Nonetheless, the failure to actively pursue those responsible meant that the case remained a high-profile judicial and political issue: 'Los Derechos Humanos Durante 1990', *El Salvador Proceso*, 11, 457, extraordinario (December 1990), p. 41; 'Preparativos Belicos', *El Salvador Proceso*, 10, 427 (9 May 1990), p. 4.

16 'Sospechoso Extravío de Pruebas en el Caso de la UCA', *El Salvador Proceso*, 10, 428 (16 May), p. 6. 'Balance Militar', *El Salvador Proceso*, 11, 457, extraordinario (December 1991), pp. 19–20, states that total aid was $4 billion for the period; a United States General Accounting Office report states that the USA provided $1 billion in military aid, $996 million in military credits and $24 million in training programmes: 'GAO', *El Salvador Proceso*, 12, 482 (24 July 1991), p. 13.

17 'Confrontaciónes Bélicas', *El Salvador Proceso*, 11, 433 (27 June 1990), p. 6; 'Convergencia de Diálogos', pp. 5–6; 'La Fuerza Armada Ante la Cuestion de la Impunidad', *El Salvador Proceso*, 11, 435 (11 July 1990), p. 10. Ponce would be named defence minister in September 1990.

18 'Acuerdo de San Jose Sobre Derechos Humanos,' in Naciones Unidas, *Acuerdos de El Salvador*, pp. 7–12; 'Editorial: Los Escollos del Proceso de Diálogo–Negociación', *El Salvador Proceso*, 11, 438 (8 August 1990), p. 2. It is worth noting that one source suggests that the GOES itself was initially more open to discussing the status of the armed forces, but caved in when faced with military pressure:

'Balance Político', *El Salvador Proceso*, 11, 457, extraordinario (December 1990), p. 8.

19 'Impunidad y Depúración (1)', *El Salvador Proceso*, 11, 440 (22 August 1990), p. 9, and, in the same issue, 'Posición del FMLN para Desmontan el Militarismo, Alcanzan el Cese de Fuego y Avanzar a la Democracia sin Armas', pp. 13–14, which also demanded that the intellectual and material authors of the UCA massacre be punished as an example.

20 'Editorial: La Fuerza Armada en la Encrucijada', *El Salvador Proceso*, 11, 441 (29 August 1990), p. 2; 'Impunidad y Depuración (2)', *El Salvador Proceso*, 11, 441 (29 August 1990), pp. 6–8. In response to FMLN demands for accountability in several notorious cases, the government proposed parallel investigations into four cases where victims were presumed to have been killed by the FMLN.

21 'Auto-depuración de la Fuerza Armada?', *El Salvador Proceso*, 11, 443 (12 September 1990), p. 6.

22 'La Ayuda Militar Norteamericana y la Guerra', *El Salvador Proceso*, 11, 450 (30 October 1990), p. 6. The military expressed fears that this would undermine its advantage over the FMLN. Military actions by both camps subsequently increased dramatically, but the balance of forces did not alter despite a significant FMLN offensive in late November.

23 'La Negociación de la Guerra', *El Salvador Proceso*, 11, 456 (12 December 1990), p. 2, and, in the same issue, 'Nueva Ayuda Militar Norteamericana a la Fuerza Armada', pp. 5–6.

24 'La Rutina de la Guerra', *El Salvador Proceso*, 11, 459 (23 January 1991), p. 4. Following the announcement, several serious right-wing acts of violence took place, including the destruction of the *Diario Latino* offices and the massacre at El Zapote, which some observers took to be a direct result of the American 'signal' of plans to unfreeze aid: 'Las Paradojas del "Proceso Democrático"', *El Salvador Proceso*, 11, 463 (20 February 1991), p. 2.

25 'El Diálogo Otra Vez en Dificultades', *El Salvador Proceso*, 11, 464 (27 February 1991), pp. 5–7. Article 248 dictated that the initiative for reform must be brought to the Organo Legislativo (legislative organ) by at least ten legislators, and that it must be approved by two consecutive legislatures, one that approves the measure by an absolute majority, and the next by a vote of two-thirds of the representatives. With looming legislative elections, the speed of completing reform proposals became critical. For an analysis of this article, see Franco Eliseo Ortiz Ruiz, 'El Procidimiento de Reforma Constitucional en la Constitución Political de 1983: Un Análisis Jurídico-Político', *Cuadernos del Instituto de Estudios Jurídicos de El Salvador*, 2 (August 1993), p. 109.

26 'El Diálogo Otra Vez en Dificultades', pp. 7–8; 'El Proceso Negociador, a Contrapelo de la Guerra', *El Salvador Proceso*, 11, 467 (20 March 1991), p. 6.

27 'La Marcha de la Guerra en el Contexto Diálogo', *El Salvador Proceso*, 11, 470 (24 April 1991), p. 5. This issue was a serious stumbling block in negotiations in the run-up to the May Mexico accords.

28 'Acuerdos de Mexico', in *Acuerdos de El Salvador*, pp. 13–19, parts I–IV. The limitation of military jurisdiction can be found in the Salvadoran constitution, article 216. Also provided for was oversight by the CNJ of the judicial school, to ensure professional judges. Article 187 of the Salvadoran constitution articulates these reforms.

29 These agreements somewhat amplify details of the Mexico accords. See 'Acuerdos Políticos para el Desarollo de la Reforma Constitutional' and 'Comisión de la Verdad', in *Acuerdos de El Salvador*, pp. 28–33; 'Anteproyecto de Reformas Constitutionales', *El Salvador Proceso*, 11, 471 (1 May 1991), pp. 8–12. The FMLN, however, expressed its dissatisfaction with the agreements, arguing that the hegemony of the army over society had been implicitly retained: 'Posición de la

Comisión Negociadora del FMLN', *El Salvador Proceso*, 11, 471 (1 May 1991), pp. 15–16. The FMLN objected, in particular, to the continued description of the FAES as a 'permanent' institution: Acuerdos de Mexico, Part VI.

30 'Luz Verde para ONUSAL', *El Salvador Proceso*, 11, 474 (22 May 1991); 'Los Derechos Humanos en El Salvador durante el Trimestre Junio–Agosto de 1991', *El Salvador Proceso*, 12, 493, supp. (6 November 1991), p. 3.

31 'Más Guerra en Perspectiva', *El Salvador Proceso*, 12, 476 (5 June 1991), p. 5; 'Mociónes a Propósito de la Ayuda Militar Norteamericana', *El Salvador Proceso*, 12, 476 (5 June 1991), p. 15; 'Visita de Cristiani a Washington', *El Salvador Proceso*, 12, 477 (12 June 1991), p. 9; 'La Marcha de la Guerra', *El Salvador Proceso*, 12, 479 (26 June 1991), p. 8.

32 'Hacia la Incorporación Política del FMLN', *El Salvador Proceso*, 12, 483 (14 August 1991), pp. 4–5; 'La Negociación Bordea el Abismo', *El Salvador Proceso*, 12, 485 (28 August 1991), p. 3; 'Momento Crucial de la Negociación', *El Salvador Proceso*, 12, 487 (11 September 1991), pp. 2–3.

33 'Momento Crucial de la Negociación', p. 4. Two court cases raised these issues in other ways: one sought indemnification against the state for UCA and the victims' families; the other challenged the constitutionality of a 1987 amnesty law: 'Caso Jesuitas: La Acción Civil', *El Salvador Proceso*, 12, 486 (4 September 1991), pp. 10–11, and 'Caso Jesuitas: La Vista Pública y la Posibilitad de Amnistía', *El Salvador Proceso*, 12, 487 (11 September 1991), pp. 10–11.

34 See 'Radiografía Cronológica de las Negociaciónes de Nueva York', *El Salvador Proceso*, 12, 489 (2 October 1991), pp. 5–8.

35 'Acuerdo de Nueva York', in *Acuerdos de El Salvador*, pp. 34–40; 'Radiografía Cronológica de las Negociaciónes de Nueva York', p.8.

36 Acuerdo de Nueva York, Articles II–V; the new doctrine, with its emphasis on the protection against internal threats, was in contrast to the doctrine of national security prevalent in the region in the 1980s.

37 Acuerdo de Nueva York, Article VII. Other issues, such as the membership of, and FMLN participation in, the new PNC, were unresolved.

38 'El Permanente Escollo de la Fuerza Armada', *El Salvador Proceso*, 12, 494 (13 November 1991), p. 5. General Vargas takes a more positive stance on police reform than he and his colleagues did in 1991: he now argues that the separation of the police from the military was good for the FAES, preventing it from being pulled into cyclical crises along with the police. He further argues that, while the entry of ex-FMLN combatants into the PNC was risky, it was necessary and the results have been acceptable: interview of General Mauricio Vargas by the author (San Salvador, 3 December 1997).

39 'La Marcha de la Negociación: Otra Vez a Nueva York', *El Salvador Proceso*, 12, 498 (11 December 1991), pp. 7–10.

40 'Acta de Nueva York', in *Acuerdos de El Salvador*, pp. 45–46; 'Acta de Nueva York II', in *Acuerdos de El Salvador*, p. 47; 'El Fin de la Guerra', *El Salvador Proceso*, 12, 501 (31 January 1992), p. 15. See also 'Central America: Efforts Towards Peace', UN Doc. S/23402 (10 January 1992).

41 'El Fin de la Guerra', p. 15.

42 'Acuerdo de Paz de El Salvador' (Chapultepec Accord), ch. I, in *Acuerdos de El Salvador*, pp. 53–5; 'El Fin de la Guerra', p. 16.

43 Chapultepec Accord, ch. II; Elisabeth Wood, in 'The Peace Accords', p. 81, states that these percentages were established in a secret annex to the September 1991 New York accords.

44 Chapultepec Accord, ch. VI.

45 Chapultepec Accord, ch. VII. ONUSAL was to have 1,100 members for the task: 'El Fin de la Guerra', p. 18.

46 See Wood, 'The Peace Accords', on this linkage.

47 Americas Watch, 'El Salvador: Accountability and Human Rights', pp. 8–9.

48 Tina Rosenberg, 'Terror, Tribunals, and Truth: El Salvador, Not The Balkans, Is the First Place to Seek Justice', *Washington Post* (14 March 1993), p. C1; David Holiday and William Stanley, 'Building the Peace', *Journal of International Affairs*, 46 (Winter 1993), p. 425; Human Rights Watch, *Human Rights Watch World Report 1993, Events of 1992* (New York: Human Rights Watch 1993), p. 109.

49 The military also attempted to move these units wholesale into the army and simply rename them rather than dissolve them. See Gino Costa, 'The United Nations and Reform of the Police in El Salvador', *International Peacekeeping*, 2, 3 (Autumn 1995), p. 370; *Human Rights Watch World Report 1993*, p. 109. Wood, 'The Peace Accords', p. 92 says that the visit of several US high-level military officers emphasizing US concern about compliance in this matter played an important role. This included the 15 officers mentioned before: see 'Letter dated 2 April 1993 from the Secretary-General addressed to the President of the Security Council', UN Doc. S/25516 (2 April 1993), and 'Letter dated 7 July 1993 from the Secretary-General addressed to the President of the Security Council', UN Doc. S/26502 (8 July 1993); Walter and Williams, *Militarization and Demilitarization in El Salvador's Transition to Democracy*, pp. 156–7.

50 *Human Rights Watch World Report 1993*, p. 106; 'Consideraciónes Sobre la Ley de Amnistía', *El Salvador Proceso*, 12, 501 (31 January 1992), p. 9.

51 Holiday and Stanley, 'Building the Peace', p. 430; *From Madness to Hope: The 12-year War in El Salvador, Report of the United Nations Commission on the Truth for El Salvador*, UN Doc. S/25500, annex (1 April 1993), p. 11 on the mandate, and p. 22 explicitly emphasizing the non-judicial nature of the commission.

52 Americas Watch, 'El Salvador: Accountability and Human Rights', pp. 10–13; Cynthia Arnson, 'Unburying El Salvador's Skeletons', *New York Times* (13 March 1993), p. 21.

53 UN Commission on the Truth, *From Madness to Hope*, p. 25.

54 Americas Watch, 'El Salvador: Accountability and Human Rights', pp. 13–14.

55 '75,000 Deaths', *Washington Post* (18 March 1993), p. A26; UN Commission on the Truth, *From Madness to Hope*, pp. 176–86; Americas Watch, 'El Salvador: Accountability and Human Rights', pp. 19–20, provides a helpful summary.

56 UN Commission on the Truth, *From Madness to Hope*, p. 185.

57 UN Commission on the Truth, *From Madness to Hope*, p. 185; Stanley Meisler and Tracy Wilkinson, 'Salvador Urged to Bar All Rights Abusers from Public Life', *Los Angeles Times* (16 March 1995), p. A6.

58 Americas Watch, 'El Salvador: Accountability and Human Rights', pp. 21–2; Douglas Farah, 'Salvadoran Ruling Party Seeks Civil War Amnesties', *Washington Post* (17 March 1993), p. A28; 'Posición de la Fuerza Armada de El Salvador ante el Informe de la Comisión de la Verdad', *Diario Latino* (24 March 1993), p. 11. The statement repeatedly refers to the 'communist attack' that the FAES confronted in the 1980s, arguing that the commission failed to take into account the nature of the threat posed to the country by the FMLN. The statement further asserts that the commission was not impartial, and had failed to investigate some 695 cases of FMLN atrocities submitted to it by the FAES.

59 Americas Watch, 'El Salvador: Accountability and Human Rights', pp. 23–4; Tracy Wilkinson, 'El Salvador Frees 2 Officers Convicted in Priest Killings', *Los Angeles Times* (2 April 1993), P. A9.

60 Sala de lo Constitucional de la Corte Suprema de Justicia, 'Resolución de la Demanda de Inconstitucionalidad para los Señores José Benjamin Cuellar Martinez y Ana Mercedes Valladares', No. 11–93 (20 May 1993), found in the computer database of the Corte Suprema de Justicia in San Salvador, printout on file with author.

61 Robert J. White, 'In El Salvador, UN Exits to Applause', *Star Tribune* (7 May

1995), p. 27A; but see Martha Doggett (Lawyers Committee for Human Rights), letter to the editor, 'El Salvador Hasn't Purged Itself of War Crimes', *New York Times* (15 August 1994), p. A14; 'National Peace Commission Closes as its Work Comes to an End', BBC Summary of World Broadcasts, EE/D2509/L, part 5 (14 January 1996); US Department of State, 'El Salvador Human Rights Practices, 1995', *Department of State Dispatch*, 7 (March 1996).

62 Dan Alder, 'UN Faulted on Vote in El Salvador', *Chicago Tribune* (24 April 1994), p. 12.

63 Howard W. French, 'As the Elections Near, Killings Shake El Salvador', *New York Times* (15 December 1993), p. A3; Pamela Constable, 'Salvadoran Deaths Spur New Worries; Election, Peace Seem at Risk', *Boston Globe* (19 December 1993), p. 1. Some 26 rebels were slain in the wave of assassinations, including two military commanders, three security guards with their intelligence operations, and two members of a logistical team. For this reason, a joint group to investigate politically motivated killings was created: see 'Letter dated 11 August 1994 from the Secretary-General addressed to the President of the Security Council', UN Doc. S/1994/989 (22 October 1994). US Department of State, 'El Salvador Human Rights Practices, 1995'; see also 'El Salvador: UN Extends Observer Mission for Six Months', *NotiSur–Latin American Political Affairs* (10 November 1995). US Department of State, 'El Salvador Human Rights Practices, 1995' puts the number of complaints at 1,844; the report of then Procuradora Victoria Marina Velasquez de Aviles, *La Seguridad Ciudadana, la Policía Nacional Civil, y los Derechos Humanos* (San Salvador, El Salvador: Procuraduría para la Defensa de los Derechos Humanos, 1997), pp. 13–14, puts the figure at 1,791, including 89 dealing with the violation of the right to life.

64 See William Stanley, 'Protectors or Perpetrators? The Institutional Crisis of the Salvadoran Civilian Police' (Washington, DC: Washington Office on Latin America, January 1996); 'El Salvador', in *NotiSur*.

65 'Letter dated 8 June 1993 from the Secretary-General addressed to the President of the Security Council', UN Doc. S/25901 (8 June 1993).

66 Physicians for Human Rights, 'Physicians launch DNA testing to reunite "disappeared" Salvadoran children with parents' (13 September 1994), at http://www.phrusa.org/research/forensics/el_salvador/fordna1.html.

67 Nathaniel Sheppard Jr, 'War-scarred Salvadorans find real enemy is inside us', *Chicago Tribune* (16 June 1993), p. 1; Douglass W. Cassel Jr, 'Wielding the Truth in El Salvador', *Chicago Tribune* (29 March 1993), p. 11.

68 Meisler and Wilkinson, 'Salvador Urged to Bar all Rights Abusers'.

69 Centro Universitario de Información, Documentación, y Apoyo a la Investigación, 'Las Elecciónes del 16 de Marzo de 1997: Quiebre de la Hegemonía de ARENA', *Estudios Centroamericanos*, 581–2 (March–April 1997), p. 221.

70 As Williams and Walter rightly point out, the military retained broad autonomy from civilian control and were unwilling to give up the networks of social control that they retained in the countryside: see *Militarization and Demilitarization*, pp. 9–11, p. 116 ff.

71 Walter and Williams, 'The Military and Democratization in El Salvador', p. 68.

72 James K. Boyce, 'External Assistance and the Peace Process in El Salvador', *World Development*, 23, 12 (1995), p. 2110; IISS, *The Military Balance: 1995–1996*, p. 216.

73 Author's interview with participants in ICITAP at the US Department of State, John Feeley and Fay Armstrong (Washington, DC, 10 June 1997); Williams and Walter, *Militarization and Demilitarization*, p. 171.

74 On the general history of military corporatism and penetration in politics in El Salvador, see Erich G. Frankland, 'Under the Gun in El Salvador: The Evolving Relationship between the Military and Democracy', *Low Intensity Conflict and Law Enforcement*, 3, 1 (Summer 1994), pp. 104–31; see also Walter and Williams, 'The

Military and Democratization in El Salvador'; Thomas K. Adams, 'Disengage, Disarm, Demobilize: The Success of ONUSAL in Implementing the 1992 El Salvador Peace Accords', *Low Intensity Conflict and Law Enforcement*, 3, 2 (Autumn 1994), p. 292. The percentages were to be: 60 per cent persons with no involvement in the prior conflict, and 20 per cent each screened former PN members and former FMLN members: Brody, 'The United Nations and Human Rights in El Salvador's "Negotiated Revolution"', p. 174.

75 Walter and Williams, 'The Military and Democratization in El Salvador', p. 67.

76 Morgan Rose, 'El Salvador: Abuse of Human Rights and the Process of Peace', *Guild Practitioner*, 50, 4 (Fall 1993), p. 121; Washington Office on Latin America, 'Reluctant Reforms: The Cristiani Government and the International Community in the Process of Salvadoran post-War Reconstruction' (Washington, DC: Washington Office on Latin America, 1993), pp. 33–4.

77 Author's interview with Escobar Galindo, who emphasized these changes as evidence of a change at the base, in the allocation of power, as opposed to mere cosmetic changes.

78 Reglamento Disciplinario de la PNC, Article 67, reprinted in ONUSAL/ Procuraduría para la Defensa de los Derechos Humanos, *Guía Sobre las Normas y Procidimientos de la Policía Nacional Civil* (San Salvador, El Salvador: ONUSAL, 1994), p. 163.

79 Ley Organica de la Policía Nacional Civil, Articles 25(4) and 27(2) reprinted in ONUSAL; *Guía Sobre las Normas*.

80 Stanley, 'Protectors or Perpetrators', p. 6, emphasizes the potentially thorny political situation. Santiago Fernandez Quezada, the secretary-general of the ANSP, says that he saw relatively little conflict engendered by the incorporation of the FMLN when he arrived in 1993, and suggests that a reason for success was that the Consejo Academico (academic council) conditioned the treatment of incoming students based on their origin and presumed capacities and shortcomings: author's interview with Santiago Fernandez Quezada, Secretario General, Academia Nacional de Seguridad Pública (Santa Tecla, 19 November 1997).

81 Author's interview with ICITAP participants at the US Department of State, John Feeley and Fay Armstrong (Washington, DC, 10 June 1997); Stanley, 'Protectors or Perpetrators?', pp. 5–6; author's interview with Santiago Fernandez Quezada; 'Strengthening of the Coordination of Humanitarian and Disaster Relief Assistance of the United Nations, including Special Economic Assistance to Individual Countries or Regions', UN Doc. A/52/433 (8 October 1997), paras 66–72; Gabriel Siri and Jenny Malmquist, 'Evaluacion del Apoyo de Suecia al Proceso de Paz y Democratización en El Salvador' (Informe de la consultoria preparado para la Autoridad Suecia para el Desarollo Internacional, December 1994). See generally also Costa, 'The United Nations and Reform', pp. 373–9 on the curriculum of the ANSP and the role of international assistance.

82 On other social and historical forces, see Raul Benitez Manaut, 'Los Militares: Viejos Caudillos, Nuevos Democratas?', in Francisco Barahona Riera and Manuel Carballo Quintana, *Reconversión Militar en Centroamerica* (San Jose, Costa Rica: Fundación Friedrich Ebert, 1995), pp. 24–5; Edelberto Torres-Rivas and Dirk Kruijt, 'Presentacion', in Kruijt and Torres-Rivas (eds), *America Latina: Militares y Sociedad – I* (San Jose, Costa Rica: FLACSO, 1991), p. 9; Kees Koonings, 'La Sociología de la Intervención Militar en la Política Latinoamerica', in Kruijt and Torres-Rivas (eds), *America Latina*, pp. 19–61. Alain Rouquie, while not disputing the role of ideology, does not see the doctrine as decisive: see Rouquie, *The Military and the State in Latin America*, trans. Paul Sigmund (Berkeley, CA: University of California Press, 1987), p. 8.

83 Kruijt, 'Politicians in Uniform: Dilemmas about the Latin American Military', *European Review of Latin American and Caribbean Studies*, 61 (December 1996),

pp. 7–19. See Coronel Prudencio Garcia, (ONUSAL human rights division chief of cooperation with the FA), 'Fuerzas Armadas y Consolidación Democrática en America Latina', in Barahona Riera and Carballo Quintana (eds), *Reconversión Militar*, p. 48.

84 Stepan, *The Military in Politics*; Koonings, 'La Sociología de la Intervención Militar', pp. 46–50. Benitez Manaut, 'Los Militares: Viejos Caudillos', p. 30. On the Argentine case, see Colonels H. P. Ballester, J. L. Garcia, C. M. Gazcon and A. B. Rattenbach, 'Fuerzas Armadas Argentinas: El Cambio Necesario, Bases Políticas, y Tecnicas Para Una Reforma Militar', in Fuerza Armada de El Salvador, *Doctrina Militar y Relaciones Ejército/Sociedad*, p. 199. See also Raul Benitez Manaut, *La Teoría Militar y la Guerra Civil en El Salvador* (San Salvador, El Salvador: Universidad Centroamericana, 1989).

85 Hector Samour, 'Las Fuerzas Armadas Salvadorenas', *Realidad: Revista de Ciencias Sociales y Humanidades* (September–October 1994), pp. 765–6; Oscar Alfredo Santamaria, 'Relación de la Seguridad Nacional Salvadoreña con el Contexto Internacional', in Centro de Estudios Democraticos (CEDEM), *El Nuevo Concepto de la Seguridad Nacional Salvadoreña* (San Salvador: CEDEM, 1994), p. 14; Coronel Omar Arturo Vaquerano, 'Efectos de la Terminación del Conflicto Este-Oeste con la Seguridad Nacional Salvadoreña', in CEDEM, *El Nuevo Concepto de la Seguridad*, pp. 28–31.

86 Samour, 'Las Fuerzas Armadas Salvadorenas', pp. 766–77.

87 Samour, 'Las Fuerzas Armadas Salvadorenas', pp. 774–5. It is worth noting that, despite the reforms to be discussed shortly, the tanda system has not been altered: *ibid*., p. 777; Williams and Walter, *Militarization and Demilitarization*, p. 150.

88 'El Fin del Militarismo: Dictadores en Busca de Escuela', *Cuadernos del Instituto de Estudios Jurídicos de El Salvador*, 7 (March 1993), pp. 135–42.

89 Author's interview with Escobar Galindo, who emphasized in particular the fact that, until the initiation of negotiations, the political power in the nation had become increasingly concentrated in the FAES, thus the key thrust of the negotiations, reinforced by domestic and international pressure, was the de-concentration of this power. See 'Nuevas Percepciones de Seguridad Nacional,' *El Salvador Boletín de Análisis e Información*, 13 (June–July 1992), p. 14.

90 Colonel Prudencio Garcia, 'Ineludible Incorporación de los Derechos Humanos a la Moral Militar Democrática y a la Nueva Relacion Ejército/Sociedad', in Barahona Riera and Carballo Quintana, *Reconversión Militar*, p. 96.

91 All the foregoing points were raised in the author's interview with David Escobar Galindo.

4 Argentina
Struggle for accountability

Introduction

Argentina provides another rich case, illustrating the role of external factors in helping to engender transition, as well as the complex set of trade-offs states must face. The central catalyst for change in Argentina is commonly agreed to have been the debacle in the Falklands/Malvinas, which weakened and embarrassed the military and encouraged it to step down. Domestic opposition was strong, but had previously posed no particular threat to the regime; the military loss seems to have been most important. Despite its weakened status, however, the military did not surrender all control over the political situation. At the same time, in contrast to other transitional experiences, external actors did not play a particularly significant role when the transition was underway. Although important and even high-level prosecutions went forward, as did a thorough report by a commission of inquiry, rebellions by the military helped force a series of procedural limitations and amnesties that largely reversed the effects of prosecutions. Some important constitutional institutional reforms were made, though they too were limited. The result was a set of compromises that partially addressed the legacy of the past and partly reformed the security forces to prevent future abuses. As with the other cases here, the outcome on the accountability/stability continuum was not an either/or trade-off: measures of both were sought and achieved.

A brief history

In March 1976, the Argentine military staged a coup and seized power in response to both political violence and the faltering economy of the country. It came to power seeking also to eliminate the threat posed by two guerrilla groups: the Montoneros and the Ejercito Revolucionario del Pueblo. During the period 1976–83, the country underwent the *Proceso de Reorganización Nacional*, or what is now referred to as the 'dirty war', ostensibly in response to terrorism and subversion but with a repressive reach far beyond the relatively small numbers of rebels and supporters. Tens of thousands of people disappeared, and almost 10,000 more were held as political prisoners by the military dictatorship.[1]

In Argentina, unlike many other countries where gross human rights abuses have occurred, the subsequent democratic regime attempted to prosecute the perpetrators, albeit with unsatisfactory results. As we shall see, despite the weakened status of the military following the Falklands/Malvinas defeat and economic crises that pushed it to initiate democratization, the military to a large degree set the terms for its own departure and continued to play a significant role in the democratizing polity.[2]

The human rights movement

I now consider the demands of the indigenous human rights movement in Argentina, and the ways in which they were translated (or not) into government policy in the face of a strong military. The most notable group pressing for human rights reform was the Madres de la Plaza de Mayo, who were mothers of 'disappeared' Argentines. This group, along with other, pressed for the accountability of the government for human rights violations, in particular demanding that the truth be told and that there be 'no impunity', that is no amnesty, for the perpetrators.[3]

Democratization: the Alfonsín regime

Human rights activists played a role in Argentina's transition to democracy, although the weakened status of the Argentine military following the Falklands/Malvinas war played a significant, perhaps decisive role. Even before the Falklands/Malvinas debacle, cracks in the military's unity were developing in part due to the strains and failures of their management of the economy. The surrender in June 1982 perhaps only sealed the fate of the junta: it undermined a nascently expansionist foreign policy, crushed the Argentine war machine, posed an embarrassment for the military in terms of both its morale and battle-readiness, destroyed the junta's plan to generate unity by whipping up nationalism, and unleashed a wave of social frustration from diverse quarters.[4] Thus, following the rout in the Falklands/Malvinas, the ruling General Galtieri was replaced with General Bignone, who was tasked with returning the nation to constitutional government.[5]

Nonetheless, democratization has been hampered by the privileged status of the military, which has also limited the government's capacity to respond to the demands of the human rights movement. There were at least four military uprisings during the period of democratization, often in response to attempts to hold members of the military accountable for human rights violations.[6] Despite these limitations, however, the government did attempt prosecutions and other forms of accountability under President Raúl Alfonsín.

The human rights movement had demanded government accountability for human rights violations, and demanded that the truth be exposed and that there be no impunity. Rhetorically, Alfonsín responded to these demands while campaigning for the presidency, promising responses to human rights abuses that included prosecuting those who had given or exceeded orders during the dictatorship. After the election, human rights groups maintained pressure on Alfonsín through mass demonstrations.[7]

The legacy of the past: Alfonsín's policies

Once in office, Alfonsín sent a bill to congress that included an annulment of the amnesty the military had granted itself, reform of the military code of justice, and a mandate for the trials of members of the first three military juntas.[8] It also sought to lay bare the legacy of the dirty war through a variant on the truth commission, the Comisión Nacional sobre Desaparición de Personas (CONADEP).

Revealing the truth: CONADEP

The commission collected testimony of survivors of mass executions and other atrocities, documenting some 9,000 disappearances. In September 1984, after 280 days work, CONADEP presented a report, *Nunca Más*, which presented the names and fates of victims; it did not name perpetrators. The report also investigated and articulated some of the underpinnings of the repression, in particular the obsessive concern with fighting subversives derived from the doctrine of national security (DNS).[9]

The report provoked a crisis in the military: it named not only some of the disappeared, but gave sensitive details such as the extent of torture and location of what some have called concentration camps, provoking the army chief of staff Arguindegui to assert that there was a plot to undermine his authority within the military.[10] Furthermore, while the report itself did not explicitly name perpetrators, the commission gave the president a list of names in a sealed envelope, which was promptly leaked to a Buenos Aires newspaper.[11] Nonetheless, the president of the Madres de la Plaza de Mayo condemned CONADEP as failing to truly bring the military to justice.[12]

The trials of the mid-1980s are discussed below, but it is worth turning briefly to other reforms that Alfonsín sought to effect. He obtained the resignations of 59 admirals and generals. Further, he proposed reforms in the command structure and doctrine of the military, in particular the deleterious doctrine of national security.[13]

Pursuit of accountability: the trials and their consequences

The trials of high-level officers for the excesses of the dirty war did not begin in civilian courts, but rather in the supreme military council. Under the reformed military justice code, with the support of Alfonsín, the council was given jurisdiction over offences that were committed by the armed forces or security forces, police or workers in the penitentiary system operated by the armed forces. However, the reformed code also stipulated that, should there be undue delays, the federal chamber would take over the cases. The supreme council delayed making decisions throughout 1984, and ultimately released a report stating that it was unable to judge the defendants because the orders given and followed were 'unobjectionable' in the context of a 'war against subversion'. The Buenos Aires appeals court then assumed jurisdiction over the cases, which took place through 1985. The trials were open to the public and press, and excerpts were shown on television, allowing a wide range of views and personal stories of the victims to be heard.[14]

During the trials, evidence was destroyed, a coup plot against Alfonsín was discovered, witnesses were threatened and harassed, and a bomb was found at the home of the president of the appeals court.[15] Ultimately, five of the nine defendants were convicted: General-Presidents Jorge Videla and Robert Viola, Admirals Emilio Massera and Armando Lambruschini, and Air Force Brigadier Orlando Agosti. Despite defences by these high-level officers that their actions were a response to terrorism and that therefore their acts were of necessity, self-defence or war, the appeals court (whose judgement was affirmed by the supreme court) ultimately rejected all defences and found that these defendants were guilty of crimes ranging from aggravated homicide and torture to robbery.[16]

The Alfonsín administration also ordered a number of exemplary trials, but victims and their families pressed for much larger-scale prosecutions. The military courts which were to hear more cases, however, were given orders by the ministry of defence constructed so that massive acquittals or immunity from prosecution would result, and in 1986 the civilian courts took up the cases.[17]

Proceedings were also initiated against high-level police officials at the same time as the trials against former junta members, and the federal appeals court assumed jurisdiction, much as it had in those earlier cases. The trials led to the conviction of two former police chiefs, Ramon Camps and Ovidio Riccheri, as well as the former Buenos Aires chief inspector in December 1986, on torture charges. However, under the due obedience legislation, passed while these cases were being processed, the sentences were reduced or eliminated altogether.[18]

Even as these trials were progressing, the Alfonsín administration sought to mediate between increasingly activist courts and a restive military. First, the judiciary was to apply a set of instructions developed by the minister of defence for judgement in the supreme council, a strategy made public in April of 1996. These instructions were seen by many as both a hidden amnesty effectively limiting the responsibility of subordinates and an overreaching by the executive power into judicial matters. Resignation threats by members of the judiciary and the general prosecutor in the trial of members of the junta, as well as vocal opposition by human rights groups and opposition political parties prompted Alfonsín to backpedal, announcing new instructions constricting the concept of due obedience.[19]

Second, Alfonsín introduced the *punto final* legislation, which was to limit trials procedurally. This legislation meant that, after 60 days, no further charges could be brought against any defendant, which was expected to severely limit any future trials. Although the human rights movement flooded the courts with cases, getting some 400 cases processed before the deadline, another 1,300–1,500 perpetrators identifiable from extant testimony could not be prosecuted. Nonetheless, the cases were significant, with some 30 per cent of the cases filed against active duty officers. Further, the courts worked in active cooperation to speed the process, suspending their holidays to clear out cases before the *punto final* law came into force.[20]

Even with these limitations on trials, the relations between the democratic government and the military remained tense. This situation was compounded by internal rifts within the military caused by the human rights trials. The rifts were based on differences of opinion among different levels of the hierarchy regarding the dirty war and the trials, and may have been a result of the tiered strategy of prosecution, which sought to punish the junta members who designed the repression and the officers who actually carried it out; those lower-ranking officers felt abandoned by their generals; they felt that those who were neither designers or direct implementers of the dirty war were, unfairly, going unpunished. The lower-ranking officers who had largely carried out the war against the guerrillas and later in the Falklands developed a strong sense of solidarity, and believed strongly that they had fought honourably for their country. These officers, now promoted to the middle ranks of major and lieutenant-colonel, felt they had become scapegoats when the trials began, and saw themselves as victims of collusion between higher-ranking generals and Alfonsin.[21]

In April 1987, a widespread military rebellion was sparked in a military complex outside Buenos Aires, Campo de Mayo. This Easter rebellion began when Major Ernesto Barreiro, an officer accused of torture, sought refuge in an airborne infantry unit in Cordoba. A few days later, Lieutenant-Colonel Aldo Rico took over the Campo de Mayo in Buenos Aires in solidarity with Barreiro, demanding the replacement of certain top officers in the army including the chief of staff, and a political solution to the human rights trials. The chief of staff, General Rios Erenu, ordered troops to put the rebellion down, and resigned when they refused, further demonstrating the divisions within the military. Meanwhile, the response of the populace was one of outrage: there were large demonstrations in the Plaza de Mayo as well as outside the Campo de Mayo regiment; legislators signed an act articulating their commitment to democracy, and labour leaders called for a strike.[22]

Alfonsin negotiated directly with the leaders of the rebellion, resolving the crisis, but shortly thereafter introduced further legislation to mitigate the prosecutions. This legislation, the Obediencia Debida (due obedience) law, introduced the presumption that all but a few high-ranking officers were 'just following orders'; the legislature reportedly passed it under fear of renewed military repression. The result, as briefly discussed above, was to reverse a number of high-profile cases and release many other officers whose cases were pending.[23] The goal of the legislation was to mitigate the sense of injustice and scapegoating felt by the middle-level officers; the timing of the legislation and the fact that Alfonsín did negotiate with the rebels has led many to assume that the legislation was a direct concession in exchange for the end of the Easter rebellion.

However, others argue that the timing of the Obediencia Debida legislation should not be too heavily weighted: the core of Alfonsín's policy towards the armed forces had already been outlined in his campaign. He had, early on, articulated the three-tiered approach that would treat differently those who planned the dirty war, those responsible for its excesses and those who had only obeyed orders. In fact, the key facets of the due obedience concept had been included in the 1984 reform of the military justice code, which included a presumption that individuals who acted under orders of high-level officers of the military or the junta had held the mistaken belief that their actions were legitimate.[24]

The Obediencia Debida legislation did not, however, bring military restiveness to an end. Two more rebellions must be noted. Lieutenant-Colonel Aldo Rico was the cause of a second rebellion in January 1988. In the face of punishment for his role in the previous rebellion, Rico occupied an infantry regiment, claiming that the demands of the Easter rebellion had not been met. The rebellion was eventually put down, but Rico's support weakened because he had been acting in defiance of a military tribunal rather than a civilian court.[25]

The third military rebellion of note took place in late November and early December 1988, instigated by Colonel Mohamed Ali Seineldín, a key figure among the rebel military officers. A unit took over the infantry school at the Campo de Mayo, claiming to be under the orders of Colonel Seineldín, who was in Panama at the time but returned to lead the rebellion. The putative causes of the rebellion were several: the refusal to promote Seineldín, seen as a snub to this sect of officers, the perception that Alfonsín's administration was soiling the honour of the armed forces, and a desire that amnesty be granted for those involved in previous rebellions.[26]

Alfonsín refused to grant the amnesty, and ordered the suppression of the rebellion. Furthermore, civilian outrage went beyond demonstrations: crowds surrounded the barracks to hurl both stones and insults. Labour and business groups called for a strike, and congress went into an emergency session to demonstrate support for democracy.[27]

Seineldín announced the officers' demands, which ranged from an amnesty to budget increases. The general in charge of suppressing the rebellion entered the base to speak to the rebels, and compromises were made, which according to the rebels included the replacement of a key general, wage increases, the sparing of the rebels from trials, a general amnesty in the next government change and a public depiction of the dirty war as a positive thing. However, not all of these demands were realized: the general in question was replaced and wages were increased, but Seineldín was arrested and accountability for the rebellion was limited to officers, rather than eliminated. The commitment made to 'restore the army's dignity' was sufficiently vague as to have no real meaning.

Seineldín survived to lead one last mutiny, in December 1990, but surrendered without negotiation, and was excluded from subsequent pardons.[28]

While Alfonsín entered office with a strong commitment to prosecute human rights violations, political tension and, more importantly, military rebellions set practical limits on the level of accountability that could be achieved. Between the *punto final* and the Obediencia Debida legislation, the number of pending cases was drastically reduced, and many convicted murderers and torturers were released. No further trials began under Alfonsin's administration, and in July 1989 President Carlos Menem assumed office.

Democratization: the Menem regime

Despite ongoing attempts to reform and democratize the military, it remained an autonomous corporate force prone to rebellion when Menem came to power. Though Menem had himself been persecuted during the dirty war and spoken out against the Obediencia Debida legislation, his defence minister favoured amnesty and Menem quickly moved to pardon military figures convicted of human rights abuses.[29]

In September 1989, Menem pardoned 18 Argentine generals and admirals facing trial, and announced the review of the convictions of six convicted earlier, including two ex-presidents. In October, Menem pardoned over 200 more officers, accused of human rights abuses or aiding military rebellions, in the name of national reconciliation. In response to those arguing that there should be no impunity, he said that, with the economy in crisis, the country could not afford the bitter social divisions fomented by the imprisonment of the military figures.[30] Although many believed that Menem felt compelled to pardon the officers in the light of the three military rebellions that had taken place in the last two years in protest against the trials, many were outraged at the act.[31] Only a small majority of Argentines agreed with Menem that such an action was necessary for reconciliation; many others feared that pardons would make the officers feel vindicated, and could perhaps encourage them to return to their repressive routines. The critics objected that the officers felt no responsibility for their crimes, and that families of the victims did not feel that justice had been done. They protested that pardons delegitimated the justice system, and would only exacerbate the conflicts between the civilians and the military. Despite both domestic and international objections, in December 1990 Menem also pardoned the former rulers convicted of human rights violations.[32]

The mixed legacy of human rights in Argentina

While the prosecutions of key perpetrators of human rights violations appear to have failed, the period of democratization witnessed an explosion of truth-telling. Newspapers, television and film featured the stories of victims, and public opinion indicates the delegitimation of the military and support for human rights. Nonetheless, the national reconciliation hoped for has failed to materialize, in part because of the continuing demands for justice by victims and their families. While the Madres have continued to demand information about their disappeared children, their status has sunk dramatically, suggesting a national desire to leave the past behind.[33] Furthermore, as democracy was defined by the human rights movement and Alfonsín as including government accountability, pardons mark the weakness of the nascent democratic state.[34]

The lack of reconciliation is made clear by the ongoing protests of the Madres, but perhaps more importantly by the recent spate of confessions by military figures involved in disappearances and killings. In early 1995, a former navy captain confessed to taking part in flights in which prisoners were thrown out of planes into the sea; this provided the country with a chance to revisit human rights issues, but was met almost immediately with nationalist rhetoric about the need to fight the left-wing insurgents. Many human rights activists interpreted this response and the dearth of other opinions as indicative of the degree to which the military still acts with impunity. Menem himself, after first encouraging people to speak out, suggested that they confess their sins to a priest rather than the public, saying that such confessions merely reopened old wounds that needed to heal.[35] Victims responded that society would be stained until justice was done.

The issue was not laid to rest as Menem had hoped. In April 1995, a first sergeant in the army came forward and discussed his role in the flights also. This ultimately sparked an apology from the army chief of staff, General Martin Balza, who stated that '[w]e must no longer deny the horror we lived through', and promised that the military would not repeat the mistakes of the past. This apology was followed by similar remarks by the heads of the navy and air force.[36] Some believed that this apology would have a cathartic effect on society, and Menem, switching positions, announced that he would look into the possibility of rescinding some Alfonsín-era laws pardoning perpetrators.[37] The revelations and apology have had an uncertain effect thus far on the victims and Argentine society in general. For some they merely spark new anger and reopen old wounds, while others feel relief at the opportunity to speak out. Few expect new prosecutions to result, but public debate on the issue has resumed, and Menem has reopened some cases.[38] For the victims and the families of victims, the past looms large and reconciliation is not complete. Many of the Madres say that they cannot rest until the truth is out, and until they know that their children did not die in vain. The desire for retaliation remains, as evidenced by repeated public physical attacks by survivors and family members of victims on retired Captain Alfredo Astiz, a renowned torturer during the dirty war.[39]

Finally, in 1998, the question of accountability arose again, in connection with the apparent kidnappings of children from detained mothers. These children were allegedly then adopted by couples who were part of the military or the police. Two former rulers, Admiral Emilio E. Massera and General Jorge Rafael Videla, have been detained in relation to these abductions. In addition, a Spanish judge is investigating abuses under Massera. These developments are noteworthy, since Massera was pardoned by Menem, but that pardon did not cover the kidnapping of babies born in prison camps.[40] This issue returned to prominence in late 1998 with the arrests of a number of military officers for past kidnappings of the babies of women killed in detention centres.[41]

Strategies of transition in the face of a recalcitrant military

A key obstacle that nascent democracies frequently face is the recalcitrant old guard, whose most powerful elements are often military officers. Whether the military previously ruled directly, or through obedient civilian governments, its members will feel insecure in a new democratic environment, having lost the protection that comes with power. I build upon claims in the literature that the key concerns they have are to do with the following three factors: treatment of their members in the face of calls for accountability for human rights violations, institutional reform and budgetary levels. An examination of the Argentine case suggests all three issues were of concern to the military, though perhaps to varying degrees.

Human rights accountability: a promise largely deferred

As can be seen from the tortured history of the trials in Argentina, in relation to this element that the military was most recalcitrant. The various coup attempts can be interpreted as responses to specific events in the judicial and political process, rather than as part of greater aspirations to bring down the nascent democratic regime.[42] While trials achieved convictions of high-level junta members and others, amnesties and procedural limitations undermined much of the impact of these judicial proceedings.

Institutional reform

Alfonsín was able to implement some substantive change in the structure and control of the military: the president was established as the commander in chief of the armed forces, the ministry of defence was re-established with a civilian at its head, and would control the joint general staff, the military planning wing, who would in turn control the heads of each of the branches of the armed forces. The Commandantes en Jefe (commanders in chief) were eliminated, the number of high-level posts in the military was reduced, and the elimination, fusion or transfer of some military units was achieved. In addition, some modification of doctrines, regulations and training was achieved, and is discussed below.[43] A key intelligence unit was also placed under civilian control. Nonetheless, Alfonsín's initiatives were met with passive resistance. Further, even when budget cuts began to take effect, most of the old military units were still intact.[44] In addition to budget and staff cuts, Alfonsín attempted to restructure the military. He transferred some military institutes and corps from the capital to the provinces, introduced new, civilian-taught courses at military institutes on the role of the military in democracy, and limited to some degree the role of the military in internal state matters.[45]

Alfonsín was also able to push through a change in the military doctrine, one that was meant to fit the military's new role in a democratic society. As in many Latin American countries, in Argentina the line between internal and external security had been so thoroughly blurred as to be nearly erased. Thus it was an important facet of the new doctrine, introduced in 1985, that the distinction between internal and external security was explicitly established in the new law of national defence. This doctrine thus specifically limited the role of the armed forces to the defence of territory and sovereignty from external attacks.[46] Two additional laws were passed in this arena: the law of national defence of 1988 and the law of internal security of 1991. Military reform is far from complete, however; in recognition of that, in 1995, congress initiated hearings on restructuring the defence system, in response to which the ministry of defence set up its own commission on restructuring.[47]

It is worth noting that the entrenchment of those reforms that have been achieved may be aided by the shift in the foreign policy of the state and thus the military: from a tradition of isolationism to engagement in regional and international security actions. Some argue that many in the military now recognize that isolationism created misperceptions that enabled the Falklands/ Malvinas debacle; thus there was a desire by some within the military to professionalize. Specifically, members of the military believed that the failure was due in part to the diffusion of military control and resources over too many aspects of the country, and began to express the desire to withdraw from politics and professionalize.[48] In addition, cooperation with other armed forces in UN actions calls for not only coordination of weapons systems and troops but doctrines.[49]

Further, advances in reform were often simultaneously undermined by back-door political compromises. In 1985, the nascent separation of the military from intelligence and other covert internal activities was undermined by decrees allowing intelligence agencies to conduct secret business activities, that consolidated military and non-military intelligence bodies, and that actually called on the military to acquire intelligence dealing with 'probable adversaries'. This last decree gave the president the right to authorize the military to resolve internal conflicts, in direct opposition to the nascent principle of excluding the military from internal security matters. The law of national defence's exclusion of military participation in internal conflicts was undermined in 1986 by the so-called firepower clause, giving it the power to act where the police or security forces were unable to control internal conflicts. And, in 1989, Alfonsín continued this trend by creating a new national security council to advise on the threat of internal subversion that included as members the chiefs of staff of the armed forces.[50]

This trend continued under Menem, who even before he took office stated that he wanted to change the defence law to give the armed forces an explicit role in internal security, which he partially accomplished by decree; a law in

1992 abolished the ban on military action in internal situations, though limited such action to that of last resort where the security forces were overwhelmed.[51] In addition, one observer has argued that the military also retained a significant degree of autonomy in the definition of its mission, doctrine and education.[52]

Budgetary concerns

Part of the platform that Alfonsín's party ran on was the promise to cut the military budget. As in El Salvador, the military budget in Argentina remained high after the transition to civilian rule. While estimates of military spending are unreliable and vary from source to source, the 1984 level of 3.3 per cent of GDP is in fact higher than at many points during the proceso. By 1986, the budget had been cut in half, but, as mentioned above, military units were intact. In 1995, the military budget's percentage of GDP was 1.7 per cent, and had increased slightly for several years. Argentina was remarkably successful in reducing the size of its armed forces overall: between 1983 and 1987, they shrank by 49 per cent.[53]

Factors enabling or inhibiting accountability

I now discuss the nature of several salient factors that may affect the level of accountability that a regime may achieve: civil–military relations, international factors and the duration and intensity of the conflict.

Civil–military relations/balance of forces

Argentina has a long history of military intervention in politics, including coups in 1966 and 1976 establishing military dictatorships in response to state crises. Thus, the 1983 transitional civilian regime faced a tough challenge: reinforcing democracy while responding to economic crises and addressing calls for accountability for past human rights abuses. The legitimate fear was that, should the new democratic regime find itself unable to address these challenges, the armed forces would impose order themselves.[54]

Even in the absence of the doctrine of national security, outlined in Chapter 1 and discussed in the Argentine context below, the armed forces would likely have been prone to intervention in politics. From their perspective, they held several advantages over other actors in politics: they were better organized, more efficient and had professional solidarity, all of which were buttressed by their monopoly of arms. As other scholars have discussed, the legacy of praetorianism is extensive in Argentina, and the nation was imbued with militarist values that held that the military was a legitimate actor in politics. The result was that democracy was shaky at best: between 1955 and 1976, no electorally empowered president completed the legally prescribed six-year term.[55] As we shall see, this organizational perspective was soon bolstered by an ideological one.[56]

Like many other countries in Latin America, Argentina was heavily influenced by the doctrine of national security. As mentioned above, the emphasis on counterinsurgency was discussed by the CONADEP report as a precursor to coups and repression by the military. For example, in 1964, in a speech at West Point, the commander in chief of the Argentine army, General Ongania, stated that the duty of the military to subordinate itself to civilians ceases when there is a threat to authority and the basic system of republican government. Under the influence of the doctrine, the military came to see itself as the last moral barrier protecting the nation.[57]

The DNS made its way into the collective psyche of the Argentine military largely through American, but also French, influence.[58] The USA trained a significant number of Argentine officers; this training focused heavily on anti-subversive activities. The DNS found fertile soil in the Argentine military, which was a coup-prone one in a country with a weak democracy at best. The coup-makers that broke with Peron in 1955 used the DNS to carve out a new mission for the armed forces: to defend the nation against internal and external aggression or subversion. The period between 1959 and 1961 saw the creation of a post-graduate course of conferences for officers on counter-subversive war and the adaptation of the organization and procedures of the army to this mode of warfare.[59] The gestation of the DNS in the military could be said to have been complete with General Ongania's speech. Theorists have seen the dirty war as merely an elaboration and actualization of the themes present in the DNS.[60]

Even prior to the coup, the military's role in internal affairs had been steadily increasing: in 1975, the government concluded that the internal security forces were incapable of combating subversion adequately, and passed legislation assigning this function to the armed forces.[61] Thus, the legislation that gave the period its name, the law of the *Proceso de Reorganización Nacional*, which emphasized the role of the military in reordering the state, did not represent a drastic break with the past. The military justified the coup by pointing to the inability of the government to wage the battle against subversion, and held itself up as the saviour of the nation, offering to restore values and promote efficiency, development and security.[62] The governing junta propagated what has been since termed the myth of the dirty war: the claim that such drastic measures were needed because of an imminent guerrilla threat. Subsequent scholarship has suggested that, contrary to the military's claim that insurgents numbered 15,000 combatants with an equal additional number of active supporters, insurgents never rose above 2,000, in marked contrast to the military's numbers, which reached 200,000. Nonetheless, members of the military expressed the view that Argentina was involved in a serious war against subversion; that if the threat were not actively combated the Soviet Union would gain another toehold in Latin America. The 'enemy' was demonized as leftist, not Argentinian. The military argued that the police were unable to face this threat; hence there was a need to work outside the normal republican institutions. To fight such an insidious enemy, secrecy was essential and it was even acknowledged that torture might be necessary.[63]

Several Argentine officers, writing in recent years, have acknowledged the power of the doctrine in the military, arguing that it turned the Argentine military against its own people and undermined its professionalism. The doctrine, meant only to be used within the nation's borders, is identified by these authors as the source of the *Proceso de Reorganización Nacional*, which they claim turned the military into an internal occupation force.[64] Professionalism was further undermined, according to these authors, because military careers began early, before men had matured as citizens, and these young men were easily indoctrinated with military propaganda.

The Falklands/Malvinas debacle profoundly shook the confidence of the military regime, signalling as it did a need for restructuring and reconsidering virtually every aspect of doctrine and practice that the DNS had enshrined. The new government in 1983 then faced a weakened military, but one with highly elaborated corporate interests and widely dispersed influence, as the military had taken control of various economic bodies and become skilled at media and information manipulation. The penetration of society and economy was so complete that the army had taken over not only the state apparatus, but institutions ranging from telecommunications to the Institute of Cinematography. The Falklands/Malvinas conflict did, however, generate a rift between the military and some of their traditional business/financial allies.[65]

While there was no significant military opposition force, there was strong domestic pressure in favour of human rights prosecutions, as discussed above. This pressure came not only from the Madres but also from support for the trials by people from all walks of life.[66] While the human rights lobby may not have been vast, two groups were linked to political parties and had great public legitimacy and dissemination of their ideas despite a lack of real direct political power. They posed a constant challenge to Alfonsín's strategy of pursuing limited accountability, issuing calls for more direct challenges to the military and for retribution based on the wrongness of past acts, not the more limited deterrent-based approach chosen by the regime.[67]

External factors

The most salient external factor in the Argentine transition appears to have been the defeat at the hands of the British in the Falklands/Malvinas. Otherwise, in contrast to many other countries that have undergone such transitions, neither the USA nor the UN was actively engaged in the transition. The implications of this relative absence during the transition of external peacebuilding actors is discussed below.

Nature/extent of abuses and conflict

The extent of abuses appears to have had a perverse effect on the strategy of prosecutions: that is to say, the number of those implicated in the abuses meant that prosecution of all those implicated in past abuses was not feasible and posed a threat to stability, such that a more limited strategy must necessarily be employed.

Absence of external actors: can peacekeepers and peacebuilders learn from Argentina?

At first sight, the relative absence of external peacebuilding actors, and the complete absence of peacekeeping actors, during the Argentine transition would seem to imply that relatively little can be learned from Argentina's experience by today's external actors. Certainly, Argentina's transition, in contrast to the others examined in detail here, began nearly a decade prior to the publication of UN Secretary-General Boutros-Boutros-Ghali's *Agenda for Peace*, a seminal document as the UN engaged in new approaches to peacekeeping and peacebuilding. However, what is of interest about the Argentine case, as with a number of the nutshell cases that also occurred before 1992, is precisely how similar it appears to transitions during the 1990s.

Specifically, not only did attempts to impose accountability meet similar challenges, but similar tools were deployed, and similar trade-offs engaged in, despite the absence of external actors. This would suggest, not that external actors are irrelevant, but that the shape of challenges remains similar. Comparison of cases where they were present and absent allows us to control for the possible bias of external actors towards particular approaches to the putative peace/justice divide. We should, in fact, be very concerned if we detect a radical difference in approaches to the dilemma given the presence or absence of such actors.

The value of external actors in such situations is not necessarily that they can or ought to make choices that are better or different to those that internal actors would make, but that they can bring resources to bear to support the advancement of peace and justice in a fashion consistent with local needs.

Lessons

Argentina demonstrates the nature of the accountability continuum as well as what makes it more or less feasible. While a unique historical moment that also briefly weakened the armed forces made transition and efforts at accountability possible, the corporatism of the armed forces would eventually place sharp limits on efforts at prosecution. The result was a virtual reversal of the successful prosecutions, as well as a halt to further proceedings. Nonetheless, an accounting of abuses was also provided by the commission of inquiry, and some important, if incomplete, steps towards restructuring the security forces were taken. What we learn again is that accountability and stability and reform in their fully elaborated forms may not be possible simultaneously, but that partial measures may well be implemented.

Notes

1 See Alejandro M. Garro and Henry Dahl, 'Legal Accountability for Human Rights Violations in Argentina: One Step Forward and Two Steps Back', *Human Rights Law Journal*, 8 (1987), pp. 287–94; Alison Brysk, *The Politics of Human Rights in Argentina: Protest, Change, and Democratization* (Stanford, CA: Stanford University Press, 1994), p. 1; compare Pion-Berlin, 'To Prosecute or to Pardon?', p. 108.

2 Garro and Dahl, 'Legal Accountability', pp. 300–1. See also J. Patrice McSherry, *Incomplete Transition: Military Power and Democracy in Argentina* (New York: St Martin's Press, 1997), p. 2. But see Munck, *Authoritarianism and Democratization*, p. 147 and *passim*.

3 Brysk, *The Politics of Human Rights*, pp. 12–16, 63–4.

4 Pion-Berlin, 'To Prosecute or to Pardon?', p. 113. See Mark Osiel, 'The Making of Human Rights Policy in Argentina: The Impact of Ideas and Interests on a Legal Conflict', *Journal of Latin American Studies*, 18 (1986), p. 142; Gary W. Wynia, 'Democracy in Argentina', *Current History*, 498 (February 1985), p. 53; Alejandro Dabat and Luis Lorenzano, *Argentina: The Malvinas and the End of Military Rule*, trans. Ralph Johnstone (London: Verso, 1984); David Pion-Berlin, 'The Fall of Military Rule in Argentina, 1976–1983', *Journal of Interamerican Studies and World Affairs*, 27, 2 (1985), pp. 55–76. See also McSherry, *Incomplete Transition*, p. 6, and Munck, *Authoritarianism and Democratization*.

5 Ronaldo Munck, *Latin America: The Transition to Democracy* (London: Zed Books, 1989), p. 103. The junta dissolved between July and September, reconstituting itself and beginning to seek reassurances regarding accountability in November 1982, in a document that was roundly rejected: see Munck, *Authoritarianism and Democratization*, pp. 147–55.

6 Brysk, *The Politics of Human Rights*, pp. 19–20; Pion-Berlin, 'To Prosecute or to Pardon?', p. 112; Alejandro M. Garro, 'Nine Years of Transition to Democracy in Argentina: Partial Failure or Qualified Success?', *Columbia Journal of Transnational Law*, 31, 1 (1993), pp. 1–102.

7 Brysk, *The Politics of Human Rights*, pp. 65–7. Compare Osiel, 'The Making of Human Rights Policy', pp. 142–3. On various political parties' stances on military reform, see Walter Little, 'Civil–Military Relations in Contemporary Argentina', *Government and Opposition*, 19, 2 (1984), pp. 207–24.

8 Brysk, *The Politics of Human Rights*, pp. 67–8; Jaime Malamud-Goti, 'Punishing Human Rights Abuses in Fledgling Democracies: The Case of Argentina', in Roht-Arriaza (ed.), *Impunity and Human Rights*, p. 161. The bill passed by Congress voiding the self-amnesty law was subsequently upheld in court: see Garro and Dahl, 'Legal Accountability', pp. 305–6.

9 CONADEP was created by Decree No. 157 of 15 December 1983, Anuario de Legislación de Jurisprudencia Argentina, 1983-B-1944. Osiel, 'The Making of Human Rights Policy', p. 136; Comisión Nacional Sobre la Desaparición de Personas, *Nunca Más: Informe de la Comisión Nacional Sobre la Desaparición de Personas* (Buenos Aires: EUDEBA, 1984), pp. 473–5; Malamud-Goti, *Game Without End*, p. 59.

10 CONADEP, *Nunca Más*; Laura Tedesco, 'The Argentine Armed Forces under President Alfonsín', *European Review of Latin American and Caribbean Studies*, 61 (December 1996).

11 Jose Luis Diaz Coludrero and Monica Abella, *Punto Final. Amnistía o Voluntad Popular* (Buenos Aires: Puntosur Editores, 1987), p. 88.

12 Diaz Coludrero and Abella, *Punto Final*, pp. 90–3.

13 Osiel, 'The Making of Human Rights Policy', p. 149.

14 Diaz Coludrero and Abella, *Punto Final*, p. 94, discusses this law, number 23.049;

Tedesco, 'The Argentine Armed Forces under President Alfonsin', p. 26. See also Kathryn Lee Crawford, 'Due Obedience and the Rights of Victims: Argentina's Transition to Democracy', *Human Rights Quarterly*, 12 (1990), pp. 21–3; and Garro and Dahl, 'Legal Accountability', pp. 306–10; Brysk, *The Politics of Human Rights*, p. 76.

15 Brysk, *The Politics of Human Rights*, p. 77.

16 See generally 'Argentina: National Appeals Court (Criminal Division), Judgment on Human Rights Violations by Former Military Leaders', *International Legal Materials*, 26 (1987), p. 317 (judgement of 9 December 1985, affirmed by the Supreme Court, 30 December 1986). See also 'Human Rights: Conviction of Former Argentine Military Commanders for Human Rights Abuses Committed by Subordinates', *Harvard International Law Journal*, 27 (1986), pp. 688, 691–8.

17 Brysk, *The Politics of Human Rights*, pp. 79–81; Osiel, 'The Making of Human Rights Policy', pp. 154–6.

18 Camps, the military commander of the Buenos Aires police, was found guilty of 600 counts of homicide and sentenced to 25 years in prison: Brysk, *The Politics of Human Rights*, pp. 80–1; Malamud-Goti, 'Punishing Human Rights Abuses', p. 162. Camps and Riccheri's sentences were reduced, while those of the inspector and others were eliminated altogether: Crawford, 'Due Obedience', pp. 28–31.

19 Tedesco, 'The Argentine Armed Forces', pp. 28–9; Garro and Dahl, 'Legal Accountability', pp. 333–4. In February 1987, a similar set of instructions was issued to federal, non-military prosecutors, again with the ostensible aim of speeding the process but with the effect of limiting the number of cases that could be pursued ibid., at pp. 336–7.

20 Pion-Berlin, 'To Prosecute or to Pardon?', p. 124; Brysk, *The Politics of Human Rights*, pp. 80–1; Tedesco, 'The Argentine Armed Forces', p. 29. Compare Crawford, 'Due Obedience', p. 25.

21 Malamud-Goti, *Game Without End*, pp. 60–2, 66; Tedesco, 'The Argentine Armed Forces', p. 30. The initial prosecution strategy was to pursue superiors who had created the repression and low-level officials who exceeded their orders: see Osiel, 'The Making of Human Rights Policy', p. 147.

22 Malamud-Goti, *Game Without End*, p. 65; Tedesco, 'The Argentine Armed Forces', pp. 30–31.

23 The Obediencia Debida legislation is law 23.521 of 4 June 1987; an English translation of the relevant portions can be found in Garro and Dahl, 'Legal Accountability for Human Rights Violations in Argentina, pp. 337–9. Malamud-Goti, 'Punishing Human Rights Abuses', p. 162; Brysk, *The Politics of Human Rights*, pp. 82–3. The Supreme Court upheld the constitutionality of this law a few weeks later; see Crawford, 'Due Obedience', pp. 17–18, and Garro and Dahl, 'Legal Accountability', pp. 339–42.

24 Tedesco, 'The Argentine Armed Forces', pp. 25–7. The final law included an amendment that excepted from such an excuse those who committed atrocious acts.

25 Tedesco, 'The Argentine Armed Forces', p. 32; Malamud-Goti, *Game Without End*, pp. 5–6, 169–70.

26 Tedesco, 'The Argentine Armed Forces', p. 32; Malamud-Goti, *Game Without End*, pp. 67–8.

27 Tedesco, 'The Argentine Armed Forces', pp 23, 32; Malamud-Goti, *Game Without End*, p. 68, suggests that the officers involved in the rebellion interpreted these civilian actions as evidence of armed subversion.

28 Tedesco, 'The Argentine Armed Forces', p. 33; Malamud-Goti, *Game Without End*, pp. 69–70.

29 Brysk, *The Politics of Human Rights*, pp. 92–106. Menem was held without charge for five years during this time. 'New Argentine Leader Won't Pardon Military', *St Louis Post-Dispatch* (16 June 1989), p. 15A; '200 Military Officers are Pardoned

in Argentina', *New York Times* (8 October 1989), p. 12; Garro, 'Nine Years of Transition', p. 17; James Brooke, 'Aide to New Argentine Chief Wants Military Trials to End', *New York Times* (12 June 1989), p. A13. Citing the need for 'unity', the defence minister to be, Italo Luder, expressed his support for amnesty.

30 'Argentines to be Pardoned', *Los Angeles Times* (19 September 1989), pt 1, p. 2. This was despite Menem's earlier announcement, largely viewed as an attempt to embarrass outgoing President Alfonsín, that the latter had asked him to co-sign an amnesty for convicted officers. James F. Smith, 'Alfonsín Reported Seeking Amnesty Deal', *Los Angeles Times* (16 June 1989), pt 1, p. 21; 'New Argentine Leader Won't Pardon Military', *St Louis Post-Dispatch* (16 June 1989), p. 15A; Brysk, *The Politics of Human Rights*, p. 84; '200 Military Officers are Pardoned in Argentina', *New York Times* (8 October 1989), p. 12.

31 George de Lama, 'Pardons Fuel the Bitterness in Argentina', *Chicago Tribune* (9 October 1989), p. 1.

32 Cesar A. Chelala, 'Has Argentina's President Granted a Privilege to Kill?', *Chicago Tribune* (17 October 1989), p. 21. 'The Ghost at Freedom's Party: Giving Amnesty to Terrorists and Torturers', *New York Times* (2 April 1990), p. A16; Brysk, *The Politics of Human Rights*, p. 84.

33 Brysk, *The Politics of Human Rights*, pp. 127–33; Andrea Malin, 'Mother Who Won't Disappear', *Human Rights Quarterly*, 16, 1 (February 1994), p. 211.

34 Brysk, *The Politics of Human Rights*, pp. 161–6.

35 Gabriel Escobar, 'Argentines Forgo Inquest on War: Confession by Participant in "Disappearances" Revived Issue', *Washington Post* (3 April 1995), p. A14.

36 Gabriel Escobar, 'Ex-Sergeant Details Role in Killings: Argentine Describes Army Abuses in '70s', *Washington Post* (25 April 1995), A13; 'Argentine Army Apologizes for "Dirty War"', *Washington Post* (26 April 1995), p. A26; Calvin Sims, 'Army Chief's Admission of "Dirty War" Rips Veil From Dark Era', *New York Times* (27 April 1995), p. A5. For the text of the interview, see FBIS-LAT-95-081 (27 April 1995) 'Army Chief Interviewed on Dirty War'. This apology was followed by an acknowledgement by the commander of the navy, Admiral Enrique Molina Pico, that mistaken methods were used during the dirty war: FBIS-LAT-95-086 (4 May 1995), 'Navy Chief Acknowledges "Mistaken Methods" During Dirty War'. The air force chief of staff, Brigadier Juan Paulik, made a similar statement: FBIS-LAT-95-086 (4 May 1995), 'Air Force Commander Regrets Dirty War "Horrors"'. However, the joint chiefs of staff head General Mario Candido Diaz said the confessors should not have spoken, and that 'We have brought up something that should have been forgotten': FBIS-LAT-95-096 (18 May 1995), 'Armed Forces Joint Staff Head Declines Dirty War Mea Culpa'.

37 Sims, 'Argentine Chief's Admission'. Just after Menem indicated that it was possible that the Obediencia Debida legislation would be reviewed, his defence minister announced that neither that law nor the amnesty laws were under review: FBIS-LAT-95-082 (28 April 1995), 'Menem May Review Abrogation of "Due Obedience Law"'; FBIS-LAT-95-082 (28 April 1995), 'Camilion: Annulling of Amnesty Laws Not Being Considered'. Menem apparently authorized this and subsequent 'mea culpas': FBIS-LAT-95-06 (4 May 1995), 'Menem on Ex-Montonero Leader's Self-Criticism, Elections'. See also FBIS-LAT-95-085 (3 May 1995), 'Menem: Navy, Air Force to Follow Suit in Self-Criticism'.

38 Pamela Constable, 'Revisiting the Horrors of Their Past: Survivors Deal with Old Pain as Argentina Comes Clean on "Dirty War"', *Washington Post* (22 May 1995), p. B1. An editorial in *La Nación* lauded the apology and argued that it would enable real reconciliation to go forward: FBIS-LAT-95-084 (2 May 1995), 'Editorial Views Value of Army Self-Criticism'; FBIS-LAT 95-112 (12 June 1995), 'Menem on Challenges, Dirty War, Economic Crisis'; FBIS-LAT-95-080 (26 April 1995), 'Menem: Charges of Atrocities in "Dirty War" to be Probed'. Indeed, the

reopening of debate may help generate a deeper consensus about the past; when former Admiral Massera, who had been convicted for human rights violations and pardoned by Menem, attempted to defend the military's past practices, he was rebuked by the army: FBIS-LAT-95-147 (1 August 1995), 'Former Junta Commander Massera on Repression, Dirty War', pp. 19–20; FBIS-LAT-95-147 (1 August 1995), 'Army Harshly Criticizes Admiral Massera's Remarks', p. 20.

39 Malin, 'Mother Who Won't Disappear', p. 212; Calvin Sims, 'Retired Torturer Now Lives a Tortured Existence', *New York Times*, (12 August 1997), p. A4.

40 'Argentina: Ex-ruler Held in Kidnappings', *New York Times* (26 November 1998), p. A10; Clifford Krauss, 'Spanish Judge Investigating Rights Abuses in Argentina', *New York Times* (29 November 1998), p. 4.

41 'Baby Theft: Argentine Hunted', *New York Times* (16 December 1998), p. A17.

42 Pion-Berlin and Lopez, 'Una Casa Dividida: Crisis, Fractura, y Conflicto en el Ejército Argentino', in Ernesto Lopez and David Pion-Berlin, *Democracia y Cuestión Militar* (Buenos Aires: Universidad Nacional de Quilmes, 1996), pp. 92–3.

43 David Pion-Berlin, 'Entre la Controntación y la Adaptación: Los Militares y la Politica Gubernamental en la Argentina Democrática', in Lopez and Pion-Berlin, *Democracia y Cuestión Militar*, p. 67. This effectively demoted the status of the heads of each force by making them accountable to the joint chiefs. The president assumed commander-in-chief functions under law 22.520; law 23.023 effected the general subordination of the heads of the forces and strengthened the role of the joint chiefs in doctrine, planning and training; see Carlos Alfredo Orgaz, *La Difícil Convivencia: Fuerzas Armadas y Sociedad Civil en la Argentina* (Buenos Aires: Nuevohacer, 1996), pp. 99–101. Moneta, 'Fuerzas Armadas', pp. 70–1, in Moneta et al., 1985.

44 Stepan, *Rethinking Military Politics*, pp. 88–9.

45 Tedesco, 'The Argentine Armed Forces', p. 25.

46 'Mensaje del Presidente Raul Alfonsín al Congreso Argentino del 17 de Abril de 1985 Presentando el Proyecto de *Ley de Defensa Nacional*, in Carlos J. Moneta, Ernest Lopez and Anibal Romero, *La Reforma Militar* (Buenos Aires: Editorial Legasa, 1985), pp. 175–206 contains the proposal of the president, much of which was eventually adopted. Marcela Donadio, 'La Construcción de una Nueva Política de Defensa en Argentina', *Fuerzas Armadas y Sociedad* (Chile), 11, 2 (April–June 1996), p. 5.

47 Donadio, 'La Construcción de una Nueva Política', p. 6. Proposals for reform that were never implemented include reform of military college curricula, and that all officials of the rank of captain or higher take civilian postgraduate courses. See David Pion-Berlin, 'Autonomía Militar y Democracias Emergentes en America del Sur', in Lopez and Pion-Berlin, *Democracia y Cuestión Militar*, p. 35; however, he simultaneously suggests that Argentina has been successful in reorienting the basic mission of the FA, pp. 45–8.

48 Horacio Salduna, *Cuadernos para la Democracia 12: La Reforma Militar* (Buenos Aires: El Cid Editor, 1985), p. 35. Deborah L. Norden, 'Democratic Consolidation and Military Professionalism: Argentina in the 1980s', *Journal of Interamerican Studies and World Affairs*, 32, 3 (1990), pp. 157–61, discusses the internal military recognition of its failings: in managing the economy, in managing counter-subversion, and in preparing for other types of war.

49 Donadio, 'La Construccion de una Nueva Politica', p. 7; Juan A. Ferreira Pinho, 'Evolución del Sistema de Defensa Argentino', *Fuerzas Armadas y Sociedad* (Chile), 11, 2 (April–June 1996), pp. 9–10.

50 This was despite a 1988 law exluding the military from internal security and intelligence activities: McSherry, *Incomplete Transition*, pp. 139–40, 166, 223–4 and 225.

51 McSherry, *Incomplete Transition*, pp. 235–7, 247–8.

52 McSherry, *Incomplete Transition*, p. 273, does not elaborate on this, although obviously with regard to mission a significant degree of autonomy did remain.
53 Stepan, *Rethinking Military Politics*, p. 77. However, it is worth noting that it may be roughly equivalent to pre-Proceso allocations: Norden, 'Democratic Consolidation', p. 165 (discussing the military budget as a percentage of GNP). Estimates of such spending fluctuate; Pion Berlin says that spending fell 40 per cent between 1983 and 1986; see 'Autonomia Militar', pp. 37–9. Such figures can vary, of course. Further, the relevant figure may be the proportion of the national budget devoted to the military: McSherry places that figure at 4.39, 3.23 and 2.84 per cent for the years 1983, 1983 and 1985 respectively, a steady decline. Further, while the number of members of the military were cut, this was achieved by slashing conscripts, not officers, whose numbers remained steady: *Incomplete Transition*, pp. 119 and 150.
54 Tedesco, 'The Argentine Armed Forces', pp. 21–2.
55 Lázara, *Poder Militar*, p. 230, also notes that in the 25 years before this period only two had completed their terms.
56 Alain Rouquie, 'El Poder Militar en la Argentina de Hoy: Cambio y Continuidad', in Peter Waldmann and Ernesto Garzon Valdez (eds), *El Poder Militar en la Argentina (1976–81)* (Frankfurt: Verveurt, 1982), pp. 67–8. Like many other militaries, the Argentine one was isolated from most of society, mixing only with civilian elites: McSherry, *Incomplete Transition*, pp. 35–6; Orgaz, *La Difícil Convivencia*, pp. 26–8. Other scholars note that there was a national history of scapegoating, including that of communism, dating to at least the 1930s: Lazara, *Poder militar*.
57 CONADEP, *Nunca Más*, p. 475. McSherry, *Incomplete Transition*, p. 53.
58 General Camps argued in a newspaper article in 1981 that the USA and France were the key propagators of the doctrine: see CONADEP, *Nunca Más*, pp. 473–4. See also Carlos J. Moneta, 'Fuerzas Armadas y Gobierno Constitucional despues de Malvinas: Hacia una Nueva Relacion Civil–Militar?', in Moneta *et al.*, *La Reforma Militar*, pp. 20–2.
59 Lopez, *Seguridad Nacional*, pp. 62–3, says that between 1950 and 1965, for example, 1,375 officers were trained in the USA, and another 256 at extraterritorial bases out of a military totalling 132,000 By 1979, some 4,017 members of the military had attended specialized US military schools through American programmes of military assistance: Lázara, *Poder Militar*, p. 172. The doctrine derived not just from the USA, but also from the French experience in Indochina: the first inter-American course on counter-revolutionary war was given in Buenos Aires with the participation of two French instructors in 1961: ibid., p. 118.
60 Lopez, *Seguridad Nacional*, pp. 174–81.
61 Garro and Dahl, 'Legal Accountability', pp. 288–9.
62 Lopez, 'Doctrinas Militares en Argentina: 1932–1980', in Moneta *et al.*, *La Reforma Militar*, p. 136. The agenda indeed extended well beyond security to the reform of education and the imbuing of Catholic doctrine. See Arnold Spitta, 'El "Proceso de Reorganización Nacional" de 1976 a 1981: Los Objectivos Basicos y su Realización Practica', in Waldmann and Valdes, *El Poder Militar*, pp. 79–80.
63 Daniel Frontalini and Maria Cristina Caiati, *El Mito de la Guerra Sucia* (Buenos Aires: CELS, 1984), pp. 6–7, 11–36. The exaggeration of the guerrilla threat was particularly ironic as the miltiary had proclaimed victory over them but a few years previously: Spitta, 'El "Proceso"', p. 80.
64 Colonels H. P. Ballester, J. L. Garcia, C. M. Gazcon and A. B. Rattenbach, excerpts from 'Fuerzas Armadas Argentinas: El Cambio Necesario. Bases Políticas y Técnicas para una Reforma Militar', reprinted in ONUSAL and Fuerza Armada de El Salvador (eds), *Doctrina Militar y Relaciones Ejército/Sociedad* (San Salvador: ONUSAL and Fuerza Armada de El Salvador, 1994), pp. 197–201. See also Osiel, 'The Making of Human Rights Policy', p. 174.

65 Moneta, 'Fuerzas Armadas', pp. 14, 20–2, 51. See also Virgilio R. Beltrán, 'Political Transition in Argentina: 1982 to 1985', *Armed Forces and Society*, 13, 2 (Winter 1987), p. 217; Salduna, *Cuadernos para la Democracia 12*, p. 38.

66 Malamud-Goti, *Game Without End*, p. 26 and *passim*, although he argues that the trials were ultimately counterproductive. On the weakness of the guerrillas, see Osiel, 'The Making of Human Rights Policy', p. 167. See also Beltran, 'Political Transition', p. 215.

67 Osiel, 'The Making of Human Rights Policy', pp. 159, 166.

5 Honduras

Justice in semi-transition

Introduction

Honduras presents a sort of transition which is different from some of the other cases examined here: transition from a military regime to a civilian regime, followed by attempts at accountability, began in the absence of a strong opposition force, civilian or military. There have been attempts to pursue domestic prosecutions of human rights violations; attempts that have thus far been slowed, but not completely thwarted, by amnesties and significant military intransigence. At the same time, the regime created the office of the national commissioner for human rights, which issued a scathing report addressing past abuses. The military's strength and political clout remained a significant limiting factor affecting efforts at accountability, but the changing international environment meant that it lost outside support and was subject to external pressure. The results of these myriad pressures were partially successful prosecutions, the report, the separation of the military and the police and the creation of a new civilian police force.

A brief history

On 3 October 1963, the military of Honduras staged a coup, making it the centre of power and only real route for political, social and even economic activity. The first change of regime came only in 1975; it was effected solely by the high command of the military, and substituted one officer for another. 1978 marked the last change of military government, when a military junta was named to rule. From then on, pressures mounted for a return to constitutionality, which was achieved with the elections of 1980. It should be noted, however, that the election was won by the Liberal Party, which was headed by a member of the previous junta, General Policarpo Paz Garcia. The 1982 elections were also won by the Liberal Party, and a formal transition to democracy took place in 1982.[1]

Until 1963, the police had been under civilian control. With the coup came the repression of the civil guard and the creation of the Cuerpo Especial de Seguridad (CES) which in 1975 became the fourth branch of the military and was renamed the Fuerza de Seguridad Pública (FSP). The unity of the police and the military continued into the new 'democratic' era, and in fact one branch of the police, the Dirección Nacional de Investigaciones (DNI) became one of the more notorious human rights abusers, routinely using unorthodox means such as torture and illegal detention to obtain information.[2]

The hope had been that with a politically spent military the installation of democracy would go smoothly. These hopes were undermined by the growing crisis in Central America and the dissemination of the doctrine of national security, which, as has been discussed above, branded as subversive the sort of opposition normal in democracies.[3] From 1980 onwards, Honduras saw a vast increase in human rights violations, many of them perpetrated by the CIA-trained Battalion 3–16. Some 184 people 'disappeared' over the course of a decade, and numerous others, largely members of the opposition – peasant organizers, trade unionists, teachers, students and Catholic clergy – were detained and tortured. From 1981 to 1984, it is undisputed that Battalion 3–16 was engaged in a systematic programme of disappearances and political murder: the Inter-American Court of Human Rights attributed the actions of plain-clothes death squads, which executed 100–150 teachers, students, unionists and travellers, to this battalion.[4] Nonetheless, until recently, no domestic action had been taken to confront the legacy of human rights abuses.

Tentative civilianization

Like many other nations in the region, Honduras has experienced long periods of authoritarianism under both military and civilian governments. Under the influence of the doctrine of national security as well as heavy external interference because of the strategic importance of Honduras in the Nicaraguan conflict, the country experienced thoroughgoing militarization.[5] Military domination was pervasive following the 1963 coup, even extending to control over the police: the FSP were structurally part of the military. This meant that, even after relinquishing formal political power, the military retained significant control over Honduran society. While the military handed over power formally in 1980–82, its domination over society continued even under civilian rule. Recently former president Roberto Suazo Cordova has strongly asserted that he had no control over the military during his presidency of 1982–86, that military control was total.[6]

Further, two amnesties passed in 1987 and 1991 continue to pose significant obstacles to the pursuit of justice against military members responsible for human rights abuses and disappearances. The first amnesty was one-sided, benefiting only agents and officials of the military tied to the repression and disappearances in the 1980s, and is not generally raised as a defence. The second amnesty, passed in July of 1991, was a wider more unconditional amnesty, benefiting members of the military involved in human rights violations as well as leftist political exiles seeking guarantees before returning to the country. A prominent criticism of this amnesty is that it was the result largely of negotiations between governments involved in the regional and domestic crisis – Honduras, Cuba and Nicaragua – and left out important groups such as human rights NGOs.[7]

In June 1992, the government created the office of the Comisionado Nacional Para la Protección de los Derechos Humanos (CNDH). In December 1993, Dr Leo Valladares Lanza issued a report, *Los Hechos Hablan por Sí Mismos* (The Facts Speak for Themselves), detailing human rights abuses and in particular disappearances perpetrated by the military. The report gives a list of the disappeared, as well as discussing some representative cases. It provides some of the testimony of the victims or their families in their own words. The report also attempts to place the domestic crisis in the context of external involvement, including the staging of contras by the USA from Honduran soil, the US involvement in the training of Battalion 3–16, and the role of the Argentinean Batallón de Inteligencia (Intelligence battalion) 601 in training Honduran officers in what is ominously referred to as the 'Argentinian method' of repression.[8] The report finally seeks to identify the units within the security forces responsible for the disappearances, concluding that they were largely the DNI and special intelligence units such as Battalion 3–16.

The new president inaugurated in 1994, Carlos Robert Reina, pledged a 'moral revolution' and an end of the armed forces' impunity from prosecution for human rights violations. He pledged to abolish the draft and to transfer authority for the police force to a civilian ministry. And, in July 1994, the first military officer was convicted for human rights violations.[9]

The tentative beginnings of transition: the Reina regime

As in many countries when periods of military domination come to a close, the question of accountability is not the only thorny, political question. Also of key significance is the future role, structure and budget of the armed forces. In Honduras, even as prosecutions of a few key figures responsible for disappearances and other abuses have gone forward, the issue of separating the police from the armed forces has been a controversial political issue.

In January 1994, when President Reina was inaugurated, the audience booed the armed forces chief, General Luis Alonso Discua. The demand for human rights is relatively new in Honduras: the public has been vocal only since the end of the Cold War, but their demands have seen some results. One of Reina's first acts was to initiate steps to fulfil his promise to end the practice of forced military recruitment, no easy task as the legislature feared military power.[10] Reina also had to face the demands of civilian pressure groups, in particular those advocating human rights, that the police be separated from the military and placed under civilian control. This process, like the prosecutions, has gone forward slowly. In May 1994, the government created the office of the special prosecutor for human rights.[11] In late 1994, General Discua acknowledged that the military bore some responsibility for the disappearances, but pointed to the Cold War in its defence.[12]

The new government also created the Comisión de Alto Nivel para la Prevención y Lucha contra la Violencia y la Delincuencia (or ad hoc commission). The commission presented its final report and recommendations after two months of work to President Reina in May 1995. Its recommendations included, *inter alia*, that the police be transferred to civilian control, that the penal code be reformed to include crimes such as kidnapping, torture and forced disappearance, and that the country ratify various international human rights conventions.[13]

From the beginning, the process of accountability was impeded by military intransigence. In June 1995, the special prosecutor for human rights, Sonia Marlina Dubon, publicly denounced the military, stating that it had burned files pertaining to the 184 disappearances of the 1980s. Dubon reported that the military claimed that the material had been burned five years before by unknown persons.[14]

Public pressure, domestic and international, on the issue of the disappearances increased with the publication of a series of articles in the USA on the clandestine actions of Battalion 3–16. In response, the military adamantly denied involvement in the disappearances, insisting that it did not possess any files pertaining to disappearances. The head of the armed forces, General Discua, acknowledged that he had been the first commander of Battalion 3–16, and stated that during that time there had existed two contenders or sides in what he referred to as a war, adding that decisions were not taken unilaterally, but with the approval of all of the authorities.[15]

In July 1995, ten military officers were indicted on charges of kidnapping and torturing six university students in April 1982, but there were delays while judges reviewed the government's evidence. General Discua declared the support of the institution of the military for those charged, while refusing to guarantee that those charged would appear in court. Meanwhile, the human rights commissioner participated in an investigation of a residence adjacent to the police academy that had reportedly served as the centre of operations of Battalion 3–16, finding evidence that files of the death squad had been removed.[16]

On 1 August, the government human rights commissioner, consistent with the expressed wishes of President Reina, asked the USA for information on the role of Honduran army officers in the disappearances of the 1980s.[17] Because of the role of the CIA in training the notorious Battalion 3–16, as well as the American role in working with the Honduran military and in training Nicaraguan *contras* in Honduras, the declassification and release of documents by both governments have been requested. However, their release has been slow and frequently unhelpful because of the blacking out of information deemed sensitive in those documents that have been released.[18]

In response to this highly publicized request for information, the military went on alert and planned a secret meeting that resulted in a campaign of intimidation. On 2 and 4 August, the army sent tanks into the streets of the capital in protest, and General Discua warned of retaliation if his men were treated unfairly. The tanks returned to their bases later, having reminded the populace and government of the army's power. The army then resorted to other means to influence politics: it sponsored a television advertisement justifying its actions in the 1980s.[19] Death threats have forced the head of the human rights commission to send his children into exile, and have been used to intimidate other human rights activists and even members of the Honduran judiciary.[20] While the army's power is undisputable, so is the increased stability of democracy, and the legal institutions for prosecution of rights abusers. Some former victims of torture have even returned to testify. Nonetheless, many Hondurans, including former president, Rafael Leonardo Callejas, expect the trials to 'create big conflicts in Honduran society'.[21] One sign of the impact of the military's pressure may be President Reina's subsequent statement that the officers charged in the disappearances would be granted amnesty if their crimes were considered 'political'.[22]

These hesitant steps towards accountability were further impeded by death threats made against the judge handling the case of the ten officers in late 1995.[23] Nonetheless, judicial attempts to air the truth went forward. In a case attempting to reveal the truth regarding a disappearance and murder, the ex-chief of military intelligence for the military was called to testify for 18 hours. In the same case, the judge announced his intent to call as a witness the current inspector of the FSP, Colonel Alexander Hernandez, whom the officer had named as the second head of Battalion 3–16. Unfortunately, that would prove impossible, as Hernandez was already a fugitive from justice in the case pertaining to the six students. The judge in the latter case issued orders for the capture of Hernandez and two other fugitives in October. The deputy director of the FSP claimed that Hernandez was on vacation and that he was unsure whether he (Hernandez) could be found in the country.[24] In February 1996, eight members of the military and 11 civilians were indicted for the murder of two persons who disappeared in 1982: they included former chief of the FSP, Castillo, as well as other high-level officers of the FSP, including Hernandez. This indictment was based on evidence recently exhumed by an Argentine forensics team.[25] A further sign of continued impunity may be the election in October 1995 of the new commander in chief of the armed forces, Colonel Mario Raul Hung Pacheco, who was implicated in human rights abuses that took place in 1993 when he headed the FSP.[26] In this selection, in keeping with tradition, the legislature chose from a trio of candidates put forth by the military.

Some small steps towards accountability were taken in November 1995, when Discua and the former president of the congress, Efrain Bu Giron, were questioned in relation to the disappearances of the 1980s, and in particular regarding the three fugitives. Discua, in speaking of Hernandez, said only that the fugitive was at the disposal of his defence lawyers. Bu Giron blamed past state security policies on the former head of the military, General Alvarez Martinez, whom he said had a phobia about communism.[27] Hernandez, still the salary-drawing inspector-general of the FSP while fugitive from an arrest warrant, was finally officially relieved of his post in November. The FSP and the military continue to plead ignorance regarding the whereabouts of the fugitive officers.[28]

As the question of past abuses has been discussed, so has the future role and structure of the security forces. Human rights advocates have been concerned both with the elimination of abusive units, whether of the police or military, but also with the permanent separation of the police and military to aid the prevention of future abuses. While the famously abusive DNI was closed in June 1994, there have been reports that some of its ex-agents have since gone to work for the police.[29] Human rights advocates have strongly advocated the separation of the FSP from the military as a crucial step towards strengthening civilian control. Beginning in 1995, progress towards that separation was made, though it has yet to be completed.

In September 1995, constitutional reforms were approved creating a new police body, and an executive decree was issued approving the transfer of funds, personnel and so on from the FSP to the new police organ. The reforms to articles 272, 273, 291 and 293 replace military domination of the police with cooperation by two autonomous bodies.[30] The reforms also establish that the police are to be professional, purely civilian and apolitical. The congress also set up commissions to draft the new ley orgánica of the police and the police code. While not directly objecting to the civilianization of the police, the inspector-general of the FSP, Colonel Hernandez, not yet a fugitive, announced that he would resign if the transfer to civilian hands didn't 'respect the hierarchy' of the institution, making clear his desire to head the new police.[31]

While various drafts of a new ley orgánica for this body were circulated, approving one was a time-consuming process. The main point of contention in the debate over the ley organica was whether the new investigative unit, the Dirección de Investigación Criminal (DIC) should be part of the police or not. The DIC was created to replace the notoriously abusive Dirección Nacional de Investigaciónes (DNI), and some have argued that uniting it with the police would be a dangerous step backwards, replicating a military, vertical hierarchy. They claimed further that, while the role of the new police is to serve and protect members of society from crime, the role of the DIC is to look for evidence for the sake of prosecution. The military, in particular, was an outspoken advocate of a unified police.[32] Thus, while the creation of a new civilian police has been agreed upon and even begun, important features of the new institution were hotly disputed.

At the same time, hesitant steps were being taken in the human rights trials to bring the ten officers charged to accountability. In September, the judge handling the cases announced the end of the summary phase of the process, remitting files on the cases to the supreme court. In October, the judge handling the cases ordered the detention of three of the accused, who would promptly become fugitives.[33] In response, defence lawyers reiterated their claim that the two previous amnesties protected their clients, General Discua announced that members of the armed forces would not come before the tribunal, and the inspector-general of the FSP threatened to sue for defamation anyone linking him with the disappearances.[34]

In January 1996, the supreme court issued a historic ruling. It reversed the decision of the appellate court that the amnesty of 1991 protected the officers, instead returning the case to the lower court for further inquiry. The supreme court found that the lower court judge, Roy Medina, had the power to find and analyse the facts and *then* determine whether the amnesty applied. Thus, rather than the amnesty becoming a bar to prosecution, the judge would have the discretion to determine how broad it was.[35] The incoming head of the military, General Mario Hung Pacheco, commenting on the trials and the fugitives, followed in the footsteps of his predecessor, claiming that he didn't know the whereabouts of the fugitives but also adding that he was not seeking to find them.[36]

Meanwhile, one of the fugitive officers held a television interview in which he acknowledged having commanded the unit that captured the six students, though denied knowing what happened to them. Further, he defiantly declared that he had nothing to regret, pointing as have many other members of the military to the existence of a two-sided war, and calling for the reconciliation of the 'Honduran family'. He named as groups with links to subversives agricultural and workers' organizations.[37] In April, despite the six-month evasion of the courtroom by the fugitive officers, another step was taken in the quest for accountability: a plan was laid out for Canadian judges to hear and authenticate the statements of ex-members of Battalion 3–16 who resided in Canada.[38]

In June 1996, Judge Celino Aguilera issued an order for the capture of 13 more officers, in addition to the already fugitive Hernandez: nine military members and five former DNI officers. These orders arose in connection with the exhumation the previous November of the bodies of two men detained by the DNI in June 1982 and found dead five days later.[39] While one officer, Lieutenant-Colonel Aben Claros Mendez, voluntarily turned himself in, others remain fugitives from justice. In a separate human rights development, a journalist announced that he would sue the state of Honduras, alleging an attack, torture, false imprisonment and forced exile perpetrated upon him by the military in 1982.[40]

In July, a plan was effected whereby military members under indictment could be detained while awaiting trial in military installations rather than prisons. This plan was subsequently upheld by the supreme court. Various observers, including the human rights commissioner, saw this decree as a concession brought about by the supreme court's fear of the military. It should not be forgotten, however, that in January the supreme court had demonstrated a new level of independence in declaring that the lower court did have the competency to proceed in trials against the officers accused of the kidnapping and attempted murder of the six students.[41]

The arrival of General Hung at the beginning of 1996 as the new head of the military brought restructuring and new appointments with ambiguous import for human rights and civilianization. On the positive side, Hung nominated a police officer to head the FSP, a move that would lead to the first police officer, rather than military man, as head of the police in 32 years. On the other hand, Hung nominated a former head of Battalion 3–16 as his proxy for head of the army. In response to Hung's announcements of restructuring, heads of human rights organizations were dubious, pointing out that most high-level posts had been given to former members of Battalion 3–16.[42] Similarly, Hung rejected the president's claim to the right to name the minister of defence and pressed ahead with his own selection, though this was a battle that he did not ultimately win.[43] Nonetheless, a positive note was struck when Hung promised to reach agreement on the transfer of the police to civilian control by the end of the year.[44]

In a significant step backwards, the outgoing head of the armed forces, General Discua, was named as Honduras' alternate delegate at the UN Security Council. Human rights organizations protested this choice vigorously, pointing to Discua's role in the founding of Battalion 3–16 and thus his implication in the perpetration of severe human rights abuses. In response to criticism, in May the president observed that there had been no proof that Discua had committed any crime.[45] Impunity would continue in other ways into 1997: as late as June the fugitive officials continued to draw salaries from the armed forces.[46]

There were other advances against the traditional prerogatives of the military in 1996. In February, President Reina bucked tradition by ignoring the three candidates proposed by the military in his selection of the new minister of defence. In response to questions about this unprecedented step, President Reina responded simply that the president could not be obligated by subordinates.[47] Nonetheless, the military would continue to reject proposals that the chief of the armed forces be replaced by the minister of defence: Reina had announced that after Hung Pacheco's departure there would be no successor.[48] Another key step was the subordination of the budget of the military to the congress, where in the past it had been set by decree. In the past, the military had not had to submit to the treasury ministry an account of expenses or of funds received; it presented only a general budget proposal. The hope was that this change would increase the transparency of the military.[49]

The civilianization of the police continued to be a key political issue in 1996. While the September 1995 constitutional reforms had raised hopes on this front, the question of the relation of the investigative unit to the rest of the police soon became salient. Shortly after the approved reforms, the military circulated a proposal that suggested, among other things, that the police be led by military officials (though those trained as police), that there be a system of social security for the police subsidized by the state, and that the new body be called the national police, not the national civilian police (PNC). Further military proposals were that the new police be under a public security secretariat rather than under the Ministerio Público (public ministry), and that members of the existing police should not be evaluated when they applied to become members of the new police. Last but not least, the military proposal called for the unification of the police with the investigative unit, the DIC, as well as other units such as the anti-drug and forest guard bodies. These proposals represented a significant step back from full civilianization, one the military would have a difficult time promoting.[50] Not only was the military suggesting maintaining as head of the police a non-civilian, it was advocating the unification of police and investigative roles, which given the disreputable history of the DNI raised strong objections from human rights advocates. As the national ombudsman for human rights, Leo Valladares Lanza, put it, the unification would be a total regression because the DIC should look for evidence in the name of society and the police should protect society from crime.[51]

Despite the absence at this point of a new ley orgánica for the police, the board handling the transfer of goods, budget and personnel to the new police began work in May 1996.[52] The military lost a key goal on its agenda in June with the creation of a new anti-drug police body to be placed under civilian control, despite the vehement objections of General Hung.[53]

The shape of the new police continued to be a matter of dispute in 1997. While the formal transfer to civilian control was made in October 1997, true civilianization could not occur until foundational legislation was in place, and this legislation remained a matter of heated debate. In April, the FSP submitted a proposal for the ley orgánica of the PNC to the legislature. Under this proposal, the PNC would be under the auspices of a ministry of public security, headed by a civilian. While the police were to be united with various other police units such as the border police under this proposal, it would fall to the legislature to determine the location of the DIC.[54]

In the legislature the leading parties, the National Party and the Liberal Party, both advocated variants on the unified police proposal, but various minority parties banded together to prevent the approval of any law without due consideration of the opinions of all political elements. The human rights group representing the families of the disappeared was particularly outspoken in opposition to a unified police.[55] In August 1997, legislation was drafted to enable a Junta Interventora (advisory board) to oversee the transfer of the police, with the mandate to direct, evaluate and purify the corps.[56]

The debate over the ley orgánica of the new police dragged on into 1998. In February, the designated drafters delivered a proposal that would create a unified police under a ministry of security. Within that ministry would be established two subsecretariats, one for investigation and one for the police. The draft law further established that the head of the DIC would be a civilian. The law also authorized the ministry of security to create special police bodies in areas such as drugs and transit. Additionally, the law provided for a new academy for the police, to be under the auspices of the police subsecretariat, which would be responsible for the technical and professional formation of the new police.[57]

This proposal was strongly denounced by the commissioner for human rights, as well as a consultative group to the president, the Foro Ciudadano de Seguridad Pública (citizen forum on public security). The Foro Ciudadano denounced the plan for a unified police as the brainchild of the military, claiming that it sought to replicate the vertical, centralized nature of the military in the police, which ought to be civilian and democratic. It argued that the investigative function should remain in the Ministerio Público, rather than being transferred to that of security, and pointed to other Central American states as exemplary.[58]

The Foro further objected that the police have not been properly 'purified', and that individuals with questionable ethics were aspiring to top posts in the new police.[59] The body created to effect purification, the Junta Interventora, has, according to many, carried out only a superficial cleansing, in part as a result of its limited powers; even some officials of the FSP have suggested the need for stronger mechanisms. In March 1998, however, the Junta was to present a list of names of corrupt officials and human rights violators to the president, Carlos Flores. It remains to be seen whether an effective purification can be carried out.[60] While objections to the new law were strenuous, positive features included making the head of the new ministry of security a civilian, and the police officially a civilian, professional, apolitical body. And although the police and DIC were placed in the same ministry, they were to be headed by separate subsecretariats. The law also created a national police council which is to include representatives from, *inter alia*, the supreme court, the commissioner for human rights, and 'civil society'.[61]

In late 1997, another significant step was taken with the imprisonment of Colonel Suarez Benavides for two 1982 disappearances.[62] Further, in 1998 several key events occurred in the trials of the military officers charged with kidnapping and torturing six university students. In February, in the case of Juan Blas Salazar, the amnesty was applied in his favour. On the positive side, however, rather than being a bar to the progress of the case and the outing of the truth, the amnesty was applied only after the facts had been established. Nonetheless, the application of the amnesty was a blow to attempts at accountability; one that the commissioner for human rights intimated might not be constitutional.[63]

Accountability through the legal process is not the only way that a government might seek to compensate victims of human rights abuses. The government of Honduras also began setting up an inter-institutional commission to provide indemnification for relatives of the disappeared of the 1980s. The commission would be made up, *inter alia*, of representatives of the ministries of foreign relations and justice, and of the commissioner for human rights.[64] Victims were also given access to greater information regarding the abuses of the past, with the release in late 1998 of a declassified, though heavily redacted, report regarding the extent of knowledge that the CIA had regarding the abuses of the Honduran military.[65]

In late 1998, the legislature also finally passed the ley organica for the new police. The final version of the law remained largely unchanged from the version of the spring, with its virtues and drawbacks. The legislation clearly established the professional, apolitical, impartial nature of the police, and the requirement that they demonstrate respect for human rights and the rule of law.

A national advisory council was established to supervise and advise the police, and an internal affairs division was created to investigate allegations of police misconduct. The DIC is part of the police but, while hierarchically and administratively under the secretary of state for security, it is to function under the public ministry. Education will be handled by an education section, an academic council and two police academies. The police, already constitutionally separated from the military, should request help from the latter only under certain emergency circumstances, and ex-military members were barred from top police positions.[66] Even before the passage of the law, efforts at transferring the police authority had begun, as discussed above. These were further aided by the US ICITAP project, which trained DIC instructors and made plans to aid the new police in the selection of officers and interpretation of police law.[67]

Trade-offs of transition

In this section I briefly assess the degree to which change has occurred in any of the three issue areas of primary concern to security forces: budgetary levels, institutional reform and accountability for human rights abuses.

Budget

The FSP budget rose significantly in 1995 and 1996. It was increased by 12 million and 25 million lempiras, respectively. The purpose of the increase was to raise salaries and pay for equipment, to help combat a rising level of crime.[68] A significant step towards civilian control of the military budget occurred in 1996 when it was made subject to the approval of the legislature. In a public demand for a higher budget in April 1996, the military's director of civilian affairs complained that it received only 0.6 per cent of the national budget, in particular calling for greater funds to feed recruits; it should be noted that his claim of the percentage of the budget the military commands appears to be a gross underestimate. In 1997, the national legislature approved an increase of 118 million lempiras for the budget of the armed forces, an increase of 36 per cent for the following year. However, it should be noted that part of the increase was due to an increase in educative voluntary military service. The 1998 budget allocated around one-third the amount spent in the previous year; however, that is no guarantee that spending would not exceed allocations.[69]

Institutional reform

The biggest blow, at least in theory, to the armed forces in Honduras, has been their constitutional separation from the police and civilian attempts to reassert control over military budgets. However, the military continued to dominate the selection process for their own leader. In addition, concerns have been raised that the new civilian police body has not been properly purified as yet.

Nonetheless, not only did President Reina make good his promise to eliminate forced military recruitment, the realm of activities that volunteers can engage in may become remarkably broad: according to a new proposal, they would include service in aid of health, literacy or forest protection.[70] In late 1998, the legislation establishing the new civilian police was finally established, institutionalizing its separation from the military, its apolitical nature, and so on.

Accountability

In this arena, too, there have been successes and setbacks. While numerous indictments have been handed down and trials have gone forward against high-ranking members of the security forces and former members of Battalion 3–16, some key individuals have remained fugitives, apparently with the collusion of the security forces. In 1996, a story in the *Washington Post* alleged that the Honduran military officers, along with other officers of the region, had accepted the loss of political power in exchange for impunity in the matter of human rights and silence regarding both personal and institutional finances. General Hung denied these charges.[71]

Relevant factors: analysis

Balance of forces

Honduras has a long history of military rule and military intervention in politics. As in other countries in the region, the doctrine of national security was disseminated in military training, although some observers argue that it did not take hold very strongly.[72] Nonetheless, the military ruled directly following the 1963 coup, and continued to have a hold on society through its own power and that of the FSP.

The effects of the doctrine and of military dominance were compounded by US aid to the armed forces, which included the training of Battalion 3–16, according to recently declassified documents. The full extent of US involvement in training may not be revealed with a fuller disclosure of documents, demanded not just by the national commissioner for human rights but by the president as well.[73]

Furthermore, not only did the military have a strong hold over politics, the challenge it faced from guerrilla groups was quite minimal. Reports of guerrilla activities have been of small-scale activities involving only tens of combatants at a time, and these groups have been easily quelled by the armed forces.[74] Whatever the underlying source of the nature of civil–military relations in Honduras, it cannot be denied that the military dominated over a weak state and weak civil society.[75] This continued autonomy and influence in the political sphere has meant that, even where change either initiated by or tolerated by the military may occasionally exceed its expectations, the reality or wide perception is that the military may rein in reform when it wishes.

It is worth noting that the Honduran military modernized relatively late: the professional military school was founded only in 1952.[76] As one observer has pointed out, the military developed institutionally during the Cold War, and was deeply affected by the fear of the spread of communism. This was fostered in particular by the Cuban revolution in 1959 and the subsequent declaration of communism there in 1961. This fear of ideological threat from within meant that those who simply questioned or criticized were viewed as enemies of the state, blurring the line between internal and external security. Such blurring of roles was undoubtedly exacerbated by the militarization of the police force beginning with the 1963 coup. Since the founding of the FSP in 1975, the police have been headed by a military officer, despite the availability of experienced police officers for the post.[77] The military continues to have a great deal of autonomy; further, despite formal steps to civilianize the police, no such transfer has as yet been achieved and many important details remain unresolved. Thus the distinction between internal and external security continues to be blurred.

International involvement

The US involvement in training the notorious Battalion 3–16 was only one of the ways that the USA influenced the shape of the Honduran military: aid and dissemination of the aforementioned doctrine of national security also played a role in forming its ideology. The USA has played less of a role in the transition to greater civilian authority and accountability, although undoubtedly the waning of the Cold War that inspired American interest in the region opened up the space for civilians to encroach on military authority. The USA has not, however, taken a very proactive role; until recently it was instead a passive party that did not advocate or aid the transition. It has only recently begun to facilitate police reform via ICITAP. Other international actors, too, have played virtually no role, beyond the early judgement of the Inter-American Court of Human Rights and pressure from NGOs (but not, notably, from international organizations).

Length and intensity of conflict

While Honduras laboured first under direct military rule and then under violence and repression despite a formally civilian constitution, for more than 30 years, its history differs otherwise from many nations in the region. Repression was widespread and military prerogatives broad, but there were 'only' 184 disappearances in that country. This may actually have made the pursuit of prosecutions easier: the narrower scope of possible prosecutions meant fewer members of the security forces were threatened and thus there was possibly a smaller threat to stability. This should not be overstated: as we have seen, the military has been fairly outspoken in defence of its own.

Conclusion

In Honduras, as in the other countries examined here, we see the divergent effects of the factors I emphasize. Military strength and intransigence posed a significant threat to attempts at accountability. However, the changing international environment and the relatively small number of disappearances may have facilitated attempts at accountability. The regime seems to have engaged in a delicate set of trade-offs, pursuing accountability and revelation of past abuses as well as police reform, but accepting a significant increase in the military budget.

Notes

1 Leticia Salomon, *La Violencia en Honduras 1980–1993* (Tegucigalpa, Honduras: Centro de Documentación de Honduras, 1993), pp. 35–6. The text of the 1982 constitution sets forth a democratic form of government, at least grants nominal control over the size of the armed forces to the congress, and articulates a set of rights that is broad, but also sets forth conditions under which these rights may be suspended. See 'Constitución de la República de Honduras', available at: http://www.georgetown.edu/LatAmerPolitical/Constitutions/Honduras/honduras.html.

2 Salomon, *La Violencia*, pp. 39–41.

3 Salomon, *La Violencia*, p. 36.

4 Amnesty International, *Honduras: Civilian Authority–Military Power; Human Rights Violations in the 1980s* (London: Amnesty International, 1988), pp. 4–5; 'President to Ask U.S. to Open Files on CIA "Operations", FBIS-LAT-95-116 (16 June 1995), p. 23; Anne Manuel, 'Death Squad Debris: Honduras Struggles with the Legacy of CIA-trained Rights Abusers', *Washington Post* (28 November 1993). Argentina also played a key role in the training of Honduran security forces that may have contributed to human rights abuses. See 'Siguen Demandas de Desclasificación de Documentos', *Los Hechos Hablan por sí Mismos* (hereafter *Los Hechos*), 19 (August 1996), p. 5. On recently declassified documents on this matter, see 'Pentagon Entrenó a Oficiales del 3–16', *Los Hechos*, 27 (May 1997), p. 7. While the numbers of disappeared are fairly small compared to the vast abuses in El Salvador and elsewhere, they made a strong impression on this tiny nation of 5 million people. The government of Honduras was found to be accountable for the involuntary disappearance of a student, Manfredo Velasquez. See Inter-American Court of Human Rights, Judgement in *Velasquez-Rodriguez* case, *International Legal Materials*, 28 (1989), p. 291; Manuel, 'Death Squad Debris'.

5 Comisionado Nacional de los Derechos Humanos (CNDH), *El Difícil Tránsito Hacía la Democracia* (Tegucigalpa, Honduras: Comisionado Nacional de los Derechos Humanos, 1996), p. 11.

6 The ex-president's assertion should not be taken entirely at face value, taken in the context of a public race by all parties to evade responsibility for the disappearances of the 1980s. Nonetheless, Cordova, arguing that he had been little more than a figurehead, displayed a number of letters to officials of the military and FSP regarding complaints of human rights abuses which were apparently never answered: 'Ni Civiles ni Militares Admiten Cuota de Responsabilidad en Desapariciónes', *Los Hechos*, 8 (September 1995), p. 10.

7 The text of the amnesty of 1991 can be found in executive decree No. 87–91', at http://www/us.net/cip/cdh/amnistia.htm. Decree 87–91 granted amnesty to those in prison for political crimes: CODEHUCA, *Informe Trimestral Sobre la*

Situación de los Derechos Humanos en Centroamerica (September 1995), p. 62; 'El Laberinto de la Amnistía', *Los Hechos*, 10 (November 1995), pp. 1–2.

8 The commission was established by executive decree No. 26–92 of 8 June 1992, and reformed by executive decree No. 51–92 of 8 September 1992. The office was formally incorporated into the constitution and implementing legislation enacted in February and October of 1995, respectively. See CNDH, *El Díficil Tránsito*, pp. 85–9; Comisionado Nacional de los Derechos Humanos, *Los Hechos Hablan por Sí Mismos* (Tegucigalpa, Honduras: Editorial Guaymuras, 1994).

9 John Otis, 'New Civilian President has Honduran Military on the Run', *San Francisco Chronicle* (1 April 1994), p. A17.

10 Reina's election and successful inauguration is itself important, as he was a lawyer with a background in human rights, and to the left of centre. In response to Reina's plans to abolish forced recruitment, Discua suggested sarcastically that the president must have been 'without advisers' when he decided to take that action. The change in the constitution's article 276 was perhaps aided by his electoral mandate and massive demonstrations against forced recruitment: Otis, 'New Civilian President has Honduran Military on the Run'.

11 Otis, 'New Civilian President has Honduran Military on the Run'; Manuel Gamero, 'Honduras:¿ Despertó La Sociedad Civil?', *Tendencias*, 36 (December 1994–January 1995), p. 18; Comité de Familiares de Detenidos Desaparecidos en Honduras (COFADEH), 'Visión General de la Situación de los Derechos Humanos en Honduras', in Comisionado para la Defensa de los Derechos Humanos (CODEHUCA), *Informe Trimestral Sobre la Situación de los Derechos Humanos en Centroamerica* (December 1996), p. 43.

12 CODEHUCA, 'Destellos Bajo las Sombras' (San Jose, Costa Rica: CODEHUCA, May 1995), p. 19. In December, General Discua stated in regard to the disappearances of the 1980s: 'Fue nada más un resultado, un producto de la guerra fría, un producto de la aplicación de la política de seguridad nacional que se aplicó en los anos 80.' This defence would be repeated by his successor, General Mario Hung Pacheco, who asserted that the disappearances were part of the past, and pointed to the Cold War as a defence: 'Jefe Electo de FFAA: Desapareciónes Forman Parte del Pasado', *Los Hechos*, 10 (November 1995), p. 5.

13 'Comisión AD-HOC Presenta Recomendaciónes al Presidente', *Los Hechos*, 4 (May 1995), p. 8.

14 'Denuncia Fiscalia: Militares Quemaron sus Archivos', *Los Hechos*, 5 (June 1995), p. 5.

15 'Reacciónes Públicas: Militares', *Los Hechos*, 5 (June 1995), pp. 8–9. These somewhat contradictory statements suggest that Discua perhaps sought to lay the foundation for a superior orders defence. Rumours circulated of an internal military report on past abuses drafted by an indicted and fugitive officer but it was not released; the military denied the official nature of the document. See 'Esperan que Informe Arroje luz Sobre Abusos de Militares', in *La Nación* (Costa Rica) (15 February 1996) at http://www.nacion.co.cr/CentroAmerica/Archivo/1996/febrero/15/honduras.html#1.

16 Ginger Thompson, 'Trial of 10 Military Officers may be at least a Month Away', *Baltimore Sun* (13 August 1995), p. 9A. The special prosecutor has gone ahead with these cases despite a decision by a commission named by the supreme court that forced disappearance was not formally a crime and the officers should be punished for other crimes: COFADEH, 'Visión General', p. 49. The text of the indictment can be found in 'Acusaciónes y Denuncias Presentadas por la Fiscalia General de la República de Honduras, en los Casos de Violaciónes a los Derechos Humanos', at http://www.us.net/cip/cdh/Acusacio. 'Armed Forces Chief to Support Accused Military Officers', FBIS-LAT-95-148 (2 August 1995), pp. 15–16; Reina, however, articulated his confidence that the military would not rebel: see 'Reaffirms

Loyalty of Military', FBIS-LAT-95–150 (4 August 1995), p. 16; 'Ministerio Público Sienta a Diez Oficiales en el Banquillo', *Los Hechos*, 6 (July 1995), pp. 8–9.

17 Honduras requested information not only on the activities of Battalion 3–16, but on CIA covert operations more generally: 'President to Ask U.S. to Open Files on CIA "Operations"', FBIS-LAT-95–116 (16 June 1995), p. 23.

18 For an account of the requests and resultant release of information, see Leo Valladares Lanza and Susan C. Peacock, *In Search of Hidden Truths: An Interim Report on Declassification by the National Commissioner for Human Rights in Honduras* (Tegucigalpa, Honduras: Comisionado Nacional de los Derechos Humanos, 1996), pp. 3–5.

19 'Honduras Tanks in Streets', *Houston Chronicle* (3 August 1995), p. 29; Tim Johnson, 'Trials May Lay Bare a Dark Time of Terror in Honduras', *Houston Chronicle* (17 August 1995), p. 25; 'Tank Mobilization in Capital Viewed as Threat', FBIS-LAT-95–150 (4 August 1995), p. 15. The request for information relating to the acts of Battalion 3–16 would be particularly disturbing to the military because, according to human rights advocates, members of that battalion now occupy 30 per cent of key posts in the military: see COFADEH, 'Visión General', pp. 48, 50. Discua denied that the military intended to intimidate anyone by sending tanks into the streets: see 'Gen. Discua on Charges Against Officers', FBIS-LAT-95–150 (4 August 1995), pp. 17–18. Other alleged acts of intimidation include threats against judges and attempts to influence victims: CODEHUCA, *Informe Trimestral* (September 1995), p. 62; Ginger Thompson, 'Tainted Honduran Army Turns to TV Ads', *Baltimore Sun* (9 August 1995), p. 1A.

20 'Amenazas Contra Funcionarios', *Los Hechos*, 4 (May 1995), p. 6. Human rights advocates claim that the campaign of intimidation and propaganda is ongoing: see COFADEH, 'Vision General', pp. 43, 46–7. See also COFADEH, 'Informe Sobre la Situación de los Derechos Humanos en Honduras', in CODEHUCA, *Informe Cuatrimestal Sobre la Situación de los Derechos Humanos en Centroamerica* (May 1997), pp. 48–50. According to Bertha Oliva de Nativi, the head of COFADEH, the group of relatives of the detained or disappeared, the campaign of intimidation against NGOs and non-military government organizations continues even as the military is slowly relinquishing control. Author's interview with Ms Oliva de Nativi, (Tegucigalpa, 24 November 1997).

21 Most recently, a reported coup plot may or may not have been linked to objections of military members to prosecution. See 'Honduras Derails Army Plot', *Sun Sentinel* (Fort Lauderdale) (30 July 1996), p. 6A; Johnson, 'Trials May Lay Bare a Dark Time of Terror in Honduras'. Indeed, General Discua, while voicing support for accused officers, has promised to follow the law, though he was ambiguous about whether some accused officers would appear for trials: 'Armed Forces Chief on Support to Accused Military Officers', FBIS-LAT-95–148 (2 August 1995), pp. 15–16. 'Gen. Discua on Charges Against Officers', FBIS-LAT-95–150 (4 August 1995), pp. 17–18. The possibility of military uprisings has repeatedly been raised, despite President Reina's attempts to calm fears abut them: 'Reaffirms Loyalty of Military', FBIS-LAT-95–150 (4 August 1995), pp. 16–17.

22 'President Comments on Amnesty, Praises Prosecutor', FBIS-LAT-95–156 (14 August 1995), pp. 18–19.

23 'Amenazan de Muerte a Juez Roy Medina', *Los Hechos*, 9 (October 1995), p. 6.

24 COFADEH, 'Exhumaciónes en Honduras: Sus Efectos Practicos' (COFADEH publication, 1996), p. 2 (case of Nelson McKay). 'Ex-jefe de Inteligencia Militar Comparece ante Juez', *Los Hechos*, 9 (October 1995), p. 11. Despite being a fugitive from justice, Hernandez would retain his post and continue to draw a salary for some time: 'Profugos de la Justicia Tres Oficiales de las FFAA', *Los Hechos*, 9 (October 1995), p. 12. General Discua denied that the military was rebelling against civilian authority in reaction to the arrest orders, but reiterated that the

judiciary should address the applicability of the amnesty decrees soon. In separate statements, Discua declared that the defence of these officers was their own concern, not that of the military, which some officers felt to be unfair, observing that those being prosecuted had been following orders: 'Oficiales Presionan a su Jefe por Defensa de Procesados', *Los Hechos*, 9 (October 1995), p. 13.

25 'Militares y Civiles Acusados de Muertes', in *La Nación* (Costa Rica) (15 February 1996), at http://www.nacion.co.cr/CentroAmerica/Archivo/1996/febrero/15/honduras.html#1; 'Juicio a Militares por Violaciónes a los Derechos Humanos', at http://www.codeh.hondunet.net/juicio.htm.

26 'Congreso Nacional Ratifica al Jefe de las Fuerzas Armadas', *Los Hechos*, 9 (October 1995), pp. 4–5.

27 'Autoridades Declaran Sobre Caso de los Desaparecidos', *Los Hechos*, 10 (November 1995), p. 10.

28 'Policía Destituye a Inspector Profugo', *Los Hechos*, 10 (November 1995), p. 11. While the DIC has made some attempts to locate the fugitives, Hernandez's lawyer threatened to seek the criminal prosecution of the heads of the DIC should they seek to execute the orders of capture. Oliva de Nativi, like many human rights activists, is sceptical of this claim, asserting that the FSP has closed ranks to help the fugitives evade capture, and that the DIC doesn't pursue the fugitives in earnest out of fear. Author's interview with Oliva de Nativi.

29 'Policía Reforzo Filas con ex Agentes de la DNI', *Los Hechos*, 6 (July 1995), p. 13.

30 'Septiembre: Los Contradictorios Pasos para la Democracia', *Los Hechos*, 8 (September 1995) pp. 1–2.

31 'Congreso Nacional Aprobo Traspaso de Policía a Civiles', *Los Hechos*, 8 (September 1995), pp. 8–9.

32 Comisionado, *El Dificil Tránsito*, pp. 65, 105. While this might seem to be an arcane distinction, much has been made of this distinction because of the abusive history of the police; many human rights groups and others seem to fear that a unified police would enable a back door remilitarization of a new civilian police.

33 Larry Rohter, 'Honduras Confronts Military Atrocities of the 80's', *New York Times* (21 December 1995), p. A10.

34 'Caso de los Desaparecidos: Oficiales no se Presentan a Tribunales, Pero la Demanda Prosigue', *Los Hechos*, 8 (September 1995), p. 12.

35 'Corte Suprema de Justicia Emite Historico Fallo', *Los Hechos*, 12 (January 1996), p. 4. The defendants claimed the court had been influenced by a leftist bias; the military had warmly greeted the earlier ruling, arguing that it would provide for reconciliation and unity: ibid., p. 5.

36 'Cambios al Interior de las Fuerzas Armadas bajo una Nueva Jefatura', *Los Hechos*, 12 (January 1996), p. 12.

37 'Capitan Prófugo se Presenta ante Medios de Comunicación', *Los Hechos*, 13 (February 1996), pp. 8–9. The captain alleged the occurrence of a number of terrorist acts, and a larger number of bank assaults that formed their financial support.

38 'Oficiales Prófugos Cumplen seis Meses de Evadir la Justicia', *Los Hechos*, 15 (April 1996), p. 9. In May of 1997, information including statements made by ex- 3–16 members was provided to Honduras by Canada: 'Canada Envia Información Sobre Ex-miembros del 3–16', *Los Hechos*, 27 (May 1997), p. 8.

39 'Ordenan Captura contra 13 Oficiales Mas de las FFAA', *Los Hechos*, 17 (June 1996), pp. 8–9. See also 'Juicio a Militares por Violaciónes a los Derechos Humanos'.

40 'Anuncian Nueva Demanda contra Estado Hondureño', *Los Hechos*, 17 (June 1996), p. 10.

41 Comisionado, *El Dificil Tránsito*, pp. 71–2, 101, 108; 'Juicio a Militares por Violaciónes a los Derechos Humanos'; 'Corte Ratifica auto Acordado que Beneficia

a Militares,' *Boletín Informativo del Comisionado Nacional de Derechos Humanos de Honduras* (hereafter *Boletín Informativo*) (30 September 1997), at http://www.us.net/cip/cdh/970930.htm. Further judicial independence was demonstrated in late 1997 when the president of the supreme court rejected the thesis that the fugitive military officers were afraid of judicial instability, stating that it was simply because they did not want to present themselves: 'Corte Suprema Garantiza Seguridad Juridica a los Militares Profugos', but compare the critique of administrative inefficiency in the judiciary in Poder Judicial es Deficiente y Precaria su Administración', in *Boletín Informativo*, 3, 709 (17 December 1997), available at http://www.us.net/cip/cdh/971217.htm.

42 'Cambios al Interior de las Fuerzas Armadas', p. 13. Shortly thereafter, in July 1996, four officers were arrested, accused of plotting to oust Hung Pacheco: see 'Honduras Derails Army Plot', *Sun Sentinel* (30 July 1996), p. 6A. 'Cupula Militar Señalado como Responsable Desapariciónes Forzadas', *Los Hechos*, 13 (February 1996), pp. 6–7, gives a list of new appointees and their history with the notorious battalion. For example, in 1996, the head of the FSP was alleged to have been involved in a variety of killings in 1988 when leading the 7th infantry battalion.

43 'Presidente Desmiente Falta de Autoridad', *La Nación* (Costa Rica) (15 February 1998), at http://www.nacion.co.cr/CentroAmerica/Archivo/1996/febrero/15/honduras.html#1.

44 'Cambios al Interior de las Fuerzas Armadas', p. 13.

45 'Ex Jefe de las Fuerzas Armadas al Consejo de Seguridad de la ONU', *Los Hechos*, 12 (January 1996), p. 16; 'COFADEH Reitera Protesta por Nombramiento de Ex-jefe de las FFAA en ONU', *Los Hechos*, 16 (May 1996), p. 6.

46 'Fuerzas Armadas Siguen Pagando Sueldos a Oficiales Profugos Denuncia Fiscal General', *Boletín Informativo*, 3, 577 (10 June 1997), at http://www.us.net/cip/cdh/970610.htm.

47 Comisionado Nacional, *El Difícil Tránsito*, p. 28; 'Por Primera Vez el Titular del Ejecutivo Nombra a su Ministro de Defensa', *Los Hechos*, 13 (February 1996), p. 3.

48 '"Despues de Hung Pacheco no Seguira Nadie: Reina", and Cargo de Jefe de las FF.AA. no sera Sustituido por Ministro de Defensa', *Boletín Informativo*, 3, 637 and 639 (4 and 8 September 1997), available at http://www.us.net/cip/cdh/970904.htm and /970908.htm.

49 Comisionado Nacional, *El Difícil Tránsito*, pp. 27–8.

50 '¿Traspaso o Reciclaje de la Nueva Policía?', *Los Hechos*, 16 (May 1996), pp. 1–2; 'Se Reaviva Discusion Sobre Traspaso de la Policía a Civiles', *Los Hechos*, 16 (May 1996), pp. 4–5; 'Inician Proceso de Traspaso de Policía', *Los Hechos*, 16 (May 1996), p. 3.

51 'Se Reaviva Discusion Sobre Traspaso', p. 5.

52 'Inician Proceso de Traspaso de Policía', p. 3.

53 'Civiles Dirigiran Policía Antinarcóticos', *Los Hechos*, 17 (June 1996), p. 3. In a move not likely to increase his credibility, General Hung, in response to a proposal for conditioning lending on military reduction, accused the USA of wanting to eliminate the militaries of Honduras and other developing countries: 'Militares Temen Eliminación de las FFAA', *Los Hechos*, 17 (June 1996), p. 3.

54 'FFAA Traspasará la Policía al Sector Civil el 21 de Octubre', *Boletín Informativo* (8 October 1997), at http://www/us/net/cip/cdh/971008.htm; 'Policía Militar Presenta su Propio Proyecto de Policía Civil', *Los Hechos*, 26 (April 1997), p. 13.

55 The head of the organization, Bertha Oliva de Nativi, argued that the goal of a unified police was to control the investigative process and protect the rest of the armed forces: 'Inician Concertación de la Ley Organica de la Policía', *Los Hechos*, 28 (June 1998), p. 9.

56 'Junta Interventora Hará el Traspaso de la Policía', *Boletín Informativo*, 3, 623 (15 August 1997), at http://www.us.net/cip/cdh/970815.htm.

57 'Una Sola Policía Establece el Proyecto del Congreso', *Tiempo* (25 February 1998), p. 8. An outline of the key points of the proposal can be found in 'La Tesis Sobre Policía del Congresa Nacional', *El Heraldo* (4 March 1998), p. 16.
58 Eduardo Lopez, 'Congreso Intenta Acatar Voluntad de FF.AA. de una Policía Vertical', *Tiempo* (25 February 1998), p. 6.
59 Leonarda Andino, 'Junta Interventora no ha Depurado la Policía', *El Heraldo* (5 March 1998), p. 15; 'Foro Ciudadano Analizará Proyecto de Ley de Policía para Proponer Reformas', *La Tribuna* (6 March 1998), p. 10.
60 Thelma Mejia, 'Depuración, la Otra Espina en la "Nueva" Policía', *El Heraldo* (8 March 1998), pp. 28–9. It was the junta that finally put a stop to the continued drawing of salaries by the three fugitives: ibid., p. 29.
61 Dagoberto Rodriguez, 'DIC Formará Parte de la Policía Nacional', *La Prensa* (25 February 1998), p. 11A. In a fine splitting of hairs, the proposal stipulates that both the police and the DIC will belong 'administratively' to the ministry of security, but that 'operationally' the DIC will be an auxiliary organ of the Ministerio Público. For the text of the part of the proposal relating to the DIC, see 'La Dirección de Investigación Acatará Ordenes de la Fiscalia', *El Heraldo* (26 February 1998), p. 4.
62 Benavides, as director of migration at the time, was charged with responsibility in the disappearances of a Nicaraguan and a Honduran near the border following their detention: '"FFAA me Dejaron Solo, soy Inocente" declara Suarez Benavides', and 'Coronel Suarez Benavides en la PC', *Boletín Informativo*, 3, 632 and 634 (27 August and 1 September 1997), at http://www.us.net/cip/chd/970827.htm and 970901.htm.
63 Eduardo Lopez, 'Delitos de les Humanidad son Imprescriptibles', *Tiempo* (4 February 1998), p. 4.
64 'Gobierno de Honduras Indemnizará a Familiares de los Desaparecidos', *Los Hechos*, 27 (May 1997), p. 8.
65 Tim Golden, 'Honduran Army's Abuses were Known to C.I.A.', *York Times*, (24 October 1998), p. A3.
66 Congreso Nacional, 'Ley Orgánica de La Policía', Decreto No. 156–98 (on file with current author), articles 2, 4–8, 10–11, 16, 22, 25, 31 and 44–8.
67 US Department of State, 'ICITAP Honduras Program Overview for Fiscal Year 1998', on file with current author.
68 'Amplian Presupuesto de la Fuerza de Seguridad Pública', *Los Hechos*, 8 (September 1995), p. 9.
69 'Militares Siguen Demandando mas Presupuesto', *Los Hechos*, 15 (April 1996), p. 12. The officer further complained that there was a lack of recruits in this new era of a volunteer military, suggesting a minimum wage that would be appealing. The claim cannot be accurate as the military appears to command 1.6–2 per cent of the total GDP: International Institute of Strategic Studies (IISS), *The Military Balance 1998* (London: IISS, 1998), p. 225; 'Más de 100 millones Aumenta Presupuesto de las Fuerzas Armadas', *Boletín Informativo*, 3, 710 (18 December 1997), available at http://www.us.net/cip/cdh/97128.htm.
70 'Servicio Militar Sigue en Proceso de Definirse', *Los Hechos*, 19 (August 1996), p. 10.
71 'Denuncia Washington Post: Militares Hondurenos Negocian su Influencia Política', *Los Hechos*, 17 (June 1996), p. 7. There is now a dispute over the ownership of a military investment fund worth some $280 million, as well as allegations of excessively high salaries in some businesses belonging to the military.
72 Gabriel Aguilera, *El Fusil y El Olivo: La Cuestión Militar en Centroamerica* (San Jose, Costa Rica: Departamento Ecumenico de Investigaciónes, 1989), p. 30.
73 'Pentagono Reconoce que Entrenó al Batallón Hondureño 3–16, Responsable de Asesinatos en Decada de los 80', *La Prensa* (23 May 1997), at http://www.

laprensahn.com/natarc/9705/n23001.htm. Further information was made publicly available in congressional hearings in May 1998, which dealt with access to government information as well as the specific facts of the Honduran experience. See United States House of Representatives, Subcommittee on Government Management Information and Technology, hearing, 'Access to Government Information and H.R. 2635, the "Human Rights Information Act"' (11 May 1998), available at http://www.fas.org/sgp/congress/hr051198/index.html and linked sites containing text of testimony by individuals ranging from Valladares to experts at the CIA and national archives.

74 Amnesty International, *Honduras: Civilian Authority – Military Power* pp. 10–11.

75 Aguilera argues that in fact the doctrine of national security did not take hold; that the 1969 war with El Salvador led the military to question the doctrine and the role of counterinsurgency, as they were thus underprepared for a conventional external conflict, but that the result was nonetheless the expansion of military power domestically, including its role in the social sphere: *El Fusil y El Olivo*, pp. 30–4.

76 Aguilera, *El Fusil y El Olivo*, p. 29.

77 Salomon, *La Violencia*, pp. 37–39.

6 South Africa

The exchange of truth for justice

Introduction

South Africa presents an interesting case where the exchange of truth for justice is made explicit, in the structure of the commission of inquiry and the provision for amnesty in the interim constitution. As with other countries, both enabling and limiting factors were at work. International condemnation of apartheid may have slowly pushed the regime towards change, and the change in the international environment with the fall of communism may also have affected the regime's threat perceptions. International observers from the UN and elsewhere played a role, but a much more limited one than elsewhere. Domestic opposition in the form of, *inter alia*, the African National Congress (ANC) and the Inkatha Freedom Party (IFP) formed a perennial threat to the legitimacy, though not the survival, of the apartheid regime. Also, many have suggested that the duration of the repression and rebellion produced exhaustion and war-weariness that made the situation ripe for transformation. While the outgoing regime negotiated its own obsolescence, it made sure to protect many of its civil servants, and of course the famous amnesty that meant prosecutions could proceed only against those who didn't confess. On the other hand, advances would be made on other fronts such as the reform of the doctrine and institutions of the security forces, as well as the alteration of the racial content of the military and police. Like most other countries in transition, South Africa found itself somewhere in the middle of the accountability spectrum, able to achieve some measures of justice (with the outing of the truth and the much rarer prosecution) and some measures of reform.

A brief history

In South Africa, as in the other nations discussed in this book, the task of coming to terms with the legacy of the past has been a difficult and highly politicized one, perhaps all the more so because of the length of white rule and apartheid, and the ways that apartheid discrimination and repression penetrated South African society. The political transition and new multiracial government provided for amnesties as well as the revelation of the truth and reparations to victims, but did so in rather unique ways: with individual rather than blanket amnesty, given only in exchange for admissions of guilt.

In this chapter, I discuss briefly the history of repression and resistance under apartheid before turning to the transition initiated by the white government. I then discuss the arrangements for amnesty and truth-telling in the context of the politics of transition. Finally, as I have done in my analyses of other cases, I discuss the internal and external considerations that appear to affect the feasible political outcomes.

Forty-plus years of apartheid

While racially discriminatory laws had existed in South Africa even before the National Party (NP) came to power in 1948, under that government the legislation extended, becoming more systematic and severe. Security forces were given broad powers of arrest and to detain political opponents without trial. The regime's dependence on the security forces and granting of wide latitude to them only increased with time and the vigour of the opposition.[1] Laws were passed outlawing marriage between whites and non-whites, and barring extra-marital intercourse between whites and other racial groups. Opposition anti-apartheid groups such as the African National Congress were outlawed in 1960 under the Unlawful Organizations Act, shortly after the Sharpeville massacre, which resulted in increased anti-apartheid activism. This act caused many groups to leave the country or go underground.[2]

Activism was renewed in the late 1970s and early 1980s, following an uprising in 1976 in Soweto after police shot schoolchildren who were peacefully demonstrating, and bolstered by the creation of an umbrella anti-apartheid organization, the United Democratic Front (UDF). Increased protests prompted President P. W. Botha to give the security forces greater authority and declare successive states of emergency between 1985 and 1989 imposing strict security laws; domestic opposition was viewed as terrorism.[3] Troops were placed in black townships, and violence escalated with both wide-scale detentions and torture as well as assassinations of anti-apartheid activists commonly attributed to the government. Hundreds of organizations were banned, as were some newspapers; the 'consolidated list' gagged some 500 people, who could not be quoted. The political transition began when Botha was replaced by F. W. de Klerk.[4]

The politics of transition

In February 1990, de Klerk announced the end of the ban on anti-apartheid parties such as the ANC; he also lifted a variety of other restrictions, and announced the limiting of detentions to six months and a halt to hangings. Perhaps of greatest political and symbolic importance, de Klerk freed Nelson Mandela, the ANC head who had been imprisoned for 27 years. In June, the four-year state of emergency was ended, and the ANC announced the end of its struggle to defeat apartheid via arms. While these events took the world by storm, they were based on a series of secret talks begun in 1985 with Mandela while he was still imprisoned: the talks covered a range of issues, from the renunciation by the ANC of violence to the release of political prisoners and the shape of future political arrangements.[5]

There are various interpretations for de Klerk's actions leading to negotiations with the ANC and other opposition groups. Some argue that the internal political stalemate, combined with economic problems brought on by sanctions and domestic instability, forced a recognition of the need for reform. A second possibility is that something of a normative sea change had taken place within the South African elite, generated by greater contact with liberal ideals in the international sphere, that led its members to conclude that apartheid was not morally defensible. Still another possibility is that the NP was manipulated into unplanned compromises by the dynamics of the negotiations. A final interpretation would argue that de Klerk's actions were strategic ones based upon his understanding of the political realities: that is, he initiated reform out of a recognition that it was inevitable, and in order to maintain some control over its shape.[6]

Meetings between the ANC and the government in May and August led to pledges for the release of political prisoners, though the government was slow to fulfil this pledge.[7] In February 1991, de Klerk initiated the elimination of key apartheid legislation. Negotiations continued through 1991, and in September the government, the ANC and the IFP signed the national peace accord, though this marked the beginning rather than the end of the negotiation process. The major players then agreed to participate in a negotiating forum, the Convention for a Democratic South Africa (CODESA). While the ANC, Inkatha and the NP did participate, along with 15 other parties, many other South African parties did not, and many that did take part in the negotiations were not representative but rather government creations.[8]

The CODESA meetings led to the signing on 20 December of the declaration of intent, in which the parties agreed that CODESA would initiate the process of drafting a non-discriminatory constitution, and agreed to the principles of universal suffrage and respect for fundamental human rights and civil liberties, to be protected by a bill of rights and impartial judiciary. Nonetheless, the parties remained far apart on the question of whether a new constitution would arise largely from negotiations or from a more representative process.[9]

While de Klerk initially suggested that a transitional government might rapidly be installed, he then retreated and instead called for a referendum among white voters regarding his policies of transition. Of the 87.6 per cent of voters who participated in the March 1992 referendum, 68.7 per cent approved, which at least theoretically gave de Klerk a mandate to continue on his path in negotiations.

A significant governmental attempt at investigating abuses[10] came as the negotiations were taking place, in response to black-on-black violence in townships that many attributed to a so-called third force controlled by the government and aimed at discrediting the ANC and IFP. The government established a commission, headed by respected jurist Richard Goldstone, then the head of South Africa's highest court, and later the chief prosecutor at the International War Crimes Tribunal for the former Yugoslavia. The commission had few resources, but was generally respected as objective. The Goldstone commission report was released in May 1992, finding no evidence of government involvement in the township violence and pinning the blame on the ANC and IFP; the commission held investigations between 1992 and 1995.

Negotiations in May 1992 (CODESA 2) stalled again over de Klerk's insistence that certain clauses of the constitution be approved by 75 per cent of the constituent assembly, which would have ensured that the NP could retain some control over outcomes. In response, the ANC launched what it called a mass action campaign.[11] A massacre of ANC supporters by IFP members in Boipatong on 17 June 1992, provoked the ANC to withdraw from the negotiating process and assign partial blame to government agents who allegedly aided the IFP killers. The Goldstone commission agreed to investigate this incident as well. In the context of rising ANC–IFP violence, the government and ANC agreed to a meeting in October, giving rise to the belief that both parties were interested in a negotiation process and political outcome that excluded other actors such as the IFP.

The October 1992 summit was repeatedly delayed over disputes about power-sharing and federalism. The historical overcentralization of power led to calls for decentralization via federalism; there was also a desire to enhance minority rights and self-determination, which some thought could be enhanced by federalism as well. However, the latter link would appear to hold only in a region like KwaZulu-Natal, a majority Zulu region. Naturally, the IFP, enjoying the strong support of Zulus in the region, advocated strong federalism in the hopes of achieving self-determination for Zulus, a goal the ANC opposed. The resultant provisional constitution would contain federal features, albeit limited ones. According to some, a key shift in the ANC's thinking regarding the allocation of power may have been effected by an August article by Joe Slovo advocating a 'sunset clause' enforcing power-sharing for a fixed period of time.[12]

In response to the continued violence and stalled negotiations, Mandela proposed UN involvement, requesting that the UN Security Council send a special envoy to investigate the sources of the violence. Former US Secretary of State Cyrus Vance was sent as that envoy; the result was that UN observers were sent to monitor and support the national peace accord. By September, some 50 UN monitors were sent. Other sources of observers and support included the World Council of Churches, the European Community, the Organization of African Unity (OAU) and the Commonwealth. The Goldstone commission helped the observers as well as using them as sources for its own investigations.[13] The secretary-general of the UN commended the commission's work and recommended that it look into other specific incidents and be given greater powers by the government; his report in August also recommended that an amnesty be granted for political offences.[14]

This recommendation came in the context of a wider debate about amnesty. Goldstone welcomed the suggestion, stating that such an amnesty would enable the revelation of greater information because people would not fear prosecution if they came forward. The ANC sought the release of all anti-apartheid activists; the government sought a blanket amnesty for all members of the security forces who had acted against the ANC. The NP attempted to link tightly the treatment of the two sides. While the NP had initially refused to release prisoners who had committed common crimes such as arson or murder for anti-apartheid groups, a change in the law altered its stance: the new regulations defined political crimes as ones in support, as well as opposition, of apartheid.[15] Thus the NP became eager to advance a blanket amnesty to protect its own with the benefit of the new classification, and offered to release political prisoners as a trade. On 13 August 1992, the ANC rejected this proposal, arguing that such an amnesty could be granted only by an interim government, and with the support of the people. The ANC argued that with any amnesty there must also be a full revelation of the abuses by security forces.[16] The ANC also rejected the linkage of the question of amnesty with the status of political prisoners.

On 16 October de Klerk introduced a bill that would give the executive broad powers to grant amnesty, though he continued to claim that the government had not, to his knowledge, engaged in crimes or fomented the township violence. He claimed, instead, that the goal of the bill was to level the playing field between the government and opposition groups. The bill, however, was defeated in the South African parliament: the White and Coloured houses passed the bill, but the Indian house would not. However, de Klerk then turned to the president's council, a body to resolve disputes among the three segregated houses of parliament, and which was dominated by the NP. It was through this rarely used body that de Klerk achieved the passage of the Further Indemnity Act on 9 November 1992.[17] The act empowered the president to grant amnesty to those who 'advised, directed, commanded, ordered or performed any act with a political object'[18] before 8 October 1990, though the president was given discretion to expand the time period. The law did not formally create a blanket amnesty, but rather created a national council on indemnity, which heard individual applications for amnesty in complete secrecy. Those granted amnesty would be immune from criminal or civil action, and their names would be published, though not information pertaining to the nature of their crimes or their victims.

The ANC adamantly opposed what it perceived to be a self-pardon by the government and stated that, should the party come to power, it would not execute the legislation. However, in a subsequent November document, *Strategic Perspectives*, which discussed the possibility of power-sharing with the NP, the party acknowledged that some sort of a general amnesty for security force members and civil servants would probably be necessary lest they disrupt the transition. Under the amnesty law, de Klerk commuted nearly 100 sentences and amnestied a number of former security officials.

During the debate over the amnesty bill, the ANC released a report by its own commission into abuses committed by the ANC itself in refugee camps in neighbouring countries. The report, released in August 1992, confirmed that there had been widespread torture and other abuses, and recommended that the ANC cleanse itself of the perpetrators. The commission further suggested that, as its own membership was majority-ANC, a more independent commission ought to be appointed. Further, the commission recommended that the victims receive compensation as well as psychological and other types of assistance. Mandela's response was to pledge to examine the recommendations and take action where needed, and to affirm that the ultimate responsibility lay with the leaders and their failure to monitor the situation better.[19] In January 1993, the ANC created a new commission to examine alleged abuses in its detention centres in exile. The report in August found that two senior ANC officials had violated the human rights of detainees: Joe Modise, the commander of the ANC military force, and Jacob Zuma, a former intelligence chief. Other security officials were found to be involved in serious violations including torture, execution and arbitrary detention. The commission recommended that the ANC not only apologize to victims of these abuses, but create a compensation agency for victims of abuse and the families of those who died. Further, it recommended keeping relatives of those who went missing in the camps informed of the investigations into their whereabouts, and granting former detainees the right to rejoin the ANC. Mandela promised to take the recommendations seriously, and many saw this as an important act of disclosure. The NP argued that it was proof of the organization's inability to run the nation itself, and argued that the ANC should hand over these cases to the judiciary, though it did not offer to do the same for NP agents accused of serious human rights violations. Further, in August there were reports that the state security council had ordered the destruction of classified documents in order to hide past abuses.[20]

In late 1992, as the negotiations seemed to stall, a new position was reportedly floated within the ANC camp by Joe Slovo, one which would allow for temporary concessions to whites during the transitional period. In February 1993, the national executive committee of the ANC approved a five-year transitional government with representation of sufficiently small parties that the ANC would effectively end up in a temporary power-sharing arrangement with the NP. This shift arguably helped pave the way for a return to the negotiating table in March and April. CODESA was replaced by the Multi-Party Negotiating Process (MPNP) in March 1993: this body consisted of a plenary body and various committees to address issues ranging from the protection of rights during the transition to the creation of a transitional executive council (TEC).[21] In September, the TEC was established to create conditions conducive to a free election, to be held the following April.[22] The TEC was made up of subcouncils to handle various issues and institutions, including one to oversee the security bodies by creating an inspectorate and an independent complaints body, and one to oversee defence and create a binding code of conduct for the military.[23]

On 26 November 1993, de Klerk announced his desire for a government of national unity that would be completely representative by the first half of 1994. A few days later, the chief of the KwaZulu homeland and head of ANC rival Inkatha Freedom Party, Mangosuthu Buthelezi, announced plans for a new constitution that would lead to the secession of the Natal province which included KwaZulu. The political situation was further destabilized by the declaration of war on all white South Africa by the military wing of the Pan-Africanist Conference (PAC), which carried out attacks on a steakhouse and a golf club. In response, the government cut off talks with the PAC. Tensions were exacerbated in the right wing of the South African political spectrum as well when, on 19 December, de Klerk suspended or sacked 23 military officials, six of whom were generals, who had allegedly perpetrated acts aimed at thwarting the peace and reconciliation process. This act may well have been a concession to the ANC, which had called for a purge in the military, but it also risked driving whites into the arms of extremists. Despite the heightened political tensions, the negotiations moved tentatively forward. In October, Mandela and de Klerk were jointly awarded the Nobel Peace Prize for their work towards a negotiated transition.

On 18 November 1993, the negotiations finally produced a new constitution that all but one of the parties still participating in the negotiations endorsed; the IFP and several right-wing parties did not endorse it. The interim constitution, which provides for majority rule but also provides protection for minority rights,[24] was to remain in force until a new parliament, to be elected in April 1994, could draft a new one. Several key issues are addressed in this interim constitution. The constitution provides protection for the jobs of white civil servants and military staff. However, it should be noted that this does not mean that they cannot be legally fired, but rather protects them as a group. This decision was apparently advocated by Joe Slovo of the Communist Party as part of a compromise over the thorny issue of power-sharing. In particular, the status of the Public Service Commission was enshrined in the transitional constitution: its actions in reviewing appointments were seen as protection of the old bureaucratic order.[25]

The constitution also enshrined a set of fundamental rights and created a constitutional court to interpret these rights. The court has the power to invalidate as inconsistent with the constitution legislative and executive acts. Greater rights were specifically articulated for persons who are arrested and detained. Other rights must be further interpreted by the court, which was immediately called upon to determine whether the death penalty was consistent with the right to life.[26]

The question of amnesty

During the negotiations, the question of amnesty was one of the most controversial. As is well-known, the ANC frequently voiced opposition to any sort of blanket amnesty. However, the stakes may have been raised when the police commissioner and the ex-head of intelligence approached the ANC, offering the promise that the security forces would 'guarantee stability' throughout the transition in exchange for an amnesty.[27] The interim constitution addresses the issue of past abuses of human rights, in particular the question of amnesty. The text states:

> These [violations] can now be addressed on the basis that there is a need for understanding but not for vengeance, a need for reparation but not for retaliation. In order to advance such reconciliation and reconstruction amnesty shall be granted in respect of acts, omissions and offenses associated with political objectives and committed in the course of the conflicts of the past.[28]

Parliament is further directed to enact a law setting a cut-off date and creating the mechanisms, which may include tribunals, to deal with amnesty. This provision created a constitutional commitment that would bind the successor regime. This promise was exacted by the security chiefs from the ANC in exchange for a promise of stability and the establishment of a truth commission.[29] The subsequent regime had to acknowledge some form of amnesty, but in order to 'restore the honour and dignity of the victims' this was not a blanket amnesty for perpetrators but contingent on their admissions.[30]

In the April 1994 elections, Mandela and the ANC rose to power, and created a government of national unity that included de Klerk and Buthelezi as cabinet members. The UN, in response, terminated the mandate of the observer mission a few days later. The Further Indemnity Act had been the prior regime's attempt to address the issue of past abuses, but was viewed by many as nothing more than an attempt by that regime to cover up, rather than reveal, the truth in pursuit of reconciliation. The newly elected ANC was bound by the provision in the interim constitution promising some form of amnesty, but claimed to want to seek reconciliation without obscuring the past. This intention would appear to be illustrated by the structure and procedure of the Truth and Reconciliation Commission (TRC).

The commission was established after a year of debate in 1995 by the Promotion of National Unity and Reconciliation Act. It was created to investigate and report on events between 1 March 1960 and 6 December 1993. The commission has three committees: one that deals with amnesty, one with human rights violations, and one with compensation and rehabilitation. In addition to its role in examining, revealing and where appropriate making reparations for the legacy of the past, the commission was also charged with making recommendations to ensure that such abuses do not recur.[31] All three committees have important implications for South African society but, because amnesty was particularly hotly disputed and is central to this investigation, I focus largely on the amnesty committee.

The TRC's amnesty provisions were unique among truth commissions. Those involved in political crimes, whether for the government, anti-apartheid groups or others, could apply for amnesty and indemnity, but these were only to be granted if the applicant made a full disclosure and the action taken had a political object that could feasibly be realized. The commission could only recommend the granting of amnesty – President Mandela was given the final say. The commission's proceedings were, with exceptions in the interest of justice or to avoid personal injury, open to the public. Further, the commission had an unusual amount of power in comparison to other bodies of its type in that it had the power of subpoena and of search and seizure.[32] Thus, what was created was not a blanket amnesty: evaluations were made on a case-by-case basis. Further, there were structural incentives for persons to come forward and apply for amnesty: those that did not do so by the cut-off date[33] were still subject to prosecution. Those who applied for amnesty were required not only to reveal their own involvement in abuses of the past but also to reveal information about those responsible for ordering these acts as well as what happened to victims. A series of criteria was then applied to determine whether the application would be successful.[34]

The constitutionality of the amnesty was challenged by the widow of Steve Biko. His killers had applied for amnesty from the commission. The constitutional court refused to invalidate the procedure, finding it consistent with the amnesty provision of the interim constitution, and pointing out that without this procedure there would be no incentive at all for perpetrators to admit to the truth. The court also pointed out that without the amnesty provision a negotiated settlement and the new constitution itself might not have come into being.[35]

The work of the Truth and Reconciliation Committee

The TRC members appointed by President Mandela came from various professions and ethnic backgrounds; they were chosen, *inter alia*, to comply with the requirement that they be 'fit and proper persons who are impartial and who do not have a high political profile'.[36] Before the cut-off date the TRC received approximately 8,000 petitions for amnesty; it then had the time-consuming task of sifting through them all; the report took longer than expected, but was finally issued in October 1998.

In addition to reviewing individual amnesty applications, analysing human rights violations and making recommendations with regard to reparations and rehabilitation, the commission also received reports from the two major players, the ANC and the NP, with regard to the legacy of the past. In August 1996, the ANC submitted a 90-page report to the TRC, which, while incomplete, was more thorough and honest than the 35-page NP report which largely articulated a justification of the government's actions. Only late in the NP report, in one paragraph, was there an apology by de Klerk for abuses under apartheid. De Klerk was to refer to his initial apology of April 1993 and those in the submissions to the TRC whenever critics suggested that he had failed to apologize for apartheid.[37] Both parties subsequently submitted further, more extensive statements to the TRC.

Amnesty

The commission has heard testimony from prominent figures from the anti- and pro-apartheid factions, as well as important testimony regarding the fates of powerful and well-known victims. As might have been expected, it was members of the NP and former regime, responsible for wide-scale atrocities, and members of the IFP, more recently found to have colluded with the NP to undermine the ANC during the run-up to the elections, who were particularly resistant to the process. De Klerk, in particular, was vocal about his fears that the commission could become a witch-hunt against himself and his party.[38]

High-level former political and military leaders stonewalled the commission for months, a pattern broken only in October 1996, when the former chief of police, General Johan van der Merwe, admitted his role in several notorious incidents, and laid the blame on the ministers of law and public order, adding that he believed the actions had been approved by then-president P. W. Botha. Some observers viewed this testimony as evidence that the procedural approach of the commission was finally working: van der Merwe was slated to be named before the commission by five police officers seeking amnesty, and thus needed to come forward to obtain amnesty for himself.[39] Mixed signals were simultaneously being sent by the judiciary: one high-level official was acquitted, and another convicted in late 1996 (see detailed discussion of the court cases below). Certainly, potential defendants could not fail to recognize that jail was a real possibility, making testimony before the TRC appealing.[40]

In another high-profile case, in December, the TRC freed a police officer already jailed for life in a massacre of civilians. Some observers suggested that this step was taken in the hope of generating more applications: up to that point few applications for truly political crimes had been received. Shortly thereafter, in January 1997, five police officers came forward with confessions in the killing of anti-apartheid activist Steve Biko, requesting amnesty. In April, former defence minister Magnus Malan, who had already been acquitted in connection with a set of politically motivated killings, came forward with an offer of testimony before the TRC. However, when he testified, he adamantly defended his past actions, in particular cross-border raids into neighbouring countries, and said that he would not seek amnesty in relation to operations that he authorized because he considered them 'legal acts of state'. Even while arguing eloquently for the need for the various peoples of South Africa to reconcile, Malan went on to warn that too much probing into the past would generate a reaction.[41]

After a slow start, then, the TRC began to receive testimony of greater political import, as well as a greater volume of applications. By the time the extended deadline for amnesty applications had passed, on 10 May 1997, 8,000 applications had been received, though former presidents de Klerk and Botha, and President Mandela, did not apply. However, other high-level members of the ANC and Mandela's government, including cabinet ministers and the deputy president, did apply for amnesty, owning up to sabotage and other political violence, partly in the hope of pushing white people to come clean as well.[42]

Former President de Klerk finally testified before the commission in May 1997. De Klerk appeared resistant, explaining that he had not applied for amnesty because he had not committed any criminal acts. He denied having knowledge of, much less having authorized, a wide range of politically motivated abuses, such as beatings, killings and kidnappings. He insisted that any violence had been committed by a 'few bad eggs'. De Klerk's testimony before the commission was strongly criticized by commission members, who questioned the former president's truthfulness. In response, de Klerk accused members of the commission of political bias and violation of its own regulations, and withdrew his party from the proceedings, stating that the National Party would not return until commission members played by the rules. Shortly thereafter, de Klerk went further, demanding an apology from TRC chair Tutu for his remarks and the resignation of deputy chair Alex Boraine, threatening to sue the TRC if his demands were not complied with. With the withdrawal of the largest opposition party from the TRC process, justice minister, Dullah Omar, publicly expressed concern about the threat to the future of the country. Tutu refused to comply, and de Klerk refused a counter-offer of a meeting with the full commission to resolve their disagreements.[43]

De Klerk has repeatedly acknowledged that apartheid was wrong, and offered a public apology to its victims.[44] However, despite evidence gathered by the TRC and available in the press to the contrary, he steadfastly denied that he or other high-level officials authorized or knew of assassinations. Rather, in his written submission, he referred to them as 'the criminal actions of a handful of operatives of which the National Party was not aware and which it could never have condoned'.[45] He offered the defence commonly heard not only in South Africa but many other nations where the legacy of the past is confronted, that the country faced a revolutionary threat requiring extraordinary actions, while affirming that murder and assassination were not justifiable.

Other cases at the TRC

Another prominent case for the TRC dealt with the fate of two men already convicted of the killing of a popular black leader, Chris Hani. Hani had been the head of the armed wing of the ANC, and subsequently became the head of the South African Communist Party. The two men convicted for respectively shooting and planning the assassination, Janusz Walusz and Clive Derby-Lewis, applied for amnesty. The Hani family strongly opposed the application, arguing that the two men had failed to disclose all information in their applications and were thus not eligible for amnesty. The TRC's amnesty committee eventually denied the killers amnesty on the grounds that they had failed to make a full disclosure and lacked a relevant political motivation as a defence.[46] In June 1997, President Mandela's ex-wife, Winnie, was subpoenaed to testify before the commission regarding her role in the political violence perpetrated by her bodyguards, who had applied for amnesty.[47] While many significant figures testified before the commission, there have been some important holdouts. There were accusations that the TRC has a pro-ANC bias. The IFP, alleging such a bias, largely refused to work with the commission. Following the commission's criticisms of de Klerk, the National Party said it would suspend cooperation with the TRC, demanding an apology from Archbishop Desmond Tutu and the resignation of Alex Boraine.

Former president P. W. Botha defied the commission's subpoena to testify before it three times. The TRC wanted Botha to provide information regarding the old State Security Council and its crackdown on anti-apartheid groups during the 1980s. In January 1998, Botha received a summons to answer a contempt charge for ignoring the commission's subpoenas, a charge that carries a sentence of up to two years. In August 1998, a court found Botha in contempt for his refusals to testify before the TRC, and sentenced him to a fine of $1,600 or a year in prison. However, the contempt conviction was ultimately reversed in mid-1999 on a technicality.[48]

While high-level police officials submitted applications to the TRC, members and former members of the military high command have refused to do so.[49] In an unusual step, the TRC denied the amnesty application of an officer who took part in the abuse leading to the death of Steve Biko on the grounds that he had not admitted to a crime.[50]

Prosecutions and the legacy of the past

An attempt was made to prosecute the former minister of defence, Magnus Malan, in 1996, for the atrocities of the past. Malan was charged with murder in relation to a 1987 attack on the home of an ANC supporter. However, in October, a court found Malan and all of his 15 co-defendants not guilty in this incident. Mandela moved to quell anger by announcing his acceptance of the ruling, but the victim's family was still outraged, and Tutu stated that the TRC might conduct its own investigation into the case.[51]

Shortly thereafter, on 30 October, another court found a police colonel, the former head of an assassination squad, guilty of a series of political killings. Colonel de Kock was given the most severe penalty allowed by South African law, two life sentences plus 200 years in prison. Immediately after the sentencing, some suggested that this outcome would reverse the sense of impunity many may have felt after the Malan case, and perhaps result in more applications to the TRC. De Kock himself has since submitted a detailed amnesty application to the TRC that runs to 4,000 pages.[52]

In an unusual and important case, a former police officer, Dirk Coetzee, was found guilty of a 1981 killing. The case is unique, however, in that he had voluntarily come forward in the 1980s to expose the abuses of apartheid, fled the country, and joined the ANC in 1989, later working for Mandela's government in the intelligence agency. Coetzee and his co-defendants applied for and received amnesty from the TRC.[53]

Reparation and rehabilitation

The reparation and rehabilitation committee of the TRC was set up to provide compensation to victims and families of victims. It is as yet unclear what the level of these reparations will be. The commission has, however, issued a statement of the criteria on which reparations and rehabilitation will be given. The commission chose to award rehabilitation and compensation rights not to all victims, some of whom could not be identified, but to a finite list that could be identified through specified means.[54]

The report

On 29 October 1998, the TRC released its final report. Comprising 3,500 pages, the report contained accounts that displeased all the major political players; even before its release it was controversial. Former president de Klerk threatened to go to court to stop the release of the report, which was said to have named him as an accessory after the fact for a 1986 church headquarters bombing. The TRC, facing the threat of this legal action, agreed to withhold its findings on de Klerk at least temporarily, until the matter could be judicially resolved. At the same time, the ANC, facing the threat of similarly unflattering disclosures, threatened to go to court to block the release of findings regarding its abuses, but would not be as successful.[55]

Not surprisingly, the report itself was highly critical of the apartheid era governments of South Africa, but also discussed the abuses committed by opposition movements and leaders. However, the report refused to equate the acts of the state with those of the opposition anti-apartheid groups, arguing that such groups were fighting a just war with a just cause. However, this did not mean that all anti-apartheid actions were therefore justified, and the report took the position that human rights violations could have been committed by both state and non-state actors like the ANC.[56]

The report ascribed responsibility to the state for the predominant part of the abuses, seeing a pattern of human rights violations committed largely by state security forces. The state then sought to cover these abuses, in particular its use of extrajudicial killings and its collusion with the Inkatha Freedom Party. Nonetheless, the ANC was held responsible for gross violations of human rights by its security forces, both in the course of armed struggle and in retaliation against defectors and informants. Finally, the IFP was found to be in collusion with the South African defence forces from the mid-1980s on, perpetrating gross violations of human rights against individuals perceived as the enemies of the state and the IFP.[57]

Prominent individuals were also named in the TRC report. Former president P. W. Botha presided over the state and security forces at a time when abuses were rampant and covert assistance was given to anti-ANC groups, according to the report. The former wife of Nelson Mandela, Winnie Madikizela-Mandela, was said to have been central to the formation of a vigilante group responsible for gross violations of human rights, to have been herself responsible for such violations. For the actions taken by Inkatha in collusion with the South African Defence Force (SADF), the commission held responsible, *inter alia*, P. W. Botha, Magnus Malan and ANC head Chief Mangosuthu Buthelezi. The report, in a noteworthy step, chose not to recommend lustration, or the disqualification of those implicated in human rights violations from holding public office.[58]

Reaction to the report was largely negative, as the commission had found fault with the three major players in the apartheid struggle as well as major post-peace political parties. President Mandela accepted the report, but noted that 'many of us' would have reservations about the report, whose release his party failed to block.[59] Shortly thereafter, talk of a general amnesty circulated: several major political parties called for one, and the ANC, while calling such talk premature, did not rule out an amnesty.[60]

Trade-offs of transition

Accountability

The question of accountability has been discussed at length above, so I recap briefly here. The TRC represented a significant jettisoning of accountability for an outing of the truth, but not a complete one. The stick that encouraged violators to take advantage of the carrot of amnesty and confession was the threat that a failure to apply for amnesty left one open to prosecution.

Institutional reform

Important changes in the security apparatus of South Africa are now being effected. There were several main strands of reform to be effected, which also ran directly counter to the self-image held by many in the previous regime and its military: these pertained to the composition of the armed forces, control of them and their mission. This was bound to be complicated because, as the head of the SADF said in his submission to the TRC, the old SADF members had strong ties, and care should be taken with reference to the old members.[61]

First, ex-ANC and PAC guerrillas as well as the armed forces of the four homelands are being incorporated into the National Defence Force. In the interim, a temporary National Peacekeeping Force was set up under the auspices of the TEC; while some hoped that this force, made up of contributions by negotiating parties, would form the basis for the new defence forces, but this was not to be.[62] A plan largely initiated by the senior officials of the various forces in early 1994 stipulated that each force was to present a registry of its personnel by 26 April 1994. After this, ex-guerrillas were to report in segments of 1,500 for training and review with the assistance of a British military assistance training team. Nonetheless, this process has not run perfectly: some guerrillas have not reported, and demobilization of large numbers of troops and guerrillas may pose a serious threat to stability.[63]

Second, officers from the apartheid era are being retired. While the armed forces do not yet represent the ethnic makeup of the nation, the number of black officers has increased dramatically, to 29 per cent in 1998, including the top posts in the South African National Defence Force (SANDF) and in the army.[64] In an attempt to gain international acceptance, the military has turned its attention to preparation for participation in peacekeeping operations.[65] However, the more general force structure has become increasingly top-heavy, with unusually few privates, which has also increased the proportion of the military budget devoted to personnel. At the same time, the military sought to both incorporate members from other security forces and reduce the overall number of personnel, reducing the force from a potential high of 135,000 to 90,000.[66] This reduced force would, however, be supplemented with voluntary part-time forces of up to 100,000.[67]

It is not just the composition of the armed forces that has begun to change, however; a sea change in the nature of oversight over the forces also took place. The Ministry of Defence is accountable directly to the president, and a civilian secretary of defence as well as the heads of the various branches of the armed forces advise the minister.[68] Civilian oversight has also become more salient in the arena of doctrine and mission definition, with a tussle between the SANDF and the defence minister exemplifying the gap between old and new approaches to both the process and content of doctrine definition. The role of the SANDF, as defined in the constitution, is defence of territorial integrity and sovereignty, and only secondarily as support for the police; the proposed code of conduct emphasizes, *inter alia*, respect for human rights, the rule of law and international law and civilian supremacy.[69]

The police were traditionally quasi-military, with their primary concern the protection of the apartheid system and taking part in covert operations and even battles outside the nation's borders. Thus institutional reform was a high priority.[70] It was initiated by the South African Police (SAP) themselves in 1990–91, out of a concern to maintain their legitimacy and buffer themselves from radical restructuring, and they maintained a high degree of control over the process for several years.[71] The peace accord mandated important doctrinal and structural changes that were implemented in 1993. These included the creation of a police board for oversight with civilian members, the creation of a code of conduct for the police, and local committees to hear complaints against the police.[72] Police reform has led to a merging of the country's various police forces and removal of military ranks. Under the auspices of the July 1995 police service bill, 11 forces were amalgamated into one force, though vetting appears to have been limited.[73] An attempt at democratizing the police through community policing, begun under de Klerk, continued, though with limited success.[74] Rights of citizens such as access to courts were enshrined in the bill of rights in the 1996 constitution; however, the constraints these rights placed on police may have been limited by the police powers contained in the Emergency Act of

1995.[75] Similarly, the Regulation of Gatherings Act enshrined the right to peaceful public expression; though passed in 1993 it was enacted after the change of regime.[76] A civilian oversight body was also set up to investigate complaints against the police, as well as keep tabs on deaths in police custody. Another institutional reform was a new organization structure that replaced military ranks with more common police titles. In another symbolic move, the ministry at the head of the police was renamed. At the same time these changes took place, however, President Mandela and the new head of the SAP took great pains to reassure the old guard that change would be gradual, not radical.[77]

President de Klerk asserted that, even before the transition, he had begun reviewing a number of covert operations, some of which were terminated, and that his regime also terminated the national security management system and reduced the role of the State Security Council. He also abolished the political branch of the police known as the security branch. Further restructuring took place with the 1992 creation of the internal stability division to replace the riot squads.[78]

Reform has also led to increased participation by persons of all ethnicities, in part through the incorporation of members of the ANC and other liberation movements into the new SAP. In particular, ex-fighters were incorporated as members of the VIP bodyguard service. The discredited intelligence organ for the police was also staffed by some ANC intelligence agents.[79] However, the white hierarchy has not been eliminated; instead a second tier of black, Indian and other non-white people has been established. Further, from March 1997, 47,000 of 50,000 white officers remained on the force. While a 1992 purge of conservatives in the military and SAP as well as early retirements by some of the old guard partially changed the face of the force, the vast majority of the officer corps (95 per cent) remained white.[80]

The police, once famous for abuse in support of apartheid, are now branded as inept and corrupt in the face of post-peace rising waves of crime. In addition, the separation from the military is not perfect: the police are still heavily reliant on the SANDF for support.[81] The police have, however, begun to pay more attention to respect for human rights, with training programmes on this issue supported by aid from, *inter alia*, some EU nations, the UN Commission for Human Rights and the International Committee of the Red Cross.[82] Police prerogatives were further limited by constitutional changes that clarified the fundamental rights that citizens cannot be stripped of in a state of emergency.[83]

Budgetary reductions

Another arena of importance to military establishments (and, by extension, elites that are closely linked to them) is budgetary levels. While the budget for defence rose slightly in 1994–95, that increase was due to the costs of transition such as demobilization and integration: on one analyst's account, the budget fell by 13 per cent when these costs were excluded. Further, there is some concern in military circles that readiness may be harmed because of the reductions combined with the increased proportion of spending devoted to personnel.[84]

Factors enabling or hindering accountability

International

The South African transition has been used by supporters of sanctions and international pressure generally as evidence that these devices can have an impact on the domestic behaviour of even a recalcitrant regime. Many international sceptics as well as many white people in South Africa deny that sanctions caused the reforms: they point instead to internal shifts in self-perception and definition. However, some have argued that these shifts were themselves provoked not only by internal unrest but also by international isolation.[85] Both the perception of risk by international lenders and investors sparked by domestic strife and the imposition of sanctions hurt the country severely.[86]

Audie Klotz examines this thesis further and comes to the conclusion that sanctions did have some effect, but that the impact on the South African elite was not merely direct economic or security harm. Klotz argues that, while it may be the case that some key economic industries were at least temporarily harmed, and the defence industry suffered setbacks, as a result of sanctions, most of these obstacles could eventually be circumvented, if at a somewhat high cost.[87] Instead, the argument is that the sanctions had effects that have been noted less, though ones that constructivist theory would predict. Klotz argues that sanctions had an important effect on legitimation processes and construction of self-identity within South African elites. Klotz points in particular to the deleterious effects that the country's reputation had on its international standing: it was pushed out of the Commonwealth in 1961, and excluded from the founding of the OAU in 1963.[88] Thus the sanctions promoted new norms of racial equality. Klotz suggests that the link between sanctions and reform is proven by the fact that the five main areas of concern put forth by sanctioners were addressed over time by the reforming elite: the repeal of the state of emergency, the release of political prisoners, the unbanning of the ANC and other political parties, the elimination of apartheid laws, and good-faith negotiations for a new political system. Finally, Klotz argues that the quest for international legitimation affected the behaviour of all three main parties to the peace negotiations.[89]

As with many of the transitions studied here, the sea change in the international environment with the end of the Cold War should not be underestimated. Like many other countries in regions of bipolar contention, the South African elite had an image of the Soviet Union as a menace that sought to destroy it. The white government and the security forces pointed to the threat, real and perceived, posed by, *inter alia*, the South African Communist Party and the ANC, bolstered by the extremity of some of their tactics. That image began to crumble with Soviet–American cooperation during the 1989 Namibia and Angola negotiations.[90]

Civil–military relations and the balance of forces generally

The NP was clearly pushed to the bargaining table by a variety of factors, not the least of which was the real threat to stability posed by the ANC and other opposition forces, both political and military. While the ANC may not have been in a position to bring apartheid down militarily, its actions as well as grass-roots opposition to the regime posed serious economic threats and threats to order and stability more generally. There was recognition that the continuing war was too costly for all sides.[91]

Nature/extent of abuses or struggle

It is less clear what impact the protracted nature of the apartheid regime and the struggle against it had on the outcomes in South Africa. Certainly it is plausible that exhaustion in the regime and the population and a recognition that rebel groups could not be eliminated played a role in the decision to reform, though it is unclear what role was played.

Lessons

South Africa provides us with yet a different instance of a country following a third path between pure accountability and pure amnesty. The balance of forces seems to have had only moderate importance in the decision to reform; more important were the effects of international pressure and the permissive effects of a changed international environment. The result, however, was that the new regime was not free to take any actions it desired; it was constrained by the interim constitution and the degree to which certain status quo forces remained entrenched. Nonetheless, despite the amnesty, a commission of inquiry with broad powers was created, and the security forces underwent a radical overhaul in structure and doctrine. Thus, as we have learned from other countries, an amount of accountability may be achieved though compromises are made, and other goods such as reform of the security forces might simultaneously be achieved.

Notes

1 For a chronology of apartheid legislation, see the text of the South African Truth and Reconciliation Report (TRC Report), vol. 1, ch. 13, available at http://www.polity.org.za/govdocs/commissions/1998/trc/. On conscription and the role of the armed forces in the state generally, see Lynn Berat, 'Conscientious Objection in South Africa: Governmental Paranoia and the Law of Conscription', *Vanderbilt Journal of Transnational Law*, 22 (1989), pp. 127–86.

2 Act no. 34 of 1960 is discussed in the TRC Report, vol. 1, ch. 13. The massacre was

followed by the Indemnity Act, no. 61 of 1961, which indemnifies the government and its agents for actions done in the suppression of internal disorder.

3 TRC Report, vol. 1, ch. 13, lists laws pertaining to internal security such as the regulations following on the declaration of a state of emergency on 12 June 1986. See also Janine Rauch, 'The Policing of Public Gatherings and Demonstrations in South Africa 1960–1994' (unpublished manuscript, on file with current author), on the major uses of violence against public demonstrations and the legislation that legitimated these actions.

4 Lynn Berat, 'South Africa: Negotiating Change?', in Roht-Arriaza (ed.), *Impunity and Human Rights*, pp. 267–8; Berat and Shain, 'Retribution or Truth-telling?', p. 164.

5 For a general narrative of these secret talks, see Allister Sparks, *Tomorrow is Another Country: The Inside Story of South Africa's Road to Change* (New York: Hill & Wang, 1995).

6 See, for example, Alex Callinicos, 'South Africa: End of Apartheid and After', *Economic and Political Weekly* (New Delhi) (3 September 1994), p. 2357–8. Whether or not international sanctions and the threat of greater ones played a role is also a point of contention: Michael MacDonald, 'Power Politics in the New South Africa', *Journal of Southern African Studies*, 22 (1996), pp. 221–3.

7 Berat, 'South Africa: Negotiating Change?', p. 268.

8 Berat, 'South Africa: Negotiating Change?', p. 269.

9 Callinicos, 'South Africa', p. 2359.

10 In 1990, the so-called Harms commission released evidence of government-sponsored hit squads and recommended judicial action, but none was taken.

11 Callinicos, 'South Africa', p. 2359.

12 Bede Harris, 'The New South African Constitution', *New Zealand Law Journal* (January 1995), pp. 20–1; Joe Slovo, 'Negotiations: What Room for Compromise?', *African Communist*, Third Quarter (1992), pp. 36–40, quoted in Bronwyn Leebaw, 'Theory out of Practice: An Intellectual History of the South African TRC', paper presented at the American Political Science Association's Annual Conference (Atlanta, GA, September 1999); Sparks, *Tomorrow is Another Country*, pp. 181–2.

13 For a brief summary of the work of the Commission of Inquiry regarding the Prevention of Public Violence and Intimidation, see the TRC Report, vol. 1, ch. 13.

14 UN Doc. S/24389.

15 Guidelines for Defining Political Offenses.

16 Berat and Shain, 'Retribution or Truth-telling in South Africa?', pp. 176–7.

17 Act no. 151 of 1992, repealed by the Promotion of National Unity and Reconciliation Act, no. 34 of 1995.

18 Quoted in Berat, 'South Africa: Negotiating Change?', p. 273.

19 Berat, 'South Africa: Negotiating Change?', p. 274.

20 Berat, 'South Africa: Negotiating Change?', pp. 275–6.

21 Callinicos, 'South Africa', p. 2360; John Hatchard, 'Towards Majority Rule in South Africa: The Transitional Executive Council Act 1993', *Journal of African Law*, 37, 2 (1994), p. 207.

22 Hatchard, 'Towards Majority Rule in South Africa', p. 208.

23 Hatchard, 'Towards Majority Rule in South Africa', p. 210.

24 The constitution attempts to strike this delicate balance through a complex method of selecting the membership in the bicameral parliament. In the house of assembly, members are elected on a purely representative basis, though half are elected from national lists and half from lists by province. The senate, on the other hand, is made up of members nominated by the provincial legislatures. Harris, 'The New South African Constitution', p. 19.

25 MacDonald, 'Power Politics in the New South Africa', pp. 228–30. The Public Service Commission was to continue under the 1996 constitution until abolished by

its specific terms, see *Constitution of the Republic of South Africa* (adopted 8 May 1996, amended 11 October 1996), Schedule 6, Sec. 24(2), available at: http://www.constitution.org.za/b34/b34b_con.htm.

26 Harris, 'The New South African Constitution', pp. 17–18. The court agreed unaimously to abolish capital punishment: John Forsyth, 'Mental Somersaults in the New South Africa', *SCOLAG: The Bulletin of the Scottish Legal Action Group*, 228 (31 October 1995), p. 150 (interview with Albie Sachs, a member of the constitutional court).

27 Berat and Shain, 'Retribution or Truth-telling?', pp. 182–3. On the question of whether to approve an amnesty and the genesis of the Truth and Reconciliation Commission generally, see Alex Boraine, 'Truth and Reconciliation in South Africa: The Third Way' (paper presented 20 October 1998, at Columbia Seminar on Justice in Transitions, on file with current author). At least briefly, the security forces may have believed that they were protected: subsequently, in January 1995, it was revealed that de Klerk had promised 'administrative indemnity' to these and other law enforcement issues, a step Mandela's cabinet reversed. See Neier, *War Crimes*, p. 41.

28 South African Constitution, available online at http://www.truth.org.za.

29 Garton Ash, 'True Confessions', p. 33; Berat and Shain, 'Retribution or Truth-telling?', p. 183.

30 For this justification, see the article by the minister of justice, Dullah Omar, 'Justice in Transition', available at http://www.polity.org.za/govdoc.

31 Promotion of National Unity and Reconciliation Act 1995, no. 34 (26 July 1995) and the acts expanding its membership and extending its mandate are available at http://www.truth.org.za/. The three committees of the TRC are created by Chapters 3–5 of the Promotion of National Unity and Reconciliation Act of 1995. See also Boraine, 'Truth and Reconciliation Commission', p. 8. On the functions of the TRC, see the Act, Chapter 2, sec. 4.

32 See the Act, Chapter 4, sections 18–22, regulating applications for amnesty and the Act, Chapter 6, secs 31–3. See also Boraine, 'Truth and Reconciliation Commission', p. 9.

33 After being extended, the deadline finally expired on 10 May 1997. The TRC was then to complete its work on the last day of July 1998, and release a report within the next three months. See Portfolio Committee Amendments to Promotion of National Unity and Reconciliation Amendment Bill, B 48A-98, available at http://www.truth.org.za/. See also Garton Ash, 'True Confessions', p. 34.

34 These include the motives of the applicant, the context of the act, the legal nature of the act, whether it was in compliance of higher orders, etc. See the Act, Chapter 4. See also Boraine, 'Truth and Reconciliation Commission', pp. 12–13.

35 See *Azanian Peoples Organization (AZAPO) and Others v The President of the Republic of South Africa*, CCT 17/96 (25 July 1996), available at http://www.truth.org.za/reading. See also Garton Ash, 'True Confessions', p. 36; Suzanne Daley, 'In South Africa, Confessions to Dark Era's Worst Crimes', *New York Times* (29 January 1997), pp. A1, A4.

36 Quoted in Garton Ash, 'True Confessions', p. 34.

37 Eddie Koch and Marion Edmunds, 'More Reconciliation than Truth', *Mail and Guardian* (23–9 August 1996), pp. 6–7. For a text of the submissions, see http://www.mg.co.za/mg/ or http://www.truth.org.za/submit/anctruth.htm and submit/np-truth.htm. For an analysis of the ANC's claims that it was engaged in a just and relatively clean war, see Tom Lodge, 'Taking Great Pains to Justify a "Clean War"', *Mail and Guardian* (23–9 August 1996), p. 7. See also the transcript of the ANC's political party recall of May 1997, further discussing the ANC's actions during the conflict, and that of the NP's political party recall doing

the same, available at http://www.truth.org.za/hrvtrans/party2/anc2.htm and party2/np2.htm.

38 Suzanne Daley, 'Panel to Investigate Atrocities of the Apartheid Era', *New York Times* (27 August 1995), p. 3.

39 This was of course because, given the terms of the commission, only those who come forward can receive amnesty; otherwise one is still vulnerable to prosecution. Suzanne Daley, 'Former South Africa Police Chief Admits Role in Terrorizing Blacks', *New York Times* (22 October 1996), pp. A1, A16. Van der Merwe's testimony carries additional importance because he was also a member of what has been referred to as a 'shadow government', the State Security Council. Donald G. McNeil, 'A "Shadow Government" with a Shadowy History', *New York Times* (22 October 1996), p. A16; Suzanne Daley, 'Settling for Truth in Place of Justice', *New York Times* (27 October 1996), sec. 4, pp. 1, 6. He was eventually granted an amnesty: see Daley, 'South Africa Commission Grants Amnesty for 2 Apartheid Cases', *New York Times* (6 August 1999), p. A6.

40 Suzanne Daley, 'South African Police Colonel Jailed for Life in Apartheid Killings', *New York Times* (31 October 1996), p. A11. The case was still outstanding in June 1998, see the TRC database at http://www.truth.org.za/scripts/database.pl?

41 Suzanne Daley, 'South Africa Frees Apartheid Killer, Hinting at Broad Amnesty', *New York Times* (11 December 1996), p. A15; John F. Burns, 'Biko's Case Now Offers Justice From a Travesty', *New York Times* (2 February 1997), sec. 4, p. 4; 'South African Ex-official to Aid Inquiry', *New York Times* (24 April 24, 1997), p. A4; Suzanne Daley, 'Apartheid-era Defense Chief Defends Role in Ordering Raids on Neighboring Countries', *New York Times* (8 May 1997), p. A16; Jillian Edelstein and Mark Gevisser, 'The Witnesses' (photo essay) *New York Times Magazine* (22 June 1997), p. 38.

42 '8,000 South Africans Apply for Amnesty', *New York Times* (12 May 1997), p. A11; Suzanne Daley, 'Party Led by Mandela Now Owns Up to Atrocities', *New York Times* (13 May 1997), p. A7.

43 Suzanne Daley, 'de Klerk Denies Authorizing Killings During Apartheid', *New York Times* (15 May 1997), p. A8. De Klerk was responding to the comments of Alex Boraine and Archbishop Desmond Tutu, who made critical remarks, leading de Klerk to accuse them of reaching their own findings outside the commission process. Suzanne Daley, 'De Klerk Pulls Party Out of Inquiry into Apartheid Era', *New York Times* (17 May 1997), p. 3. For the text of the NP's second submission, accusing the TRC of at least the appearance of bias, see Second Submission of the National Party to the TRC, available at http://www.truth.org.za/submit/np2.htm. Suzanne Daley, 'Divisions Deepen on Apartheid Inquiry', *New York Times* (8 June 1997) p. 6; Suzanne Daley, 'Tutu, Head of Apartheid Inquiry, Refuses to Apologize to de Klerk', *New York Times* (20 June 1997), p. A3.

44 See, for example, the NP's submissions to the TRC as well as the NP party political recall.

45 Quoted in Garton Ash, 'True Confessions', p. 36. The same stance was taken by de Klerk and General Magnus Malan: that apartheid was wrong, but also that they had no knowledge of or responsibility for many 'dastardly deeds'. See the NP's political party recall.

46 Suzanne Daley, 'Apartheid Inquiry Takes Up the Killing of Mandela Associate', *New York Times* (12 August 1997), p. A7. The case was still outstanding in March 1998, see the database of the TRC, available at http://www.truth.org.za/scripts/database.pl?; 'Amnesty Denied to Hani Killers', (7 April 1999), available through trc-list@www.truth.org.za.

47 Suzanne Daley, 'Panel to Call Former Wife of Mandela', *New York Times* (25 June 1997), p. A3.

48 'Botha to Face Charges over Apartheid Inquiry', *New York Times* (8 January 1998), p. A6; Suzanne Daley, 'Ex-South Africa Leader Guilty of Contempt for Refusing to Testify before Truth Panel', *New York Times* (22 August 1998), p. A8; Donald G. McNeil, 'Appeals Court Reverses Botha's Apartheid Panel Conviction', *New York Times* (2 June 1999), p. A6.

49 Garton Ash, 'True Confessions', p. 36.

50 Suzanne Daley, 'Officer is Denied Amnesty in the Killing of Steve Biko', *New York Times* (11 January 1999), A4.

51 Suzanne Daley, 'Former Officials Cleared by Court in South Africa', *New York Times* (12 October 1996), pp. 1, 7.

52 Daley, 'South African Police Colonel Jailed for Life'; Neier, *War Crimes*, p. 42; Suzanne Daley, 'South Africa Confronts Brutalities of One Man', *New York Times* (19 July 1999), p. A3.

53 Dirk Coetzee (Application No. 0063/96) *et al.*, available at http://www.truth.org.za/amnesty/32.htm. Suzanne Daley, 'Ex-policeman Who Told of Apartheid Crimes is Guilty of Killing', *New York Times* (16 May 1997), p. A5.

54 One report suggests that the reparations offered might be as high as about $11,000 a person for perhaps some 20,000 victims. Garton Ash, 'True Confessions', p. 38; 'Policy Framework for Urgent Interim Reparation Measures', available at http://www.truth.org.za/reports/policy.htm; TRC Report, vol. 1, ch. 4, secs 133–6.

55 Suzanne Daley, 'South Africa Braces Itself for Report by Truth Panel', *New York Times* (27 October 1998), p. A8; Suzanne Daley, 'Truth Commission to Withhold its Findings on de Klerk', *New York Times* (29 October 1998), p. A3; Suzanne Daley, 'South African Panel's Report Arrives in a Swirl of Bitterness', *New York Times* (30 October 1998), pp. A1, A14.

56 Suzanne Daley, 'South African Panel's Report Arrives in a Swirl of Bitterness', pp. A1, A14. See TRC Report, vol. 1, ch. 4, esp. secs 70, 74, and 77.

57 'Pretoria's Words: "Extrajudicial Killing"', *New York Times* (30 October 1998), p. A14.

58 'Foreword by Chairperson', TRC Report; Daley, 'South African Panel's Report'.

59 Daley, 'South African Panel's Report'.

60 Suzanne Daley, 'Next Up for Amnesty: The Unrepentant', *New York Times* (8 November 1998), p. 1. Such an amnesty would benefit figures such as Botha and many IFP members who have not applied for amnesty.

61 Robert J. Griffiths, 'South African Civil–Military Relations in Transition: Issues and Influences', *Armed Forces and Society*, 21, 3 (Spring 1995), p. 396. This somewhat opaque statement falls short of articulating the possible consequences of harsh treatment of old SADF members. See the TRC Armed Forces Hearing: SADF available at http://www.truth.org.za/hrvtrans/forces/sadf.htm. The same statement goes on to refer to an assessment by the National Assessment Service asserting that the SADF could stage a coup if the negotiations went the wrong way, but rejects this claim. For a further statement by the same individual, now head of the new SANDF, see 'Panel Discussion between Gen. G. Meiring of SANDF and TRC Panel', available at http://www.truth.org.za/hrvtrans/forces/sandfpan.htm. On the belief by some members of the security forces that the TRC was pursuing a witch hunt, see TRC Armed Forces Hearing: South African Police (9 October 1997), available at http://www.truth.org.za/hrvtrans/forces/sap.htm.

62 Griffiths, 'South African Civil–Military Relations in Transition', pp. 399–400.

63 Jakkie Cilliers, 'Security and Transition in South Africa', in Diamond and Plattner, *Civil–Military Relations*, pp. 92–3, says that the optimal size for the new South African National Defence Force is 90,000, but that there are 95,000 former SADF, 11,000 members of homeland armies and 34,000 guerrillas to be either incorporated into the new force or demobilized. The service corps' plan to offer vocational training and ease the strain of demobilization has also been lagging.

64 Ronnie Kasrils, 'Progress in Transformation', *Continuity in Change: The SA Army in Transition*, monograph 26 (August 1998), available at http://www.iss.co.za/Pubs/MONOGRAPHS/No. per cent2026/Kasrils.html.
65 Donald G. McNeil Jr, 'South Africa's New Army is All Soft and Cuddly', *New York Times* (28 March 1997), p. A4. A small purge was carried out under de Klerk in 1992; issues of civilian control are still salient even with the removal of some officers involved in past repression: Griffiths, 'South African Civil–Military Relations in Transition', p. 400.
66 Jakkie Cilliers, 'Rethinking South African Security Architecture', *African Defence Review*, 20 (December 1994), p. 25; 'The SANDF', available at www.southafrica.net/government/safety/sandf.html. For more on 'rationalisation', the process of reduction through both natural attrition and voluntary or compulsory severance, see L. B. von Stade, 'Rationalisation in the SANDF: The Next Challenge', *African Security Review*, 6, 2 (1997), available at http://www.iss.co.za/Pubs/ASR/6.2/van per cent20Stade.html.
67 'The SANDF'; 'The South African Army', available at www.southafrica.net/government/safety/army.html.
68 Dr Martin Edmonds, 'South African Defence: In Transition', available at www.cdiss.org/safrica1.htm.
69 Edmonds, 'South African Defence Policy'; 'The SANDF'; Kasrils, 'Progress in Transformation'.
70 Nadia Levin, Kindiza Ngubeni and Graeme Simpson, 'Meeting the Challenge of Change? Notes on Policing and Transition in South Africa', Centre for the Study of Violence and Reconciliation, available at http://www.wits.ac.za/csvh/papnk&gs.html.
71 Janine Rauch, 'State, Civil Society and Police Reform in South Africa', Centre for the Study of Violence and Reconciliation, available at http://www.wits.ac.za/csvr/papstate.html; Janine Rauch, 'Police Reform and South Africa's Transition' (paper presented at the June 1999 meeting of the Academic Council on the United Nations System, on file with current author), p. 2.
72 Rauch, 'State, Civil Society, and Police Reform in South Africa'. These included a new code of conduct, bodies to receive and investigate complaints about police, and attempts to improve relations with local communities: Rauch, 'Police Reform', p. 3.
73 Cilliers, 'Rethinking South African Security Architecture', p. 17; 'The South African Police Service', available at www.southafrica.net/government/safety/police.html.
74 Jeffrey Lever and Elrena van der Spuy, 'Challenges Facing Democratic Policing in South Africa' (unpublished manuscript, on file with current author), pp. 2, 4–5.
75 Lever and van der Spuy, 'Challenges Facing Democratic Policing', pp. 6, 8.
76 Rauch, 'The Policing of Public Gatherings', p. 29.
77 Lever and van der Spuy, 'Challenges Facing Democratic Policing', p. 7; 'The South African Police Service'. The law and order ministry became the ministry for safety and security: Rauch, 'Police Reform', p. 4–7.
78 Submission to the TRC by Mr F. W. de Klerk for the NP, available at http://www.truth.org.za/submit/np-truth.htm. Lever and van der Spuy, 'Challenges Facing Democratic Policing', p. 18.
79 Rauch, 'Police Reform', p. 10.
80 Rauch, 'State, Civil Society and Police Reform in South Africa'; Rauch, 'Police Reform', p. 9.
81 Suzanne Daley, 'Apartheid's Feared Police Prove Inept and Corrupt', *New York Times* (25 March 1997), pp. A1, A13. On current police priorities and strategies, see South African Police Service, 'Policing Priorities and Objectives 1998/1999', available at www.saps.co.za/17_policy/priority/. Cilliers, 'Security and Transition', pp. 90–1. US Department of State, 'South Africa Country Report on

Human Rights Practices for 1998' (26 February 1999), available at http://www.state.gov/www/global/human_rights/1998_hrp_report/southafr.htm.

82 See generally Elrena van der Spuy, 'Foreign Donor Assistance and Policing Reform in South Africa' (unpublished manuscript, presented at the Sociology Association Conference, 6–9 July 1999, University of Stellenbosch, on file with current author). See 'Human Rights and Policing,' available at www.saps.co.za/17_policy/19_humanrights/index.html or /detained.html, an educational poster listing the rights of detained persons, for an example of these materials. See also Lever and van der Spuy, 'Challenges Facing Democratic Policing', pp. 15, 18 on attempts to imbue a new sense of professionalism.

83 Donald G. McNeil Jr, 'New Charter Passed', *New York Times* (12 October 1996), p. 7.

84 Cilliers, 'Rethinking South African Security Architecture', p. 24.

85 Heribert Adam and Kogila Moodley, *The Negotiated Revolution: Society and Politics in Post-Apartheid South Africa* (Johannesburg: Jonathan Ball, 1993), pp. 52–8.

86 Adam and Moodley, *The Negotiated Revolution*, pp. 57–8.

87 Audie Klotz, *Norms in International Relations: The Struggle Against Apartheid* (Ithaca, NY: Cornell University Press, 1995).

88 Klotz, *Norms in International Relations*, pp. 9–10, 30–1.

89 Klotz, *Norms in International Relations*, p. 159.

90 See, for example, the comments of General Johan van der Merwe in the TRC Armed Forces Hearing: South African Police (9 October 1997), available at http://www.truth.org.za/hrvtrans/forces/sap.htm. On the same perception held by the white government, see the submission to the Truth and Reconciliation Commission by Mr F. W. de Klerk for the NP, at http://www.truth.org.za/submit/np-truth.htm, on the relationship of the ANC to the South African Communist Party and the aid it received from the Soviet Union and other eastern bloc countries. See also Submission IRO the Former SADF, available at http://www.truth.org.za/submit/sadf.htm. For the justification proffered by former SADF head General Magnus Malan, see General M. A. de M. Malan, submission to the Truth and Reconciliation Commission, available at http://www.truth.org.za/submit/malan.htm. Adam and Moodley, *The Negotiated Revolution*, pp. 48, 166–7.

91 MacDonald, 'Power Politics', p. 224; Adam and Moodley, *The Negotiated Revolution*, p. 47.

7 Sri Lanka

Justice in the midst of war

Introduction

Although Sri Lanka diverges in significant ways from the other cases examined here, many of the lessons we can learn from its experience remain the same. In a very different context it has had to face the same balancing act as other, clearly transitional states, and it has made similar compromises. In Sri Lanka, the key international player has been India, rather than the USA or the UN; India even sent a peacekeeping force into the civil war in 1987. However, in recent times it has maintained a rather studied silence with respect to events on the small island to its south. As with many other cases, while the military is numerically much larger than the rebels, and has made great gains, it has been unable to eradicate a guerrilla force skilled in terrorist attacks. It also appears that a different tradition of civil–military relations has made action on past abuses more feasible. Finally, the protracted and bloody nature of the conflict may finally be pushing those on both sides of the ethnic divide towards compromise: the results of the 1994 election are seen in part as a result of war-weariness, and the population seeking a separate state is said to have waned in its fervour for the rebels.

Nonetheless, the war goes on and negotiations have repeatedly stalled. At the same time, the government has taken some steps to address past abuses, creating commissions of inquiry to investigate them and proceeding with several high-profile prosecutions. It has not, beyond some minimal human rights training sessions, impinged at all on the domain of the security forces, perhaps for the usual reasons, but also because they are still needed to prosecute the war. As we shall see, then, while conflict continues, Sri Lanka has begun to face some of the hard choices of postwar societies, making greater strides on accountability but lesser ones on reform. But, as recent events, including the rebels' July 2001 raid on the international airport and adjacent military base in Colombo have shown, the fighting continues in virulent fashion, and has the power to derail peace initiatives and constitutional reforms.

Overview

Sri Lanka, like most of the other cases I have already discussed, has suffered a protracted civil war that has resulted in significant military and civilian losses as well as disappearances and other human rights atrocities. Sri Lanka is unique, however, in that it has had a functioning democracy since independence (technically, adult suffrage and democratic procedures were introduced 17 years *before* independence) with relatively peaceful transfers of power from one ruling party to another.[1] It is an important case because it differs from the other countries I examine in this book: it illustrates the limits faced even by democratic governments, and the types of compromises that they are likely to make with respect to accountability and reform. It also provides a very different type of limitation placed on the government: in Sri Lanka there has been relatively little concern that the military was coup-prone; instead the concern has been that the security forces must remain strong and with a high morale in order to pursue the war against a domestic rebel group. It helps to demonstrate, then, that the claims regarding the compromises of transition are not tautological, that is, that governments make concessions even when they do not fear a coup. In the absence of a coup threat in Sri Lanka, we still see the basic trade-offs at work.

Despite the protracted struggle between government forces and Tamil rebels calling for independence in the north and the east of the country, as well as intermittent conflicts between the government and Sinhalese extremists in the south, as well as widened powers for the armed forces, the military has not sought to seize political control. In addition, Sri Lanka differs from the Latin American countries and South Africa in that the key external power influencing domestic politics is not the USA or the UN but a regional great power, India, which even sent its own troops into the north of Sri Lanka in 1987 as a peacekeeping force to quell the conflict. Indian troops not only failed in this goal but committed atrocities themselves and earned the enmity not only of Tamils but of Sinhalese nationalists who accused the Sri Lankan government of being little more than the puppet of India.

Thus Sri Lanka comes to the central dilemma that my research addresses with a different history that may well be enlightening. While the military continues to enjoy broad power, it has not intervened directly in electoral politics. That it has failed to do so is interesting in light of new governmental policies, following the election of the party of Chandrika Kumaratunga (now president) in 1994, which led to the creation of three regional truth commissions, scattered prosecutions for past abuses, and renewed negotiations in earnest with the Tamil rebels.

History of the conflict

As has already been mentioned, Sri Lanka poses an intriguing case of a new regime seeking to address old abuses because it is not an instance of a new democracy investigating the crimes of an authoritarian predecessor, but rather a newly elected government in a country that has been a continuously functioning democracy instigating such an investigation.[2] The situation is yet more unusual because of the tense ethnic relations in the country that have spawned the separatist Liberation Tigers of Tamil Eelam (LTTE) in the north and east, who seek an independent Tamil homeland, as well as the Sinhalese extremists of the Janata Vimukthi Peramuna (JVP), both of whom have carried out terrorist acts. It is therefore worth briefly reviewing the country's post-colonial history before addressing the war that began in the 1980s.

While Sri Lanka did not gain independence from British rule until 1948, the colonizers granted adult suffrage 17 years earlier. The result was a longer tradition of democratic structures than other post-colonial south Asian countries. However, as some analysts have noted, there was no large anti-colonialist movement in what was then known as Ceylon as there was in India: the British transferred power to a political and administrative elite, largely Sinhalese, who were loyal to their rulers in the colonial era.[3] A number of deleterious effects to national unity have been observed to result from this history. First, the absence of a strong anti-colonial movement, like that in India and elsewhere, has been blamed in part for the failure to generate a general concept of the nation, enabling the ethnic splintering that has occurred subsequently.[4] Second, the transfer to a dominant elite (Sinhalese) that also represented a significant majority of the population (approximately three-quarters) invited further fissures among ethnic and linguistic groups.[5] While ethnic tensions existed prior to the early 1970s, resulting in a significant anti-Tamil ethnic riot in 1958, it was only at the later time that the fissures truly became salient.[6] At this point it is worth detailing the features of the constitution that deal with fundamental rights and their limitations.

The constitution, emergency and restrictions on fundamental rights

Sri Lanka has a constitution that recognizes many human rights as fundamental rights, and has become a signatory to important international human rights instruments. However, that is only half of the story, as legislation for emergencies and to prevent terrorism have progressively infringed on those freedoms. The constitution's chapter III deals with fundamental rights, enshrining freedom of thought, conscience, religion and freedom from cruel, inhuman or degrading punishment. It also provides for equality before the law, non-discrimination, protection for arrestees or detainees and the presumption of innocence.[7] However, the constitution goes on, in article 15, to provide for restrictions on many of these rights in the interest of national security, public order and 'the protection of public health and morality'. As we shall see, such restrictions have not only turned out to be rather extensive, but have facilitated abuses of rights.

The Public Security Ordinance (PSO) was passed in 1947, just before the independence of Sri Lanka, but has remained in force through post-independence constitutions and provides the basis for the emergency regulations that are discussed below. Under the PSO, the president can proclaim that the ordinance will come into operation, and this declaration cannot be challenged in a court of law. Once the PSO is in operation, the president can make emergency regulations as necessary for public security and order; these regulations can override existing law but not the constitution.[8]

In 1979, the Prevention of Terrorism Act was passed, legislation that gave the police and armed forces broad powers and essentially put the northern territory under martial law. The act defined as unlawful the speaking or writing of words meant to cause religious, social or communal disharmony, reversed a previous rule that no confession in police custody is valid unless made in the presence of a magistrate, was retrospective, permitted arrest without a warrant and stop and search of anyone, and allowed for holding suspects incommunicado without trial for long periods of time. In 1983, regulation 15A was introduced: terrorism suspects could be held up to 18 months without trial; search without a warrant was acceptable, as were confessions obtained through torture. In August 1983, the 6th amendment to the constitution was passed, which deprived of their seats all members of parliament who refused to take an oath of loyalty renouncing secessionist beliefs, thus depriving Tamil United Liberation Front (TULF) legislators of their seats.[9]

The new Kumaratunga regime moved quickly to pass legislation to give effect to the UN Convention against Torture, which the previous regime had signed, but some provisions of the convention were undermined by the continuance in force of emergency regulations dealing with arrest and detention. Similarly, though the country had acceded to the International Convention on Civil and Political Rights (ICCPR), the lack of, *inter alia*, a guarantee of a right to life undermined that action. Proposed constitutional drafts presented from 1995 onwards added the right to life, but with the limitation that it could not be *arbitrarily* deprived.[10]

The two main parties that have traded positions in power in the post-independence period are the United National Party (UNP) and the Sri Lankan Freedom Party (SLFP): the former was originally more diverse and tolerant, while the latter had a wider labour base and tended to make both socialist and Buddhist chauvinist appeals. However, it was an SLFP prime minister, Bandaranaike, who would reach an agreement with the Tamils over language, only to be assassinated in 1959, apparently by radical Buddhist monks. The pact he reached with the Tamil leader, known as the Bandaranaike–Chelvanayagam pact, would have allowed for some use of Tamil and created regional councils; although it was abrogated under duress, it is still a common reference point in current discussions over the Tamils' claims. It was in 1962, in this environment of heightened ethnic tensions, that military officers launched a coup attempt that ultimately failed; however, it appears not to have been a result of ethnic divisions, but rather of a sense that the government was wrongly emphasizing such divisions and contributing to a national crisis.[11]

In 1971, the SLFP returned to power: it had strengthened its ties to marxist and Tamil groups, and faced an uprising by leftist Sinhalese youth who had also supported the party. Under the auspices of the JVP, there was a significant revolt, put down militarily by the government with foreign aid. As a result some 5,000 died, 16,000 were arrested, and a two-year state of emergency was imposed that would eventually stretch to six years during which thousands of suspects were detained without trial. While some have pointed out that the motivations for the uprising were as much economic as ethnic (if not more so), the actions came at a time of increasingly aggressive Buddhist nationalism.[12]

During the 1970–77 period, governmental policies towards Tamils became increasingly restrictive and discriminatory, pushing Tamils to define themselves ethnically and increasingly stridently, eventually leading to a call for an independent Tamil homeland. In particular, Tamil access to higher education was progressively restricted, and debates over textbooks intensified controversies over language. The result was a 1977 call by the Tamil United Liberation Front for a separate *eelam* (or homeland) for Tamils.[13] 1977 also saw the return of the UNP to power, this time headed by J. R. Jayewardene, a political pragmatist who promised some economic privatization but also promoted a Buddhist revival and demonstrated little concern for the status of the Tamil minority.[14] The UNP would hold power until 1994, during which time inter-ethnic relations deteriorated significantly. Meanwhile, the LTTE gained power. It was formed in 1972 as the student wing of the TULF, but eventually broke away. Following anti-Tamil riots in 1977, the LTTE escalated military activity and moved further away from the TULF, which failed to push for a homeland. In 1978, the LTTE was officially banned, but continued to draw ever-greater numbers of Tamil youth.[15]

Also in 1978, the centralization of power was increased with a new constitution. An executive presidency was created that was able to bypass parliamentary objections. Even the 1980 introduction of the so-called district development councils, intended to help only development but which could have aided in a slow process of devolution, were to be controlled by the president and were ultimately ineffective.[16]

In 1979, the Prevention of Terrorism Act (PTA) was passed, legislation that, as has already been discussed, gave the police and armed forces broad powers and essentially put the northern territory under martial law and facilitated the suppression of fundamental rights enshrined in the constitution. In 1983, emergency regulation 15A was passed under the auspices of the PSO and PTA, further limiting the rights of arrestees. In August 1983, the 6th amendment to the constitution was passed, which not only appeared to be a suppression of freedom of speech but also had the effect of depriving TULF legislators of their seats.[17]

Despite formal democracy, the UNP government tightened its grip on government with the December 1982 referendum on the extension of the president's term. The measure was passed following a campaign in which the populace was flooded with pro-government propaganda while opposition activities were curtailed or even broken up violently by pro-government groups, and many opposition papers were closed.[18]

These actions set the stage for the anti-Tamil riots in Colombo in 1983. The short-term cause of the riots was ostensibly the killing of 13 Sinhalese soldiers by the LTTE near Jaffna in July. The bodies were brought to the capital by fellow soldiers, sparking an outburst against Tamils by both local civilians and the soldiers themselves. The result was widespread and systematic destruction of Tamil-owned homes, businesses and factories. While accurate estimates of fatalities are difficult to obtain, the government estimate was about 470, while others place the number at between 2,000 and 3,000. In addition, between 80,000 to 100,000 Tamils were displaced to refugee camps in the Colombo area alone; other estimates place the number of Tamils made homeless at 150,000.[19] Simultaneously, there was a rise in JVP-perpetrated terror in the south, as the group accused the government of being India's pawn and of failing to deal firmly enough with Tamils.[20] A disturbing feature of the riots was the apparent failure of the military and police to even attempt to halt them; in some cases they actively encouraged these criminal acts, as President Jayewardene subsequently admitted. In the eastern territory, near Trincomalee harbour, civilians and members of the military rioted. On 25 and 27 July, some 53 Tamil 'terrorists' were killed in Colombo jail, presumably with at least the collusion of their jailers. According to S. J. Tambiah, many Tamils perceive a significant shift in the response of the security forces to rioting over time: from 1958, when some apparently saved Tamils, to 1977, when they evinced indifference, to the riots of 1981 and 1983, when at least some members took part in the anti-Tamil violence.[21]

India, not surprisingly, has taken a great interest in events affecting its tiny neighbour to the south for a number of reasons. In particular, India's southernmost state of Tamil Nadu shares at least broadly the same ethnicity as the Tamils in Sri Lanka, and the riots in Colombo generated an influx of refugees into Tamil Nadu. Even before this crisis, however, India had apparently trained and supplied a different Tamil guerrilla group, the Tamil Eelam Liberation Organization, and apparently trained some LTTE guerrillas.[22] India was then heavily involved in pushing for negotiations. In February 1987, however, it withdrew its good offices as the talks broke down. India became increasingly identified with the Tamil camp in the negotiations; this culminated in the dispute between the nations over India's shipment of food and medicine to the Jaffna peninsula in early June. India announced its intent to send such goods on unarmed ships; the prime minister of Sri Lanka called these moves provocative, and stated that the military would protect the island and its territorial waters. After 20 supply ships were turned back by the Sri Lanka navy, India delivered the goods by airdrop. In a move that further allied it with the Tamils, the Indian government, while pursuing negotiations with the Sri Lankan government, allegedly made a number of key promises to the LTTE leader, including, *inter alia*, that an interim government would be formed with the LTTE playing a prominent role and that the government of India would pay compensation to the LTTE to keep up the organization once the rebels ceased to collect taxes.[23]

However, the agreement that was finally reached between India's Prime Minister Rajiv Gandhi and Jayewardene, the 'Indo-Sri Lanka Agreement to Establish Peace and Normalcy in Sri Lanka', was rejected by the LTTE because it was not consulted as well as for substantive reasons. The agreement, signed on 29 July 1987, provided for an Indian peacekeeping force (IPKF) in the north and east; the plan was for the force to remain until elections could be held for a regional council through which some power would be devolved to the Tamils. The accord also called for the shift to a federal state structure through the 13th amendment and a merger (temporarily at least) of the northern and eastern provinces, as well as a recognition of Tamil as one of the official languages of the nation.[24]

The Tamils objected that the pact would not entail any real autonomy for the region.[25] The LTTE was therefore uncooperative, handing over only a small number of weapons to the IPKF. Further, the IPKF engaged in battles with the rebels, and the populace at large was alienated by the excesses of the force, which engaged in human rights abuses, indiscriminate shootings, rapes and massacres. By the time the force left in March 1990, 1,155 Indian soldiers and 711 Tamil rebels had died, and India's intervention had earned it the enmity of both main ethnic groups. When India pulled out its forces, the LTTE quickly destroyed the rival rebel militias that it had set up.[26] On the other side, the accord sparked Sinhalese rioting in the capital; the majority arguing that the government had given too much to the Tamils. It is noteworthy that prominent among the initially peaceful protesters were leaders of the SLFP, as well as members of the JVP. These riots resulted in significant police crackdowns. The insurrection between 1987 and 1989 resulted in killing by the military and related unofficial armed groups of an estimated 40,000 Sinhalese suspects. In the environment of growing political violence, President Premadasa was assassinated in May 1993. Disappearances also took place outside the heart of the JVP uprising in the south.[27]

Nascent attempts at reform

The question of devolution

Not surprisingly, the question of devolution of power to any degree to the Tamils has been a thorny political issue. The question is increasingly polarized, with the LTTE generally, though not all Tamils, insisting that only full autonomy will do, while the government meanwhile fears a Sinhalese backlash in response to any appearance of concessions to the Tamils. This has meant that not only is the war a salient political issue, but so are devolution measures and questions of constitutional reform such as weakening the executive presidency. As we discuss below, questions of accountability for past abuses and curtailing future abuses have recently been thrown into this already volatile political mix.

In late 1991, a parliamentary select committee began work on potential solutions to the so-called national question, largely seeking to craft institutions to enable a degree of devolution.[28] These attempts were stalled by Tamil insistence on a single merged unit in the northern and eastern provinces where they dominated. An alternate Tamil proposal was that the constitution, defined by 'unity', become a 'federal' document. While this term is loaded in the Sri Lankan context, frequently seen as a euphemism for secession, the shift in focus has apparently helped spark more productive discussions; in late 1992, there was provisional agreement within the parliamentary select committee on an Indian-style federal system, though it remains to be seen to what degree this concept can be implemented, given continued suspicion by many Tamil politicians.[29]

Following the May 1993 assassination of President Ranasinghe Premadasa, the successor government moved away from some of the excesses of its predecessor, disbanding a quasi-official police group that had been used to terrorize opponents. Scheduled provincial elections held shortly after the assassination were generally fair and resulted in a split between the UNP and the SLFP with the former dominating.[30] The military high command was somewhat revamped, with a new head that many expected to have fewer political ties. Local elections in early 1994 passed fairly peacefully, even in LTTE strongholds where a boycott was declared, which many took as a positive sign.[31]

On 16 August 1994, parliamentary elections took place following an election campaign marred by serious violence, fraud and actions by the police demonstrating their partiality towards the ruling UNP.[32] Nonetheless, the People's Alliance (PA), of which the SLFP was a member, replaced the UNP government. Chandrika Kumaratunga became the new prime minister, with the PA as part of a larger ruling coalition in a campaign that saw some violence as usual, but was relatively more open than those in recent years. The PA ran on a platform of negotiating an end to the conflict, dealing with human rights abuses and corruption and strengthening democracy, and more generally depicted itself as the party of change; it probably benefited from a general war-weariness in the population.[33] Another key feature of the PA's campaign was that the executive presidency was too strong and undermined democracy; while it seeks to abolish the presidency and return to a parliamentary system, it lacks the two-thirds majority to pass such a measure at this time.[34] The ceasefire and peace negotiations called in 2002 continued through mid-2003, but the final shape of any post-accord state remained to be determined.

The PA under Kumaratunga had progressively modified its stance on ethnic questions, coming to support the modification of local provincial councils to allow for more Tamil autonomy and possibly the Tamil call for a unit in the north-east. Kumaratunga had also criticized military excesses in the war in the north, winning further minority support, as well as building coalitions with Muslims and liberal Sinhalese. Shortly after the parliamentary elections, the new government announced plans to limit the emergency powers that the military and police had possessed with regard to search, arrest and detention since the early 1970s. The new government also suspended a $72 million arms contract with Russia, and began easing the embargo against Jaffna.[35]

Despite UNP attempts to characterize the PA as the party that would lead the country to a division, and the PA's pledge in its platform to create new administrative units to aid devolution, the PA won a clear majority among Sinhalese voters, suggesting that they were willing to look for new solutions to the problems in the north and east; in addition, the UNP crackdown on the JVP and the PA's emphasis on human rights probably aided the latter among some JVP sympathizers. Nonetheless, the new government's options would be limited: while it sincerely sought a solution to the ethnic strife, it could not count on the support of all Sinhalese, many of whom may have wanted to oust the UNP more than they actually supported PA ethnic policies.[36]

The parliamentary elections were followed by presidential elections on 9 November. Mrs Kumaratunga became president and appointed her mother (a former prime minister) as prime minister, decisively ending the UNP's 17-year rule, and giving the government an apparent mandate to negotiate with the LTTE. The PA's victory was interpreted as a sign that the populace sought an end to the protracted conflict, and that the PA was the most likely to achieve that, not least because Kumaratunga's late husband 'was the only leader of a major Sinhalese party to have ever visited the north-east and shown a genuine interest in reconciliation'.[37] Kumaratunga came to office with at least perceived support for her negotiation platform; similarly, the LTTE may have had incentives to negotiate because of economic weakness, the costs of continued war, and the lack of international recognition for their claims. The rebels began to suggest that they would accept devolution in place of a homeland.[38] Kumaratunga would still be somewhat hamstrung by the political influence of the armed forces, who formed a strong lobby not least because of their integral role in the maintenance of public order. The military was particularly vocal in its refusal to agree to rebel demands like the closure of a key base or to a formal ceasefire before the start of peace talks. According to some, the military had an interest in perpetuating the war because of the increased status and economic benefits that accrued to it. On the other side, there remained the risk that the LTTE could always return to guerrilla warfare, and that it would be unwilling to lay down its arms in the absence of significant government demilitarization. Nonetheless, Kumaratunga negotiated with the LTTE, reaching a ceasefire and agreement on development for the north and east in early 1995; and talks generated hope for a confederate state.[39]

However, the peace process that began optimistically soon foundered. The LTTE demanded substantive concessions before further discussions; in particular, it sought the dismantling of a major army camp, an end to the embargo on food and other supplies to the north, allowing Tamil fishermen to fish certain waters, and permission for the LTTE to carry guns for self-protection in the government-controlled eastern territory. When Kumaratunga refused to dismantle the base, and rejected the request to carry guns, the Tigers questioned her commitment. The food embargo was lifted but this step was difficult to implement.[40] In mid-April, the LTTE broke the truce and returned to the battlefield, taking advantage of the government being off guard. As a result, the government was embarrassed, and found it more difficult to advocate a negotiated solution. The attempted counter-offensive was huge, but was widely considered an unmitigated disaster.[41] Unlike in 1987, when the Indian government took an active part in the conflict by sending in the IPKF, there was little official Indian response to the escalation in the conflict.[42]

These developments scuttled the government's plan to propose a new devolution package in negotiations, but it was officially announced in August. The plan proposed a union of regions in which much power would devolve to regional authorities, with powers like defence, foreign affairs and currency reserved for the centre. In essence, the plan was federalism under the less loaded name of devolution. One analyst has suggested that this relatively concessional plan was a government attempt to bypass the LTTE and appeal directly to the war-weary Tamil people. The plan faced some serious opposition from the Sinhalese, in particular the Buddhist clergy, which was compounded by a simultaneous government proposal to abolish the executive presidency; any such constitutional reforms would require an approval by two-thirds of parliament. Further, the reservation of defence and national security powers to the centre was of concern to Tamils who feared a Sinhalese-dominated military. A further critique was that the emphasis was on decentralization rather than reform of central institutions to reflect the political and ethnic realities. Other Tamils objected that it was insensitive of the government to propose the package while carrying out the military offensive; the government presented the offensive as a war to achieve peace, that is, to convince the LTTE that a resolution could not be reached through force.[43]

Even as initiatives took place both on the battlefield and in the negotiations, the government was fulfilling another campaign promise by creating three regional investigative commissions into deaths and human rights abuses. The commissions, set up largely to investigate complaints of rights abuses resulting from the JVP revolt and widespread government crackdown in the 1988–90 period, heard tens of thousands of complaints; some 60,000 'disappeared' may have died at the hands of the government during this period; the JVP also perpetrated human rights abuses. While these commissions may represent a step forward, there were limits to the steps that the government could take against the security forces on which it depended to wage war; indeed, some police officials implicated in disappearances continued to hold high-level posts. The commissions' activities and reports are discussed in more detail below.[44]

In January 1996, a modified version of the peace and devolution plan, which gave the central government some authority to remove regional governments that seek to split, was proposed to parliament. This formulation was modified to appease the Sinhalese, adding the word 'indissoluble' before the formulation 'union of regions' to describe a future state structure. The proposal would give regional councils greater power than the extant provincial ones, thus giving ethnic groups greater control over issues like land, law and order, and taxation. It did not, however, address the Tamil demand that the north and east be merged; in addition, some Tamil parties charged that this proposal on devolution would leave more power with the centre than others had.[45] Contemporaneous with these political overtures, in a two-track approach, the government launched offensives that had significant success in taking Jaffna city and other LTTE strongholds. It is worth noting that there have been reports that these advances were aided by the help of US and western military advisers.[46] Developing constitutional reform packages dealt with the question of devolution, the question of the fate of the executive presidency, and that of fundamental rights.[47] We have discussed the fundamental rights chapter of the constitution, inroads made into it through various acts and regulations, and the obligations of the government under international law; let us turn now to the development of the new draft constitution.

By mid-1997, some analysts saw a significant decline in support for the PA government: it still won in regional elections in March, but by a narrowed margin. Negotiations over constitutional reform continued to stall because of disagreements between the government and the opposition UNP over federalism, the degree of authority to be granted to regional councils, and the combining of the north and east into one body.[48] The government continued, in conference with the opposition, its attempts to craft a new draft constitution that would address the issues of devolution, the executive presidency and fundamental rights. Following a public relations debacle in March 1997 when the government proudly unveiled a draft that was promptly disavowed by the opposition UNP, the government retreated, and in October–November 1997 unveiled another draft constitution for which it took sole responsibility.[49]

The new draft contained several innovations. First, it sought to democratize state institutions by abolishing the executive presidency and establishing a constitutional council for key appointments; second, the fundamental rights chapter was strengthened; finally, further mechanisms were developed to devolve power to regions.[50] Under the 1978 constitution, Sri Lanka had moved from a parliamentary system to one where the president was dominant: the presidential system, with concomitant centralization of power and diminution of the power of other institutions. The president could not only appoint and remove the cabinet and heads of the armed forces, she could dissolve parliament with relatively few impediments and possessed the vast powers given under the Public Security Ordinance. The hope of many is that by abolishing the executive presidency, allocating some of the president's functions to other bodies and creating greater checks on the president, the tendency towards authoritarian rule by the president could be curbed. Under the draft, the prime minister is made the head of the cabinet, the president's wide immunity is removed, and the president's power of appointment to a range of offices must be done in consultation with a constitutional council. However, she retains the power to dissolve parliament and the powers under the Public Security Ordinance; and if she wishes to dissolve a regional council she needs only the support of a simple simple parliamentary majority.[51]

The addition of a right to life, which cannot be arbitrarily denied, is a key innovation in fundamental rights in the 1997 draft, but not the only one. The right to privacy was also enshrined, as well as expansion of freedom of expression and freedom from arbitrary arrest or detention.[52] In addition, under the current constitution one can only challenge a bill on the grounds that it violates fundamental rights within a week of its introduction to parliament; once it becomes a law no challenge can be made. The new constitution would allow for such challenges to bills within two weeks of introduction, and laws that contravene the fundamental rights chapter of the constitution can be challenged for up to two years after passage.[53]

Devolution is the thorniest political issue in the country and the constitutional package, with many arguing that it is but a precursor to the dissolution of the state through the secession of the north and east. This has led one commentator to argue that there is an 'almost morbid fear in Sri Lanka, of any arrangement which even remotely resembles a federal structure'; this fear will make it difficult to achieve the support of two-thirds of parliament and a simple majority of the people that constitutional reform requires.[54] The devolution in the proposed constitution is symmetrical: the same set of powers would be handed over to each regional council, which takes the place of the provisional councils established after the 1987 Indo-Sri Lankan accord and the 13th amendment. The difficult issue of whether to merge the northern and eastern regions was to be resolved by a referendum in those areas. While detractors objected that the centre still held too much power, a key advance was the protection against arbitrary dissolution of local government; in the new constitution a tribunal would have to approve the dissolution.[55]

This constitution took its share of criticism as well, from both ends of the political spectrum. The UNP was concerned that the extent of devolution was too far-reaching, and drafted counter-proposals that emphasized the need for a unitary state. It would limit devolution, and the scope of powers of local government. It would instead establish a second parliamentary chamber that would ensure that 'the minority communities would be adequately represented'; representation for minorities in the cabinet; and a president and two vice-presidents to represent the three main communities (Sinhalese, Tamil and Muslim).[56] On the other side, human rights groups have expressed concern about the way in which the fundamental rights chapter of the draft constitution continues to fall short of the guarantees provided in the ICCPR. They have expressed concern that there are not attempts to curb the wide powers granted by emergency regulations, nor are there specific provisions to guarantee minority rights.[57] In any event, the proposal continued to be stalled; there was some hope of its revival in September 1999[58] but, in early 2003 it had not been passed, though current peace negotiations may give cause for hope.

The question of accountability

Kumaratunga's government moved quickly to carry out the campaign promise of investigating disappearances and killings, though the small regional commissions encountered resistance from the military and police who denied knowledge of abuses.[59] Other steps towards protection of human rights included plans to have senior military officers investigate claims of disappearances in the north and east, and the government's creation of a human rights commission under the president's direct supervision to monitor complaints that the military, police and other state bodies have violated human rights.[60] In September 1997, the final reports of the three commissions of inquiry were handed over to the president, and it was announced that their contents would be made public. In September 1997, the government publicly acknowledged that between 16,000 and 17,000 had disappeared during the crackdown on the JVP, and promised to prosecute the perpetrators. Even a military commander in Jaffna made an unusual public promise to guard against future abuses.[61]

The reports were released in September 1997; they addressed political violence by both sides around the country dating back to 1988. The commissions apparently inherited 5,000 complaints from a 1991 commission of inquiry into 'involuntary removal' of persons.[62] A key concern of human rights advocates was that they did not inquire into violence before 1988 or (according to them) after the Kumaratunga administration came into power. In July, the government appointed a unified nationwide commission to address 12,000 complaints not addressed by the previous reports, but its mandate did not include these previously excluded events.[63] The reports were extensive, although the degree of investigation varied significantly by region.[64] The creation of three commissions rather than one was, in fact, the source of considerable criticism by human rights groups. While the mandates were the same, some commissions appear to have undertaken to extend their inquiries to later dates, or even name names, while others have not. Thus, for example, the commission investigating disappearances in the north and east had considerably less information, largely because of the security situation at the time in which it began its work. In particular, in Jaffna, the LTTE stronghold, the situation was such that the commission could not go to the region and investigate complaints, but instead invited Tamils residing outside the region to come to the capital and file with the commission at the ministry of justice.[65] Another obstacle to reporting was that military uniforms do not contain the name or rank of the person wearing them, making definitive identification of perpetrators difficult save in those exceptional cases of particularly notorious perpetrators. Further, even in instances where the name of the perpetrator was known, the army was less than forthcoming with information.[66]

There was no consistency among reports regarding identification of perpetrators. While the report for the northern and eastern provinces provided a list of victims and individuals alleged to be perpetrators, the two other reports did not; the report for the western and southern region explicitly ruled out such a list citing the need for confidentiality pending further investigations.[67] There was also no consistency with regard to methodology or marshalling of information. All three commissions used the same form to solicit information from relations of the disappeared, but only one commission utilized extensive statistical analysis to identify those hardest hit. It was this commission, then, that went the furthest in attempting to identify not just the victims (and perpetrators) of disappearances, but the pattern of violence in general, an important key to addressing the foundations of such crimes.[68] The commissions also did not all address the same period of time. While the mandates for all referred to the investigation of disappearances 'at any time after 1 January 1988',[69] one report addressed disappearances up to 1991, another up to 1996, and one was less clear about its cut-off.[70] Nonetheless, the initial accusations by human rights advocates that the commissions would be loath to examine any abuses under the Kumaratunga administration appear to have been somewhat excessive, although the record after 1994 is spotty.

The reports made suggestions (again with varying degrees of thoroughness) regarding steps to be taken to redress past abuses and prevent future ones. These included punishment of perpetrators, an overhaul of the emergency regulations that facilitated the abuses, education of the police and armed forces in human rights and humanitarian norms, and compensation to victims and their families.[71]

On 30 April 1998, the president established a new, nationwide commission, whose mandate was investigate those reports of disappearances that the previous three commissions had been unable to address or resolve.[72] Again, the commission faced heavy criticism for its limited mandate. While it did not address complaints before January 1988, it would investigate complaints that continued to be received until shortly before the previous commissions completed work in September 1997.[73]

A small step was taken with regard to the disappearances in Jaffna following the government's recovery of it in 1996. In November 1996, the government established a board of investigation at the ministry of defence; by November 1997, only 180 of 760 complaints were traced. The Ministry of Foreign Affairs subsequently stated that the newly established human rights commission, discussed below, was investigating 274 cases of disappearances in Jaffna. The US Department of State states that there were 350 confirmed disappearances in Jaffna in 1996. Nonetheless, the unified commission has yet to follow up on the disappearances in Jaffna, cancelling a trip there in late 1998 on the grounds that it could not trace many complaints.[74]

The commissions of inquiry into disappearances were not the only attempts to address human rights that the government initiated. A complaint mechanism was set up in the form of the office of the ombudsman as early as 1981, though that proved to be woefully ineffective, not least because of a forbidding procedure for registering complaints. Even prior to the Kumaratunga regime, there had existed within the ministry of defence a committee to monitor detention centres.[75]

In 1996, the parliament passed a bill establishing the human rights commission, which was empowered to inquire into complaints regarding procedures of government bodies with a view to ensuring their compliance with the constitution; to inquire into complaints regarding infringements or imminent infringements of human rights, and to provide for resolution via conciliation and mediation; to advise the government in formulating legislation to further human rights; to make recommendations to the government regarding human rights treaties; and to promote awareness and education with regard to human rights. If conciliation fails, the commission can recommend to the state that redress be offered to the victim and the practice in question modified, but it cannot impose binding orders.[76]

The commission bill and ultimate act drew fire from human rights advocates, who viewed it as too weak. A key concern was that the commission covered only the fundamental rights enshrined in the Sri Lankan constitution, not the wider rights of the International Convention on Civil and Political Rights to which the country was a party. Other objections were that the human rights commission would take over the duty of its predecessor, the human rights task force, in monitoring the welfare of detainees, but that the regulations surrounding detention would be weakened; and that the commission would be limited to addressing individual allegations, and would be unable to look into larger situations, incidents and administrative practices. Finally commentators pointed to the large number of human rights bodies extant and expressed concern that there would be a proliferation of bodies that were not particularly effective.[77] In defence of the commission, it was a more efficient and less expensive way of having fundamental and human rights complaints addressed than bringing a case to the supreme court. In addition, fundamental rights cases had to be brought before the supreme court within one month of the violation; complaints brought to the commission first could be brought before the court up to one year later.[78]

The human rights commission began operating on 17 March 1997; a key feature of the new rules pertaining to human rights is that the police and army must report all arrests to it within 48 hours, including arrests under the Prevention of Terrorism Act. However, it has faced the criticism that it has failed to take any significant action. It has yet to exercise its power to initiate and intervene in legislation, and according to one commentator failed to take any drastic actions in its first year of operations. Most of its work has been devoted to monitoring the treatment of those placed in custody under the PTA and emergency regulations.[79]

Finally, in response to complaints regarding abuses occurring through the use of checkpoints and late-night sweeps, in 1998 the president set up the president's committee on unlawful arrests and harassments, to which arrestees or their proxies could bring complaints regarding mistreatment in such circumstances, and which could recommend disciplinary action for police officers or military members responsible for abuses.[80]

Accountability and prosecution

Initial steps to curb human rights abuses by the security forces took place in 1995, with the arrests of 18 members of the security forces and seven civilian informants; ten of those arrested were members of the special task force, a security body in the police that performed military functions and had acted with particular impunity. A total of 22 members of the special task force were arrested in 1995, but were released on bail and soon resumed police duties; the case has been delayed several times by the failure of the prosecution to appear at court proceedings.[81]

Prosecutions for abuses in the north against Tamils took place in mid-1998. While the government admits that some 500 Tamil civilians have disappeared since the retaking of LTTE territory in mid-1996, a key case dealt with the killings of four Tamils. In it, six soldiers and a reserve police officer were convicted and sentenced to be executed in the September 1996 killings. A soldier convicted in the case claimed to know the location of a mass grave containing 400 victims; while the government ordered a police investigation little progress was made.[82] In other cases of abuse involving the security forces, however, those charged remained free and even on the job. On a more positive note, in August 1998, five senior police officers were suspended in connection with charges of torture and extrajudicial execution at a government detention centre at the Batalanda housing estate.[83] In February 1999, another landmark case was concluded. In the case involving the disappearance of 32 schoolboys in Embilipitiya, seven of the nine persons accused, all but one security personnel, were convicted and sentenced to about ten years in prison.[84]

Reactions of the security forces to commissions and prosecutions

Unlike many other countries examined in this book, the police and armed forces have not publicly expressed significant opposition to the commissions of inquiry or prosecutions, though, as has already been discussed, they were frequently intransigent in refusing to aid such investigations. What threats there were appear to have been posed by individual members of the police to witnesses in judicial cases and even to members of a commission, but not posed by the branches of service themselves.[85] As I discuss below, this may result from the traditional separation of the military from politics in Sri Lanka; unlike many countries in Latin America, there is in doctrine and practice, civilian control over the military. Additional pressure was put on the government, and the security forces by extension, in mid-1998 by a scathing report by the UN Human Rights Commission's special rapporteur, which stated that 'extrajudicial, summary, or arbitrary executions amongst the civilian population have become an almost ubiquitous feature of daily life in Sri Lanka'.[86]

Even as the government sought to reveal and punish past abuses, there was a crackdown on civil liberties in the country. The arrest and detention of Tamils based solely on ethnicity escalated, political assassinations continued and restrictions on journalism tightened. On 4 August 1998, the government imposed a state of emergency and cancelled elections scheduled for 28 August. This continued the trend of 1997, when emergency rule was progressively applied across the country and strictures on publishing increased, most notably with a large number of defamation actions brought by the government (including the president) against the press.[87]

Trade-offs: the security forces, reform and accountability

Accountability

Surprising advances in the area of accountability have been made, with the conclusion of a number of notorious cases. However, the prosecution of high-profile cases should not be confused with a broader attempt at accountability: many more instances of abuse and even massacre remain unaddressed. Nonetheless, it is significant not only that the commissions of inquiry proceeded but that the prosecutions did as well with a minimum of backlash by those targeted.

Institutional reform: context and progress

To understand the impediments to reform of the security forces one must understand the nature of the military in Sri Lanka: security forces completely lack minority representation, facilitating impunity. This is the case even though, at independence, minorities were in fact *over*represented in the armed forces, comprising three-fifths in 1949. This would change, however, because of amendments to the recruitment system, which resulted in the overrepresentation of Sinhalese: by 1960, they comprised 100 per cent of the armed forces. As important as the makeup of the military, however, is its conception of its role and mission: it has never fought a foreign power, so it is conceptualized entirely as an internal security force. While it exists formally to deter external aggression, the conflict with the LTTE provides it with its true *raison d'être*. The military thus views its mission as internal security, viewing itself as the key player in conflict resolution. It is worth noting that it was not only the LTTE threat that created this internal emphasis; most of the senior military officers were mid-level officers during the JVP uprising, so their embattled mentality will be slow to change.[88]

In addition, not only do makeup and mission lead to a biased and overly politicized military; the military's war in the north and east commands a huge budget, which one might expect them to be loath to give up. Civilian control has also been progressively limited; until the 1980s, the secretary of defence was a civilian; now the post is held by military officers. Further, the need to prosecute the war has limited even civilian oversight and knowledge: parliament cannot scrutinize the military budget or planned acquisitions.[89]

Nonetheless, the difference between the Sri Lankan military and some of the Latin American militaries already discussed should be emphasized. As one observer put it, the Sri Lankan military inherited from the British the Sandhurst tradition, through which they were imbued with professionalism and subordination to civilian rule, unlike the Latin American cases, in which militaries were never properly subordinated to civilian rule. In fact, the problem was the reverse: that the security forces were used as political tools by cunning civilian politicians.[90] Excesses occurred, according to one observer, as a result of overreactions from above. Fighting an insurrection, first in the south and later in the north and east, the government demanded results on a significant scale: as a result, police and military netted large numbers of 'suspects' in an attempt to catch real rebels. On this account, the civilian government developed something of a dictatorship mentality, facilitated by the executive presidency. The military and the civil service were heavily influenced by this environment, with few institutional limitations placed on the abuses that proliferated.[91] The reason, then, that high-level military officers have not been prosecuted in Sri Lanka is not that there is a fear that they will stage a coup or otherwise disrupt civilian rule, but that the civilian rulers are dependent upon the military to prosecute the war against the LTTE rebels.[92]

The police, also in a significant divergence from the Latin American pattern, were initially purely peace officers; their role changed drastically after the 1971 JVP uprising, when the police suddenly found themselves in the role of defending national security and granted extraordinary powers under the emergency regulations. In the process they became increasingly militarized and politicized, taking direct orders from politicians.[93] The police need not only to be disengaged from military activities, but made more sensitive to human rights issues: efforts are being made to educate police that are parallel to those efforts to educate the military and, according to the trainers, at least, some headway has been made.[94] In addition, some analysts have argued that the police need to be restructured internally as well: they currently have responsibility for information/intelligence, investigation and prosecution, and the claim is that the prosecution role needs to be placed in separate hands. This is the case because otherwise there is a perverse incentive for the police not to investigate, but simply to seek a conviction.[95]

Fewer advances have been made in the area of reform of the security forces: attempts have been made only at the margins in the arena of education about human rights. A nascent attempt at curbing human rights abuses has begun with a joint effort between the centre for the study of human rights and the Kotalawela defence academy. Training seeks to teach both cadets and their teachers to be more respectful of human rights. The first efforts were made in a pilot programme in 1993 for armed forces and police; these have continued to the present date in altered forms despite the fact that many in the armed forces are suspicious of human rights rhetoric, seeing it as driven by partisan interests. In fact, some organizers argue that the response of the participants has demonstrated that learning and attitudinal changes are taking place.[96]

Military budgets

In 1998, the budget allocated to defence reached 45 billion rupees, more than the combined budget for the final seven years of UNP rule, apparently part of the government's push to retake large chunks of Jaffna. The projected budget for 1999 was yet higher, 47 billion rupees, continuing a spike in the defence budget, which stood at 24 billion in 1995.[97]

Discussion: key elements of political change

International factors

The role of India in the conflict should not be underestimated, both for its role as mediator and intervener. Because some 60 million Tamils live in India, the majority in Tamil Nadu, India's politicians cannot afford to ignore the crisis in Sri Lanka on purely domestic political grounds. Others have argued that India's interest in the conflict is also socio-cultural because of the historic links between the nations; at the very least India is concerned not only with politics in the state of Tamil Nadu but also the fate of the Tamils in Sri Lanka who are of Indian origin. Finally, India's security perception, according to some, necessitates that such regional conflicts be kept under control; its leaders feel that, as a major regional power, it must act.[98] However, while India played a central role in the conflict in the past, it has maintained a studied silence with regard to the conflict of late. K. M. de Silva argues that India's involvement had significant impact, as sponsor and supplier of one side. More importantly, de Silva notes that international involvement can cause a hardening or softening of positions, a lengthening or shortening of conflicts.[99] This case is unusual in that the presence of the USA does not loom large either in the war or prospects for peace. However, there may yet be some role to play: one analyst notes that the USA has traditionally had close ties to UNP governments, and might be able to use its influence upon the opposition UNP to compromise.[100]

Duration of conflict

While the 'hurting stalemate' may not be as apparent to the relevant political actors in Sri Lanka as it was in, say, El Salvador, there can be no question that after a decade and a half of war and 55,000 deaths many are questioning the utility of fighting, on both sides. Some analysts would argue that this sentiment was behind the election of Kumaratunga and her platform of negotiation, accountability and reform. Nonetheless, the war continues as negotiations have failed to produce lasting agreements.

Balance of forces/civil–military issues

While the military's offensive in 1995 eventually led to the recapture of the LTTE's de facto seat of government, Jaffna City, after five years, it has proven less easy for the military to defeat the rebels. The assassinations, bombings and battles are thought to have led to 55,000 deaths over the years; while the Tigers have been pushed out of Jaffna and many civilians have begun to return, the LTTE is not defeated militarily, and it continues to carry out terrorist bombings.[101]

Between 1978 and 1982, the government had an army of about 13,000, though it was inexperienced and initially ill-disciplined. The country also had 14,000 police. While the Tamils appeared to be overmatched, they learned guerrilla warfare skills and soon posed a real threat to government control over the north and east. By 1987, it was estimated that there were 5,000 Tamil activists with another 8,000 reserves. On some accounts, these guerrillas were able to inflict a hurting stalemate, both through direct attacks and creating an environment harming aid, investment and tourism.[102] The security forces in 1997 comprised a police force of 50,000, which has been used not only for internal security but also in anti-LTTE military operations, and military bodies comprising an army of 118,000, navy of 12,500 and an air force of 10,000. In addition, there existed the special task force to battle the LTTE, 5,000 'home guards' of local communities that gave security to Muslim and Sinhalese villages near the war zone, and the government-armed Tamil militias opposed to the LTTE. This represented a steady increase from the 1995 and 1996 numbers of 50,000 police and 80,000 army; it was in 1995 that the home guards were increased from 1,000 to 5,000.[103]

Lessons

Sri Lanka is an unusual case in several respects: it is a case of a continuing democracy facing an ongoing civil war that has sought to come to terms with past and ongoing abuses through the creation of commissions of inquiry, a human rights commission and some prosecutions. Nonetheless, as this chapter has shown, even a democratic country without a coup-prone military will have some difficulty in addressing the legacy of the past. Even war-exhaustion has not been sufficient to end the conflict and generate true reform, and international factors have not aided reform. Here, concerns about continuing to support the institutions necessary to prosecute the war in the north were more prominent than fears of a coup; as a result, as in many other countries, some compromises were necessary. While advances have been made in addressing the legacy of the past through a significant, if incomplete, outing of the truth and some high-profile prosecutions, institutional and constitutional reform has been much more difficult to achieve, as has a negotiated solution to the situation in the north and east.

Notes

1 K. M. de Silva, 'Sri Lanka: Surviving Ethnic Strife', *Journal of Democracy*, 8, 1 (January 1997), p. 97.

2 As becomes clear below, the fact that there has been enfranchisement and voting does not mean that there has not been intimidation and manipulation of the polity through propaganda, but the formal structures have remained.

3 Sumantra Bose, *States, Nations, Sovereignty: Sri Lanka, India, and the Tamil Eelam Movement* (New Delhi: Sage, 1994), p. 45; Dennis Austin, *Democracy and Violence in India and Sri Lanka* (London: Pinter, 1994), p. xvii; for a general journalistic view, see William McGowan, *Only Man is Vile: The Tragedy of Sri Lanka* (New York: Farrar, Straus & Giroux, 1992).

4 Jonathan Spencer, *A Sinhala Village in a Time of Trouble: Politics and Change in Rural Sri Lanka* (Delhi: Oxford University Press, 1990), p. 18; Spencer, 'Introduction: The Power of the Past', in Spencer (ed.), *Sri Lanka: History and the Roots of Conflict* (London: Routledge, 1990), p. 9; Howard Wriggins, 'Sri Lanka: Negotiations in a Secessionist Conflict', in Zartman (ed.), *Elusive Peace*, p. 36.

5 Austin, *Democracy and Violence*, p. 62. The Sinhalese, who speak Sinhalese and are largely Buddhist, comprise approximately 74 per cent of the population, while the Tamils, who speak Tamil and are largely Hindu, comprise about 18 per cent of the population, largely concentrated in the north and east, though with a significant minority in the capital. For a general overview of the religious/ethnic divisions and their relationships to conflict, see Douglas M. Johnston, 'Religion and Conflict Resolution', *Fletcher Forum of World Affairs*, 20, 1 (Winter/Spring 1996), pp. 53–61.

6 Stanley J. Tambiah, *Sri Lanka: Ethnic Fratricide and the Dismantling of Democracy* (Chicago, IL: University of Chicago Press, 1986), p. 13; Tambiah, *Leveling Crowds: Ethnonationalist Conflicts and Collective Violence in South Asia* (Berkeley, CA: University of California Press, 1996), pp. 15–16. On the rise of Tamil identity assertion, see Ambalavanar Sivaraja, *Politics of Tamil Nationalism in Sri Lanka* (New Delhi: South Asian Publishers, 1996).

7 *Constitution of the Democratic Socialist Republic of Sri Lanka*, Articles 10, 11, 12 and 13.

8 Nadesan Centre, *Emergency Law*, Docinform 41 (1992), pp. 3–4. The most salient of these regulations for our purposes are those pertaining to the repression of subversion and maintenance of public order, though the regulations are used in myriad ways, encompassing the creation of universities and validation of drivers' licences. See also the update of the regulations, Docinform 65 (1994); and see further regulations in emergency regulations No. 4 of 1994, *The Gazette of the Democratic Socialist Republic of Sri Lanka*, Extraordinary (4 November 1994).

9 Bose, *States, Nations, Sovereignty*, pp. 74, 79 ; Tambiah, *Sri Lanka*, pp. 42–5, argues that the Act has progressively generated the very militancy and separatist sentiments it was meant to repress.

10 Amnesty International, 'Security Measures Violate Human Rights' (July 1995), AI Index ASA 37/12/95, p. 3; Ministry of Justice, Constitutional Affairs and National Integration, *The Government's Proposals for Constitutional Reform* (Colombo: Department of Government Printing, 1997); Amnesty International, 'Sri Lanka: Security Measures', p. 17; for more on the relation of new draft rights to extant law, see Nayana, 'New Rights Clash with Existing Laws', *The Island* (4 May 1997), p. 16. Legal analysts have concluded that there is a general failure to incorporate international human rights instruments by legislation or judicial precedent, see Asian Legal Resource Centre Limited, *Human Rights Related Legal Reforms in Sri Lanka: The Final Document* (Hong Kong: ALCRL, 1996), p. 3.

11 Robert A. Denemark, 'Democracy and the World System: The Political Economy of Sri Lanka's Vicious Electoral Cycle', in Chronis Polychroniou (ed.), *Issues and Perspectives in International Political Economy* (Westport, CT: Praeger, 1992), pp. 194–6. On the assassination more generally, see A. C. Alles, *The Assassination of a Prime Minister* (New York: Vantage Press, 1986); Donald L. Horowitz, *Coup Theories and Officers' Motives: Sri Lanka in Comparative Prespective* (Princeton, NJ: Princeton University Press, 1980) *passim* and pp. 146, 208.

12 Denemark, 'Democracy and the World System', pp. 203–4; Tambiah, *Sri Lanka*, pp. 13–14.

13 Bose, *States, Nations, Sovereignty*, pp. 46, 68–72; Bruce Matthews, 'Devolution of Power in Sri Lanka', *The Round Table*, 330 (1994), p. 233.

14 Steven Kemper, 'J. R. Jayewardene, Righteousness, and *Realpolitik*', in Spencer (ed.), *Sri Lanka*, pp. 191, 200–1.

15 Bose, *States, Nations, Sovereignty*, pp. 74, 94.

16 Matthews, 'Devolution of Power in Sri Lanka', p. 234; de Silva, 'Sri Lanka', p. 103.

17 Prevention of Terrorism Act, *Gazette* (1979), no. 48, and Prevention of Terrorism, Amendment to the Prevention of Terrorism Act, *Gazette* (19 March 1982), pt II, supp.; Bose, *States, Nations, Sovereignty*, pp. 74, 79; Tambiah, *Sri Lanka*, pp. 42–5, argues that the act has progressively generated the very militancy and separatist sentiments it was meant to repress.

18 Tambiah, *Leveling Crowds*, pp. 226–9.

19 Bose, *States, Nations, Sovereignty*, p. 73; Tambiah, *Sri Lanka*, pp. 15, 22; Tambiah, *Leveling Crowds*, pp. 94–100; Denemark, 'Democracy and the World System', p. 206; Marshall R. Singer, 'Sri Lanka's Ethnic Conflict: Have Bombs Shattered Hopes for Peace?', *Asian Survey*, 36, 11 (November 1996), p. 1149.

20 Austin, *Democracy and Violence*, p. 74.

21 Tambiah, *Sri Lanka*, pp. 16, 25 and 26.

22 Bose, *States, Nations, Sovereignty*, pp. 139–41; S. D. Muni, *Pangs of Proximity: India and Sri Lanka's Ethnic Crisis* (New Delhi: Sage, 1993), pp. 74–5; see Ponmoni Sahadevan, *India and Overseas Indians: The Case of Sri Lanka* (New Delhi: Kalinga Publications, 1995).

23 Muni, *Pangs of Proximity*, pp. 94–5, 102–3 and 201.

24 Bose, *States, Nations, Sovereignty*, pp. 131, 153–6. For the text of the accord, see Austin, *Democracy and Violence*, pp. 87–92; Partha S. Ghosh, 'Sinhala–Tamil Ethnic Conflict and India', *Economic and Political Weekly* (24 June 1995), p. 1486; Muni, *Pangs of Proximity*, p. 105, points out that pride of place is still given to the Sinhalese language. Under the amendment, the president can dissolve the administration of a province: see International Centre for Ethnic Studies, *Sri Lanka: The Devolution Debate* (Colombo: International Centre for Ethnic Studies, 1996), p. 232.

25 These provincial councils, while ostensibly meant to begin the devolution of power to Tamils, were instead used to aid decentralization of government in general. Matthews, 'Devolution of Power in Sri Lanka', p. 235. Other regional councils, set up in other legislation that year, the Pradeshiya Sabhas, have shown somewhat more promise: ibid., pp. 235–6.

26 See Barnett R. Rubin, *Cycles of Violence: Human Rights in Sri Lanka since the Indo-Sri Lanka Agreement* (Washington, DC: Asia Watch, December 1987); Bose, *States, Nations, Sovereignty*, pp.131–4, 157–8, 166. On the other side, the JVP was angered by the presence of a foreign force on its soil, believing it another sign that the government was too soft towards the Tamils and a pawn of India: Austin, *Democracy and Violence*, pp. 74–5.

27 Tambiah, *Leveling Crowds*, p. 271; Mick Moore, '"Guided Democracy" in Sri Lanka: The Electoral Dimension', *Journal of Commonwealth and Comparative*

Politics, 32, 1 (March 1994), p. 1; S. Guhan, 'Indo-Sri Lanka Discord', *Economic and Political Weekly* (7 January 1995), p. 35.

28 Matthews, 'Devolution of Power in Sri Lanka', p. 237.

29 Matthews, 'Devolution of Power in Sri Lanka', pp. 238–40.

30 Moore, '"Guided Democracy"', pp. 1–2.

31 'Sri Lanka: In the Tigers' Den', *The Economist* (5 March 1994), pp. 38–9, discusses the appointment as commander of Gerry de Silva, a Roman Catholic married to a Tamil, as a positive signal; see also Manik de Silva, 'Silent Tigers', *Far Eastern Economic Review* (17 March 1994), p. 28. See also John-Thor Dahlburg, 'Sri Lankans got to Polls in East Despite Tamil Boycott', *Los Angeles Times* (2 March 1994), p. A9. These elections also showed a surprising surge in support for the People's Alliance in the south: see Manik de Silva, 'Southern Surprise', *Far Eastern Economic Review* (7 April 1994), p. 20.

32 Inform, 'Parliamentary Elections 1994: Special Report 1: Polls Related Violence' (Colombo: Inform/Movement for Free and Fair Elections photocopy, July 1994), p. 13; Movement for Free and Fair Elections, 'Interim Report on the Sri Lanka Parliamentary Elections of August 16th 1994' (Rajaginya, Sri Lanka: Movement for Free and Fair Elections photocopy, October 1994), pp. 2–19; International Human Rights Law Group, 'Report of the International NGO Observer Mission to the Sri Lanka Parliamentary Elections' (Washington, DC: International Human Rights Law Group, 1994), pp. 1–6.

33 Mrs Kumaratunga, the daughter of two former prime ministers, had left the country for a few years following the assassination of her husband in 1988, apparently by the JVP: S. W. R. de A. Samarasinghe, 'The 1994 Parliamentary Elections in Sri Lanka: A Vote for Good Governance', *Asian Survey*, 34, 12 (December 1994), pp. 1019, 1021–2, 1024–6. See also, from the perspective of an election monitor, Richard Bourne, 'Observing Sri Lanka's Parliamentary Election', *The Round Table*, 333 (1995), pp. 67, 69–71; Mervyn de Silva, 'New Broom', *Far Eastern Economic Review* (1 September 1994), p. 16. She also took a big symbolic step by publicizing the mass grave of students killed by security forces during the 1989 crackdown: see Gamini Keerawella and Rohan Samarajiva, 'Sri Lanka in 1993', *Asian Survey*, 34, 2 (February 1994), p. 171; Singer, 'Sri Lanka's Ethnic Conflict', p. 1150; Hu Guangyao, 'Why the Sri Lankan People's Alliance Won', *Beijing Review* (5–11 September), p. 21; John F. Burns, 'Long-ruling Sri Lanka Party Makes Way for 3rd in Dynasty', *New York Times* (19 August 1994), p. A8.

34 Samarasinghe, 'The 1994 Parliamentary Elections', p. 1031; Bourne, 'Observing Sri Lanka's', p. 67; de Silva, 'Sri Lanka', p. 104.

35 Chandra R. De Silva, 'The Elections of 1994 in Sri Lanka: Background and Analysis' *The Round Table*, 34 (1995), pp. 211–12; John F. Burns, 'Sri Lankan Rebels and New Government Agree to Talks', *New York Times* (5 September 1994), sec. 1, p. 5.

36 Samarasinghe, 'The 1994 Parliamentary Elections', pp. 1027, 1032.

37 De Silva, 'The Elections of 1994', pp. 207, 212; de Silva, 'Sri Lanka', p. 109; 'Sri Lanka: Vote for Reconciliation', *Economic and Political Weekly* (20 August 1994).

38 Sumantra Bose, 'Tamil Self-determination in Sri Lanka: Challenges and Prospects', *Economic and Political Weekly* (24 September 1994), p. 2537; A. G. Noorani, 'Challenge of Power-sharing in Sri Lanka', *Economic and Political Weekly* (25 March 1995), p. 622.

39 Mervyn de Silva, 'War and Peace: Army Halts Offensive as Peace Process Gets Under Way', *Far Eastern Economic Review* (13 October 1994), p. 32; Bose, 'Tamil Self-determination', pp. 2537–9. This was a concern also raised by the military in objection to peace talks: see Mervyn de Silva, 'The Lady's Mandate: Kumaratunga Sees Her Win as a Vote for Peace', *Far Eastern Economic Review*

(24 November 1994), p. 24; De Silva, 'The Elections of 1994', p. 214; John-Thor Dahlburg, 'Sri Lanka Truce Raises Peace Hopes', *Los Angeles Times* (7 January 1995), p. A12. In addition to the ceasefire, the parties agreed on a plan to rebuild the north worth some $816 million.

40 Howard B. Schaffer, 'Sri Lanka in 1995: A Difficult and Disappointing Year', *Asian Survey*, 36, 2 (February 1996), p. 217; Singer, 'Sri Lanka's Ethnic Conflict', pp. 1150–1; 'Darkness Visible', *The Economist* (4 March 1995), p. 37.

41 Schaffer, 'Sri Lanka in 1995', pp. 217–18; Manik de Silva, 'Back to War: Tamil Rebels Break Truce with Major Attacks', *Far Eastern Economic Review* (25 May 1995), p. 21; Singer, 'Sri Lanka's Ethnic Conflict', p. 1151; Sumantra Bose, 'War and Peace in Sri Lanka: Government's Reform Proposals and Beyond', *Economic and Political Weekly* (30 September 1995), p. 2426.

42 Meanwhile, India had apparently intercepted arms shipments bound for the Tamils in Jaffna and prevented rebels from coming into India: see 'This Time, Delhi is Keeping Quiet', *Asiaweek* (17 November 1995), p. 34.

43 Singer, 'Sri Lanka's Ethnic Conflict', pp. 1151–2. On the offensive in Jaffna, see Suzanne Goldenberg, 'Retreat for the Tigers of Jaffna', *The Guardian* (7 November 1995), p. T6; Schaffer, 'Sri Lanka in 1995', pp. 219–1; Lakshman Marasinghe, 'Some Thoughts on the Devolution Package', in International Centre for Ethnic Studies, *Sri Lanka: The Devolution Debate*, p. 16. Rumours have circulated that, to that end, Kumaratunga 'informally agreed to the formation of a Tamil "regiment" or "brigade" in the army': Sumantra Bose, 'War and Peace in Sri Lanka: Government's Reform Proposals and Beyond', *Economic and Political Weekly* (30 September 1995), pp. 2424–5; G. G. Ponnambalam (General Secretary, All-Ceylon Tamil Congress), 'Package Not a Matter to Laugh at', *Sunday Times* (10 September 1995); Jayadeva Uyangoda, 'Extremism Pays Not; Moderation Does', *Sunday Times* (3 September 1995); Reggie Fernando, 'War to Persuade LTTE to Talk Peace', *Sunday Observer* (11 June 1995), p. 3.

44 'Voices of the Dead', *The Economist* (15 April 1995), p. 37; Molly Moore, 'Sri Lanka: A Nation Divided', *Washington Post* (9 May 1993), p. A25. For a journalistic account of the so-called death squads, see Steve Coll, 'Silence in the Killing Zone', *Washington Post Magazine* (16 January 1994), p. W16; John F. Burns, 'Sri Lankans Hear Details of Decade of Slaughter', *New York Times* (21 May 1995), sec. 1, p. 10.

45 For the text of this proposal, see International Centre for Ethnic Studies, *Sri Lanka: The Devolution Debate*, Appendix C. See also 'An Indissoluble Solution?', *The Economist* (20 January 1996), p. 34; Neelan Tiruchelvam, 'Rough Edges', *Far Eastern Economic Review* (15 February 1996), p. 28; Neelan Tiruchelvam, 'Devolution of Power, the Problems and Challenges', in International Centre for Ethnic Studies, *Sri Lanka: The Devolution Debate*, pp. 40–1. See also Manik de Silva, 'Carrot and Stick: Colombo Proposes to Give Tamils Greater Autonomy', *Far Eastern Economic Review* (1 February 1996), p. 21.

46 Singer, 'Sri Lanka's Ethnic Conflict', pp. 1152–3. In an apparent response to the government advances in Jaffna, a bomb was placed in Colombo, killing 80. See Manik de Silva, 'Cornered in Colombo', *Far Eastern Economic Review* (15 February 1996), pp. 14–15. Uli Schmetzer, 'Tide Runs Against Sri Lanka Rebels; US Advisers Help Government in Drive to Defeat Tamils', *Chicago Tribune* (8 August 1996), p. 10.

47 For a cogent analysis of the politics and the jurisprudence surrounding the existing constitution, see Radhika Coomaraswamy, *Ideology and the Constitution: Essays on Constitutional Jurisprudence* (Colombo: International Centre for Ethnic Studies, 1997).

48 'Sri Lanka: Uneasy Calm', *Economic and Political Weekly* (14 June 1997), p. 1388; 'Sri Lanka: Movement without Progress', *Economic and Political Weekly* (21 June

1997), p. 1434. On the 1997 draft and negotiations with the opposition, see G. L. Peiris, minister of justice and constitutional affairs, 'Constitutional Reforms: A New Point of Departure for Sri Lanka', available at www.slt.lk:80/news/GLrele.html.

49 *The Government's Proposals for Constitutional Reform.*

50 See Dinusha Panditaratne and Pradeep Ratnam (eds), *The Draft Constitution of Sri Lanka: Critical Aspects* (Colombo: Law and Society Trust, 1998), p. vi.

51 Pradeep Ratnam, 'The Question of Executive Presidency in Sri Lanka', in Panditaratne and Ratnam, *The Draft Constitution*, pp. 41–4. On the experience and relative merits of presidential and parliamentary systems in Sri Lanka, see Radhika Coomaraswamy, 'Parliamentary Democracy v. the Presidential System: A Realist Approach', *Law and Society Trust Fortnightly Review*, 3, 42 (August 1992), pp. 2–6, and H. L. de Silva, 'Some Comments on Dr (Ms) R Coomaraswamy's Paper on Parliamentary Democracy v. Presidential System', in the same issue, pp. 14–15. Rohan Edrisinha, 'Critical Overview: Constitutionalism, Conflict Resolution and the Limits of the Draft Constitution', and C. S. Dattatreya, 'The Proposal for a Constitutional Council', in Panditaratne and Ratnam, *The Draft Constitution*, Ratnam, 'The Question of Executive Presidency', pp. 47–53. See generally *The Government's Proposals for Constitutional Reform*, chapters VII and XXIII; Leo Fernando, 'Position of Ministry Secretaries under the New Constitutional Proposals', *Daily News* (17 February 1999), p. 8.

52 Deepika Udagama, 'Fundamental Rights: The Need for a Futuristic Vision', in Panditaratne and Ratnam (eds), *The Draft Constitution*, pp. 119–20. See also *The Government's Proposals for Constitutional Reforms*, chapter III, as well as the limitations on those rights for national security, public order, etc.

53 G. L. Peiris, 'Introductory Overview: Constitutional Reform and Devolution of Power', in Panditaratne and Ratnam, *The Draft Constitution*, p. 6. See also Edrisinha, 'Critical Overview', pp. 19–21. However, another provision validates existing laws even if they are inconsistent with fundamental rights provisions; this was an attempt to preserve 'traditional' Muslim, Tamil, and Kandyan law; see *The Government's Proposals for Constitutional Reform*, Arts 165 and 168.

54 Tressie Leitan, 'Regional Councils and the Devolution of Power', *Daily News* (9 September 1995); 'Graduating to Mediation', *The Island* (23 August 1998), p. 11. In a recent interview, President Kumaratunga, while refusing to give details, stated that she had found a way to circumvent UNP opposition without violating the constitution: see Nalin de Silva, 'Deviousness and the Package', *The Island* (12 August 1998), p. 15. On the positive side, a recent poll by the University of Colombo found that 77 per cent of those polled and a majority of Sinhalese favoured a peaceful end to the conflict and rejected a military solution: 'Business Offer Peace Plan', *Sri Lanka Monitor* (October 1998); and Jehan Perera, 'Is Sri Lanka Ready for Peace Talks Again?', *Tamil Times*, 17, 12 (15 December 1998), p. 11.

55 *The Government's Proposals for Constitutional Reform*, chapter XV; Edrisinha, 'Critical Overview', pp. 27–30.

56 UNP constitutional proposals (photocopy, 1997, on file with current author), section on 'National Power Sharing'; see also 'UNP Seeks New Political Culture' (photocopy, 1997, on file with current author). The UNP draft, unlike the PA draft, includes provisions for a police ombudsman and human rights experts on an independent police commission. Compare *Government's Proposals*, chapter XXII, with 'UNP Seeks New Political Culture', section on 'An Independent National Police Commission and Provincial Police Commissions'; see also '[Text of the] Proposals to the Parliamentary Select Committee on Constitutional Reform by the United National Party, 29th January 1998', in Panditaratne and Ratnam, *The Draft Constitution*, p. 344.

57 Sumudu Atapattu, 'A Commentary on the Draft Fundamental Rights Chapter', in Law and Society Trust, *Sri Lanka: State of Human Rights 1998* (Colombo, Sri Lanka: Law and Society Trust, 1998), pp. 174–5; Mario Gomez, 'Sri Lanka's Proposed Bill of Rights: Lacking in Imagination and Vision', *Law and Society Trust Fortnightly Review*, 7, 113 (March 1997), p. 24.

58 This following the killing by a suicide bomber of one of its drafters and key supporters, an MP of the TULF, Dr Neelan Tiruchelvam: 'A Leading Sri Lankan Moderate is Killed', *New York Times* (30 July 1999), p. A10.

59 Burns, 'Sri Lankans Hear Details of Decade of Slaughter'. For the text of the relevant law, see Special Commissions of Inquiry, *Gazette of the Democratic Socialist Republic of Sri Lanka* (23 September 1994), pt II, supplement; the underlying legal basis for the commissions can be found in the Commissions of Inquiry Act, *Gazette* (1948), law no. 17 and Special Presidential Commissions of Inquiry Act, *Gazette* (1978), law no. 7, amended by Act, *Gazette* (1978), law no. 4.

60 Gaston de Rosayro and Matthew Chance, 'Military Officers to Probe Cases of "Disappearances"', *South China Morning Post* (16 December 1996), p. 15.

61 'Sri Lanka: Amnesty International Welcomes News that Reports of Commissions will be Made Public' (4 September 1997), available at http://humanrights.tqn.com/b1AIasa372397.htm; 'News in Brief: Sri Lanka's Disappeared', *The Guardian* (4 September 1997), p. 12; John F. Burns, 'Unable to Beat Rebels, Sri Lanka Eases Stance', *New York Times* (5 November 1997), p. A3.

62 'Sri Lanka: Human Rights Developments', *Human Rights Watch World Report 1999*, available at http:www.hrw.org/hrw/worldreport99/asia/srilanka.html. Amnesty International, 'Sri Lanka: Time for Truth and Justice', (April 1995), AI Index 37/04/95, pp. 13–14. This earlier commission spanned the period between January 1991 and January 1993: see Permanent Mission of Sri Lanka, 'Situation Report' (Colombo/Geneva: Permanent Mission, 1993), p. 8, a statement of the human rights situation to the UN HRC.

63 In particular, human rights advocates were concerned about the exclusion of disappearances of Tamils from the east in 1984–8 and disappearances after the government retook Jaffna in mid-1996: 'Sri Lanka: Human Rights Developments', available at http://www.hrw.org/hrw/worldreport99/asia/srilanka.html. See also Inform, 'Lobby Document: UN Commission on Human Rights, 1995' (Colombo: Inform, 1995), p. 3. The civil rights movement argued that the commissions should examine incidents since 1984; Inform argues that events since 1979, the year that the Prevention of Terrorism Act entered into force, should be examined; Civil Rights Movement, 'The Investigation of "Disappearances" in Sri Lanka' (Colombo: Civil Rights Movement, 1998); see also Imran Vittachi, 'That Time of Terror', *Sunday Times* (15 March 1998), pp. 1, 10. Author's interview with the chair of the southern commission and the new island-wide commission, Mrs Manouri Muttetuwegama, 15 February 1999, Colombo.

64 The reports of the three commissions into disappearances are: *Final Report of the Commission of Inquiry into the Involuntary Removal of Persons in the Central, Northwestern and Uva Provinces*, Sessional Paper No. VI (Colombo, Sri Lanka: Department of Government Printing, 1997); *Final Report of the Commission of Inquiry into the Involuntary Removal or Disappearance of Persons in the Northern and Eastern Provinces*, Sessional Paper No. VII (Colombo, Sri Lanka: Department of Government Printing, 1997); and *Final Report of the Commission of Inquiry into Involuntary Removal or Disappearance of Persons in the Western, Southern, and Sabaragamuwa Provinces*, Sessional Paper No. V (Colombo, Sri Lanka: Department of Government Printing, 1997). Additional reports addressed a number of high-profile political killings, including that of the president's

husband. See *Report of the Presidential Commission of Inquiry into the Assassination of Mr Vijaya Kumaratunga* (Colombo, Sri Lanka: Department of Government Printing, 1996) and *Report of the Special Presidential Commission of Inquiry Regarding the Assassination of the late Lalith Athulathmudali PC and Connected Events* (Colombo, Sri Lanka: Department of Government Publications, 1997). One observer has said that the manner of setting up the commissions was 'clumsy' and that not enough human rights experts were consulted; in addition many complainants felt let down because before some of the commissions they were not treated with compassion. Author's interview, not for attribution (Colombo, 9 February 1999).

65 *Final Report in the Northern and Eastern Provinces*, p. 57. Thus, while the commission received 537 complaints it investigated only around 100, of which half were of disappearances of soldiers. To be sure, a significant number of Tamils have left Jaffna, in addition to being 'disappeared': the population dropped from 850,000 to 500,000 between 1981 and 1997, see University Teachers for Human Rights (Jaffna), *Information Bulletin* (24 August 1997), p. 1.

66 *Final Report in the Northern and Eastern Provinces*, pp. 3–4.

67 *Final Report in the Northern and Eastern Provinces*, pp. 94–7; *Final Report in the Western, Southern, and Sabaragamuwa Provinces*, pp. 12, 29. The latter commission submitted a list of those implicated under separate cover to the president. On the question of due process and justiciability of the findings of such commissions, see Mario Gomez, *Emerging Trends in Public Law* (Colombo: Vijitha Yapa Bookshop, 1998). pp. 246–7 and 257–8.

68 This was the *Final Report in the Western, Southern, and Sabaragawuma Provinces*, pp. 5–97. The other reports offered some rudimentary figures by year, ethnic group and marital status, but this report addressed, *inter alia*, occupation, the mode of disappearance/death, and evidence of the political nature of the disappearance. The chair of this commission is now the chair of the consolidated island-wide commission.

69 The mandate is reprinted in *Final Report in the Western, Southern, and Sabaragumawa Provinces*, pp. 179–81.

70 These are, respectively, *Final Report in the Western, Southern and Sabaragawuma Provinces; Final Report in the Northern and Eastern Provinces*; and *Final Report in the Central, Northwestern, North Central and Uva Provinces*. The logical explanation for this disparity is, in part, that in the west and south the JVP rebellion and attendant government crackdown had subsided, and therefore disappearances did as well.

71 *Final Report in the Western, Southern, and Sabaragamuwa Provinces*, pp. 75–97; and *Final Report in the Central, Northwestern, North Central and Uva Provinces*, pp. 2–3.

72 'By Her Excellency Chandrika Bandaranaike Kumaratunga, President of the Democratic Socialist Republic of Sri Lanka', Ref. No. SP/6/N/214/97 (photocopy on file with current author).

73 Author's interview with Manouri Muttetuwegama, chair of the new island-wide commission and of the previous southern commission (Colombo, 15 February 1999).

74 Amnesty International, 'Sri Lanka: Government's Response to Widespread "disappearances" in Jaffna' (27 November 1997), AI Index ASA 37/24/97, pp. 1–2. The numbers vary: the US Department of State puts the number of complaints at 2,500: see *Sri Lanka Country Report on Human Rights Practices for 1997*, available at http://www.state.gov/www/global/human_rights/1997_hrp_report/srilanka.htm, p. 5. According to one lobby group, the president met with relatives of the disappeared in late 1997 and promised to appoint a commission to inquire into the disappearances; this group views the Board of

Investigation as insufficient. Civil Rights Movement of Sri Lanka, 'The Investigation of "Disappearances" in Sri Lanka: A Review at Mid-July 1998' (1998), CRM photocopy; 'News Review', *Tamil Times*, 17, 12 (15 December 1998), p. 7. The commission received another 500 names of disappeared persons more recently, but it is unclear whether that falls within its mandate: see 'SLMC Submits List of 500 Missing Persons to Presidential Disappearances Commission, *Daily News* (23 February 1999), p. 1.

75 Citizens could not petition the ombudsman directly until 1994; before that they had to petition through their member of parliament: Deepika Udagama, 'A Case Study of the Office of the Ombudsman', in Law and Society Trust, *Sri Lanka: State of Human Rights 1997* (Colombo: Law and Society Trust, 1997), pp. 113–37; author's interview with Justice Jayalath and assistant legal secretary to the Minister of Defence Jinasena (Colombo, 18 February 1999), both of whom had been part of this effort; the latter continues in this capacity.

76 Parliament of the Democratic Socialist Republic of Sri Lanka, 'Human Rights Commission of Sri Lanka Act, No. 21 of 1996', *Gazette*, pt 2 (23 August 1996), p. 4, Art. 10. For a brief history of the bill, see Mario Gomez, 'Sri Lanka's New Human Rights Commission', *Rights Link*, 1, 1 (1997), p. 5; Gomez, 'The Sri Lankan Human Rights Commission', *Law and Society Trust Review*, 9, 13 (September 1998), p. 31; Gomez, 'Sri Lanka's New Human Rights Commission', *Human Rights Quarterly*, 20 (1998), pp. 281–302.

77 Neelan Tiruchelvam, 'A Perspective on the Human Rights Commission Bill', *Sri Lanka Express* (21 July 1996); Deepika Udagama, 'Human Rights Commission Bill (1995)', *Law and Society Trust Review* (October 1995), pp. 13–17; Suriya Wickremasinghe, 'A National Human Rights Commission for Sri Lanka?', *Tamil Times* (April 1996), pp. 16–18; Wickremasinghe, 'A National Human Rights Commission for Sri Lanka?', *Law and Society Trust Fortnightly Review*, 6, 100 (February 1996), p. 7; see also Deepika Udagama, 'Human Rights Commission Bill (1995)', 6, 96 (October 1995), p. 13; Amnesty International, 'Sri Lanka: The Human Rights Commission Bill' (December 1995), AI Index ASA 37/25/95, p. 3; see the *Constitution of the Democratic Socialist Republic of Sri Lanka*, chapter III, the fundamental rights chapter, which does not articulate a right to life. The human rights task force had covered a significant number of complaints into illegal detention and torture: see, for example, Human Rights Task Force, *Annual Report* (Colombo: HRTF, 1994) for incident accounts, cases before the supreme court, and response by military and police personnel (obstructive, but not threatening). The task force visited detention centres around the country; its former head said it did face some obstructionism from the military and police masters of these centres: author's interview with Justice JSA Soza (retired) (Colombo, 19 February 1999).

78 Author's interview with M. D. R. A. M. Senanayake, formerly of the HRC, 22 February 1999, Colombo.

79 T. Abaratham, 'Human Rights Commission in Operation', *Daily News* (18 March 1997), pp. 1, 20; Gomez, 'Sri Lanka's New Human Rights Commission', p. 295; Gomez, 'The Sri Lankan Human Rights Commission', pp. 31–2. Author's discussion with Sri Lankan politicians, human rights activists and others involved with the commission, not for attribution, confirm that there is a widespread impression that the commission has been relatively ineffectual, in part because of a dearth of resources, but also in part because of the calibre of the staff; others have suggested that the chair of the commission is particularly unmotivated: author's interviews in Colombo, February 1999.

80 That committee is composed of five cabinet members and three members of parliament, and can inspect detention centres, demand information regarding detainees, and make recommendations with respect to particular cases. Of the

181 complaints received to date, all but thirteen have been resolved, frequently through a prompt release of the detainee. Five police officers and one member of the army face disciplinary action for abuse of power over detainees: author's interview with MP and Minister of Science and Technology Batty Weerakoon, (Colombo, 18 February 1999), and KMM Sherriff, senior assistant secretary, ministry of justice, constitutional affairs, ethnic affairs and national integration (Colombo, 23 February 1999). See also 'Performance Report – July 12, 1998 to December 31, 1998: President's Committee on Unlawful Arrests and Harassments' (photocopy on file with current author); see also 'President's Committee on Unlawful Arrests and Harassments – Meeting No. 31' (Colombo: Ministry of Justice, Constitutional Affairs, Ethnic Affairs and National Integration, 1999) (photocopy on file with current author) for examples of complaints and actions taken.

81 Amnesty International, 'Sri Lanka: Amnesty International Welcomes Government Action to Stop Death Squad Activities' (1 September 1995), AI Index ASA 37/17/95, reporting that the head of the STF was rumoured to have been suspended by the president; US Department of State, *Sri Lanka Country Report on Human Rights Practices for 1997*, available at http://www.state.gov/www/global/ human_rights/1997_hrp_report/srilanka.htm, p. 4.

82 A 'Misstatement' led observers to believe that the grave would be excavated beginning 5 March 1999, but the foreign ministry quickly retracted that statement: 'Foreign Ministry Corrects Information on Chemmani', *Daily News* (19 February 1999), p. 18. The investigation was delayed again in March due to the mysterious 'absence' of the judge that was to hear the case: 'Judge's Absence Aborts Chemmani Hearing' (26 March 1999), available at http://www.tamilnet.com/.

83 Civil Rights Movement of Sri Lanka, 'The Alleged Mass Burials at Chemmany in the North' (Colombo: Civil Rights Movement, July 1998); 'Executions Ordered for Rights Abuses', *Chicago Tribune* (4 July 1998), p. 4. This was the disappearance of a schoolgirl, Krishanthy Kumaraswamy, and family members and a neighbour who sought to find her. 'Sri Lanka: Human Rights Developments', available at http://www.hrw.org/hrw/worldreport99/asia/srilanka.html. It should be noted that reports are inconsistent regarding the number of indicted and convicted: see V. Varathasuntharam, 'Nine Soldiers Indicted on Abduction and Murder Charges', *The Island* (3 July 1997), and Sharmini Fernando, 'Bitter Victory: Krishanthi Kumaraswamy, The Women's Vigil, and the Verdict', *Options*, 14 (1998), p. 17 (says that five were given the death sentence and one released due to lack of evidence).

84 P. D. A. S. Gunasekera, 'Ten Years RI for Seven Accused, Two Acquitted', *Daily News* (11 February 1999), pp. 1, 20; J. Antony, 'Seven Accused Including Ex-principal Sentenced to 10 years', *The Island* (11 February 1999), p. 1. See also Gunasekera, 'Witness Describes how Torture Instrument was Used', *Daily News* (11 June 1996); and Gunasekera, 'First Accused Told Her that a Few Children should be Kidnapped, Witness Says', *Daily News* (26 February 1996); 'Tragedy, Trauma and Finally Justice at Embilitpitiya', *Daily News* (17 February 1999), p. 3.

85 Jhalapandithagedera Jayaratne *et al.* v. Chandrananda de Silva *et al.*, Supreme Court of the Democratic Socialist Republic of Sri Lanka, no. 609/96 (21 September 1998) (11 police officers arrested based on allegations that they had threatened a commission of inquiry); 'S. Dooriyakande: Evidence Postponed after Attorney Pleads Threats', and 'Widow gets Death Threat after Evidence', *Daily News* (18 January 1994); P. D. A. S. Gunasekera, 'Army men in Plain Clothes Hovering around Witnesses', *Daily News* (28 February 1996).

86 P. S. Suryanarayana, 'UN Agency Flays Killings in Sri Lanka', *The Hindu*

(14 June 1998); 'Sri Lanka: The Role of the International Community', *Human Rights Watch World Report 1999*, available at http://www.hrw.org/hrw/worldreport99/asia/srilanka3.html.

87 These can be found in Nadesan Centre, *Emergency Law*, Docinform 103, 104, 108, 110, and 112 (1988). See also 'Sri Lanka: Human Rights Developments', available at http://www.hrw.org/hrw/worldreport99/asia/srilanka.html; see also 'Balancing Security Interests with Rights of Citizens', *Sunday Observer* (12 April 1998), an interview with Attorney-General Sarath Silva, who sought to justify the mass arrests; Kumar Wethasinghe, 'Sunday Times Defamation Case: Date Given to Consider Judge's Order', *Daily News* (10 June 1996); Suriya Wickremasinghe, 'Emergency Rule', pp. 42–3, and Lakshman Gunesekera, 'Freedom of Expression and Media Freedom', pp. 113–14, in Law and Society Trust, *Sri Lanka 1998*; Elizabeth Nissan, 'Reform at Risk? Continuing Censorship in Sri Lanka (March 1997)', *Law and Society Trust Fortnightly Review*, 7, 114 (April 1997), pp. 1–2. Not only were there limitations on reporting regarding the war, some newspaper operations were harassed by police raids as well as the defamation charges already mentioned. The defamation case brought by the president should not be overemphasized, however, as many support the claim that the newspaper wilfully misrepresented the facts of the case, playing on the president's gender. Author's conversations with human rights activists, feminists and academics (Colombo, February 1999).

88 Imtiaz Ahmed, 'Rebuilding Sri Lankan Security', *Peace Review*, 8, 2 (1996), pp. 275–6; Wriggins, 'Sri Lanka: Secessionist Conflict', p. 39; US Department of State, *Sri Lanka Country Report 1997*, p. 3.

89 Author's interview with Batty Weerakoon (Colombo, 18 February 1999). According to one analyst, military spending has been as much as 40 per cent of total governmental spending: Ahmed, 'Rebuilding Sri Lankan Security', p. 277; de Silva, 'War and Peace'.

90 Author's interview with Deepika Udagama, (Colombo, 17 February 1999), and other interviews, not for attribution (Colombo, February 1999).

91 Author's interview with retired military officer, not for attribution (Colombo, February 1999).

92 Author's interviews with Sri Lankan politicians and human rights experts, not for attribution (Colombo, February 1999).

93 I am grateful to Deepika Udagama for this point. She points out that members of the police prosecuted for human rights violations have found themselves in something of a catch-22: while they were frequently acting under the direction of politicians, now that the courts have begun to come down on them, the [new] government refuses to bail them out. Author's interview (Colombo, 17 February 1999).

94 Sri Lanka Foundation Institute, 'Training Programme for Law Enforcement (Police) Officers on Human Rights and Gender Awareness: Progress Report: January 1999', (Colombo: SLFI, 1999) (photocopy on file with current author); for the proposal for the training, see 'Training of Law Enforcement (Police) Officers on Law, Society, and Human Rights' (Colombo: SLFI, 1997) (photocopy on file with current author), emphasizing the role of police in a democratic society, human rights and gender issues. For the text of presentations made to the participants, who are officers-in-charge, not cadets, see photocopies from the training binder (Colombo: SLFI, 1999, on file with current author). See also Sri Lanka Foundation, *Seminar on Law Enforcement Agencies and their Role in the Implementation of the International Bill of Human Rights* (Colombo: Sri Lanka Foundation, 1987); and Sri Lanka Foundation, *The Role of the Law Enforcement Officer in the Protection of Human Rights* (Colombo: Sri Lanka Foundation, 1987); author's interview with Deepika Udagama (Colombo, 17 February 1999).

95 Asian Legal Resource Centre Limited, *Human Rights Related Legal Reforms*, pp. 20–2.
96 Centre for the Study of Human Rights, 'Human Rights and Wrongs: A Human Rights Awareness Programme: For Passing Out to Cadets at Kotalawela Defence Academy 28th November 1998' (Colombo: Centre for the Study of Human Rights, 1998), photocopy on file with current author. See Centre for the Study of Human Rights, *Annual Report 1994* (Colombo: University of Colombo, 1994), p. 3, as well as the reports for 1995, p. 7, and 1997, p. 10, detailing the training efforts; author's interviews with Somasiri Devendra, coordinating the training from the CSHR (Colombo, 8 February 1999 and 19 February 1999).
97 Dayan Jayatilleka, 'The Tamil National Question Revisited: The Package and Globalisation', *The Island* (24 February 1998). In addition, actual spending consistently outpaced allocated spending: see K. T. Rajasingham, 'Government Should Grab LTTE's Offer to Negotiate', *Tamil Times*, 17, 12 (15 December 1998), p. 17.
98 Muni, *Pangs of Proximity*, pp. 13, 21–46, also emphasizes an ideological affinity that the Indian government claims with democracies, but fails to flesh this point out.
99 De Silva, 'Sri Lanka', p. 106.
100 Ruth Wedgwood, 'South Africa's Peaceful Transition a Model for Sri Lanka?' (11 January 1999), available at http://www.csmonitor.com/durable/1999/01/11/p9s2.htm.
101 Burns, 'Unable to Beat Rebels, Sri Lanka Eases Stance'.
102 Wriggins, 'Sri Lanka: Secessionist Conflict', pp. 39–41, 49.
103 US Department of State, *Sri Lanka Country Report 1996* (Washington, DC: US Government Printing Office, 1996), and *Country Report 1995*, same data; US Department of State, *Sri Lanka Country Report 1997*, available at http://www.state.gov/www/global/human_rights/1997_hrp_report/srilanka.htm.

Conclusion

Compromises of transition

Introduction

I began this inquiry with two questions: 'What makes accountability for past abuses more or less possible for transitional regimes that still face serious resistance from elements of the old regime?' and 'Against what other goals is accountability likely to be balanced?' I have reached two key conclusions, each of which challenges and/or contributes to the literature on transitional justice. First, there are two and possibly three key factors that affect the range of accountability that a nation might hope to achieve. Second, there are certain strategies that a nation might pursue to achieve more or less accountability, but these necessarily involve trade-offs and compromises with elements that may help create future stability.

I turned to studies of civil–military relations, transitions and the shift of the military 'back to the barracks' to inform hypotheses about what conditions make accountability more or less feasible. This investigation, as well as lessons from the subsequent case studies, generated further hypotheses regarding the trade-offs and strategies of transition that brought me full circle to the issue of alternate goods. Lessons from the cases about trade-offs may enrich the literature regarding what goods exactly might be obtained in compromising somewhat with accountability.

It is important to note that while external environmental changes, or changes in the behaviour of certain key actors, contributed to the possibility of transition significantly in every case except that of Sri Lanka, external actors themselves did not play an extensive role in every case. In particular, they did not play a significant role in Argentina's transition. However, the balancing act seems to apply whether it is engaged in by domestic actors alone, or with the support of external actors: Argentina's choices are not dissimilar from those of the other four cases examined closely here, or from those of the countries examined in Chapter 2. Its experiences, as with those of the other countries examined, can help to guide policy for countries that choose to go it alone, but also for the UN, bilateral donors, the World Bank, NGOs and myriad other actors that are involved in transitions.

Beyond peace vs. justice: a continuum

The key finding of this study is that, contrary to popular belief and many scholarly debates about transitional justice, transitional regimes do not face a simple either/or decision whereby they can have justice or peace, but not both simultaneously. Instead they have a wide range of options to choose from, ranging from pure amnesty to extensive prosecution. While this fact should be obvious, given the experience of recent transitions, debates about transitional justice have often continued to dissolve into simple oppositions of peace and justice, without taking account of the rich range of choices that regimes face.[1]

What does it mean to argue that justice and peace are not as dichotomously opposed in times of transition as many have alleged? Even where they have been severed, where injustice has been a cause of conflict, and conflict a cause of injustice, there is a need to relink the peace and justice that exist in tandem, to greater or lesser degrees, in stable societies. This is difficult, though not impossible if we acknowledge not that one must be given up for the other, but rather that each may be somewhat compromised. The result is that partial justice may be sought in order to simultaneously ensure that partial stability can begin to obtain. Of course, neither partial peace nor partial justice is an ideal long-term solution. However, in the short-to-medium term pursuit of both should help them to develop in tandem, in a mutually reinforcing relationship, such that in the longer term there is greater peace and justice. Transitional situations, and their aftermath, are *dynamic*, and there is no reason to assume that compromises made at the outset ought to endure permanently, but rather that they serve interim purposes. A range of choices can thus be made about accountability, in the hope of ultimately sacrificing neither too much peace nor too much justice.

However, even given that this range of choices exists, that does not mean that they are all (or all equally) morally defensible. I have argued elsewhere that there is a range of morally defensible policy choices relating to transitional justice; here I argue that there is a wide range of what is *possible* in a given country. I have articulated factors that make accountability more or less possible and strategies that regimes can and do engage in to achieve more of a desired good, whether that be accountability or the kind of reforms that can engender future stability. I turn now to a more detailed account of my findings.

Choices of transition: the ethical dilemma

In the Introduction I set out the common dilemma facing transitional regimes: the previous regime has engaged in serious violations of human rights, sometimes but not always in the context of a civil war. The new regime must steer between calls for it to prosecute violators to the full extent and resistance by elements of the old guard, frequently the military or security forces more generally. Those who favour punishment base their arguments on claims about deterrence, retribution, concern for victims or pedagogic effects. Those who favour amnesty make reference to social peace and national reconciliation. Some ethicists suggest that commissions of inquiry, while still entailing moral sacrifice, achieve at least some justice.

Choices of transition: pragmatic practice

Naturally, the fact that a wide range of options exists for transitional regimes in general does not mean that each country is in a position to choose any of these options. Governments will be constrained by their country's history and context, as will external peacekeepers and peacebuilders, so it is important to examine what factors affect the degree of accountability that a country might reasonably hope to attain. However, it is not preordained that a regime can only attain *x* level of accountability. There are choices leaders might make to achieve more accountability, or to build the foundation for another coveted goal for many states that have never known reliable governments: stability.

In Chapter 1, I hypothesize that there are three factors that affect the level of accountability that a new regime might hope to achieve: the international context, the balance of forces, and the nature of past abuses, which is largely a function of the duration and intensity of the conflict or repression. As we have seen through the examination of the case studies, the first two factors appear to have been considerably more important than the third, which has some anecdotal evidence to support it.

International factors

International factors seem to have worked to encourage transitions and frequently some measure of accountability. The international context may create a permissive space for political change. Such a historical moment may be said to have occurred at the end of the Cold War, with the waning of the bipolar rivalry having a profound effect on states in the orbit of both superpowers. States in the US sphere of influence, many of whom had dogmatically followed the anticommunist doctrine of national security suddenly lacked an external bogeyman/conspiracy to justify internal repression. At the same time the USA became less supportive in economic and military terms of some of its abusive client regimes. The same can be said of states in the former Soviet bloc, only to an even greater extent. States that had become virtual puppets of the Soviet Union were suddenly no longer under its sway and the repressive regimes it put in place or fostered fell. International factors also may play more active roles: for example, the USA began to push its former clients to change their behaviour, threatening to withhold crucial military aid if necessary. Finally, international organizations (and some NGOs) played a role, from embarrassing regimes for their human rights records to playing rather active roles in negotiations of peace accords and monitoring of their implementation.

The balance of forces

This factor, too, played much the role expected. First, it seems obvious that where a military remains strong and has no serious opposition, guerrilla or military, it will be in a stronger position to set the terms of its withdrawal from power. Clearly this control would extend to the matter of accountability, which is why we see self-amnesties by outgoing military dictatorships. This may not yet bar all prosecutions, as inventive courts will occasionally find loopholes to enable them to pursue some measures of accountability. Attempts at such accountability, however, will likely be threatened by a military that refuses to stay in the barracks, so what matters is not only the balance of forces prior to and at the moment of transition but shortly thereafter when such crucial decisions are being taken.

The nature and extent of past abuses and repression

It has been suggested, based on anecdotal evidence, that the extent of a conflict or severity of repression may have some impact on the degree of accountability that is ultimately attained. However, the logic of these arguments frequently points in contrary directions. Some argue that having few violations makes prosecution easier, while numerous violations that beget numerous prosecutions tend to generate instability and fail. Others suggest that the very fact of extensive abuses generates a societal demand for action and forces accountability. However, upon examination of the detailed case studies as well as the nutshell cases, support for these claims remains anecdotal at best.

Strategies of transition

Claims about the ways that extant factors drive near-term outcomes run the risk of being not only static, but overly deterministic. Further, they do not reflect the full nature of the choices that regimes actually confront. Instead, regimes and those who seek to assist them have some options with regard to transitional policies. I examine these options in Chapter 1 with the aid of insights from civil–military relations scholarship. I follow these theories in suggesting that, not surprisingly, militaries (though by analogy any status quo force is liable to have similar concerns) will be concerned not only with whether or not their members (especially officers) face punishment, but also with the continued maintenance of high military budgets and retaining control over doctrine, institutional structure and education. Not surprisingly, these areas of corporate concern to the military are all areas where transitional regimes will try to take action. While the virtues of achieving justice are obvious, we have also seen that there are perils both practical and normative. Further, other goods such as entrenchment of stability and democracy might be furthered with measures such as the reduction of military forces and budgets and educational and doctrinal reform that emphasize the purely defensive role of the military, the subordination of the military to civilian leaders and human rights norms. This is not to say that accountability ought to be abandoned in pursuit of these other goods, but that regimes often rightly strike a delicate balance among several goods, seeking accountability and reform simultaneously. Lowered levels of one good will generally be necessary to achieve elevated (or any) levels of another good.

The wider array of cases

This study examines only a small subset of five cases, far fewer than the number of regimes that have confronted questions of transitional justice. Thus Chapter 2 examines the larger set of cases in nutshell form. Nearly 30 countries are discussed in terms of the history of the conflict or repression they experienced, the form that the transition took, the factors affecting accountability, and the outcomes resulting. One can see from these brief examinations that certain factors such as the balance of forces and international involvement continue to be salient. One can also see that regimes find themselves at various points on the accountability spectrum in terms of what is feasible. And outcomes vary significantly based on these extant conditions and strategies deployed by the regimes.

The balance of forces was the most commonly salient factor in the wider array of transitions. Not surprisingly, the relative strengths of government and opposition, military and guerrillas affected the degree to which new (and frequently newly civilian) rulers could pursue accountability and reform. However, international factors nearly as frequently played a role, and appear to have been slightly more important when they did so. In particular, the end of the Cold War was frequently a (and sometimes the most important) factor enabling transitions, particularly in the former Soviet bloc. International intervention in the form of peacekeeping missions, direct intervention and even aid and the threat to withhold it played important roles in the transitions and peace negotiations in many countries. By contrast, the nature of past abuses was only raised as potentially important in the level of accountability in a few cases, and the case was not strongly made. This factor may deserve further investigation, however, because it only appeared to be salient in cases that had been examined in further depth, as opposed to simply as nutshell cases.

A somewhat surprising discovery arises from an examination of the outcomes in the nutshell cases. Prosecution occurs much more frequently than the 'punish vs. pardon' debate would lead us to believe. It also occurs in tandem with other measures such as commissions of inquiry or lustration. However, this does not mean that prosecution is both widespread and successful: many countries saw prosecutions curtailed by amnesties and other political and procedural roadblocks.

Finally, in the realm of transition, we see that all three of the issues traditionally of corporate concern to militaries were subjects of action or significant debate by new regimes. In particular, reforms of the institutions dealing with security were common, as was accountability, if only at the lowest level in the form of naming names. Budgetary levels appear to have been less salient, both in terms of actual change or salient governmental debate about them, although they were not completely insignificant.

The nutshell case studies do not, as I also make clear with regard to the in-depth case studies, provide us with strict causal logic, such as 'greater international involvement yields greater accountability'.[2] They can only point out salient factors, as the substantive content of each affects the outcome: for example, you must know not only that international actors are involved, but what their goals are. Causal arguments would be further muddled by the presence of an important intervening variable: the strategies that the regime (and international actors who seek to assist it) deploy with regard to the security forces. I turn now to the in-depth case studies, which illustrate the findings of the nutshell cases in greater detail.

The case studies

Chapters 3–7 examine five countries in detail, three in Latin America (Argentina, Honduras and El Salvador) and South Africa and Sri Lanka. I provide detailed narrative accounts of the experience of each with civil war, domestic repression or military rule. Sri Lanka is an unusual case in some senses, in that the war has not been concluded and that it is an established democracy, but is still pursuing commissions of inquiry, prosecutions and very limited reform. The countries were chosen from the larger set for a number of reasons. Certainly, they had undergone serious civil strife, suffered extensive human rights violations, undergone a transition of some sort and faced serious demands for accountability. Any of the countries in Chapter 2 fit those criteria. However, I did not pursue the eastern European cases in greater detail both because the unique nature of many of the transitions meant that a serious threat to accountability virtually dropped away, and because the more commonly heard objection to prosecutions was based on rule of law considerations. I did seek to achieve some level of geographic balance: while the majority of my cases are in Latin America, so are the majority of (non-east-European) cases that have arisen in recent decades. Further, the countries chosen varied across my independent variables: while international factors were salient in El Salvador, for example, they were less relevant in Sri Lanka. There was also variance across the other two factors. Not surprisingly, then, the countries display different strategies and outcomes in the face of their dilemmas, helping to provide an illustrative microcosm, if not a purely representative sample, of the experiences of transitional states more generally.

El Salvador

El Salvador provides one of the classic and most-cited examples of the use of a commission of inquiry rather than prosecutions to address the legacy of the past. The most salient factors were the balance of forces and protracted nature of the conflict, which led to the so-called hurting stalemate, and international factors such as a changed environment and active pressure as well as the facilitative role of the UN. Following a decade-long war that resulted in around 75,000 casualties, the realization emerged that neither side could definitively defeat the other. The negotiations that ensued were enabled by the end of the Cold War, active US pressure and UN mediation and observer missions.

Despite these factors enabling the transition, pure accountability was not politically feasible. The military remained politically strong during and after the transition, as it had reached a stalemate, but not been defeated, on the battlefield. As a result, compromise would be necessary on several fronts. The new regime simultaneously pursued a commission of inquiry, a commission to enable lustration, and institutional reform and force reduction. Thus it balanced the same set of issues that many transitional regimes must: it sought to pursue stability and accountability while faced with a recalcitrant military that was concerned to protect its sphere of influence over budgetary matters, but more importantly institutional reform and the treatment of its members for their past actions.

Argentina

Argentina experienced extended periods of military rule and abuses, but the period of the dirty war was particularly brutal. A salient factor in the transition was the defeat of the ruling junta in the Falklands/Malvinas, which temporarily weakened its status. The transition to democracy that ensued was still heavily controlled by the military, which staged several serious coup attempts. As a result, while landmark prosecutions went forward and garnered convictions, even of former junta members, military rebelliousness soon forced procedural limitations on prosecutions. Subsequent pardons further reversed accountability efforts. The state also created a commission of inquiry that reported on past abuses, and pursued some military reform and serious force reduction. Budgets remained artificially high for some time, in part due to the costs of demobilization.

Argentina, then, reached its transition for somewhat different reasons than El Salvador, with different salient factors enabling or inhibiting transition. External defeat affected the balance of forces temporarily, but otherwise external factors played little role. On the other hand, the balance between a restive military and a reformist civilian regime was a delicate one, and the latter was ultimately forced into numerous compromises after the initial prosecutions. The result, then, was a somewhat different set of trade-offs as Argentina pursued both stability and accountability simultaneously, with relatively little involvement by external actors. It is noteworthy that, while external actors were not actively involved in aiding the Argentinian transition, the balancing act engaged in by domestic actors does not appear significantly different from that engaged in by local and international actors in the Salvadoran transition.

Honduras

Honduras experienced significant repression, but relatively few casualties compared to its neighbours undergoing civil war, with 'only' 184 disappearances. While the regime was formally civilian, the military retained significant political power, which placed limits on accountability and reform. While the balance of forces placed limits on accountability, some have argued that the very limited nature of the disappearances made accountability more possible. Limited abuses meant limited numbers of perpetrators, and hopefully less disruption both in society and in the security forces should accountability be sought. While the latter hope was clearly misplaced, it may have made the decision to go forward with prosecutions somewhat easier. The international or external factors are somewhat harder to identify. While the USA was a significant power in pre-transition Honduras, it does not appear to have actively lobbied the government for reform, nor has the UN been actively involved in the ways it was in El Salvador. The USA became actively involved in reform only quite recently through its assistance to police reform programmes. The main international factor may have been a permissive one, the end of the Cold War that brought the doctrine of national security and attendant local and US policies into question.

The government was able to create a commission of inquiry into past abuses as well as institute prosecutions and reform. However, the prosecutions have been hamstrung by difficulties in gaining custody of fugitive indicted officers. The security forces have not only made clear their continued power with a showy parade through the capital, but have apparently destroyed records and hidden some of the fugitives. Reform efforts stalled for some time, but the separation of the forces was finally enshrined in the constitution and a reform law passed. Budgets have actually increased, though perhaps for justifiable reasons.

Thus, while Honduran transition has developed out of a different context, its government too has been forced to make the familiar trade-offs among goods of reform and accountability though, because of different enabling and inhibiting factors and different political choices, the outcomes there have been different. The middle ground of compromise is a wide one, and encompasses a variety of experiences.

South Africa

South Africa experienced over 40 years of apartheid, which included severe repression and violent rebellion. Extensive international condemnation may have played a role in pushing the white regime to initiate reform, both because sanctions took economic aim (though their impact remains hotly disputed) and because the challenges led the white rulers to question their own legitimacy. The protractedness of repression and rebellion may also have led to exhaustion and self-doubt among the white ruling elite. Nonetheless, the regime remained firmly in control of most of the transition, resulting in limits to accountability.

An amnesty written into the transitional constitution ensured that prosecutions would be difficult if not impossible, and some guarantees were made for the continuance of civil servants in their posts. However, prosecution for past abuses was not entirely impossible. Through the mechanism of the commission of inquiry, the legacy of the past has been revealed in extensive detail, but the commission also served another purpose. It placed leverage on abusers to confess, lest they be prosecuted, and some prosecutions have successfully gone forward. There were also reforms of the doctrine and institutions of the security forces. Some advances have also been made with regard to the racial balance, although these have made the least inroads at the upper echelons. Budget reductions have yet to be seen, but that has at least partially been a result of the costs of demobilization.

Again, what we see is that historically specific circumstances constrain a new regime in particular (but identifiable) ways. The negotiated transition and the strength of the old regime meant that many compromises were built into the accords and the transitional constitution. South Africa played yet a different balancing game from its fellow transitional states in Latin America, with unique compromises.

Sri Lanka

Sri Lanka is of course in a very different situation from the other regimes examined here. A civil war continues, and the nation has not had a transition in the traditional sense because it is a democracy of long standing. However, since the 1994 electoral regime change a series of important steps have been taken to address past abuses and limit current ones.

The factors affecting accountability also differ significantly from those in other contexts. The only major international player is India, but, while it was actively involved with its peacekeeping force in 1987, it has maintained its distance in recent years. Other international players such as the USA and the UN have also played minimal roles. At the same time, the balance of forces and civil–military relations play a role, though somewhat different. The military may be able to capture and hold strategic territory, but it cannot completely eliminate the rebels, so a stalemate of sorts exists. However, the military, while prone to abuses, does not, for historical reasons, appear particularly prone to intervene in politics. The security forces may often be handled delicately, but this is more because of their importance in the prosecution of the war than fears of a coup. Finally, the duration of the conflict may have had some effect on the election of a president and a party with a platform emphasizing peace negotiations.

Thus Sri Lanka has taken some unusual measures in an unusual situation, creating commissions of inquiry to investigate past disappearances and a human rights commission, and pursuing prosecutions in several high-level disappearance cases. Reform has lagged far behind, with the most notable measures being efforts to educate the military and police about human rights and to monitor and report abuses. The military budget has risen dramatically, the force sizes less so, but in the context of an ongoing civil war military expansion should not be surprising.

Sri Lanka provides us with a final instance of a country facing tough decisions about how to treat past violations, but, given its unique circumstances, responding in its own fashion. Again we see certain limiting and enabling factors, here war-weariness (a function of perhaps both the balance of forces and the nature and extent of abuses) helping spark the transition, but limiting factors such as the continuing need for the armed forces. These force the regime to compromise as it acts to pursue accountability and very limited reform, and to pursue a war simultaneously.

Lessons

Each of these cases is unique. There is no typical transitional regime, but rather regimes make decisions after armed conflict, during armed conflict, after formal regime change, and in the absence of formal complete regime change. Each of these cases represents one of these possibilities, leading to the suggestion that perhaps 'transitional regime' is an incorrect term for most of the countries lumped under this rubric. Nonetheless, the choices faced by these regimes, and the balances struck by them and by those who have sought to assist them, are interestingly similar.

The key general lesson that we might take from this examination of the dilemmas that transitional regimes face is that there is a continuum of options with no definitive one 'right' answer. At first blush this may seem a hopelessly vague lesson, and the details of the study are devoted to fleshing out the meaning of this statement for particular cases. There is a continuum of options from which transitional regimes and those who work with them might choose. While their options may well be constrained by their particular circumstances, they are generally not completely without choices. The factors that I have discussed – international/external factors, the nature and extent of the abuses, and the balance of forces – all play a role, but need not completely determine a country's fate.

Instead, a government or those who seek to assist it may make strategic choices about what values it wishes or needs most to pursue. Extensive legal justice may not be accomplished, but only lesser measures of accountability like truth-telling or lustration/purification. However, at the same time a regime may pursue measures that will help entrench the new democracy, provide for future stability and safeguard human rights, through the reduction and reform of the security forces, so often the source of the most heinous abuses.

We cannot generalize with any certainty much less predict with lawlike regularity what 'type' of transitional situation results in what 'level' of accountability, because each nation has a distinct history, culture and set of political problems. However, we can identify issues, factors and strategies of particular salience for transitional regimes, from which we can deduce likely policy choices. As I have shown, we can identify a set of salient normative concerns that are likely to partly drive a regime's choices. We can also identify salient factors that are permissive factors or barriers to greater accountability: the most important of these being international factors and the balance of forces, a less clear one being the nature of past abuses. These factors may be permissive or inhibitive, so we may not simply assume that because, say, international players are involved in a transition that more accountability will result: instead we must look not just to the fact that particular factors are salient but the content of these factors (for example, what are international actors advocating? what are they contributing?). Similarly, we see that there are a number of 'goods' that regimes may wish to pursue, but that they may need to strike a delicate balance among their pursuits. Again, we cannot predict exactly what balance a state will or should strike but rather claim that some balance will have to be struck and identify the sorts of goods that will be exchanged in trade-offs (accountability, reform, budgetary levels).

In closing, this book has sought to challenge the common treatment in the transitional justice literature of the peace/justice trade-off as overly simplistic, if not a false dichotomy. I have sought to illustrate the more nuanced set of choices that regimes face, and describe the contexts and strategic choices that make accountability more or less possible. In this way I hope to enrich the literature that describes as well as prescribes what transitional regimes concerned with past abuses can or should do by providing richer descriptions of the variety of paths they may pursue. What we find through this examination of the cases is that there is a real continuum of options that dichotomies obscure. Regimes may have to make certain strategic trade-offs to achieve more or less accountability or stability, but this does not mean that one must be completely jettisoned in favour of another.

Notes

1 A very recent exception to this artificial divide is Mani, *Beyond Retribution*.
2 Again the case of Argentina is illustrative – external factors played a role in enabling transition, but external actors were virtually absent from the transition itself. Nonetheless, some significant measures of accountability were pursued.

Bibliography

Books

Adam, Heribert and Kogila Moodley, *The Negotiated Revolution: Society and Politics in Post-Apartheid South Africa* (Johannesberg: Jonathan Ball, 1993).

Aguilera, Gabriel, *El Fusil y El Olivo: La Cuestión Militar en Centroamerica* (San Jose, Costa Rica: Departamento Ecumenico de Investigaciónes, 1989).

Alles, A. C., *The Assassination of a Prime Minister* (New York: Vantage Press, 1986).

Almond, Gabriel and Sidney Verba, *The Civic Culture: Political Attitudes and Democracy in Five Nations* (Princeton, NJ: Princeton University Press, 1963).

Amnesty International, *Honduras: Civilian Authority – Military Power; Human Rights Violations in the 1980s* (London: Amnesty International, 1988).

Asian Legal Resource Centre Limited, *Human Rights Related Legal Reforms in Sri Lanka: The Final Document* (Hong Kong: ALCRL, 1996).

Aspen Institute, Justice and Society Program, *State Crimes: Punishment or Pardon?* (Wye Center, CO: Aspen Institute, 1989).

Austin, Dennis, *Democracy and Violence in India and Sri Lanka* (London: Pinter, 1994).

Barahona de Brito, Alexandra, *Human Rights and Democratization in Latin America* (Oxford: Oxford University Press, 1997).

Barahona Riera, Francisco and Manuel Carballo Quintana, *Reconversión Militar en Centroamerica* (San José, Costa Rica: Fundación Friedrich Ebert, 1995).

Bass, Gary, *Stay the Hand of Vengeance: The Politics of War Crimes Tribunals* (Princeton, NJ: Princeton University Press, 2000).

Batt, Judy, *East Central Europe from Reform to Transition* (London: Pinter, 1991).

Benitez Manaut, Raul, *La Teoría Militar y la Guerra Civil en El Salvador* (San Salvador, El Salvador: Universidad Centroamericana, 1989).

Bienen, Henry (ed.), *The Military Intervenes: Case Studies in Political Development* (New York: Russell Sage Foundation, 1968).

Bienen, Henry (ed.), *Armies and Parties in Africa* (New York: Africana Publishing, 1978).

Bose, Sumantra, *States, Nations, Sovereignty: Sri Lanka, India, and the Tamil Eelam Movement* (New Delhi: Sage, 1994).

Boyce, James K. (ed.), *Economic Policy for Building Peace: The Lessons of El Salvador* (Boulder, CO: Lynne Rienner, 1996).

Brysk, Alison, *The Politics of Human Rights in Argentina: Protest, Change, and Democratization* (Stanford, CA: Stanford University Press, 1994).

Carr, Raymond and Juan Pablo Fusi Aizipurua, *Spain: Dictatorship to Democracy* (London: George Allen & Unwin, 1981).
Casper, Gretchen, *Fragile Democracies: The Legacies of Authoritarian Rule* (Pittsburgh, PA: University of Pittsburgh Press, 1995).
Centro de Estudios Democráticos, *El Nuevo Concepto de Seguridad Nacional Salvadoreña* (San Salvador, El Salvador: CEDEM, 1994).
Cherñavsky, Moisés, *La Seguridad Nacional y el Fundamentalismo Democrático* (Buenos Aires: Centro Editor de America Latina, 1993).
Clapham, Christopher and George Philip (eds), *The Political Dilemmas of Military Regimes* (Totowa, NJ: Barnes & Noble Books, 1985).
Comisión Nacional Sobre la Desaparición de Personas, *Nunca Más: Informe de la Comisión Nacional Sobre la Desaparición de Personas* (Buenos Aires: EUDEBA, 1984).
Comisionado Nacional de los Derechos Humanos, *Los Hechos Hablan por Sí Mismos* (Tegucigalpa, Honduras: Editorial Guaymuras, 1994).
Comisionado Nacional de los Derechos Humanos, *El Difícil Tránsito Hacia la Democracia* (Tegucigalpa, Honduras: Comisionado Nacional de los Derechos Humanos, 1996).
Consejo Episcopal Latinoamericano, *La Seguridad Nacional: Doctrina o Ideologia?* (Bogota: CELAM, no date given).
Coomaraswamy, Radhika, *Ideology and the Constitution: Essays on Constitutional Jurisprudence* (Colombo, Sri Lanka: International Centre for Ethnic Studies, 1997).
Cousens, Elizabeth M. and Chetan Kumar (eds), *Peacebuilding as Politics: Cultivating Peace in Fragile Societies* (Boulder, CO: Lynne Rienner, 2001).
Dabat, Alejandro and Luis Lorenzano, *Argentina: The Malvinas and the End of Military Rule* (London: Verso, 1984).
Danopoulos, Constantine P. (ed.), *From Military to Civilian Rule* (London: Routledge, 1992).
Diamond, Larry and Marc F. Plattner (eds), *Civil–Military Relations and Democracy* (Baltimore, MD: Johns Hopkins University Press, 1996).
Diaz Coludrero, Jose Luis and Monica Abella, *Punto Final: Amnistía o Voluntad Popular* (Buenos Aires: Puntosur Editores, 1987).
Doyle, Michael W., *UN Peacekeeping in Cambodia: UNTAC's Civil Mandate* (Boulder, CO: Lynne Rienner, 1995).
Finer, Samuel E., *The Man on Horseback: The Role of the Military in Politics* (Boulder, CO: Westview, 1962, 1988).
Frontalini, Daniel and Maria Cristina Caiati, *El Mito de la Guerra Sucia* (Buenos Aires: CELS, 1984).
Gomez, Mario, *Emerging Trends in Public Law* (Colombo, Sri Lanka: Vijitha Yapa Bookshop, 1998).
Goodman, Louis W., Johanna S. R. Mendelson and Juan Rial (eds), *The Military and Democracy: The Future of Civil–Military Relations in Latin America* (US: Lexington Books, 1990).
Hamber, Brandon (ed.), *Past Imperfect: Dealing with the Past in Northern Ireland and Societies in Transition* (Derry/Londonderry, Northern Ireland: INCORE, 1998).
Hampson, Fen Osler, *Nurturing Peace: Why Peace Agreements Succeed or Fail* (Washington, DC: United States Institute of Peace, 1996).
Hayner, Priscilla, *Unspeakable Truths: Confronting State Terror and Atrocity* (London: Routledge, 2000).

Henkin, Alice H. (ed.), *Honoring Human Rights and Keeping the Peace: Lessons from El Salvador, Cambodia, and Haiti* (Washington, DC: Aspen Institute, 1995).

Hesse, Carla and Robert Post (eds), *Human Rights in Political Transitions: Gettysburg to Bosnia* (New York: Zone, 1999).

Horowitz, Donald, *Coup Theories and Officers' Motives: Sri Lanka in Comparative Perspective* (Princeton, NJ: Princeton University Press, 1980).

Huntington, Samuel P., *The Soldier and the State: The Theory and Politics of Civil–Military Relations* (Cambridge, MA: Belknap/Harvard University Press, 1964).

Huntington, Samuel P., *The Third Wave: Democratization in the Late Twentieth Century* (Norman, OK: University of OK Press, 1991).

International Centre for Ethnic Studies, *Sri Lanka: The Devolution Debate* (Colombo, Sri Lanka: International Centre for Ethnic Studies, 1996).

International Institute of Strategic Studies, *The Military Balance* (London: International Institute of Strategic Studies, 1972–99).

Janowitz, Morris, *The Professional Soldier: A Social and Political Portrait* (Glencoe, IL: Free Press, 1960).

Johnstone, Ian, *Rights and Reconciliation: UN Strategies in El Salvador* (Boulder, CO: Lynne Rienner, 1995).

Keohane, Robert O., *After Hegemony: Cooperation and Discord in the World Political Economy* (Princeton, NJ: Princeton University Press, 1984).

King, Gary, Robert O. Keohane and Sidney Verba, *Designing Social Inquiry: Scientific Inference in Qualitative Research* (Princeton, NJ: Princeton University Press, 1994).

Klotz, Audie, *Norms in International Relations: The Struggle Against Apartheid* (Ithaca, NY: Cornell University Press, 1995).

Kritz, Neil J. (ed.), *Transitional Justice: How Emerging Democracies Reckon with Former Regimes*, 3 vols (Washington, DC: United States Institute of Peace Press, 1995).

Lanza, Leo Valladares and Susan C. Peacock, *In Search of Hidden Truths: An Interim Report on Declassification by the National Commissioner for Human Rights in Honduras* (Tegucigalpa, Honduras: Comisionado Nacional de los Derechos Humanos, 1996).

Law and Society Trust, *Sri Lanka: State of Human Rights* (annual) (Colombo, Sri Lanka: Law and Society Trust, 1996–8).

Lázara, Simon, *Poder Militar: Origen, Apogeo y Transición* (Buenos Aires: Editorial Legasa, 1988).

Lederach, John Paul, *Building Peace: Sustainable Reconciliation in Divided Societies* (Washington, DC: US Institute of Peace, 1997).

Lopez, Ernesto, *Seguridad Nacional y Sedición Militar* (Buenos Aires: Editorial Legasa, 1987).

Lopez, Ernesto and David Pion-Berlin, *Democracia y Cuestión Militar* (Buenos Aires: Universidad Nacional de Quilmes, 1996).

Lutz, Ellen, Hurst Hannum and Kathryn J. Burke (eds), *New Directions in Human Rights* (Philadelphia, PA: University of Pennsylvania Press, 1989).

Malamud-Goti, Jaime, *Game Without End: State Terror and the Politics of Justice* (Norman, OK: University of Oklahoma Press, 1996).

Mani, Rama, *Beyond Retribution: Seeking Justice in the Shadows of War* (Cambridge: Polity Press, 2002).

McAdams, A. James (ed.), *Transitional Justice and the Rule of Law in New Democracies* (Notre Dame: University of Notre Dame Press, 1997).

McGowan, William, *Only Man is Vile: The Tragedy of Sri Lanka* (New York: Farrar, Straus & Giroux, 1992).

McSherry, Patrice J., *Incomplete Transition: Military Power and Democracy in Argentina* (New York: St Martin's Press, 1997).

Ministry of Justice, Constitutional Affairs and National Integration, *The Government's Proposals for Constitutional Reform* (Colombo, Sri Lanka: Department of Government Printing, 1997).

Minow, Martha, *Between Vengeance and Forgiveness: Facing History after Genocide and Mass Violence* (Boston, MA: Beacon Press, 1998).

Moneta, Carlos J., Ernesto Lopez and Anibal Romero, *La Reforma Militar* (Buenos Aires: Editorial Legasa, 1985).

Munck, Gerardo, *Authoritarianism and Democratization: Soldiers and Workers in Argentina, 1976–83* (University Park, PA: Pennsylvania State University Press, 1998).

Munck, Ronaldo, *Latin America: The Transition to Democracy* (London: Zed Books, 1989).

Muni, S. D., *Pangs of Proximity: India and Sri Lanka's Ethnic Crisis* (New Delhi: Sage, 1993).

Murphy, Jeffrie and Jean Hampton, *Forgiveness and Mercy* (Cambridge: Cambridge University Press, 1988).

Naciones Unidas, *Acuerdos de El Salvador: En El Camino de La Paz* (New York and San Salvador: United Nations, 1992).

Neier, Aryeh, *War Crimes: Brutality, Genocide, Terror, and the Struggle for Justice* (New York: Random House/Times Books, 1998).

Nordlinger, Eric, *Soldiers in Politics: Military Coups and Governments* (Englewood Cliffs, NJ: Prentice-Hall, 1977).

Nunn, Frederick M., *The Time of the Generals: Latin American Professional Militarism in World Perspective* (Lincoln, NE: University of Nebraska Press, 1992).

Oakley, Robert B., Michael J. Dzidzic and Eliot M. Goldberg, *Policing the New World Disorder: Peace Operations and Public Security* (Washington, DC: National Defense University, 1998).

O'Donnell, Guillermo and Philippe C. Schmitter *Transitions from Authoritarian Rule: Tentative Conclusions about Uncertain Democracies* (Baltimore, MD: Johns Hopkins University Press, 1991).

ONUSAL and Fuerza Armada de El Salvador, *Doctrina Militar y Relaciones Ejército/Sociedad* (San Salvador, El Salvador: ONUSAL, 1994).

ONUSAL/Procuraduría Para la Defensa de los Derechos Humanos, *Guía Sobre las Normas y Procidimientos de la Policía Nacional Civil* (San Salvador, El Salvador: ONUSAL, 1994).

Orgaz, Carlos Alfredo, *La Difícil Convivencia: Fuerzas Armadas y Sociedad Civil en la Argentina* (Buenos Aires: Nuevohacer, 1996).

Orr, Robert C., *Paradigm Lost? US Approaches to Democracy Promotion in Developing Countries* (PhD dissertation, Princeton University, Woodrow Wilson School of Public and International Affairs, Princeton, NJ, November 1996).

Osiel, Mark, *Mass Atrocity, Collective Memory, and the Law* (New Brunswick: Transaction Publishers, 1997).

Panditaratne, Dinusha and Pradeep Ratnam (eds), *The Draft Constitution of Sri Lanka: Critical Aspects* (Colombo, Sri Lanka: Law and Society Trust, 1998).

Polychroniou, Chronis, (ed.), *Issues and Perspectives in International Political Economy* (Westport, CT: Praeger, 1992).

Putnam, Robert D., *Making Democracy Work: Civic Traditions in Modern Italy* (Princeton, NJ: Princeton University Press, 1993).
Raby, D. L., *Fascism and Resistance in Portugal: Communists, Liberals, and Military Dissidents in the Opposition to Salazar, 1941–1974* (Manchester: Manchester University Press, 1988).
Ratner, Steven R. and Jason S. Abrams (eds), *Accountability for Human Rights Atrocities in International Law: Beyond the Nuremberg Legacy* (Oxford: Oxford University Press, 2001).
Rawls, John, *Political Liberalism* (New York: Colombia University Press, 1993).
Roht-Arriaza, Naomi (ed.), *Impunity and Human Rights in International Law and Practice* (New York: Oxford University Press, 1995).
Rotberg, Robert I. and Dennis Thompson (eds), *Truth v. Justice: The Morality of Truth Commissions* (Princeton, NJ: Princeton University Press, 2000).
Rouquie, Alain, *The Military and the State in Latin America*, (trans. Paul Sigmund) (Berkeley, CA: University of California Press, 1987).
Rubin, Barnett R., *Cycles of Violence: Human Rights in Sri Lanka since the Indo-Sri Lanka Agreement* (Washington, DC: Asia Watch, December 1987).
Rubin, Barry, *Modern Dictators: Third World Coup-makers, Strongmen, and Populist Tyrants* (New York: McGraw-Hill, 1987).
Sahadevan, Ponmoni, *India and Overseas Indians: The Case of Sri Lanka* (New Delhi: Kalinga Publications, 1995).
Salduna, Horacio, *Cuadernos para la Democracia 12: La Reforma Militar* (Buenos Aires: El Cid Editor, 1985).
Salomon, Leticia, *La Violencia en Honduras 1980–1993* (Tegucigalpa, Honduras: Centro de Documentacion de Honduras, 1993).
Shriver, Donald W., Jr, *An Ethic for Enemies: Forgiveness in Politics* (New York: Oxford University Press, 1995).
Sivaraja, Ambalanavar, *Politics of Tamil Nationalism in Sri Lanka* (New Delhi: South Adian Publishers, 1996).
South African Truth and Reconciliation Commission, *Report of the Truth and Reconciliation Commission*, available at: http://www.polity.org.za/govdocs/commissions/1998/trc/.
Sparks, Allister, *Tomorrow is Another Country: The Inside Story of South Africa's Road to Change* (New York: Hill & Wang, 1995).
Spencer, Jonathan, *A Sinhala Village in a Time of Trouble: Politics and Change in Rural Sri Lanka* (Delhi: Oxford University Press, 1990).
Spencer, Jonathan (ed.), *Sri Lanka: History and the Roots of Conflict* (London: Routledge, 1990).
Sri Lanka Foundation, *Seminar on Law Enforcement Agencies and their Role in the Implementation of the International Bill of Rights* (Colombo: Sri Lanka Foundation, 1987).
Sri Lanka Foundation, *The Role of the Law Enforcement Officer in the Protection of Human Rights* (Colombo: Sri Lanka Foundation, 1987).
Stepan, Alfred, *Rethinking Military Politics: Brazil and the Southern Cone* (Princeton, NJ: Princeton University Press, 1988).
Tambiah, Stanley J., *Sri Lanka: Ethnic Fratricide and the Dismantling of Democracy* (Chicago, IL: Univeristy of Chicago Press, 1986).
Tambiah, Stanley J., *Leveling Crowds: Ethnonationalist Conflicts and Collective Violence in South Asia* (Berkeley, CA: University of California Press, 1996).

Torres-Rivas, Edelberto and Dirk Kruijt, *America Latina: Militares y Sociedad*, 2 vols (San José, Costa Rica: FLACSO, 1991).
United Nations, *From Madness to Hope: The 12-year War in El Salvador, Report of the United Nations Commission on the Truth for El Salvador*, UN Doc. S/25500 (1 April 1993).
United Nations Development Programme, *Human Development Report* (New York: Oxford University Press, 1996–98).
Velasquez de Aviles, Victoria Marina, *La Seguridad Ciudadana, la Policía Nacional Civil, y Los Derechos Humanos* (San Salvador, El Salvador: Procuraduria para la Defensa de los Derechos Humanos, 1997).
Waldmann, Peter and Ernesto Garzon Valdez (eds), *El Poder Militar en la Argentina (1976–81)* (Frankfurt: Verveurt, 1982).
Weschler, Lawrence, *A Miracle, A Universe: Settling Accounts with Torturers* (New York: Pantheon, 1990).
Wesson, Robert G., *The United States and Brazil: Limits of Influence* (New York: Praeger, 1981).
Wilkie, James W. and Jose Guadalupe Ortega (eds), *Statistical Abstract of Latin America*, vol. 33 (Los Angeles, CA: UCLA Latin American Center Publications, University of California, 1997).
Williams, Philip J. and Knut Walter, *Militarization and Demilitarization in El Salvador's Transition to Democracy* (Pittsburgh, PA: University of Pittsburgh Press, 1977).
Zartman, I. William (ed.), *Elusive Peace: Negotiating an End to Civil Wars* (Washington, DC: Brookings, 1995).

No author given

Acuerdos de Paz (Guatemala City, Guatemala: Universidad Rafael Landivar – Instituto de Investigaciónes Economicas y Sociales, 1997).
Constitution of the Democratic Socialist Republic of Sri Lanka.
Constitution of the Republic of South Africa (adopted 8 May 1996, amended 11 October 1996), available at http://www.constitution.org.za/.
Final Report of the Commission of Inquiry into the Involuntary Removal or Disappearance of Persons in the Western, Southern, and Sabaragamuwa Provinces, Sessional Paper No. V (Colombo, Sri Lanka: Department of Government Printing, 1997).
Final Report of the Commission of Inquiry into the Involuntary Removal or Disappearance of Persons in the Central, Northwestern, and Uva Provinces, Sessional Paper No. VI (Colombo, Sri Lanka: Department of Government Printing, 1997).
Final Report of the Commission of Inquiry into the Involuntary Removal or Disappearance of Persons in the Northern and Eastern Provinces, Sessional Paper No. VII (Colombo, Sri Lanka: Department of Government Printing, 1997).

Articles

Adams, Thomas K., 'Disengage, Disarm, Demobilize: The Success of ONUSAL in Implementing the 1992 El Salvador Peace Accords', *Low Intensity Conflict and Law Enforcement*, 3, 2 (Autumn 1994).
Ahmed, Imtiaz, 'Rebuilding Sri Lankan Security', *Peace Review*, 8, 2 (1996).
Alfonsín, Raúl, 'Never Again in Argentina', *Journal of Democracy*, 4, 1 (January 1993).

Baloyra, Enrique, 'Salvaging El Salvador', *Journal of Democracy*, 3, 2 (April 1992).

Bassiouni, M. Cherif and Morris, Madeline H. (eds), 'Accountability for International Crimes and Serious Violations of Fundamental Human Rights', *Law and Contemporary Problems*, 59 (1996) (special issue).

Beltran, Virgilio, 'Political Transition in Argentina: 1982 to 1985', *Armed Forces and Society*, 13, 2 (Winter 1987).

Benomar, Jamal, 'Justice After Transitions', *Journal of Democracy*, 4, 1 (January 1993).

Berat, Lynn, 'Conscientious Objection in South Africa: Governmental Paranoia and the Law of Conscription', *Vanderbilt Journal of Transnational Law*, 22 (1989).

Berat, Lynn and Yossi Shain, 'Retribution or Truth Telling? Legacies of the Transitional Phase', *Law and Social Inquiry*, 20, 1 (1995).

Bourne, Richard, 'Observing Sri Lanka's Parliamentary Elections', *The Round Table*, 333 (1995).

Brody, Reed, 'The United Nations and Human Rights in El Salvador's "Negotiated Revolution",' *Harvard Human Rights Journal*, 8 (Spring 1995).

Buergenthal, Thomas, 'The United Nations Truth Commission for El Salvador', *Vanderbilt Journal of Transnational Law*, 27, 3 (October 1994).

Centre for the Study of Human Rights, *Annual Report 1994* (Colombo: University of Colombo, 1994), p. 3.

Cilliers, Jakkie, 'Rethinking South African Security Architecture', *African Defence Review*, 20 (December 1994).

Civil Rights Movement, 'The Investigation of "Disappearances" in Sri Lanka' (Colombo, Sri Lanka: Civil Rights Movement, 1998).

Cohen, Stanley, 'State Crimes of Previous Regimes: Knowledge, Accountability, and the Policing of the Past', *Law and Social Inquiry*, 20, 1 (Winter 1995).

Costa, Gino, 'The United Nations and Reform of the Police in El Salvador', *International Peacekeeping*, 2, 3 (Autumn 1995).

Crawford, Kathryn Lee, 'Due Obedience and the Rights of Victims: Argentina's Transition to Democracy', *Human Rights Quarterly*, 12 (1990).

Crocker, David A., 'Reckoning with Past Wrongs: A Normative Framework', *Ethics and International Affairs*, 13 (1999).

De Silva, Chandra R., 'The Elections of 1994 in Sri Lanka: Background and Analysis', *The Round Table*, 334 (1995).

De Silva, K. M., 'Sri Lanka: Surviving Ethnic Strife', *Journal of Democracy*, 8, 1 (January 1997).

Dix, Robert H., 'The Breakdown of Authoritarian Regimes', *Western Political Quarterly*, 35, 2 (1982).

Donadio, Marcela, 'La Construcción de una Nueva Política de Defensa en Argentina', *Fuerzas Armadas y Sociedad* (Chile), 11, 2 (April–June 1996), p. 5.

Drzemczewski, Andrew, 'Ensuring Compatibility of Domestic Law with the European Convention on Human Rights Prior to Ratification: The Hungarian Model', *Human Rights Law Journal*, 16, 7 (November 1995).

Dwyer, Susan, 'Reconciliation for Realists', *Ethics and International Affairs*, 13 (1999).

Ensalaco, Mark, 'Military Prerogatives and the Stalemate of Chilean Civil–Military Relations', *Armed Forces and Society*, 21, 2 (Winter 1995).

Ferreira Pinho, 'Evolución del Sistema de Defensa Argentino', *Fuerzas Armadas y Sociedad* (Chile), 11, 2 (April–June 1996).

Forsyth, John, 'Mental Somersaults in the New South Africa', *SCOLAG: The Bulletin of the Scottish Legal Action Group*, 228 (31 October 1995).

Frankland, Erich G., 'The Evolving Relationship between the Military and Democracy', *Low Intensity Conflict and Law Enforcement*, 3, 1 (Summer 1994).

Gamero, Manuel, '¿Honduras: Despertó La Sociedad Civil?', *Tendencias*, 36 (December 1994–January 1995).

Garro, Alejandro M., 'Nine Years of Transition to Democracy in Argentina: Partial Failure or Qualified Success?', *Colombia Journal of Transnational Law*, 31, 1 (1993).

Garro, Alejandro M. and Henry Dahl, 'Legal Accountability for Human Rights Violations in Argentina: One Step Forward and Two Steps Back', *Human Rights Law Journal*, 8 (1987).

Gomez, Mario, 'Sri Lanka's New Human Rights Commission', *Human Rights Quarterly*, 20 (1998).

Griffiths, Robert J., 'South African Civil–Military Relations in Transition: Issues and Influences', *Armed Forces and Society*, 21, 3 (Spring 1995).

Grindle, Merilee S., 'Civil–Military Relations and Budgetary Politics in Latin America', *Armed Forces and Society*, 13, 2 (Winter 1987).

Harris, Bede, 'The New South African Constitution', *New Zealand Law Journal* (January 1995).

Hatchard, John, 'Towards Majority Rule in South Africa: The Transitional Executive Council Act 1993', *Journal of African Law*, 37, 2 (1994).

Hayner, Priscilla, 'Fifteen Truth Commissions – 1974 to 1994: A Comparative Study', *Human Rights Quarterly*, 16 (1994).

Holiday, David and William Stanley, 'Building the Peace: Preliminary Lessons from El Salvador', *Journal of International Affairs*, 46 (Winter 1993).

Huntington, Samuel P., 'How Countries Democratize', *Political Science Quarterly*, 106, 4 (1991–92).

Huntington, Samuel P., 'Reforming Civil–Military Relations', *Journal of Democracy*, 6, 4 (October 1995).

Huyse, Luc, 'Justice After Transition: On the Choices Successor Elites Make in Dealing with the Past', *Law and Social Inquiry*, 20, 1 (Winter 1995).

Inform, 'Parliamentary Elections 1994: Special Report 1: Polls Related Violence' (Colombo, Sri Lanka: Inform/Movement for Free and Fair Elections, July 1994).

International Human Rights Law Group, 'Report of the International NGO Observer Mission to the Sri Lanka Parliamentary Elections' (Washington, DC: International Human Rights Law Group, 1994).

Johnston, Douglas M., 'Religion and Conflict Resolution', *Fletcher Forum of World Affairs*, 20, 1 (Winter/Spring 1996).

Karl, Terry, 'Dilemmas of Democratization in Latin America', *Comparative Politics*, 23 (October 1990).

Keerawella, Gamini and Rohan Samarajiva, 'Sri Lanka in 1993', *Asian Survey*, 34, 2 (February 1994).

Kruijt, Dirk, 'Politicians in Uniform: Dilemmas about the Latin American Military', *European Review of Latin American Studies*, 61 (December 1996).

Leebaw, Bronwyn, 'Theory out of Practice: An Intellectual History of the South African TRC' (APSA Annual Conference, Atlanta, GA, September 1999).

Levin, Nadia, Kindiza Ngubeni and Graeme Simpson, 'Meeting the Challenge of Change? Notes on Policing and Transition in South Africa', Center for the Study of Violence and Reconciliation, available at http://www.wits.ac.za/csvr/.

Little, David, 'A Different Kind of Justice: Dealing with Human Rights Violations in Transitional Societies', *Ethics and International Affairs*, 13 (1999).

Little, Walter, 'Civil–Military Relations in Contemporary Argentina', *Government and Opposition*, 19, 2 (1984).

MacDonald, Michael, 'Power Politics in the New South Africa', *Journal of Southern African Studies*, 22 (1996).

Mackie, J. L., 'Morality and the Retributive Emotions', *Criminal Justice Ethics*, 1, 1 (Winter/Spring 1982).

Mainwaring, Max G. and Court Prisk, 'A Strategic View of Insurgencies: Insights from El Salvador', *Small Wars and Insurgencies*, 4, 1 (Spring/Summer 1993).

Malamud-Goti, Jaime, 'Punishment and a Rights-based Democracy', *Criminal Justice Ethics*, 10 (Summer/Fall 1991).

Malin, Andrea, 'Mother Who Won't Disappear', *Human Rights Quarterly*, 16, 1 (February 1994).

Matthews, Bruce, 'Devolution of Power in Sri Lanka', *The Round Table*, 330 (1994).

Mendez, Juan E., 'National Reconciliation, Transnational Justice, and the International Criminal Court', *Ethics and International Affairs*, 15, 1, (2001), pp. 25–50.

Montgomery, T. S., 'Getting to Peace in El Salvador: The Roles of the United Nations Secretariat and ONUSAL', *Journal of Interamerican Studies and World Affairs*, 37, 4 (1995), at p. 139.

Moore, John J., Jr, 'Problems with Forgiveness: Granting Amnesty under the Arias Plan in Nicaragua and El Salvador', *Stanford Law Review*, 43 (February 1991).

Moore, Mick, '"Guided Democracy" in Sri Lanka: The Electoral Dimension', *Journal of Commonwealth and Comparative Politics*, 32, 1 (March 1994).

Movement for Free and Fair Elections, 'Interim Report on the Sri Lanka Parliamentary Elections of August 16th 1994' (Rajaginya, Sri Lanka: Movement for Free and Fair Elections, October 1994).

Newman, Edward and Schnabel, Albrecht (eds), 'Recovering from Civil Conflict: Reconciliation, Peace, and Development, *International Peacekeeping*, 9, 2 (Summer 2002) (special issue).

Nino, Carlos S., 'A Consensual Theory of Punishment', *Philosophy and Public Affairs*, 12, 4 (Fall 1983).

Nino, Carlos S., 'The Duty to Punish Past Abuses of Human Rights Put into Context: The Case of Argentina', *Yale Law Journal*, 100 (1991).

Norden, Deborah L., 'Democratic Consolidation and Military Professionalism: Argentina in the 1980s', *Journal of Interamerican Studies and World Affairs*, 32, 3 (1990).

Offe, Claus, 'Disqualification, Retribution, Restitution: Dilemmas of Justice in Post-communist Transitions', *Journal of Political Philosophy*, 1, 1 (1993).

Orentlicher, Diane, 'Settling Accounts: The Duty to Prosecute Human Rights Violations of a Prior Regime', *Yale Law Journal*, 100 (1991).

Osiel, Mark, 'The Making of a Human Rights Policy in Argentina: The Impact of Ideas and Interests on a Legal Conflict', *Journal of Latin American Studies*, 18 (1986).

Paris, Roland, 'Peacebuilding and the Limits of Liberal Internationalism', *International Security*, 22 (1997), pp. 54–89.

Parlevliet, Michelle, 'Considering Truth: Dealing with a Legacy of Gross Human Rights Violations', *Netherlands Quarterly of Human Rights*, 16 (1998), pp. 141–74.

Peceny, Mark, 'Culture, Congress, and the Promotion of Democracy in Reagan Policy toward El Salvador: 1981–1984', *Low Intensity Conflict and Law Enforcement*, 4, 1 (Summer 1994).

Physicians for Human Rights, 'Physicians launch DNA testing to reunite "disappeared" Salvadoran children with parents' (13 September 1994), at <http://www.phrusa.org/research/forensics/el_salvador/fordna1.html>

Pion-Berlin, David, 'The Fall of Military Rule in Argentina, 1976–1983', *Journal of Inter-American Studies and World Affairs*, 27, 2 (1985).

Pion-Berlin, David, 'Military Autonomy and Emerging Democracies in South America', *Comparative Politics*, 25, 1 (October 1992).

Polakiewicz, Jorg, 'The Application of the European Convention on Human Rights in Domestic Law', *Human Rights Law Journal*, 17, 12 (December 1996).

Popkin, Margaret and Naomi Roht-Arriaza, 'Truth as Justice: Investigatory Commissions in Latin America', *Law and Social Inquiry*, 20, 1 (Winter 1995).

Popkin, Margaret and Nehal Bhuta, 'Latin American Amnesties in Comparative Perspective: Can the Past be Buried?', *Ethics and International Affairs*, 13 (1999).

Roht-Arriaza, Naomi, 'The Developing Jurisprudence on Amnesty', *Human Rights Quarterly*, 20 (1998).

Rose, Morgan, 'El Salvador: Abuse of Human Rights and the Process of Peace', *Guild Practitioner*, 50, 4 (Fall 1993).

Roth, Brad R., 'Peaceful Transition and Retrospective Justice: Some Reservations', *Ethics and International Affairs*, 15, 1 (2001), pp. 25–50.

Ruhl, J. Mark, 'Social Mobilization, Military Tradition, and Current Patterns of Civil–Military Relations in Latin America: Testing Putnam's Major Conclusions', *Western Political Quarterly*, 35, 2 (1982).

Rychlak, Ronald, 'Society's Moral Right to Punish: A Further Exploration of the Denunciation Theory of Punishment', *Tulane Law Review*, 65, 2 (December 1990).

Sadurski, Wojciech, 'Distributive Justice and the Theory of Punishment', *Oxford Journal of Legal Studies*, 5, 1 (1985).

Samarasinghe, S. W. R. de A., 'The 1994 Parliamentary Elections in Sri Lanka: A Vote for Good Governance', *Asian Survey*, 34, 12 (December 1994).

Schmitter, Philippe C., 'The International Context of Contemporary Democratization', *Stanford Journal of International Affairs* (Fall/Winter 1993).

Siegel, Richard Louis, 'Transitional Justice: A Decade of Debate and Experience', *Human Rights Quarterly*, 20 (1998), pp. 431–54.

Siegelman, Peter, 'The Problems of Lustration: Prosecution of Wrongdoers by Successor Regimes', *Law and Social Inquiry*, 20, 1 (Winter 1995).

Singer, Marshall R., 'Sri Lanka's Ethnic Conflict: Have Bombs Shattered Hope for Peace?', *Asian Survey*, 36, 11 (November 1996).

Skauge, Tom, 'Contraction and Detraction: Non-equilibrium Studies of Civil–Military Relations', *Journal of Peace Research*, 31, 2 (1994).

Sriram, Chandra, 'Truth Commissions and Political Theory: Tough Moral Choices in Transitional Situations', *Netherlands Quarterly of Human Rights*, 18, 4 (December 2000).

Sriram, Chandra Lekha, 'Contemporary Practice of Universal Jurisdiction: Disjointed and Disparate, yet Developing', *International Journal of Human Rights*, 6, 4 (2002).

Sriram, Chandra Lekha, 'Externalizing Justice Through Universal Jurisdiction – Problems and Prospects', *Finnish Yearbook of International Law*, (2001).

Stanley, William, 'Protectors or Perpetrators? The Institutional Crisis of the Salvadoran Civilian Police' (Washington, DC: Washington Office on Latin America, January 1996).

Tedesco, Laura, 'The Argentine Armed Forces under President Alfonsin', *European Review of Latin American and Caribbean Studies*, 61 (December 1996).
Van Dyke, Jon M. and Gerald W. Berkley, 'Redressing Human Rights Abuses', *Denver Journal of International Law and Policy*, 20, 2 (1992).
Varela, Carlos, 'The Referendum Campaign in Uruguay: An Unprecedented Challenge to Impunity', *Human Rights International Reporter*, 13, 1 (Spring 1989), pp. 16–18.
Von Stade, L.B., 'Rationalisation in the SANDF: The Next Challenge', *African Security Review*, 6, 2 (1997).
Washington Office on Latin America, 'Reluctant Reforms: The Cristiani Government and the International Community in the Process of Salvadoran Post-war Reconstruction', (Washington, DC: Washington Office on Latin America, 1993).
Weiner, Myron, 'Empirical Democratic Theory and the Transition from Authoritarianism', *PS*, 20 (Fall 1987).
Welsh, Helga A., 'Dealing with the Communist Past: Central and Eastern European Experiences after 1990', *Europe–Asia Studies*, 48, 3 (1996).
Wynia, Gary W., 'Democracy in Argentina', *Current History*, 498 (February 1985).
Zalaquett, Jose, 'Balancing Ethical Imperatives and Political Constraints: The Dilemma of New Democracies Confronting Past Human Rights Violations', *Hastings Law Journal*, 43 (1992).

No author given

'Accountability for State-sponsored Human Rights Abuses in Eastern Europe and the Soviet Union', (panel discussion), *Boston College Third World Law Journal*, 12, 2 (Summer 1992).
'Argentina: National Appeals Court (Criminal Division), Judgment on Human Rights Violations by Former Military Leaders', *International Legal Materials*, 26 (1987).
'Human Rights: Conviction of Former Argentine Military Commanders for Human Rights Abuses Committed by Subordinates', *Harvard International Law Journal*, 27 (1986).
'Symposium: Transitions to Democracy and the Rule of Law', *American University Journal of International Law and Policy*, 5, 4 (Summer 1990).

Newsletters, journals and information services

Asiaweek (Online. Available HTTP: <http://www.asiaweek.com>)
Baltimore Sun (Baltimore, USA)
Boston Globe (Boston, USA)
Chicago Tribune (Chicago, USA)
Comisionado Nacional de Derechos Humanos, *Boletín Informativo del Comisionado Nacional de Derechos Humanos de Honduras*, available at: http://www.us.net/cip/cdh/.
Comisionado para la Defensa de los Derechos Humanos (CODEHUCA), *Informe Trimestral Sobre la Situación de los Derechos Humanos en Centroamerica* (San Jose, Costa Rica: CODEHUCA).
Comisionado para la Defensa de los Derechos Humanos (CODEHUCA), *Informe Cuatrimestral Sobre la Situación de los Derechos Humanos en Centroamerica* (San Jose, Costa Rica: CODEHUCA).

Cuaderno de Trabajo (San Salvador, El Salvador: Colegio de Altos Estudios Estrategicos).
Cuadernos del Instituto de Estudios Juridicos de El Salvador (San Salvador, El Salvador: Instituto de Estudios Juridicos de El Salvador).
Daily News (Sri Lanka)
Department of State Dispatch (USA)
Diario Latino (El Salvador)
Docinform (Colombo, Sri Lanka: Nadesan Centre).
Economic and Political Weekly (New Delhi).
El Heraldo (Honduras)
El Salvador Boletín de Analisis e Información (San Salvador, El Salvador).
El Salvador Proceso (San Salvador, El Salvador: Universidad Centroamericana).
Estudios Centroamericanos (San Salvador, El Salvador, Universidad Centroamericana).
Far Eastern Economic Review.
FBIS-LAT (Foreign Broadcast Information Service-Latin America).
International Legal Materials (USA)
La Prensa (Honduras)
La Tribuna (Honduras)
La Nacion (Argentina)
Law and Society Trust Fortnightly Review (Colombo, Sri Lanka: Law and Society Trust).
Law and Society Trust Review (Colombo, Sri Lanka: Law and Society Trust).
Los Angeles Times (Los Angeles, USA)
Los Hechos Hablan por sí Mismos (Tegucilgalpa, Honduras: Comisionado Nacional de Derechos Humanos)
New York Times (New York)
NotiSur-Latin American Political affairs
Realidad: Revista de Ciencias Sociales y Humanidades (San Salvador, El Salvador: Universidad Centroamericana).
Revista Tendencias (San Salvador, El Salvador).
San Francisco Chronicle (San Francisco, USA)
Sri Lanka Express (Sri Lanka)
Sri Lanka Monitor (Sri Lanka)
Sunday Observer (Sri Lanka)
Sunday Times (Sri Lanka)
Tamil Times (Sri Lanka).
The Economist (UK)
The Gazette of the Democratic Socialist Republic of Sri Lanka.
The Guardian (UK)
The Hindu (India)
The Island (Sri Lanka)
Tiempo (Honduras)
US Department of State website www.state.gov
Washington Post (Washington, USA)

Index

For Product Safety Concerns and Information please contact our EU
representative GPSR@taylorandfrancis.com
Taylor & Francis Verlag GmbH, Kaufingerstraße 24, 80331 München, Germany

www.ingramcontent.com/pod-product-compliance
Ingram Content Group UK Ltd.
Pitfield, Milton Keynes, MK11 3LW, UK
UKHW011004180926
475701UK00004B/549

9780415407588